THE ASTD HANDBOOK OF TRAINING DESIGN AND DELIVERY

THE ASTD HANDBOOK OF TRAINING DESIGN AND DELIVERY

A Comprehensive Guide to Creating and Delivering Training Programs—Instructor-Led, Computer-Based, or Self-Directed

Edited by

GEORGE M. PISKURICH
PETER BECKSCHI
BRANDON HALL

McGraw-Hill
New York San Francisco Washington, D.C. Auckland Bogotá
Caracas Lisbon London Madrid Mexico City Milan
Montreal New Delhi San Juan Singapore
Sydney Tokyo Toronto

Library of Congress Cataloging-in-Publication Data applied for.

McGraw-Hill

*A Division of The **McGraw-Hill** Companies*

1 2 3 4 5 6 7 8 9 0 DOC/DOC 9098765432109

ISBN 0-07-134310-5

The sponsoring editor for this book was Richard Narramore, the editing supervisor was Patricia V. Amoroso, and the production supervisor was Elizabeth J. Strange. It was set in Palatino by Carlisle Communications.

Printed and bound by R. R. Donnelley & Sons Company.

This book is printed on recycled, acid-free paper containing a minimum of 50% recycled de-inked fiber.

CONTENTS

Chapter 25

Chapter 26

Chapter 27

The purpose of this book is simple: to help you design and deliver better training programs in less time. It does this by presenting a short overview of each of the major topics that constitute training design and delivery and discussing how trainers and instructional designers typically approach the topic in their work.

This is not a book to take to bed at night and read cover to cover. It is a reference source to help you review a training topic when you have a need to know. By itself it will not make you an expert in any of the elements of training design and delivery, but it provides a sound overview and gives you a benchmark for how other trainers typically approach a problem. The books and articles in the bibliography at the end of each chapter provide learning that will flesh out that framework.

This book began its life as the second edition of *The ASTD Handbook of Instructional Technology*. Our concept at the time was simply to update the 1993 edition, particularly in the technology-based instruction section, as a lot has changed in the past 5 years. For example, in 1993 the term *Internet-based training* was seldom heard in conversation, let alone commonly used to refer to a delivery system.

However, when we convened an expert panel to help identify the topics that needed updating at the 1998 ASTD International Conference, we realized that even the term *instructional technology* has evolved. Its usage has become so general in the last few years that *The Handbook of Instructional Technology* no longer seemed an appropriately descriptive title.

In fact, the process of designing training has changed. The complexity of the new technologies has created a need for the training design team, a group of practitioners each one an expert in one aspect of the training process. This team approach has filtered down into every aspect of training, from analysis teams to team instruction.

After considerable discussion, we decided to reorganize the book into three key categories and give it a simpler title: *The ASTD Handbook of Training Design and Delivery: Instructor-Led, Technology-Based, and Self-Directed.*

We have kept only 20 percent of the original book—the few chapters that our expert panel felt had handled the years well. A few others have been revised significantly, but the majority are published here for the first time.

We've divided the book into three sections based on the three concepts in the subtitle. However, there is some overlap; if the topic you are looking for is not where you expected to find it, check the other sections. The instructor-led section looks at everything from analysis to the evaluation of instructor-led training. Along the way you will find chapters loaded with hints on designing and implementing better classroom instruction. The technology-based section will give you up-to-date information on the vast array of training technologies available today. It includes the "old" multimedia technologies and the cutting edge of virtual reality training. The self-directed section includes a few chapters that could as easily have been in the other sections, as they deal with the foundations of training. To close the book and at the same time move us ahead, we've included two chapters by experts in human performance technology, each discussing from a different viewpoint how the training design and delivery relates to HPT.

This book is the product of the collaborative effort of many leading practitioners in the training industry. We hope it will prove to be a significant, valuable tool for our readers and fellow trainers.

George Piskurich

Katherine V. Beauchemin has 20 years' experience designing training programs and writing corporate publications for businesses. She has served as a consultant to client firms in developing strategic plans, writing and editing technical literature, and developing manuals, brochures, "how-to" texts, and scripts to support training initiatives.

Beauchemin's project experience includes serving as project manager for pharmaceutical, manufacturing, safety, and other programs. She has also conducted needs assessments, task analyses, and levels 1 through 4 evaluations for a variety of industries. Beauchemin received a doctorate at Widener University and received master's and bachelor's degrees at Temple University. She is cofounder along with David A. Gallup of the Training and Communications Group in Berwyn, Pennsylvania.

www.traincomm.com

Peter F. Beckschi joined Merck-Medco as director of training and education in March 1997 and has close to 30 years' experience as a training and human performance specialist in industry and government. His initial assignment as a trainer was for the U.S. Navy, where he learned instructional systems development (ISD) and conducted team training for U.S. and NATO forces. After several years as a marketing specialist for GATX Corporation, Beckschi was selected to develop and provide technical training for turnkey operations around the world. He started the first training department for this organization and introduced competency-based methodologies for headquarters and field personnel.

In 1982 Beckschi joined the faculty at the American University in Cairo, Egypt, where he served as director of commercial and industrial training. His unit was responsible for providing technical and commercial skills for clients throughout the Middle East. Upon completion of this contract, he returned to developing and conducting training programs as a senior human resources and development consultant for Holderbank Management and Consulting out of Switzerland. He provided training and organizational development services (primarily team training) for a variety of the firm's clients, including the World Bank. Projects were based in Iraq, Saudi Arabia, India, Egypt, Korea, Japan, Brazil, Germany, Costa Rica, the Baltic states, and Pakistan.

Returning to the United States, Beckschi undertook research and development training projects for the Air Force Human Resources Laboratory in the application of cognitive psychology to modern training methods while employed by

Pacer Systems, a training systems developer. During this period he coauthored the *Handbook for Instructional Technology* published by the American Society for Training and Development.

Beckschi performed training design as a solutions integrator for Astra Merck and produced workshops for executives at SmithKline Beecham, Baxter Healthcare, Bristol-Myers Squibb, Bellcore, Sprint, Avon, Ford 2000, GE Finance, and the World Bank. He provides pro bono workshops for a number of organizations, including the Philadelphia Museum of Art.

Beckschi was awarded the American Society for Training and Development Technical Trainer of the Year award in 1982 and the International Leadership Award in 1995.

Beckschi is a graduate of the University of California, Berkeley, with a master of science degree from Temple University in Philadelphia and is embarked on a doctoral program that will be completed when he decides to stop traveling so much. His wife, Trudy, would like that too.

www.peter-beckschi@merck.com

Dale Brethower is a psychology professor at Western Michigan University (A.B. University of Kansas; A.M. Harvard University; Ph.D. University of Michigan). He serves as an editor for several professional journals, is widely published, and is a regular presenter at professional conferences. He is a member of the board of directors of Triad Performance Technologies and the recipient of a Lifetime Achievement award from the Organizational Behavior Management Network. One of the pioneers of HPT, he has been a consultant for more than 30 years, primarily in the United States. He is the 1998–1999 President-elect of the International Society for Performance Improvement.

DaleBrethower@Compuserve.com

Dr. Mary L. Broad, with "Performance Excellence," specializes in organizational visioning and strategic planning, high-performance work organizations, professional competencies to support workforce performance, full transfer of learning to the job, and Future Search facilitation.

Mary is an adjunct associate professor for George Washington University's graduate Human Resource Development program, and was elected to the board of directors of the American Society for Training and Development. She is coauthor of *Transfer of Training: Action-Packed Strategies to Ensure High Payoff from Training Investments* (1992, 8th printing) and editor of *In Action: Transferring Learning to the Workplace* (1997). Recent clients include LG Electronics (Korea), IKON Office Solutions, Lexis-Nexis, Vitro Comercial (Mexico), Burlington Northern Railroad, U.S. Agency for International Development, Food and Drug Administration, Department of Defense, and the U.S. Marshal's Service.

Michael "Mike" G. Doty has developed training systems for a number of organizations, including the U.S. Air Force Pilot Instructor Training, the U.S. Department of Transportation (Drug and Alcohol Abuse), Philco Ford (NASA Space Shuttle/747 Transport Maintenance), ARAMCO (Gas and Oil Operations), the Kuwaiti Ministry of Education (vocational training), Champion International Paper (pulp manufacturing), Rollins Environmental Services (landfill management), and Merck-Medco (Customer Service).

Doty has written, directed, and produced over 1500 hours of video instruction, including subjects such as flight training, hospital staff recruitment, gas and oil engineering, and Operations concepts, along with many other industrial process subjects.

When asked about milestones in his career, Mike said, "My most rewarding experience was developing certification training for repatriated USAF pilots. That training enabled returning prisoners of war to get back on flying status. The most challenging work I've ever been involved with was managing a 'systems approach' to the operations and maintenance of Taif Air Base, Royal Saudi Air Force, Taif, Saudi Arabia. At that time training development had turned into management of training contracts. Normal contractor rotation created the need for someone to move into the president's chair, and so I inherited overall project responsibility for 1500 employees on the O & M contract."

Doty is vice president and chief financial officer of Stone Mountain Training Systems in Edgewater, Florida.

www.freeyellow.com/members2/smtsinc

Lance Dublin is President of Dublin Group, an EPS solutions business in San Francisco. He founded Dublin Group in 1984 to improve individual and organizational performance in business. He has more than 20 years of experience in the exploration and practical application of ideas aimed at improving performance. For over 10 years Dublin group has provided innovative solutions for the people side of implementing organizational change and improving performance. Solutions focus on helping people become ready, willing, and able to meet the challenges of the future. Dublin is a noted lecturer and author.

Idublin@dublingroup.com

Richard Durr received a doctorate in educational leadership in 1993 from Florida Atlantic University in Boca Raton, with his dissertation topic focusing on self-directed learning. Since then he has presented at many conferences and symposia and authored and coauthored several articles on self-directed learning and its application in the workplace.

Durr has been involved in the corporate training and education field with Motorola, Inc. since 1982. In 1994 he implemented a process to integrate self-directed learning into the current learning process throughout the facility. To assure that resources were available to the self-directed learner, he managed the implementation of a 40-seat computer and video learning resource center that provides individualized instruction in a wide range of courseware for all job functions. Since then, the use of Internet and live instructor learning has been implemented to the desktop outside the resource center.

Durr consults with other Motorola facilities around the world to integrate the self-directed learning concept into the learning process, assist in measuring readiness for SDL at those facilities, and advise on the implementation and use of technology-delivered learning. He also manages the Motorola University Instructional Design and Multimedia Development Centre in Boynton Beach, which provides custom-developed classroom-delivered and technology-delivered learning products.

John Endicott is a performance technologist at DLS Group, Inc., and as such he writes, edits, and troubleshoots computer-based and systems documentation, on-line help systems, and sales and product knowledge training. Aside from his role in designing and developing the KICS EPSS, Endicott has created award-winning performance interventions for the National Association of Securities Dealers, USWEST, the Farm Credit Bank of Baltimore, and Mincom. He is an expert at Internet search strategies and at weaving on-line help into performance support systems, especially using hypertext. Endicott has a masters degree in scientific and technical communication from Miami University of Ohio.

jendicott@dis.com

Sam Field is program director for several training and simulation programs involving virtual reality, interactive courseware, and other technologies. His clients have primarily been military training organizations in the United States and abroad. Field has extensive experience in simulator design and development and defense contracting. He has degrees in electrical engineering and finance.

sfield@rti.org

David A. Gallup is a faculty member of the PDA (a professional organization serving the pharmaceutical manufacturing industry) and has 20 years' experience designing, producing, and evaluating training programs. His background includes conducting needs analyses and task analyses and evaluating training programs for client firms. Gallup currently teaches and advises in Pennsylvania State University's training design and development graduate program at that school's Great Valley campus.

Gallup's project experience includes establishing and managing the first educational media center at Denison University, providing general policy and long-range planning for that center, developing a training cost-effectiveness model for the Cincinnati Public School District, serving as project manager and consultant to design and produce technical skill training programs for businesses and universities, evaluating training needs, conducting job and task analyses, evaluating features of classroom design, assessing the advantages of various media and audiovisual equipment, and managing an instructional development project for physicians at Hahnemann Medical College and Hospital in Philadelphia.

Gallup received a doctorate at Pennsylvania State University and received his undergraduate and master's degrees at Westminster College. Along with Katherine V. Beauchemin, Gallup founded the Training and Communications Group, Inc., which provides training and communications services.

www.traincomm.com

James J. Goldsmith is a manager at Andersen Consulting in St. Charles, Illinois. His primary responsibility is to leverage design and technology to support critical education and performance initiatives. A learning technologist and corporate trainer since 1982, Goldsmith has managed or participated in more than 100 electronic-based interactive education projects. Goldsmith received an MBA from the University of Connecticut. He writes and speaks frequently about training issues and is writing a book about multimedia and Web project management. He is a Pericles and multiple Apex award recipient and was named one of *Multimedia Producer* magazine's Top 100 multimedia producers.

james.j.goldsmith@ac.com

Dr. Lucy M. Guglielmino is a professor of adult education in the Department of Educational Leadership at Florida Atlantic University. She has written more than 100 books, chapters, articles, and monographs on various aspects of adult education, most related to self-direction in learning. Her Self-Directed Learning Readiness Scale has been widely used since 1978 and is available in 12 languages. It is the most frequently used instrument for assessment and research on self-direction in learning.

Dr. Guglielmino is listed in *Who's Who in the World* and a number of other similar publications and has received a number of awards for her teaching, research, and service.

lguglielmino@rocketmail.com

Paul Guglielmino is an associate professor of management at Florida Atlantic University in Boca Raton. He received a doctorate in adult education with a focus on management education and development from the University of Georgia. Guglielmino has served as a consultant to companies such as Motorola, Walt Disney World, AT&T, and Pratt and Whitney. He is a reviewer for the *Human Resource Development Journal* and was selected for inclusion in the International Directory of Business and Management Scholars by the Harvard University, Graduate

School of Business Administration. In 1993 Guglielmino received the Coleman Award for Research Excellence in Entrepreneurial Education at the 38th World Conference on Small Business in Las Vegas. He is a member of the Academy of Management and has been inducted into Phi Kappa Phi and Beta Gamma Sigma. In 1998 he was selected University Distinguished Teacher of the Year at Florida Atlantic University.

  guglielmino@rocketmail.com

Brandon Hall is editor of brandon-hall.com, an independent research organization on technology for training. He is a frequent speaker at conferences on industry trends and advises organizations on strategic issues related to on-line learning. Hall is recognized as an independent analyst, and his publications include *Training Management Systems* and *The Web-Based Training Cookbook*. He chairs an annual awards program that recognizes the best on-line learning programs. Hall has been a columnist for *Inside Technology Training* and a contributing editor to ASTD's *Training & Development*. He has been interviewed by *Fortune, The New York Times, The Wall Street Journal, Business Week*, and other magazines.

  brandon@brandon-hall.com

Donald L. Kirkpatick, Professor Emeritus at the University of Wisconsin, is a widely respected teacher, author, and consultant. He is the author of eight management inventories and five books: *How to Manage Change Effectively, How to Improve Performance through Appraisal and Coaching, How to Train and Develop Supervisors, How to Plan and Conduct Productive Business Meetings, and No-Nonsense Communication.* He is best known for developing the internationally accepted four-level approach for evaluating training programs. He received his BBA, MBA, and PhD from the University of Wisconsin–Madison. He is past president of the American Society for Training and Development (ASTD) and the 1997 inductee into *Training* magazine's Hall of Fame. Don is retired and enjoys mentoring and lecturing.

  414-784-8348, fax 414-784-7994

Ann Kwinn earned a PhD in Instructional Technology at the University of Southern California in 1990 and was chosen to be a research fellow at the ETS. After graduation, she created multimedia training programs and consumer titles for Darox, HSC Software, ASK International, and the Graphix Zone. As a project manager/enterprise manager for Learning Systems Sciences, she manages the development of multimedia training programs for corporate clients. She is a contributing writer for *Boxoffice* magazine and has spoken at IICS, ASTD, and SALT events. In 1997 Kwinn was named one of *Multimedia Producer* magazine's top 100 producers and won a gold CINDY.

  akwinn@lss.net

Karen Lawson is an international consultant, speaker, and author. As founder and president of Lawson Consulting Group, Inc., Lawson built a successful consulting firm specializing in organization and management development. She has extensive consulting and workshop experience in the areas of management, team development, communication, and quality service.

In her consulting work with Fortune 500 companies as well as small businesses, she uses her experience with and knowledge of human interaction to help leaders at all levels make a difference in their organizations. A much-sought-after speaker, she informs, inspires, and involves her audiences as she shares her insights on influencing others. She is one of about 250 people worldwide to have earned the Certified Speaking Professional (CSP) designation awarded by the 3500-member national Speakers Association.

Lawson is the author of six books: *Improving On-the-Job Training and Coaching, Improving Workplace Performance through Coaching, The Art of Influencing, The Trainer's Handbook, Train-the-Trainer Facilitator's Guide,* and *Involving Your Audience: Making It Active.* She is also coauthor of *101 Ways to Make Training Active* and has published dozens of articles in professional journals. She has presented at many regional and national professional conferences and is on the adjunct faculty of several colleges and universities.

Solutions@Lawson CG.com

Roger E. Main is president of F & M Innovative Solutions, Inc., a performance consulting firm specializing in helping training organizations' transitions to a performance focus, leveraging technology for improved employee performance, and designing ISO 9000 compliant quality system designs. He earned his B.A. in management and human relations from Mid-America Nazarene University and is currently completing graduate work on his MBA. Main has been a teacher, trainer, researcher, machinist, manager, and consultant for more than 25 years. In addition, Main has worked over 21 years in the U.S. defense industry. Main has authored several articles, reports, and manuals on various aspects of instructional and performance technology. He is a frequent speaker and presenter for major companies and professional associations. He has won several awards for innovation and teamwork.

REMain@worldnet.att.net. or phone 816-322-8518 in the United States.

Nancy Maresh is chief executive officer and wizard of Maresh Brainworks in Boulder, Colorado. Her current work in accelerated brain-to-brain communication consists of lecturing to audiences in business and education, consulting marketers and training professionals, and coaching curriculum designers and presenters. Her particular interests lie in helping clients build intellectual capital through accelerated acquisition of learning assets. She is currently authoring two books: *The Art and Science of Web-Based Training* and *Ten Steps toward Personal Genius.*

Maresh is coauthor of *Building Financial Fitness* and has been featured in numerous journal and magazine articles, including the front page of *The Wall Street Journal.* She is cocreator and developer of *The Accounting Game* and *The Internet Game.*
Mbrainworks@earthlink.com

David S. Metcalf II is director of development at Merrimac Interactive Media Corp. He is responsible for development activities combining creative, instructional, and technical disciplines to produce technology solutions for training and knowledge management applications. Metcalf came to Merrimac from the Kennedy Space Center, where he was lead multimedia designer and ran the Web Interactive Training (WIT) project. The project produced several web-based training applications that were given a Gold Award in the 1997 Multimedia and Internet Training awards. Metcalf has a BA in computer graphics from the University of Texas and a master's in computer-based learning and a doctorate in information systems from Nova Southeastern University.
dsm@merrimac.com

Carol Gunther Mohr is program manager for virtual reality learning systems. She works with clients to define appropriate advanced technologies to apply to learning and performance problems and then manages the development of applications that employ these technologies. She has worked with clients in the automotive, airline, and utility industries. Her background includes human resource development and instructional design.
cgm@rti.org

Scott B. Parry is a psychologist, consultant, and trainer who is chair of Training House, Inc., creators of instructional programs and assessments. His Managerial Assessment of Proficiency (MAP) has been translated into five languages and is used throughout the world.

He has published numerous articles in training and management journals and is the author of four books and dozens of published training courses. To date, he has run more than 400 train-the-trainer workshops and has addressed human resource development conferences in several dozen countries.

Parry has conducted workshops for managers and trainers worldwide under the sponsorship of UNESCO, the Ford Foundation, and private corporations. His consulting clients have included corporate giants such as AT&T, IBM, Ford, Coca-Cola, and American Express.

In private life, Parry plays the organ and harpsichord, has published three collections of music, and has given a carillon concert tour in Europe. He and his wife live in Princeton, New Jersey.
TrngHouse@aol.com

Jack J. Phillips has more than 27 years of corporate experience in human resource development and management, and has served as training and development manager at two Fortune 500 firms, senior human resources executive at two firms, president of a regional bank, and management professor at a major state university.

In 1992 Phillips founded Performance Resources Organization (PRO), an international consulting firm specializing in accountability issues, including ROI. PRO provides a full range of services and publications to support assessment, measurement, and evaluation. In 6 years PRO has become the global leader in accountability and has pioneered the application of ROI to a wide variety of nonfinancial processes.

Phillips consults with clients in the United States, Canada, the United Kingdom, Belgium, Germany, Sweden, Italy, South Africa, Mexico, Venezuela, Malaysia, Hong Kong, Indonesia, Australia, New Zealand, and Singapore. Among his clients are some of the world's most respected companies, including Andersen Consulting, AT&T, Bell Atlantic, Bristol-Myers Squibb, Canadian Imperial Bank of Commerce, Compaq, DHL Worldwide Express, Deloitte & Touche, Federal Express, First Union National Bank, Lockheed Martin, Motorola, Nortel, Singapore Airlines, Volvo of North America, and Xerox.

A frequent contributor to management literature, Phillips has authored or edited 20 books, including *A New Vision for Human Resources* (with Jac Fitz-Enz, 1998) and *Return on Investment in Training and Performance Improvement Programs* (1997). He also has written more than 100 articles for professional, business, and trade publications.

Phillips earned undergraduate degrees in electrical engineering, physics, and mathematics from Southern Polytechnic State University and Oglethorpe University, a master's in decision sciences from Georgia State University, and a doctorate in human resource management from the University of Alabama. In 1987 he won the Yoder-Heneman Personnel Creative Application Award from the Society for Human Resource Management for an ROI study of a gain-sharing plan.

George M. Piskurich is presently consulting in instructional design and technology-based training implementation. He has been in the training profession in various positions and industry settings for over 20 years. His areas of special interest include self-directed learning, performance improvement, customer service, and management/supervisory development.

He has been a presenter at over 30 conferences and symposia, including the International Self-Directed Learning Symposium and the ISPI and ASTD international conferences, speaking on topics ranging from mentoring systems to interactive distance learning to telecommuting.

He has authored books on learning technology, self-directed learning, and telecommuting, written extensively in his areas of interest for a number of periodicals, and is currently working on a book on practical instructional design.

Currently residing in the Raleigh/Durham area of North Carolina, he can be reached at 919-968-0878.

GMP1@Compuserve.com

Harvi Singh cofounded Empower Corporation to marry the best of computer and Internet technologies with the best of learning and human performance to create enterprise learning solutions. He has over 10 years of experience in technology-based learning and knowledge management. He is the primary designer of KaleidoScope and Online Learning Infrastructure, a network-based application for on-line learning and knowledge management. He has consulted on on-line learning initiatives with Microsoft, Sun Microsystems, GlaxoWellcome, Apple, IMS, ADL/DoD, Oracle, and others. Singh received a BS in computer science from North Carolina State and graduate degrees in both computer science and education from Stanford University.

Harvis@empower-co.com

Robert A. Steinmetz received an MA in human factors psychology from California State University at Northridge and a doctorate in instructional technology from the University of Southern California. Steinmetz began his professional career at Hughes Aircraft Co. as a member of the technical staff for field training and support. After serving in various Instructional design capacities for other firms, Steinmetz founded Learning Systems Sciences (LSS) in 1979. The firm has designed and produced over 150 technology-based instructional programs. In May 1998 LSS joined Provant Inc., a provider of performance improvement services. Steinmetz continues to serve as the LSS group president.

rsteinmetz@LSS.net

Deborah L. Stone is president and founder of DLS Group, Inc., in Denver and has received 17 professional Awards of Excellence for her work in instructional design, technology-based training, and performance support systems. A frequently published author and presenter at international conferences, Stone completed her graduate work in instructional technology at San Francisco State University. She served as vice president of technology applications for the International Society for Performance Improvement from 1991 to 1993 and currently serves on the Advisory Board of the University of Colorado's Graduate Division of Instructional Technology.

dstone@dls.com

Steve Sugar holds a BA in economics from Bucknell University, Lewisburg, Pennsylvania, and an MBA from George Washington University, Washington, D.C. He served as deck watch officer in Operation Market Time in Vietnam. He is the author of *Games That Teach* (Jossey-Bass) and five game systems actively used in the United States and 20 other countries. His current projects include *Games That Teach*

Teams (Jossey-Bass) and a board game system to accompany the book, *The Leadership Challenge* (Jossey-Bass).

Sugar is editor-contributor to four ASTD INFO-LINE publications, contributor to *The 1999 Team and Organization Development Sourcebook* (McGraw-Hill), and contributor to *The ASTD Handbook of Instructional Technology.* He has contributed to every national training publication and has been interviewed on learning games by *Personnel Journal, Training & Development* and *TRAINING* magazines.

Sugar has presented at virtually every national training conference and has been on the faculties of Johns Hopkins University; the University of Maryland, University College; New York Institute of Technology; Interamerican College of Physicians and Surgeons; and the U.S. Department of Agriculture Graduate School.

Sugar received the ASTD D.C. Metro chapter's Outstanding Contribution to the HRD Profession award for his health performance games developed for Dr. Koop, surgeon general of the United States. He received Special Recognition Awards for his community service work from the chief engineer of the U.S. Public Health Service and the Interamerican College of Physicians and Surgeons. He is co-founder and president of the Game Group of Ellicott City, Maryland.

410-418-4930
FX: 410-418-4162

Sivasailam "Thiagi" Thiagarajan owns and operates Workshops by Thiagi and specializes in the design and delivery of public and in-house workshops on different aspects of performance and instructional technology. Thiagi's long-term clients include AT&T, Arthur Anderson, Chevron, Harris Bank, IBM, Intel, Intelsat, and Liberty Mutual. On a long-term basis, Thiagi has worked with more than 50 different organizations in the high-tech, financial services, and management consulting areas. For these clients Thiagi has consulted and conducted training in areas such as rightsizing, diversity, creativity, teamwork, customer satisfaction, total quality management, and organizational learning.

Thiagi has conducted hundreds of workshops, made hundreds of presentations, published hundreds of articles (but only 20 books), and designed hundreds of instructional games. He has directed instructional technology projects in many countries in Asia, Africa, and Central America, including a project for revamping the primary education system in Liberia. He has produced instructional materials in print, computer, radio, audiovisual, and video media.

Thiagi has been president of the North American Simulation and Gaming Association (NASAGA), the Association for Special Education Technology (ASET), and the National Society for Performance and Instruction (NSPI), which has honored him with six different awards, including its most prestigious Honorary Life Membership Award. He is listed in the *Who's Who* (Worldwide).

www.thiagi.com

W. Wayne Turmel is the Western Regional Director of Client Services for PACE (a division of Sylvan Learning Systems) based in Pasadena, CA. Wayne's background is truly unconventional, including a 15-year stint as a writer and stand-up comedian. His area of expertise is presentation skills and training the trainer, where he has developed material and taught for numerous Fortune 500 clients. His work has appeared in numerous publications in Canada and the United States.
    PACEGPLA@aol.com

J. Patrick Whalen is a senior consultant for the Performance Resources Organization (PRO). Whalen consults with a broad range of organizations on evaluation methodology, establishing evaluation strategies, conducting business impact studies, and identifying needs and return on investment (ROI) projects. He conducts both public and in-house workshops on needs analysis, assessment, measurement, evaluation, and the ROI process. His primary experience has been as an internal and external consultant on human resource and performance enhancement programs across various industries. His principal consulting focus has been measuring the performance of individuals, teams, and systems and the overall business impact of human resource interventions. Whalen has a master's in industrial organizational psychology and a master's in counseling and sports psychology and is licensed as a human resource professional.
    918-760-7703
    patrickwhalen@worldnet.att.net

Saundra Wall Williams is an assistant professor of training and development in the Department of Adult and Community College Education at North Carolina State University in Raleigh. She has been involved in the design, development, implementation, evaluation, and management of technical training and instructional technologies, specifically Web-based training, since 1990. Williams teaches instructional design, instructional technologies, training and development research, and training management and has directed research and development projects in the area of adult learning and Web-based training. Her research activity is evidenced by her publications and by her being named a Cyril O. Houle Scholar in Adult Education.
    Before entering the professorate, Williams held several positions in business and industry, including director of technical training at Syntel, senior training specialist at Broadband Technologies, and instructional designer and trainer at Nortel.
    Wmscorp@Mcione.com

Bill Withers leads Rosenbluth International's Learning Frontiers team in the creation, customizing, and marketing of the firm's successful learning experiences to organizations around the world. He headed up Rosenbluth's internal global learning and development team for two years, leading its transformation from a traditional training department to a "consultative facilitator of individual and organizational learning." He had developed successful train-the-trainer and professional development video leader's guides in South Africa, implemented customer service training programs in Russia and China, and coordinated Total Quality Management and team-development programs for clients in Canada and Hong Kong. Withers's team is currently working with clients in health care, manufacturing, education, and the public and private service industry.

Withers has presented at the American Productivity and Quality Center, the Department of Labor, the Office of the New American Workplace, the International Alliance for Learning, the Training Directors' Forum, TRAINING, and Seton Hall University Graduate School, among others. He is coauthor with Frank Hoffmann of the article "Shared Values: Nutrients for Learning" in the recently released *Learning Organizations: Developing Cultures for Tomorrow's Workplace*. He is currently collaborating on a workshop and an accompanying test for interveners in organizational, ethnic, and political conflicts.

bwithers@rosenbluth.com

Dorman Woodall, a graduate of the University of Arkansas, lives just outside of Charlotte, North Carolina, with his wife and their young son. He is a seasoned training professional who has presented at several national training conferences, including Interactive '96, Influent's Training IT '97 conference series, ASTD '98, various IQPC conferences, and several regional and local conferences. Over the last three years he presented the "Implementing Multimedia Learning Programs" workshop series to more than a thousand people. He is currently the program director for the NETglobal '99 Customer Conference.

Before joining NETg as its director of field education, Woodall held key information technology management roles in major U.S. and Canadian corporations. These firms included Colgate-Palmolive and Burlington Industries, where he designed and developed major on-line customer service systems. He also had oversight of the training for both technical and user teams.

Woodall has developed several programs, methods, materials, and tools that have been very effective in improving training quality and productivity in several training programs. His views are consistently from the customer's perspective, and he can be counted on to apply the appropriate training technology to solve a business problem. Woodall uses his unique style and sense of humor in all his work.

Dwoodall@netg.com

THE ASTD HANDBOOK OF TRAINING DESIGN AND DELIVERY

Instructor-based Section

Peter Beckschi

To borrow a quotation from Hippocrates that is cited in Chapter 12, "Life is short, the art long, opportunity fleeting, experience treacherous, judgment difficult," and so goes it for the training professional who is challenged in today's work environment to do it cheaper and faster. Training has emerged as both an art and a science enhanced by new and exciting tools and technology. The authors in this section provide a reflection on design issues that affect the development and delivery of training as we know it today and as it might look in the future. The authors are seasoned professionals who are willing to share their wisdom and knowledge by describing the experiences that shape the way they look at training within the global context of human performance. Their experience serves as a knowledge base or reference for further elaboration and interpretation in dialogue with others attempting to achieve exceptional results with the provision of training.

There is some old stuff and some new stuff in this section. The old stuff provides the foundation for training such as Chapter 2 by Mike Doty and myself on ISD (instructional systems development) and Donald Kirkpatrick's four levels of evaluation in Chapter 9. ISD provides a framework on which to create, deliver, and evaluate training. A basic knowledge of these principles and relationships promises rewards by helping you know why and what you are doing. And who doesn't know the "four levels"?

Thiagi, in his inimitable manner, is able to derive short, practical rules of thumb in looking at instructional processes such as ISD in Chapter 4. He permits and draws on multiple actions while reinforcing the basic process for developing sound training. This leads us to three other authors who provide "creative" inputs and solutions: Nancy Maresh (Chapter 1) is extremely adept in examining how the human context derives the kind of approaches supported by Karen Lawson (Chapter 3) on making training an active process (learner-centered), and Steve Sugar (Chapter 7) has found games and gaming to be productive training solutions. It is this area that has challenged traditional thinking about training the most over the past decade. Having fun while learning has crossed over to acceptability, but judging by training in many organizations, it still seeks respectability when "spray and pray" seems so much more businesslike (and cheaper). Anybody try to find a local telephone number lately or seek information about where to get information? Creativity needs to be embedded not only in the design of training but also as an outcome.

If you left it to Wayne Turmel (Chapter 6), he would want to use Velcro to ensure that training is transferred, at least from the perspective of technology: AV, video, and so on. Turmel suggests that the medium is not the message, especially in the age of technique saturation. How many flying screens are enough? One might be better focused if it related directly to the job, according to David Gallup and Kate Beauchemin in Chapter 8. You mean to say people can really learn outside the classroom and on the job? However, if you've decided to develop and use instructors, Bill Withers (Chapter 5) invites you to consider what he values.

The end game of training is a change in human performance. Did we get what was intended? How do we measure it? What did it cost us? Donald Kirkpatrick (Chapter 9) provides the simplicity and elegance of his four-level model of evaluation. As a user and advocate of ISD, Kirkpatrick elaborated what we all needed in this very difficult area. Scott Parry (Chapter 10) demonstrates how one can pull this model through a case history. Parry speaks the language of business through logical analysis and data. It is this area which supports the basic principle of why we need training: the bottom line.

That's not all, folks. You can't stop now. There is so much happening in training today: some old, some new, some good, and a lot not so good. The proliferation of information makes, as Hippocrates said, "experience treacherous and judgment difficult." I hope this selection of topics and authors makes the journey enjoyable and successful.

CHAPTER 1

Breathing Life into Adult Learning

Nancy Maresh

Make a loop that looks like a rabbit's ear and pinch the bottom. Loop the other string around the bottom of the ear and then slowly pull it back through the hole so that you make a second ear. Pull the ears apart to make a knot. You've tied your own shoes for the first time! You're really a big kid now.

Chances are, this is how you learned to tie your shoes. You didn't consult a step-action table written by a technical writer. You didn't learn from a book; you couldn't, since you probably weren't reading on your own yet. Instead, you learned by example and analogy. You learned by experimenting and doing. You mastered a new skill because it was emotionally important to do so. Best of all, you immediately applied this new skill in your daily life.

This is how children learn, and in many ways this is how adults learn best too. However, many of these learning strategies are set aside as we move through school, college, and vocational training. In the place of the richly creative methods the best parents and teachers use with children, the majority of adults are put in a chair, handed a textbook or manual, and told to pay attention as a lecturer or computer screen presents information.

The next frontier in business evolution is the growth of the human capacity for generating and manifesting new ideas, and it's high time for traditional training methods to evolve as well. By understanding how adults *really* learn, learning how the brain functions at its peak, and applying this understanding to instructional design and delivery, trainers can create cost-effective programs with extraordinary creativity and power that will accelerate learning while producing retention rates that approach 90 percent.

This chapter tells trainers exactly how to increase learning speed, bring information alive, expand understanding and retention, and explain why these methods work. Regardless of the method of course delivery, instructor-led, self-paced, and computer- or Web-based training can be improved and accelerated by connecting curriculum content to the complex and demanding brain of the learner.

HOW ADULTS LEARN

As people move through life, new information and skills are imprinted in the brain by linking what is being learned to the rest of the learner's past experience, prior knowledge, and current experiences. In fact, learning doesn't happen without these connections. The creation and access of memory are a chemical and electrical process that links new pieces of information to existing pieces. While this may seem obvious, many trainers do not appreciate its importance.

The brain has a predisposition to search for how things make sense and *automatically* looks for meaning in every experience. This quest for personal meaning translates directly into the search for common patterns and relationships. The essential function of adult learning is to find out how what is being learned relates to what the learner already knows and values and how that information and the learner's prior experiences connect.

Trainers must capitalize on this innate capacity of the brain to seek and perceive patterns, create meanings, integrate sensory experience, and make connections so that they can become more proficient at designing and delivering a dynamic curriculum, assessing learning, and effectively administering true education. In the process trainers will release learners' intrinsic drive to acquire knowledge, an admirable outcome from any training.

How can a trainer create learning experiences that capitalize on these brain functions? The first step is to create common ground at the very start of a program and the beginning of each learning segment. Participants enter a classroom with varying degrees of background, knowledge, and expertise that relates to the subject matter. Creating common ground means entering into a dialogue with the audience members that acknowledges their experience and speaks directly to the familiar frustrations, joys, and challenges that link up to the learning task at hand.

By asking a series of "How many people have ever _____" questions, a trainer spotlights the audience members' background and connects them to the information being taught, a process that creates personal meaning for the participants. As a result, learners feel included and begin committing themselves early and wholeheartedly to the process. Presenters should not accept a show of hands as an adequate response but should ask for more information and comments. The responses to these questions should be repeated by the trainers for all to hear and, in the process, validate the persons who offer comments. The trainers will then get a quick read on the audience's skill levels and readiness to learn.

The process of enrollment and the creation of common ground is fundamental to students' personal involvement with the subject matter. When people begin learning together as a group, they start to relax and develop a sense of belonging. This common ground forms the basis of group awareness, which enhances interaction and collaboration and expands the opportunities for new learning.

I cocreated and developed *The Accounting Game*, the most successful accelerated-learning seminar in the world. This game teaches a semester's worth of basic accounting in one day. Because of the way it is taught, the participants not only learn much more quickly but retain and utilize the information longer than they would if they had learned through traditional means. *The Accounting Game* uses the metaphor of a kid's lemonade stand to teach its content. Participants can revert to the safety and fun associated with childhood by using a game board and colored game pieces. The concepts are not abstract but simple and concrete.

The following series of enrollment questions have been used effectively with hundreds of thousands of students around the world. At the very start of the program *The Accounting Game* uses the method of creating common ground and personal meaning described above. The presenter starts off by asking open-ended enrollment questions:

- How many people have had some kind of formal background in accounting? Could I please see a show of hands? Thank you.
- Who doesn't have a formal background but has learned through his or her own experience on the job or somewhere else? Thank you.
- Who doesn't have any background at all in accounting? Thanks.
- Can I see a show of hands if there are any CPAs in the class today? Thank you.
- Whether you are a CPA, have a background in accounting, have learned on the job, or don't have any background at all, how many people have some confusion about accounting? If you look around the room, you will see that almost everyone has some confusion about accounting.

At this point everyone in the room has raised his or her hand in response to these simple questions and has been enrolled in participating; a basic level of common ground connectedness to the subject has been established. After creating a sense of association and safety with the material, the trainer can address the "big why" in the minds of the students: the purpose, method, and desired results of the training program. Why is this subject important? How is it relevant to the learner's life? What will people do when they return to the job? An explanation of the methodologies and purpose satisfies the brain's intellectual and social needs. The whole enrollment process, though, should go deeper than the rational mind, penetrating into the emotional and physical maintenance parts of the brain, the home of feelings and instinct. I'll explain later why this is essential.

After the opening enrollment process and big picture explanation, the leader needs to share something about his or her background, preferably by telling a personal story about an experience with the subject matter that is being covered. This connects the leader to the participants in an essential way. People's experiences are dramatic. They include emotion, mystery, tension, climaxes, and humor. When personal stories are recounted, learners emotionally identify with the parts that have meaning to them, and this confirms their commitment to participate. Personal stories bond the audience to the instructor, the course content, and the other participants.

Adults need to know the relevance and specific details of what they're being asked to learn. When they do, a sense of anticipation and value is instilled from the start. Specifically, this means passing out an agenda or a list of the course objectives to satisfy the learners' need to know where they'll be at the end of the course. This fulfills the logical, content-focused, time-conscious parts of the brain and relaxes the learner's mind.

To this point we've spent less than 30 minutes of training time, but the success of the first day's program is assured.

The following steps have been discussed to this point and are important principles of accelerated learning:

- The brain automatically searches for meaning, patterns, and relationships based on prior knowledge and experience.
- Asking "how many" questions starts the enrollment process.
- Creating common ground stimulates personal meaning and intrinsic motivation.
- Stating the big picture, including purpose, methods, and intended results, provides the necessary global overview.
- Telling personal stories creates a connection and common ground.
- Handing out an agenda and clarifying objectives satisfies the analytic brain.

Using these tools will upgrade course design and presentation. However, there is a world of knowledge waiting for trainers' use that will bring information to life and deliver true value to adult learners.

HOW WORKPLACE LEARNING DIFFERS FROM OTHER FORMS OF EDUCATION

Are there ways in which adults learn at work that are different from other kinds of learning? The answer is a qualified yes. People of all ages can benefit from learning that employs all the tools described in this chapter. However, in today's fast-paced corporate environments there are special considerations for building curricula that work.

Employees may feel tremendous pressure to do well in workplace training. They may have little choice about which training to take, and their career success may hinge on the results. Adult learners often have resistance to or anxiety about a highly technical curriculum. Course designers and presenters alike must reckon with this uneasy anticipation.

Training professionals must ensure that courses and their delivery work for very diverse work forces and across significant geographic distances. Frequently, trainers are required by employers to "do more with less" and put training together with inadequate lead time. These realities may challenge students and instructors alike. The good news is that accelerated learning works for everyone. It makes the most of the magnificent organ between our ears.

THE LEARNING BRAIN

To respond successfully to the challenges of business, today's best trainers understand how to maximize time and effort because they know how the learning brain works. This knowledge is the result of research conducted by psychologists and brain researchers over the last few decades. Although all learning is brain-based, accelerated learning acknowledges the brain's predisposition for rapid, meaningful learning so that teaching can be organized to trigger quick acquisition and long-term retention. Accelerated learning is a multisensory, brain-compatible methodology that can be incorporated into *every* aspect of the teaching and learning process from design to delivery.

To accelerate learning, there are three fundamental theories that help us see the whole brain in action:

- Left brain–right brain theory
- Triune brain theory
- Multiple intelligences theory

Left Brain–Right Brain Theory: Two Brains in One

Perhaps the best known of these theories—the left brain–right brain theory—was put forth in the early 1970s, when Dr. Roger Sperry of the University of California discovered that the lateral lobes of the cerebral cortex function very differently from each other.

Sperry found that the left side of the brain is more active than the right side when people use language, write, read, solve math problems, and process information in a linear, sequential manner. Sometimes the left brain is referred to as the "analytic" brain.

The right side of the brain is more active than the left when people engage in nonverbal activities such as listening to music, drawing, and daydreaming. The right brain is stimulated by the use of color, graphics, movement, and rhythm. As a result, the right brain often is referred to as the "creative" brain. A whole range of personal growth seminars and books teach people how to better utilize the right side of the brain.

While the left brain is busy separating out the parts that constitute the whole—in other words, analyzing—the right brain specializes in *combining* those parts to create a whole. The right brain is engaged in *synthesis* precisely because it does not move linearly but processes information in toto.

Clearly, people need and use both sides of the brain in a seamless unity. People don't think solely with one hemisphere or the other. The more stimulated and connected the two halves of the brain are, the greater the brain's potential for learning is. *Together* the brain hemispheres process and communicate information more clearly than either one could alone.

Traditional training and education were designed for predominantly left-brain functions. Think for a moment how you learned math. Probably you were given multiplication tables to memorize. Today innovative math teachers use "manipulatives": tangible objects that students can use physically and spatially to experience the grouping of items. Manipulatives provide an example of using the right brain to help the left brain learn.

Although I did not know it at the time, my commitment to developing *The Accounting Game* was a perfect example of how both sides of my brain had to work together for me to learn accounting. My first exposure to any kind of accounting was serendipitous. To that point I had been an athlete and an artist, and accounting was a subject I dreaded. When I encountered the rudiments of *The Accounting Game*—colored pieces of paper that could be moved to create a balance sheet—I realized that even I could learn the basic concepts and language of accounting. My left brain could not conceptualize accounting principles by itself, but my right brain learned from color coding and my body loved the movement of pieces that represented a whole construct. The energy that was liberated from my knowledge breakthrough propelled me through many years of personal and professional development.

The point is that trainers need to pay careful attention to the power of the *whole* brain in designing and presenting information. The "two-brain" doctrine is most valuable as a metaphor that helps educators acknowledge these two separate but simultaneous tendencies in the brain. Curriculum designers can benefit by reviewing their course material to ensure that reducing information into parts is bal-

[handwritten note:] Super 8 78.29 + tax 7 85.79 Sunday noe R /noe 75.87 total

...s as a whole or a series of wholes. ...l always be balanced with right-...y.

s Are Better Than Two

...ers—the triune brain model—has ...y known or utilized by trainers. It ...IacLean, chief of the Laboratory of ...itute of Mental Health in Bethesda, ...the others mentioned in this chap-...nd learning by identifying power-...e evolved over millions of years.

In particular, MacLean's model helps us understand and apply how the brain is organized intellectually and emotionally. The word *triune* alludes to MacLean's breakthrough understanding that the human brain has evolved through three primary stages:

- The reptilian
- The limbic
- The neocortex

According to MacLean, the core area of the brain is also the oldest and smallest area. He named it the *reptilian* brain, comparing it to the kind of brain possessed by the hardy reptiles that preceded mammals roughly 200 million years ago. This region, at the top of the brainstem, is "preverbal" but controls life itself. Its work is to initiate and monitor every autonomic function. Impulses cannot be expressed through language; rather, they are instinctual and ritualistic. The reptilian brain is concerned with fundamental needs such as survival, physical maintenance, hoarding, social dominance, preening, and mating.

To satisfy and assure this most basic essence of each class participant, presenters should provide for the physical well-being of the students. Breaks need to be scheduled regularly, about 50 to 90 minutes apart. Students should be encouraged to move around and get fresh air. Lunch should be leisurely, not rushed. Lunch foods and break snacks should be healthy, not sugar-laden.

Instructors can avoid a "reptile aversion" by allowing people to stay in their chosen seats for at least the first morning of a course. The reptilian brain is territorial, and moving too quickly or working with several different groups too early in a class will create discomfort. If you let the participants feel grounded in the environment and with each other, once safety is assured, they will willingly make the moves you request.

Presenters need to build into each training day opportunities to help anxious students relax: "Let's all take a deep breath now. Thank you." Since breathing and heart rates are controlled by the reptilian brain, physical and mental relaxation ensures a receptive mind-body state. Further, relaxation relieves muscle tension and fatigue, carries more oxygen to the brain, and promotes increased concentration, receptivity, and memory.

As an example, after a long or challenging class session or at the beginning of a new session, the presenter can lead the whole class in standing, stretching, and taking several slow, deep breaths. The use of relaxation rituals is an extremely powerful suggestive tool that helps learners become fully present and open to new information.

In training design it is important to respond to the reptilian need for rituals and patterns. Rituals play a key role in creating an atmosphere in which the participants feel connected to one another and are comfortable in the learning environment. Classroom rituals include mutual events such as arrival and starting routines (where you can use upbeat music and fanfare), positive greetings, hugs, high fives, and special handshakes. Special team and group rituals involve chants, gestures, team names, and games. Other possibilities include cheers, songs, affirmations, and slogans as well as special claps to celebrate when a session is closing or a program is ending. Some of the most effective affirmations are given by instructors and class members in response to participation and contribution. The wary reptile is calmed by being affirmed, appreciated, and validated through repetition.

The brain is a physiological organ that functions according to physiological rules. Stress management and exercise create safety, connection, and social cohesion (instead of competition and a concern for personal survival), ensuring that reptilian needs are satisfied. As a result, learners are able to absorb information at the deepest levels of understanding and retention.

MacLean named the middle layer the *limbic* brain, and it is common to all mammals; it developed after most reptiles of the dinosaur age perished, about 60 million years ago. It houses the primary centers of emotion. Like the reptilian brain, the limbic system is involved in primal activities, but it is particularly involved with food and sex, the sense of smell, and bonding needs, including emotions linked to attachment and bringing up the young. Centered in the midbrain, the limbic system monitors the immune and hormonal systems and metabolism.

For designers and presenters, MacLean's view of the work of the limbic system has great relevance: This system acts as the brain's emotion factory, creating the chemical messages that connect information and memory. MacLean believed that for anything to be memorable it must have an emotion associated with it. When learners are emotionally stimulated, even technical information is embedded into long-term memory. Pleasurable learning experiences generate opiatelike chemical connectors that associate pleasure with the subject matter being learned. The converse is true too. Anyone who learned to drive first with an easygoing, confident teacher and then with a critical nervous wreck knows the difference.

The interconnectedness of information and emotions is a central principle of accelerated learning, capitalizing on the knowledge that the limbic system mediates both emotion and memory. Consider the many examples of this in life: the pleasurable memories of family and achievement, the memories connected with grief and loss, the learning blocks people pick up about math and computers, and the tremendous amounts people remember about the subjects that fascinate them.

Here are some accelerated learning techniques that can be used to affect the limbic system positively:

- Creating familiar and pleasant associations through stories, myths, and fables
- Building an upbeat emotional and social environment using plants, flowers, and other attractive physical features in the classroom
- Using positive suggestion to help learners transcend limiting self-concepts, beliefs, and fears
- Playing games, engaging in interactive exercises, and having fun
- Incorporating music, graphics, and art
- Facilitating meaningful exchanges with others
- Developing interactive activities using analogies, themes, and metaphors

People learn when they have a compelling, personal emotional reason to do so. Most students long to make sense of what they have to learn and strive to make a personal, emotional connection to the content.

If such a reason for learning is not apparent, you have to suggest it. For instance, a hotel chain wanted its housekeeping staff to improve its performance, yet a needs assessment suggested that one reason the housekeeping staff didn't always perform well was that some housekeepers viewed the work as menial or "beneath" them. Unfortunately, this perception was fueled by how other employees treated the housekeepers and their work. Many employees never cleaned up a spill or even swept up broken glass because "that's housekeeping's responsibility."

To counter both the housekeepers' sense of inferiority and the hotel staff's view of housekeeping, a comprehensive training program was designed and delivered. The program started with everyone thinking about and sharing his or her view of "home." Home is one of the most powerful emotional triggers in our culture. Think of *E.T., The Odyssey, The Wizard of Oz*, almost all war stories, and even *Little House on the Prairie*. Many of the greatest stories and myths have to do with finding or getting home: "Auntie Em, there's no place like home!"

This exercise was designed for the limbic brain. It succeeded in redefining the hotel employees' attitude toward their work home and the keepers of that home, the housekeepers. As a result, a new sense of individual pride and shared purpose was instilled, thanks to training targeted at the limbic system.

According to MacLean, the youngest brain region is the *neocortex*. It surrounds both the reptilian brain and the limbic brain. While found in all mammals, it is most developed in *Homo sapiens*. The neocortex constitutes five-sixths of the total brain mass that evolved over the last million years to produce the human brain. It houses about 70 *billion* neurons and controls high-level thought processes such as logic, creative thought, language, and the integration of sensory information.

The neocortex is divided into the left and right cerebral hemispheres, referred to earlier as the left brain and right brain. A bridge called the corpus callosum, consisting of 200 million or more nerve fibers, connects these halves. The complementary functions of the two hemispheres give the neocortex its power, flexibility, and ability to transfer information into the limbic system's long-term memory bank.

Unlike the limbic brain, which processes emotions and sensory input internally, the neocortex receives information from the external environment through signals received by the eyes, ears, and other sense organs. It alone among the three regions allows people to see ahead and plan for the future. It can abstract and insinuate and daydream. It makes compassion and empathy possible because it enables one to imagine oneself in another person's place.

We would have no Mozart, Einstein, Martha Graham, or Mother Theresa without the neocortex. Why? It is the neocortex that gives people genius and uniqueness. All people have the same set of systems, including the senses and basic emotions, but they are integrated differently in every brain. It is the neocortex that makes people individuals. While educators and trainers have long targeted the neocortex as the "thinking" brain, many still do not maximize its potential.

The neocortex thinks in patterns. When a pattern isn't available, it creates one. When a pattern is familiar, it uses it to absorb new information. The most powerful boost the learning neocortex can use is a framework for a system being taught. Frames work as structures to organize complex material because the neocortex searches for patterns within a body of information. The following example shows the value of presenting a framework for learning new information. In Fig. 1–1 a series of numbers and a simple shape are presented to a class for memorization.

Without an organizing framework, most students diligently try to find a way to remember each number along with its associated shape, taking several minutes to do so without having much short- or long-term success. Unless the student can "invent" a meaning, the exercise is difficult and meaningless.

FIGURE 1-1

Relearning to Count: I

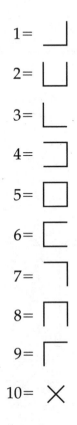

With a framework such as the omnipresent telephone keypad or the familiar tic-tac-toe grid (Fig. 1–2), the new numbering system makes perfect sense. The new numbering system is thus connected to what we already know and grasp. Most participants can remember the numbers and shapes within 10 seconds of seeing them and never forget this pattern.

Tapping the pattern-seeking, organizing principle of the neocortex is an especially humane tactic for presenting technical information. The neocortex likes to see things in familiar places and in relationship to other things it knows. It is through this processing that new information is quickly and easily absorbed, understood, and retained.

How can instructors put these two theories together? What is a good approach to reach the left and right brains and the three capacities of the ancient brain?

FIGURE 1–2

Relearning to Count: II

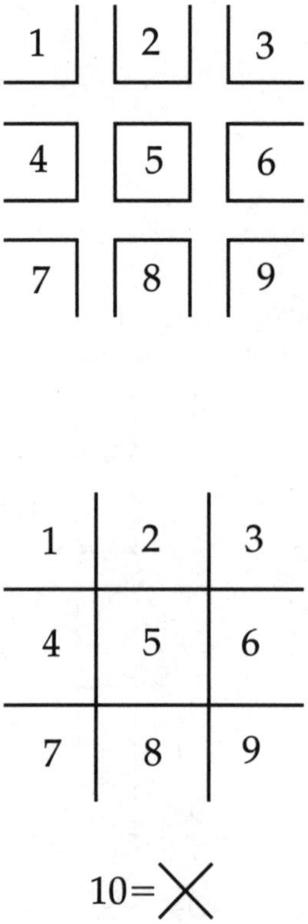

The following example illustrates how to take technical information and present it in an engaging manner that appeals to all the parts of the brain. *The Internet Game* teaches people the big picture and the technical details of how to take full advantage of the Internet. Briefly, my objective was to present highly technical information by using a wide variety of teaching and learning strategies. Before the instruction starts, the participants are immersed in the content because the room is filled with large blowups of Web pages and covers of *Time, Newsweek, U.S. News and World Report*, and other magazines with feature stories about the Internet. There's a giant display board of "Planet Internet," which serves as the governing theme.

Sending messages via the Internet is not as simple or straightforward as some people think. Information gets broken up into separate packets, coded, and sent to the final destination through a variety of electronic routes. After this minilecture on Transmission Control Protocol/Internet Protocol (TCP/IP), the same information is delivered through an analogy: "Consider a 500-piece jigsaw puzzle. Sending a message via the Internet is like sending your friend across the country 500 envelopes each containing one puzzle piece. Because of handling methods at the post office, the envelopes take different routes to your friend's home. But it is the Internet, not your friend, that has the task of putting all 500 pieces back into the correct organization again."

So far information has been presented through a lecturette and analogy, taking advantage of the brain's desire and ability to make multiple connections between what is new and what is known. A third method is a visual presentation that uses colored pens to trace the individual packets as they travel via a series of different routers to the destination computer. Finally (and most fun), the participants *become* the individual packets of information and routers, moving around the room on an imaginary electronic highway until they find the correct path and destination, acting out the process for themselves.

The best training teaches both sides and all three brain regions together. When trainers "work" the content in various ways and have the learners physically, emotionally, and intellectually experience it in different modes, all the parts of the brain are satisfied. The synergy of all the parts working together allows the whole brain to realize its full learning potential and is satisfying for the students.

One, Two, Three: All Together Now!

One of the most effective single tools for providing a supportive and exciting milieu for accelerated learning works to bring the whole brain together. What powerful force could possibly integrate both halves of the brain and all three developmental "compartments" of human gray matter? What great leveler can join all people of all cultures, ages, and backgrounds together? It's music.

Music is an essential tool for adult learning. Playing music before class, especially Baroque or classical recordings, establishes an elevated, relaxed tone that can't be achieved any other way (Table 1–1). Breaks deserve upbeat, rhythmic music (Table 1–2), while working alone or in small groups benefits from string ensembles (Table 1–3). Funny tunes and songs that fit the course metaphor or theme make presentations special and memorable.

Music influences heart rate and breathing (the reptile's job) and stimulates the limbic system's emotional core. Music acts as a carrier to imprint new information with rhythm, pattern, tempo, and tone. Hearing the works of Mozart has been shown to integrate the brain's two hemispheres and help develop the neocortex in newborns. Music directly encodes information into both the conscious and unconscious memory systems, stimulating receptivity and perception. In the original accelerated-learning research done by Dr. Georgi Lozanov, music was a key element in speeding

TABLE 1–1

Suggested Music List

Classical			
Composer/Artist	**Album**	**Label**	**Notes**
Handel	*Fireworks / Water Music*	NAXOS	Start with no. 7
Shahin and Sepehr	*One Thousand and One Nights*	Higher Octave	Start with no. 2
Relax with the Classics	Vol. 3: *Pastorale*	Lind	
Mozart	*In the Morning*	Philips	
Mozart	*For Monday Mornings*	Philips	
Haydn	*String Quartets*	Seraphim	
Violin classics		Seraphim	
Vivaldi		L'ouiseau -lyre	
Bach	*Sonatas*	RCA	
Officium		ECM	
Learning Music			
Music for the Mozart Effect	*Strengthen the Mind*, Vol. I *Relax, Daydream and Draw*, Vol. II		
Music for the Mozart Effect	*Heal the Body*, Vol. II		
The Mozart Effect	*Music for Children*, Vol. 2		
Eagles	*Greatest Hits 1971–1975*	Asylum	Good for working alone
Mozart	*For Your Mind*	Philips	
Mozart	*Makes You Smarter*	Sony	
Break Music			
Somewhere in Time		MCA	
Various artists	*Television's Greatest Hits*	TeeVee Toons	
Cole Porter	*Anything Goes: Cole Porter Songbook*	Verve	
Various artists	*Television's Greatest Hits: 70's and 80's*	TeeVee Toons	
Irving Berlin	*Capital Sings Irving Berlin*	Capitol	
Various artists	*That's Entertainment! The Best of MGM Musicals*	Rhino	
ABBA	*Arrival*		
Various artists	*Thunder on the Steel*	Railcraft Recordings	
Marvin Gaye	*Greatest Hits*	Motown	
Kenny G	*The Moment*	Arista	
Olivia Newton-John	*Olivia's Greatest Hits*, Vol. 2	MCA	
Patsy Cline	*The Patsy Cline Story*	MCA	
Various artists	*Forest Gump: The Soundtrack, Disc One and Two*	Sony	

TABLE 1–1

Suggested Music List continued

Johnny Nash	*I Can See Clearly Now*	Epic	
Various artists	*Zydeco Music*	Rhino	
Bob Marley and The Wailers	*Legend*	Tuff Gong	
Various artists	*St. Elmo's Fire*	Atlantic	
James Taylor	*Greatest Hits*	WB	Mellow break

World Music

Ottmar Liebert + Luna Negra	*Euphoria*	Sony
Prem Joshua	*Tales of a Dancing River*	New Earth Music
Asian Fusion	*Ancient Future*	BMI
KO	*Alter Ego*	Higher Octave Music
Willie and Lobo	*Fandango Nights*	Mesa
Quincy Jones	*Back on the Block*	Qwest
Mickey Hart	*Planet Drum*	Rykodisc
Various artists	*Big Noise*	Rykodisc
Various artists	*Big Noise 2*	Rykodisc
Various artists	*Yoga: A Way of Life*	Silverline

TABLE 1–2

Music for Breaks

Composer/Artist	Album	Label
Various artists	*Forest Gump: The Soundtrack*	Sony
Johnny Nash	*I Can See Clearly Now*	
Marvin Gaye	*Greatest Hits*	Motown
Al Green	*Al Green*	Motown
Bob Marley and the Wailers	*Legend*	Tuff Gong
Quincy Jones	*Back on the Block*	Qwest
Cole Porter	*Cole Porter Songbook*, Vols. 1 and 2	Verve
Cole Porter	*Cole Porter Songbook, Instrumentals*	Verve
Eagles	*Greatest Hits 1971–1975*	Asylum
Patsy Cline	*The Patsy Cline Story*	MCA Records
Olivia Newton-John	*Olivia's Greatest Hits*, Vol. 2	MCA Records
Paul Simon	*Graceland*	WB Records
Enya	*The Memory of Trees*	Reprise
Shahin and Sepehr	*One Thousand and One Nights*	Higher Octave
Willie and Lobo	*Fandango Nights*	Mesa
Asian Fusion	*Ancient Future*	Narada Equinoz
EKO	*Alter Ego*	Higher Octave
Prem Joshua	*Tales of a Dancing River*	New Earth

T A B L E   1–3

Music for Learning

Composer/Artist	Album	Label
Handel	*Fireworks/Water Music*	NAXOS
Haydn	*String Quartets*	Seraphim
Mozart	*In The Morning*	Philips
Mozart	*For Monday Mornings*	Philips
Mozart	*Makes You Smarter*	Sony
Mozart	*For Your Mind*	Philips
Mozart	*The Mozart Effect*	Spring Hill Music
	I: Strengthen the Mind	
	II: Heal the Body	
	III: Unlock the Creative Spirit	
Mozart	*The Mozart Effect*	Spring Hill Music
	Music for Children	
	Vols. 1, 2, and 3	
Vivaldi	*Six Cello Concertos*	L'Oiseau-lyre
Vivaldi and Boccherini	*Cello Concertos*	Deutsche Grammophon
Corelli	*Concerti Grossi*	Seraphim
Various composers	*Relax with the Classics*	Lind
	Vols. 1, 2, 3, and 4	
Telemann	*Suites: Concerto in D Major*	Archiv

up the learning of foreign languages—by a factor of 5 or more. Music and sound effects can be used in many ways to enhance the classroom experience and create an environment of relaxed concentration. You can use music in the following ways:

- In the background during interactive exercises and projects
- While telling stories, myths, and fables
- During reading and reflection
- During creative and journal writing
- To add special effects or excitement during an assignment
- To relax during a guided visualization
- To enliven breaks, stretches, and rituals
- To make special moments more memorable and create a sense of ceremony and celebration
- To enliven a metaphor or theme

Developing music for a program can be a challenging and enjoyable process. Start simply and build your collection gradually. Take an experimental approach in selecting different kinds of music. Use a variety of types of music, note the response from the participants, and keep experimenting. After you've integrated music into the program, you'll never want to be without it.

We have discussed brain "mechanics" in a functional way. Now we can move to the richess of brain power applied: the genius in every person.

Multiple Intelligences Theory:
Eight Kinds of Smart and Counting

The last of the crucial accelerated-learning theories is the multiple intelligences theory. This theory was developed by the Harvard psychologist Howard Gardner and his team of researchers at the Graduate School of Education. (Books by Gardner and others about multiple intelligences are listed at the end of this chapter.) What Gardner and his team put forth is the fact that there is no single way in which everyone thinks and learns. Instead, there are many forms of intelligence, many ways by which people learn, understand, think, problem solve, and relate to the world. Gardner proposed a system of eight distinct intelligences. (Not to be outdone, other researchers have suggested up to 150 different types of intelligences.)

In brief, here are Gardner's multiple intelligences:

1. *Verbal-linguistic.* This is perhaps the most universal of the multiple intelligences, since everyone learns to speak and most people can read and write. In our culture language ability ranks among the most highly esteemed intelligences, along with logical-mathematical thinking. Were you ever impressed or intimidated by someone with a large vocabulary? If so, you're not alone. This intelligence shows up in writers, storytellers, lawyers, politicians, and television talk-show hosts.

2. *Logical-mathematical.* This form of intelligence is most often associated with "scientific" reasoning. This intelligence easily recognizes logical patterns, makes connections, and masters abstract symbols and concepts. Obvious possessors are scientists, statisticians, and computer programmers.

3. *Visual-spatial.* People who are visual-spatial perceive the world through its spatial arrangements: line, shape, positive and negative shape, volume, balance, light and shade, harmony, and color. Think of architects, graphic designers, painters and sculptors, decorators, film directors, chess players, and engineers as examples of this type of brilliance.

4. *Bodily-kinesthetic.* This form of intelligence involves the control and interpretation of muscular and other physical sensations, touch impressions, and visceral reactions to set a person's relationship with the world. Geniuses here may be actors, athletes, dancers, physical therapists, mechanics, carpenters, jewelers, and craftspeople.

5. *Musical-rhythmic.* What outsiders call a gift comes naturally to people with the capacity to recognize and use rhythmic and tonal patterns. If you learn best when music is playing, harmonize with every song you hear, or play rhythms on your briefcase, you may have this form of intelligence. Musicians, disc jockeys, and studio engineers make a living from this intelligence, and others who gain energy and expression from music and rhythm may be high on this scale.

6. *Interpersonal.* This type of intelligence involves the ability to work cooperatively with others, which in turn involves the ability to communicate verbally and nonverbally. This intelligence finds nuances in the feelings, motivations, intentions, and moods of other people. Because of this, it comes naturally to understand, help, and motivate others. This form of intelligence is highly developed in teachers, therapists, politicians, managers, arbitrators, salespeople, public relations specialists, and religious leaders.

7. *Intrapersonal.* To know oneself and to trust one's intuition are aspects of this type of intelligence. Intrapersonal intelligence processes individually rather than in groups. This intelligence entails a keen ability to watch oneself as an outside observer. Some people who appear highly motivated have this intelligence simply because they know themselves so well that they can set a clear direction. This form of intelligence shows up in theologians, entrepreneurs, philosophers, and therapists.

8. *Naturalistic.* Gardner added this eighth form of intelligence recently, perhaps in response to the ecology movement and the recognition that for some people the natural world is a central organizing principle. We all know those who "like animals better than people," but the naturalist is drawn to all elements of the physical world. This type of genius has the ability to see organic systems and their interrelatedness. Charles Darwin is no doubt the best example of this intelligence. Nature writers, anthropologists, biologists, physicians, natural healers, conservationists, and natural scientists are among the people who are strong in this intelligence.

Here are some other key points to keep in mind:

- Everyone possesses all eight intelligences to a greater or lesser degree. It's the combination of how all eight operate that is unique to each person.
- Most people can develop each intelligence to an adequate level of competency. Some people can develop all eight and enjoy a rich level of performance.
- Intelligences work together in complex ways that are defined by individual, social, and cultural proclivities. In a culture that doesn't value logic, a person with this natural intelligence is not likely to emphasize it.
- There is no standard set of attributes that one must have to be considered intelligent in a specific area. For example, an illiterate person may be a fine storyteller.

Gardner's work is having an effect beyond the classroom. *Business Week* reports that writers for *Sesame Street* use his theory to present information through music, animation, dance, and the manipulation of forms. All the automaker Saturn's employees are required to take courses based on the theory. The hard-core scientists at Los Alamos National Laboratory are designing a new work model that incorporates the different intelligences.

For our purposes, a person's learning style consists of the intelligences put to work. Thus, trainers should keep in mind that there are at least eight ways to design and present content area to achieve instructional objectives.

Essentially, multiple intelligences theory offers a means of building curriculum or training plans for maximum learning impact in which all students can have some of their intelligences addressed at least some of the time. The more intelligences you can incorporate into a program, the deeper, more inclusive, and more thorough the learning will be. Here's a "brain buffet" for you to use, giving representative learning activities for the respective intelligences:

Verbal-Linguistic
These people are "word-smart" and prefer

- Debates
- Lectures
- Large and small group discussions
- Brainstorming
- Crossword puzzles and word games
- Audiotapes

Logical-Mathematical
These people are "math- and logic-smart" and prefer

- Socratic questioning
- Scientific demonstrations
- Logical and mathematical problem-solving exercises
- Creating and "breaking" codes
- Calculations and other math operations
- Logical-sequential presentations of content
- Computer programming languages

Visual-Spatial
These people are "picture-smart" and prefer

- Charts, graphs, diagrams, and maps
- Visualization

- PowerPoint presentations
- Mind mapping and visual organizers
- Painting, collages, and visual arts
- Graphic symbols
- Visual pattern seeking

Bodily-Kinesthetic
These people are "body-smart" and prefer

- Creative movement, dance, and mime
- Physical awareness exercises
- Sports that teach
- Hands-on learning
- Manipulatives, tactile materials, and experiences
- Competitive and cooperative games
- Using body language, gestures, and hand signals to communicate
- Stretching and physical relaxation exercises

Musical-Rhythmic
These people are "music-smart" and prefer

- Singing, humming, or whistling
- Putting information into chants and raps
- Hearing songs that teach
- Using music in the background
- Playing all kinds of musical instruments
- Linking old tunes with new concepts

Interpersonal
These people are "people-smart" and prefer

- Paired sharing
- Conflict mediation
- Role playing
- Interactive games and exercises
- Group and peer teaching
- Group brainstorming sessions
- Social gatherings
- Simulations

Intrapersonal
These people are "self-smart" and prefer

- Individualized instruction
- Independent study
- Self-paced learning
- Private time for study, reflection, or meditation
- Options for working on one's own
- Reflection and journal-keeping time
- Personal connections
- Self-esteem activities

Naturalistic
These people are "nature-smart" and prefer

- Field trips and time outdoors
- Expeditionary activities
- Classification and activities that locate the connections
- Hands-on experiments
- Activity write-ups

On one level, multiple intelligences theory applied to course design and presentation may be used as a loose and diverse collection of strategies such as those listed in this chapter. When used in this way, this theory represents a model of instruction that has no distinct rules other than to fulfill the needs of the individual and the interrelated qualities of the intelligences. You can pick and choose freely from all the suggestions above, matching the theory to your unique teaching style and adapting its principles to any educational setting. On a deeper level, the theory suggests a set of criteria that can be included when you create new programs. In fact, it provides a context within which you can address any skill, content area, or instructional objective and develop at least eight ways to teach it.

In summary, curriculum designers and presenters are obliged to offer training that works in today's society. While modern employees are the best educated in history, they are required to absorb tremendous amounts of information and apply vast amounts of knowledge. We must use every theory, tool, and technique that will help employees learn while unleashing every available type of intelligence, gift, and aspect of humanity at their disposal.

The expansive view of using all the mind's talents encourages trainers to help learners make important connections, turning information into knowledge quickly while forming long-term memory. Learners can comply, respond, and make the most of these learning opportunities. Some will try to grow the underdeveloped parts of themselves that are honored and validated through whole-brain, accelerated-learning techniques.

CREATING A CONTEXT FOR LEARNING

There is one last concept that can shore up even a beginner's efforts to bring accelerated learning to the workplace: creating the learning context. Put simply, as children learn, they absorb the entire experience, including feelings. Thus, the whole context, as well as the content, is learned. Context is the entire physical, social, and emotional place in which learning takes place. Context should not be confused with content. Context is the envelope, the container, and the environment, that holds the course content.

Building a context for learning uses all the techniques and suggestions previously discussed: a safe and supportive physical environment, an emotionally rich milieu, and an intellectual framework where connections between old and new information can flourish. The most effective unifying force for creating the ultimate learning context is to use metaphors to deliver course material.

Metaphors are intrinsic to the construction of new knowledge and lie at the heart of the creation of meaning. Metaphors compare the meaning and attributes of one thing to the meaning and attributes of another. Here are some familiar examples of metaphor:

- Time is money.
- Love is war.
- Life is just a bowl of cherries.
- A faithful friend is the medicine of life.

We hear sayings like these and instinctively know what is meant by them because metaphor provides a familiar "playing ground." We are able to make connections between two different things by recognizing that they share common traits.

Learning by metaphor is like climbing a spiral staircase. We start with a base of knowledge and move up through the metaphor, comparing what we know to what we don't know. The result of the climb is new knowledge, which gives us a new base to work from. When we forge a connection between a new concept and a past experience, the concept is clarified and the mind is encouraged to explore it further. Metaphor becomes a means to effectively engage all the systems of the brain and, in so doing, creates a dynamic context for learning.

Metaphor has a wide range of uses in designing and presenting a course. It can be used to introduce a particular concept, and it also can become the overall theme for the program. For example, when we discussed left brain–right brain theory, we could have likened the left brain to a computer and the right brain to a kaleidoscope. If you are familiar with those things, you will make quick connections, speed up your learning, and deepen your understanding.

Let's take this a step further and see how it can be used to create a framework for an entire program. How does a course designer develop a metaphor that will work, that is, one that is familiar to the participants and contains sufficient parallels to the course's subject? If you're fairly intuitive, it may just come to you. If it doesn't, it's productive (and fun) to brainstorm ideas with others.

Here's a process to follow:

- Decide exactly what you want to teach and what the general principle of the course is.
- See if the content itself suggests a metaphor or theme.
- Brainstorm as many metaphors as you think might work.
- Select the metaphor that best communicates the information you're teaching and start experimenting with designing the content.
- Clarify the discrepancies, or the ways in which the metaphor doesn't fit the subject.
- Choose a "working metaphor" and formally begin the design process.

When a metaphor fits, everything else seems to fall into place. When it doesn't, you're facing a square peg and round hole. One key is to find a metaphor to which the content can be connected seamlessly. Another key is to make sure the metaphor creates a positive context and/or environment. If you haven't consciously included metaphoric teaching in program design or delivery before, it may seem a little difficult at first. But as you practice, you'll see that the possibilities are unlimited.

An effective metaphor can provide the designer and the presenter with a constant source of associations, analogies, props, characters, music, and games. Choosing a metaphor for a course can introduce a multitude of comparisons between a common experience and the subject matter being taught. Consider these ideas as stimuli:

- Popular movies, plays, and television shows
- Genres such as westerns, science fiction, fables, game shows, sporting events, and myths
- Major events such as elections and holidays
- Historical time settings and futuristic fantasy
- Literary classics
- Geographic settings
- Familiar settings such as a cruise, courtroom, family life, or movie set

The Accounting Game uses the metaphor of a kid's lemonade stand to teach the basics of accounting. Since it's a lemonade stand, numbers and concepts are kept simple: The inventory is lemons and sugar, the finished goods consist of lemonade, and accounts payable is the money you owe the grocer. The learning is conducted with color-coded game pieces and a game board (a financial statement) that allows for easy organization. The green pieces represent cash, the red pieces represent accounts payable, and so forth. Participants are given separate name tags and told to invent nicknames for themselves. The instructor wears a beanie with a propeller. The music consists of golden oldies from baby boomers' youth.

In many successful training programs a metaphorical theme dictates the design and delivery of the content while setting and maintaining an upbeat and sensory-rich context. This theme is chosen carefully to elicit a deep and appropriate emotional response that in turn accelerates learning and the retention of information. Once selected, the metaphor or theme is woven through all the instructional material, the learning environment, the language, the form of learning activities, break and background music, leader costumes, snacks—everything!

The fastest learning with the best retention occurs in a sensory-rich metaphoric learning context in which the learner is engaged and relationships are built and reinforced. The most effective trainers make sure that the participants fully connect with themselves and with others, taking complete responsibility for their own and others' learning.

BRAIN-BASED LEARNING IN ACTION

An understanding of how the adult brain learns is very important, but it's not the be-all and end-all. *Applying* that understanding to training design and delivery is the goal. This chapter has given you a start toward a practical understanding of the best modern training approaches.

Although this takes more creativity and attention to detail up front, accelerated learning and other whole-brain training technologies have enormous long-term benefits to curriculum designers and trainers. Learners will respond to the approach and be much easier to teach. Programs will receive excellent long-term evaluations and feedback. Retention rates will approach 90 percent, and finally, while perhaps being more labor-intensive and financially intensive to create, this type of program costs less over time thanks to its effectiveness.

In the most exciting accelerated-learning corporate classrooms there is an atmosphere of excitement and activity that is set up initially by the trainers and then driven by the students. Learners who thrive on a deliberately constructed context of thoughtful design and uplifting teaching techniques can clearly focus on their own learning objectives, be open to growth and development, and help their colleagues do the same.

Such learning experiences are never forgotten, and like the first time a youngster ties a shoe, they become an important part of an individual's confidence and contribution to the world.

CHAPTER 2

Instructional Systems Design: A Little Bit of ADDIEtude, Please

Peter Beckschi

Mike Doty

Not long ago a friend of the authors decided to build the home of his dreams. Sam had just gotten a new job in Phoenix and was looking forward to bringing his family along after he built the home. Wanting to save money, Sam decided to build his new home just the way Marge and the kids wanted it. Sam was good: He had refurbished a dilapidated house back east that had earned him a nice profit. When we told Sam that his plans sounded interesting and mentioned that he'd never built a house from the ground up, he replied, "I just purchased some house plans, and with a few modifications here and there I can pull it off." To make a long story short, Sam did build his house, but it did not turn out to be the home of his dreams. It cost him considerable time, money, and aggravation trying to retrofit his ideas into the existing architecture he purchased. Old plumbing lines, electrical overload, structural dead ends. . . all defeated his end goal. His attitude was terrific, but if he had known more about architecture, he would have foreseen the problems that he later experienced.

This tale is similar to many we've heard over the years about training. The attitude of most trainers is positive and obliging; they want to help and learn from others. We like to think it is one of the things that sets our profession apart from the others. However, one of the things we experienced that caused us concern is that many people in our field don't have what we call ADDIEtude. By ADDIEtude we mean the architectural knowledge of how to develop training from the ground up. The word is based on the primary phases of the instructional systems development (ISD) process: *a*nalyze, *d*esign, *d*evelop, *i*mplement, and *e*valuate (Fig. 2–1).

In an age when fast is better, many training programs are likely to go the way of Sam's dream house unless sound architectural thinking is in place. If you've ever

FIGURE 2-1

Basic ISD Model

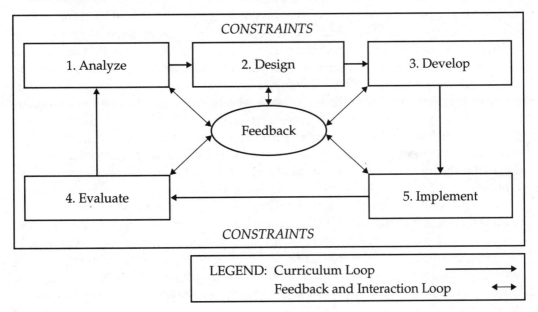

seen a video program converted to CD-ROM so that it could be called "interactive," you know what we mean. If you ever sat watching a computer-based training (CBT) program and were bored to tears turning electronic pages, you know what we mean. If you ever sat in a seminar wondering when the leader would get to the substance, you know what we mean.

Understandably, there is little time to do the job, and so we buy ready-made training packages or take shortcuts in building a training program. This is fine if you are backing it up with sound reasons and have expertise available to tweak the content to your needs. Most of our colleagues in business, industry, and the military have faced the challenge of delivering the training on time and at minimal cost using off-the-shelf programs and shortcutting the ISD process. Many take a calculated risk based on years of experience and their knowledge of Murphy's law.

Our belief is that armed with a basic knowledge and application of ISD, trainers can organize and develop a better training program or curriculum. They also can identify the critical factors and devote the time and investment required to do it right the first time.

BACKGROUND

Since its inception in the early 1960s, ISD has undergone very little change. ISD was designed to provide a template for the development of instruction by the U.S. military, where it remains the foundation for courseware. Recent discussions with educational researchers and users underscore the fact that the basic ISD model and its underlying systems approach are relevant and sound. ISD is used extensively in U.S. government agencies to develop courseware, especially for highly critical training. It is employed by utilities, process plants, and human health systems. Although the models employed by these users are highly elaborated, most training programs can use the basic model to provide an architectural blueprint or guide, ensuring that essential components have been addressed. Intrinsic to the ISD system is the ability to create an audit trail to evaluate and modify a program. ISD has been adapted for the development of multimedia programs in which contractual obligations with vendors are stated to include ISD components such as learner analysis, design limitations, development plans, delivery, and methods of learner evaluation. (It makes sense to know what you ordered and what you're getting.)

The ISD model is atheoretic, offering a generic framework with established tasks for the instructional designer to perform in preparing training programs. However, the procedures specified to complete each stage of a training program's development were based on psychological principles derived mainly from behaviorism and are being updated with recent advances in cognitive science (see below).

NEW FRONTIERS AND OLD CHALLENGES

In light of technological advances such as CBT and computer-aided instruction (CAI) and training presented on the Internet, one might ask, Doesn't the new presentation technology imply the need for a companion advancement other than the basic ISD model to achieve transfer? Some would answer that hybrid training, combining an instructor and all the new media, mandates a more sophisticated design approach. Others might observe that the logical progression of ISD curriculum dovetails nicely with equally logical CBT. Consider the following excerpt from the November 1998 edition of *Inside Technology Training*. The quote comes from an article by Constantine von Hoffman entitled "What Kind of Training Is This Anyway?"

> Fifty employees at Amdahl Corp. are serving as guinea pigs in an experiment that is in many ways a microcosm of these trends (hybrid training). George Purnell, chief learning officer for the Sunnyvale, California-based computer maker, combines lectures from Knowledge Pool, an international corporate training consortium, with CBT from NETg to train employees to take Microsoft certification exams. " [The student] signs up into a 'client zone' on the Web, which is basically an enrollment system," says Purnell. Once into the client zone, the student takes a Web-based skills as-

sessment test. The test, says Purnell, specifies a "learning path," that should take the student on the quickest route to certification. It's a step in the right direction—but the computer's ability to specify a different and accurate curriculum for each student isn't perfect. It generates the learning path, says Purnell wryly, "hopefully without redundancy."

Opting for the potential cost-effectiveness of newer, more technological modes of presentation may not necessarily provide for all student or training system needs. More likely is a scenario in which new methods supplement proven approaches to transfer, such as ISD. A fair conclusion can be made: Basics still apply and should be accomplished to maximize performance competency in those being trained. What follows is a quick review of the *essential* components of the basic ISD model.

ANALYZE, DESIGN, DEVELOP, IMPLEMENT, EVALUATE (ADDIE)

The authors acknowledge that there is nothing new here. We attempt only to remind the reader of ISD fundamentals that often are overshadowed in the interest of conserving resources. Sam was going to save money by building his dream house without sufficient architectural experience or knowledge. He did build his house, but it did not turn out as he envisioned it. Figure 2–1 illustrated the top-level architecture of ISD, centering on the core element of continual feedback between the model elements. This model mirrors the version applied by the U.S. Department of Defense (DOD) and organizations with critical training needs (Fig. 2–2).

Analyze

This phase requires that the developer first become familiar with every aspect of the operational system, job, or educational situation for which there is thought to be a need for instruction: Do we need to teach something? What is the subject all about? What should the learner be able to do?

Analysis will help determine whether there is a need for instruction, what will be taught, and what behaviors and processes the learner should exhibit. This part of the process is dedicated to the collection of data, which should be used to determine the purpose of the operational system, job, or educational situation to be taught, including the following elements:

- Functional responsibilities of personnel working within the operational system, job, or educational situation to be taught
- Operational subsystems structure or knowledge base to be taught

FIGURE 2–2

ISD Model Developed by the US Air Force

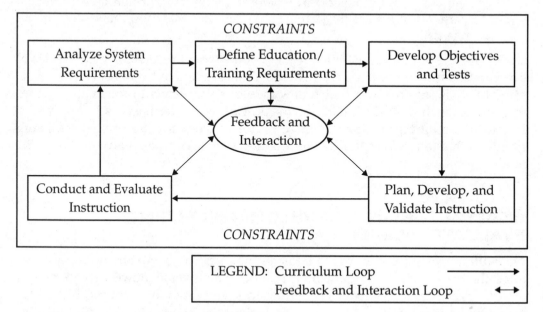

- Support equipment or materials
- How information about the system or educational situation is maintained or used

The products of analysis should include:

- The basic human physical and mental processes required
- A list of all job tasks and procedures
- The equipment and materials involved in each task
- The conditions under which the task must be done
- The performance standards (degree of competency) to be demonstrated

In the final phases of analysis a developer should determine

- How often a task needs to be accomplished
- Task criticality
- Task complexity
- Difficulty level required to learn and teach each task

Figure 2–3 provides a graphic flowchart of the analysis-to-design phase. You can use this figure as a template to prepare your own flowchart.

FIGURE 2-3

Typical Flowchart of Analysis-to-Design Phase

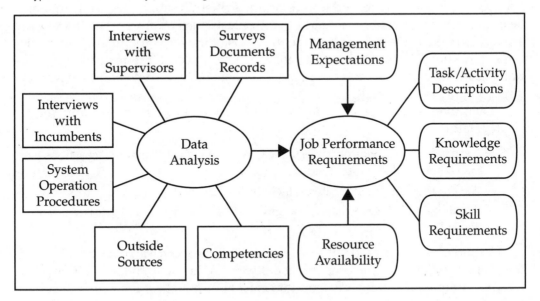

Design

Once the job performance requirements are known, the developer must determine the difference between the skills possessed by those targeted for training and the skills required to operate the system or master the educational challenge. The resulting data constitute the training or education requirements. The developer will use the initial data to build the course design by considering the following:

- What training is needed most
- Criticality of tasks and knowledge
- Frequency of performance
- Complexity of tasks
- Difficulty of learning
- Time interval between initial training and initial performance
- Availability of time, instructors, equipment, facilities, and funding

The first design activity constructs terminal learning objectives for each task. These objectives contain three parts: statement of the action, conditions, and standards of performance. Each terminal learning objective is classified into one of four learning categories and analyzed to determine specific learning objectives and the learning steps necessary to master them. The four learning categories are mental skills, information, physical skills, and attitudes.

Next, criterion-referenced test items are written to satisfy the needs for entry tests, pretests, unit posttests, or end-of-course tests. One or more test items usually are written for each learning objective. Analysis of the target population identifies the skills, knowledge, and attitudes that learners have before instruction. Additional learning objectives may be included, or some may be deleted (if the learners already know the material).

Objectives should be meaningful, measurable, and observable and should clearly state

- The expected behavior or performance, using active verbs that reflect actions that can be observed and measured
- The limits or conditions within which the students will perform
- The standards of performance that indicate that a student can perform a task to the desired level of proficiency

Experience indicates that if a developer cannot produce an objective that contains all three elements, the problem usually lies in the fact that the analysis phase was not completed and insufficient data exist about the task for which the objective is being written.

Objectives and learning steps should be arranged in the sequence in which instruction is presented to the learner. Relationships between objectives should be examined to determine those which are independent of each other, those which are dependent, and those which are supportive (Fig. 2–4).

With the framework of the educational and training requirements known and the learning objectives sequenced in a way that produces the desired learning, tests can be developed. Thoroughly developed objectives tell the instructor and the student where they are going. Corresponding tests should tell the instructor whether proper instruction or learning has been achieved. If you have no idea of where you are going, you probably will not get there.

A poorly developed objective might look like this:

Understand Ohm's Law

A stronger objective statement might be

Use Ohm's Law to determine applied voltage when amperage and circuit resistance are known.

This type of objective statement can easily be tested for competency.

Measurement devices must evaluate both supporting knowledge and the behavior of the objective under the conditions and subject to the standards as they are stated in the objective. To teach one thing and measure another is not acceptable.

FIGURE 2-4

Relationships Among Learning Objectives

DEPENDENT	INDEPENDENT	SUPPORTIVE
Skills and knowledge in one learning objective are closely related to those in the other learning objectives. It is necessary to master one before the other.	Skills and knowledge in one learning objective are unrelated to those in the other learning objective. Mastering one of the learning objectives does not simplify mastering the other.	Skills and knowledge in one learning objective have some relationship to those in the other learning objective. The mastery of one transfers to the other, making learning easier.
EXAMPLES: ❖ Before driving a vehicle, the learner demonstrates knowledge of rules of the road. ❖ Before answering a customer, the caller should know the FAQs (frequently asked questions).	**EXAMPLES:** ❖ The administrative assistant needs to know Word and Excel. ❖ Auditors need to develop problem-solving skills and how to communicate.	**EXAMPLES:** ❖ Keyboard skills are very useful in sending e-mail. ❖ To analyze the profit-loss ledger, using the calculator would be helpful.
SEQUENCE: The learning objectives must be arranged in the sequence indicated.	**SEQUENCE:** The learning objectives can be arranged in any sequence without loss of learning.	**SEQUENCE:** The learning objectives should be placed close together in the sequence to permit optimum transfer of learning from one learning objective to the other.

As with any building project, the foundations must be constructed so that they carry a specific load. Beams, trusses, and load-bearing walls must be constructed according to well-tested and proven codes. It is a bit late to correct deficiencies in the roof of a shopping mall when a sudden downpour destroys a roof that was not built to code. Sam should have done it right the first time.

Experience indicates that for budgetary planning purposes, creating a formal design document that incorporates the analysis and design phases provides an essential document for vendor development and production. This document can be labeled a training design report (TDR) or personnel training concept (PTC). The importance lies not in the label but in the information it provides to management and vendors for the next ISD phase.

Develop

Some instructional designers consider this the fun phase of ISD. Once the data, objectives, and proofs (or tests) have been established, how we translate this into learning events and activities can be enjoyable but also frustrating, since experience and judgment play a critical role.

This is also the phase when inexperience can lead to the selection of inappropriate materials from vendors. For example, a "generic" problem-solving video may not provide the appropriate context unless special "customization" is included. Another example is using an off-the-shelf time-management program for call center supervisors. Anybody who has visited or works in a call center will know what it means when we say "context, context, context."

One of the purported limitations of ISD mentioned earlier in this chapter is that it originally was based on behaviorism and that not until recently was cognitive science introduced to provide a more robust approach to developing the knowledge, skills, and attitudes that result in the desired human performance. Through understanding and experimenting with recent developments in cognitive science, designers have been able to enhance procedural (behavior-based) as well as mental skills by applying unique and creative designs to training. Other chapters in this book provide useful guidelines for incorporating a variety of learning approaches that relate to adult learning theory, active training techniques, accelerated learning, facilitation instead of instruction, self-directed learning, and so forth. Again, be aware of context not only in terms of the learner but also in terms of possibilities within the organizational culture. Ever wonder why so few training conferences and seminars are held in Hawaii?

This is also the phase where media selection can limit the development of instruction. Consider and select methods appropriate to the learning (and price tag). The range available today is enormous, from simple, soundly developed instruction to CBT and workplace simulations (Fig. 2–5).

FIGURE 2-5

Representative Instructional Media

INSTRUCTIONAL MEDIUM GROUP	REPRESENTATIVE EXAMPLES
Instructor with instructional aids ❖ Instruction ❖ Instructional aids	Lecture Demonstration Tutoring/coaching Overhead projector (1 in this category) Whiteboard Powerpoint presentation Posters
Multimodal media	Video Computer-based training Multimedia
Print	Books Computers (words and numbers only) Programmed instruction booklets Microfiche
Peer (or peer group)	Role playing Discussion groups Tutoring/coaching
Training devices and simulators	Actual equipment trainers Gaming Interactive computer (simulation) Training simulators (full-scale)

The rule of thumb is that the closer the medium is to the real work environment, the better the knowledge transfer is.

Our advice is to go for the type of creativity that enhances the delivery and retention of learning but takes into account cost, time, and the delivery method that is "appropriate." There is no substitute for experience and sound judgment (read return on investment here).

In the ISD model completed objectives and tests or units of instruction should be presented to typical members of a target population to ensure that the objectives and tests are valid. There are many different ways to do this, from small group try-outs (pilots) to a large-scale presentation or "dry run" of the entire curriculum. Even though a proficient ISD project will be updated constantly through feedback, the initial project should be as near to final as possible before the first presentation.

Implement

At one time or another, most trainers have received requests (excuses) for training that sound like this:

> Our sales force is getting together next week. Could you provide some training between 9 and 10 a.m. on Monday? Something inspiring?

> Our customer service people are not meeting their targets. We need to send them back for training.

> My supervisors haven't had any training for a while. What can I send them to?

These statements imply that any training will solve a "problem." This is the Band-Aid approach to training implementation and falls outside the realm of any advice we can offer using ISD other than "good luck."

However, if you've developed most of the processes and products from the previous phases, you're ready to launch the training. Depending on the urgency of the request for training, you should have conducted a pilot to validate the design and development. In many cases, the transition from pilot to final training product is imperceptible not so much because of the quality of the product but because of the urgency that follows the request for training.

Depending on the size of the training effort, the following implementation plan requirements need to be situated in this phase of the ISD process. Actually, many of these requirements need to be identified in the analysis phase to provide the resources necessary for successful implementation.

An implementation plan, also called a master training plan, should include the following:

- Administrative details
- Audience to be trained (demographics)

- Schedules and venue (logistics)
- Curriculum path, map, and modules
- Test and evaluation procedures
- Trainers assigned
- Budget

Other support factors to be considered prior to training include:

- Trainer competencies
- Records and reports (systems)
- Regulatory and legal considerations
- Overall project management

The actual conduct of the training should make most of the noninstructional aspects of implementation transparent to the learner.

Evaluation

Ensure that evaluation instruments are in place that measure both instruction and how well the students do. Measurement takes many forms, however. As was stated in the development step, measurement devices must evaluate both supporting knowledge and the behavior of the objective under the conditions and subject to the standards as they are stated in the objective. The best instructional systems take the student through an experience that mirrors the work environment and maximizes student activities that are identical to job functions.

This fifth or final phase of ISD evaluation consists of two major activities:

1. *Internal evaluation* basically provides inputs based on the experience of trainers, staff, and learners that measure points of quality, including learner knowledge and performance checks. The overall purpose is to provide immediate or nearly immediate feedback to the instructional developers so that changes and/or modifications can be made to the curriculum. This is where "formative evaluation" applies.

2. *External evaluation* is directed fundamentally to application on the job; it includes Kirkpatrick's four levels as well as Parry's return on investment (ROI) (Chapters 9 and 10). This is where "summative evaluation" techniques apply; it is also where instructional objectives can be demonstrated through changes in human performance.

At a recent conference Kirkpatrick surveyed the audience in terms of which of the four levels were in play at the different organizations represented. All the hands went up for *level 1 (reaction)*, about 80 percent for *level 2 (learning)*, about 50 percent for *level 3 (behavior)*, and only one hand for *level 4 (results)*. This random survey corroborates our experience in the field, which indicates that most organizations are at level 2. However, with today's increased accountability and justification for budgets, heads of training operations are driving level 3 and 4 evaluations. Demonstrating the training effect as ROI satisfies management's need for data and leads to continued support.

A FINAL REALITY CHECK

The use of the ISD process may require compromises. Some training media may cost too much. Sufficient time to do a thorough analysis may not be available, or there may not be enough time to try out the instruction. These constraints must be considered in the design of the system. The developers' goal is to build an instructional system that is the best possible considering all the alternatives, where *best* is defined as the most cost-effective way possible. The need to deal with valid constraints is not a license to bypass major parts of the system development process for frivolous reasons. Compromises and the reasons for them must be documented.

Although ISD has the appearance of a linear system, it is best utilized as an interactive process in which sequencing and fine-tuning objectives are possible. There are no prohibitions against incorporating "fun activities" or music, and evaluations can be changed with reference to other changes. Once you begin using ISD as a working template (Fig. 2–6), you will be able to create the right training program and justify the resources needed. It works!

ISD Job Aid

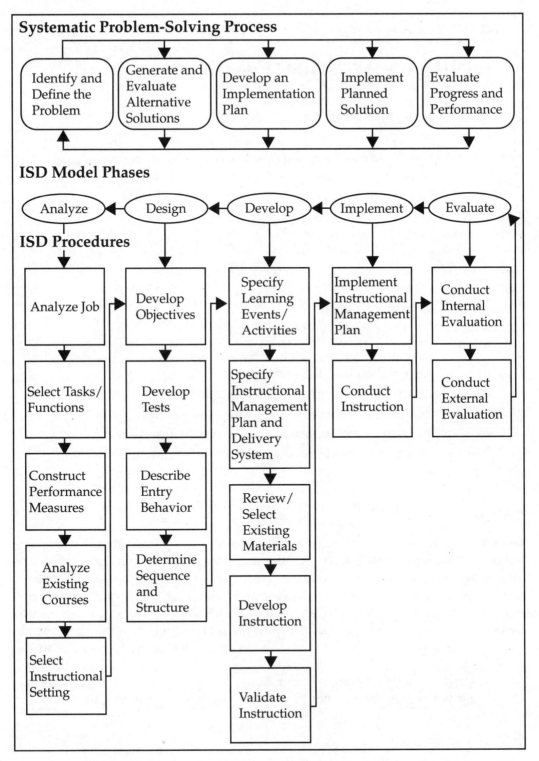

Systematic Problem-Solving Process

| Identify and Define the Problem | Generate and Evaluate Alternative Solutions | Develop an Implementation Plan | Implement Planned Solution | Evaluate Progress and Performance |

ISD Model Phases

Analyze ◄ Design ◄ Develop ◄ Implement ◄ Evaluate

ISD Procedures

Analyze
- Analyze Job
- Select Tasks/Functions
- Construct Performance Measures
- Analyze Existing Courses
- Select Instructional Setting

Design
- Develop Objectives
- Develop Tests
- Describe Entry Behavior
- Determine Sequence and Structure

Develop
- Specify Learning Events/Activities
- Specify Instructional Management Plan and Delivery System
- Review/Select Existing Materials
- Develop Instruction
- Validate Instruction

Implement
- Implement Instructional Management Plan
- Conduct Instruction

Evaluate
- Conduct Internal Evaluation
- Conduct External Evaluation

CHAPTER 3

Making Training Active

Karen Lawson, PhD, CSP

Objectives

After reading this chapter, you will be able to:

- Use active-training techniques to increase retention, build understanding, and improve the skills of the participants
- Involve all the participants in the learning process
- Adapt active-training methods to any course content
- Use active-training techniques to gain 100 percent participation
- Introduce, conduct, and process an activity for maximum learning effectiveness

OVERVIEW

A growing concern among trainers is getting participants interested and involved in training sessions. It's becoming increasingly difficult to gain and maintain program participants' attention and interest. Conditioned by computer games, MTV, and interactive media, corporate classroom audiences expect and demand to be entertained as well as trained. They want the learning experience to be both meaningful and enjoyable. Although challenging, meeting these needs and expectations is not difficult if you incorporate interactive techniques in the training design.

Research shows that people understand concepts better and retain information longer when they are actively involved in the learning process; therefore, the most effective means of delivering training are active-training techniques. Active training is "the process of getting participants to do the work," according to active-training expert Mel Silberman. Active training is based on a well-researched, proven approach to learning called cooperative learning. This is an approach to learning in which participants learn from each other in pairs or small groups.

STRATEGIES AND TECHNIQUES

Based on learning, teaching, and motivation theories as well as research findings, the following strategies and techniques create the underpinnings of active-learning methods.

Structure and organization. Active training requires structure. The trainer places participants in specific groups and gives specific assignments with clear instructions and time limits. These assignments may include group tasks as well as individual roles such as recorder, timekeeper, and spokesperson. Since people take in and process information differently, trainers should first form the groups to avoid confusion and then give instructions in both oral and written form by displaying them on a flip chart, transparency, or handout.

Moderate level of content. Active training focuses more on process than on content; therefore, trainers should determine "need to know" versus "nice to know." Content no longer is limited to facts, dates, formulas, definitions, and so on. It has been redefined to include skills and understanding, thus ensuring a balance among the cognitive, affective, and behavioral domains of learning. When you clearly define what you want participants to know and be able to do by the end of the session, you clarify the content and select appropriate learning strategies. These expectations must be communicated clearly to the participants at the beginning of the session, preferably before presession memos, questionnaires, assignments, and so on.

High level of participation. The trainer's role is that of a facilitator whose primary function is to manage the learning process. Learners are actively engaged in activities from the start, continuously involved in doing, discussing, and reflecting.

Interdependence. Active training creates interdependence among group members. To facilitate that outcome, the trainer requires all group members to master the content of the assignment. This might be accomplished by a jigsaw design in which the group learning activity is structured so that each group member is responsible for learning a specific piece of the content and then teaching it to the other participants.

Minimal lecturing. Although there is a place for lecturing as a training method, it should be used in small doses of 10 to 15 minutes. Uninterrupted trainer discourse results in confusion, boredom, and low retention. Lectures, however, can be interactive. Participants can be involved through interactive techniques that promote both understanding and retention. These techniques are addressed later in this chapter.

Variety of methods. The active-training approach incorporates a variety of methods and techniques. These activities focus primarily on the use of small groups, pairs, and trios.

Peer teaching. Adults bring a wealth of experience and expertise to the learning environment. Active training encourages them to draw on and share their experiences with others in the group.

Iterative process. Throughout an active-training session, the trainer arranges activities that build on and repeat concepts and skills that were learned earlier. Therefore, learning is reinforced and the participants have more opportunities to digest and integrate the learning into their current body of knowledge and understanding.

Real-world application. Active training enables participants to use real-life situations in learning new concepts and skills. Sometimes the trainer solicits examples of hypothetical or real problems for the participants to use throughout the session. In addition, before the session ends, the trainer allows the participants to develop individual action plans, identifying how they are going to apply what they have learned in the real world.

This chapter will help you identify ways to involve the participants in the learning process actively by using learner-centered activities and structured experiences and providing the earners with many opportunities to master the content.

DESCRIPTION OF BASIC TECHNIQUES

Get Them Active from the Start

People learn by doing, not by being told. This basic principle of adult learning should be your guide in designing any training program, from the highly technical to the so-called soft skills addressed in human resource development programs.

Participants need to be engaged from the beginning. You can create immediate involvement with a variety of enjoyable yet content-related activities and techniques. Opening activities can accomplish several goals: (1) involving the participants immediately in the learning experience, (2) creating a risk-free learning environment, (3) communicating personal responsibility for learning,

(4) introducing the content, (5) building group cohesiveness, and (6) assessing participants' needs and expectations.

Choose an opening activity that will accomplish several goals or objectives. For example, one successful technique is called "What Do You Want to Know?" The trainer posts flip chart pages on the wall, each with a heading that corresponds to a major topic of the training program. Then the trainer gives a packet of Post-It notes to each participant and asks the participants to write down any questions they have about any of the topics. They may fill as many notes as they want but may put only one question on each note. The participants then get up and place their questions under the appropriate headings. The trainer can then categorize the questions and compare them to the learning objectives of the session. This method gives participants an opportunity to express their expectations anonymously. They are also immediately engaged in the process, thinking about the content, and beginning to take ownership of their learning. The only goal this activity does not address is building group cohesiveness.

The trainer needs to create many opportunities for the participants to interact with each other. Often this may involve asking people to work in pairs to come up with a joint answer to a question posed by the trainer, prepare a list of guidelines related to the topic, or discuss individual responses. Pairs ensure 100 percent participant involvement in a low-risk environment.

The use of small groups is a very effective way to get people involved. Use small groups to generate ideas, discuss concepts, solve problems, or work on case studies. Small groups provide more opportunities for people to contribute and participate. Often those who are reluctant to speak up in a large group seem to come alive in a small group setting.

Alternatives to Lectures

Trainers who have to present a lot of information in a short period argue that the only way to communicate information effectively and efficiently is to lecture. This is not so. Cognitive information can be taught actively by using cooperative-learning techniques. The following designs, adapted from *101 Ways to Make Training Active* by Mel Silberman and Karen Lawson, can be used to present content without lecturing.

Group Inquiry

This technique is particularly useful when you have a somewhat complicated graphic, such as a diagram, flowchart, model, or numerical table. The traditional approach would involve the trainer showing the item on a slide or transparency and "going over it," that is, explaining it to the group. A more active approach is to put participants in pairs or small groups and ask them to study and discuss the piece with their partner or partners, placing question marks and making notes on the things they do not understand. After a while you reconvene the entire group and begin answering the questions the participants have generated during the study period. The purpose of this is to arouse interest and stimulate questions.

Information Search
By nature, people are curious. Capitalize on this by making participants find the information for themselves instead of giving it to them. This technique is similar to the homework worksheet assignments you may have used in grammar school. Create a worksheet listing a number of questions related to the information you want the participants to learn. Also provide resource materials where they can find the answers to the questions. These materials can be brochures, manuals, job aids, and so on. Put people into pairs or small groups, give them the study sheets and resource materials, and ask them to search out the information. At the end of the designated time period, reconvene the entire group, ask the small groups to report, and discuss the information.

Guided Discussion
Guided discussion can be traced back to Socrates, who guided his students in the learning process by asking them a series of questions. You too can guide your participants by posing questions that draw on their knowledge and experience. Your job is to provoke thought and discussion about the concepts and ideas you are presenting.

Jigsaw Design
When you have learning material that can be broken into several parts, such as an article with several sections, use a jigsaw design to help the participants learn the content. Divide the group into small groups according to the number of segments. Each group becomes a study group that will master one section of the text. Each group studies its "chunk" of material, with the group members reading, discussing, and deciding how to teach the information to others. After an adequate study and preparation period, form cooperative or "jigsaw" learning groups by taking one representative from each study group to become part of a new group. Each new group has a person who has studied a particular segment. Each member of the new cooperative group will teach his or her segment to the other group members. Reconvene the full group to review and answer questions. This design ensures accuracy and uniform understanding and also creates interdependence among the group members, who are responsible for combining separate pieces of information to create a single, coherent body of knowledge.

Learning Tournament

A learning tournament, a variation of the classic study group, combines individual accountability with cooperation and competition. Create teams of five to seven people. Give the teams time to study, discuss, and coach each other, using material they have been given during the session. At the end of the study period reconvene the entire group and distribute a handout with quiz items that each participant will complete and score individually. After each team computes a team average, post the team scores and repeat the process for as many rounds as you want to conduct; three rounds seem to work well. At the end of the designated number of rounds, total each team's score and award prizes to the winning team.

Card Sort

This method helps participants learn information that has multiple sections or parts and can be easily "chunked." Some examples are the four stages of team development (forming, storming, norming, performing), the five approaches to dealing with conflict (competition, accommodation, avoidance, compromise, collaboration), and the four interpersonal influence behaviors (assertive, aggressive, passive, passive-aggressive). You create a deck of cards that consists of "header" cards indicating the major categories and four or five descriptors for each category, putting each descriptor on a separate card. During the session, form teams of four to six people and give each team a set of shuffled cards. Ask the teams to sort the cards, putting the descriptors under the appropriate headings.

Role Plays

Many trainers use role playing as a skill-building technique in training programs. More often than not, this technique does not achieve the desired results because of participant resistance. An effective, nonthreatening way of using role playing is to conduct a demonstration role play. Prepare a scripted role play depicting either the right way or the wrong way to use a skill, technique, or process. Early in the session select two "actors" from the group and give them the script so that they can familiarize themselves with their parts before the demonstration. At the appropriate point in the program, ask the "players" to come forward and read their scripts while the rest of the group observes the interaction for various dos and don'ts that illustrate the learning points.

Another nonthreatening technique involves the trainer as one of the role players. Ask for a volunteer to assume the role of the other person. For example, in a "customer service" session you want to demonstrate how to deal with an irate customer. You assume the role of the customer service representative and ask for a volunteer to play an irate customer who is returning a piece of merchandise for a full refund. The "employee" (played by the trainer) is not permitted to give a refund, only store credit. As the role play begins, the customer demands a refund. At this point you stop the action and turn to the participants for coaching. When the action resumes, you follow the group's suggestions in responding to the customer. This stop-action technique is used several times throughout the role play.

A third technique is to create three different scenarios to use in three rounds of activity. Divide the participants into trios and assign the roles of primary player, secondary player, and observer. After the first scenario has been played out and the observer gives feedback to the "players," ask the people in each trio to rotate roles and distribute a new scenario. Repeat the process for the third round.

ENCOURAGING PARTICIPATION

A big problem trainers face is getting people to respond to questions during a full-class discussion. In many cases, only a handful of people participate. To guarantee 100 percent audience response, use response cards. Hand each participant cards to use in responding to multiple-choice (A, B, C, D) or true-false (T, F) questions. Develop three or four statements or questions to which the participants will respond with their cards. As you read or show each item, the participants respond by holding up the card of their choice.

You also might choose four or five statements designed to elicit the participants 'opinions about the topic. They can indicate whether they agree or disagree with a statement by holding up a card (A = agree; D = disagree). You also can ask them to stand if they agree and stay seated if they disagree. After each statement, ask a few people to explain why they agreed or disagreed before moving to the next statement.

BRINGING IT TO A CLOSE

Endings are as important as the rest of the training program: It's not what you give them but what they take away that counts. Many activities can make the training unforgettable. Remember the "What Do You Want to Know?" activity in which the participants wrote their questions and expectations on Post-Its? To bring the training session full circle, ask the participants to get up and reclaim or take off their notes if their questions or expectations were addressed. If you've done your job, the flip chart pages on the wall will be empty. Not only does this activity bring closure to the session, it reinforces the learning. By reclaiming their questions, the participants take ownership and acknowledge that their needs have been met.

Another effective closing technique is the human continuum. At the end of a training session post two signs, one at each end of a long wall. For example, one sign might read "Competent," and the other "Clueless." Ask the participants to envision the wall as a continuum. Ask them to think about where they were in terms of their knowledge and/or skill level at the beginning of the session. Then ask them to stand up and place themselves where they think they were on the continuum. Then ask a few participants to explain why they placed themselves where they did. Next, ask them to think about where they are on the continuum at the end of the program and place themselves accordingly. Once again, ask the participants to share the reasons for their placement. Most people will have moved from "Clueless" to "Competent." Sometimes, however, the reverse happens. Those who come to the session thinking they know it all often discover that they didn't know as much as they thought they did. Consequently, they will indicate a movement in the opposite direction. In either case, this activity is a powerful way to help participants assess how much they perceive they have learned.

A successful training session is the result of careful planning, preparation, and practice. Effective trainers use a skillful blend of content and participant interaction to create a program that not only involves and informs but influences others to assimilate new information, modify attitudes, and change behaviors in both their professional and personal lives.

DOCUMENTS, JOB AIDS, AND HELPFUL HINTS

Not only must all training activities (role plays, case studies, assessment instruments, small group discussions, and other structured experiences) be positioned within the context of the overall session, they must be structured and facilitated carefully. Many trainers make the mistake of engaging participants in activities without helping them "harvest" the learning. For the activity to be meaningful, you must follow a three-part format: introducing the activity, conducting the activity, and processing the activity. Here are some guidelines for facilitating any learning activity.

Introducing the Activity
- Give a purpose and objectives for the activity you are introducing. Be careful not to provide too much information. If you are focusing on discovery learning, don't tell the participants what they're supposed to learn from doing the activity. That would defeat the purpose of inductive or discovery learning.
- Rearrange the furniture and regroup the participants as is appropriate for the activity. Your goal is to group people as quickly and efficiently as possible.
- After the participants are settled in their small groups, provide specific instructions about what the participants are to do during and after the activity.

- Make appropriate role assignments (timekeeper, spokesperson, recorder) and give time limits.
- Define terms and distribute materials, carefully going over printed material. Display on a flip chart or transparency a brief step-by-step outline of the activity. For lengthy or complicated activities, include the time associated with each step.
- To prevent the same people from assuming the leadership role for every activity, request that the assignments be rotated.
- Solicit questions and make sure all the participants understand what they are to do before you continue. You can do this by asking a participant to review the steps for the group.
- Model what you want them to do by demonstrating rules or procedures.
- Begin the activity and circulate around the room to determine whether everyone knows what to do.

Conducting the Activity

- As you circulate around the room, listen carefully to the discussion. Don't be concerned if the participants express confusion or frustration. Clarify as needed and appropriate, but don't do their work for them.
- Continue to move from group to group to make sure the participants are on track.
- Maintain the role of the facilitator. Resist giving participants the answers or getting directly involved in the activity. You can give suggestions or ask guided questions if you find that the participants are way off the mark.
- Constantly observe how individuals and small groups are working on the task or problem as well as how the members work together. Intervene only when absolutely necessary.
- Remind the participants of time passing, giving them signals halfway through a particular stage and 2-minute warnings for each deadline.
- You may have to be flexible about time limits. In some cases you may need to allot extra time; in other situations the groups may finish earlier than expected. In either case you should be ready to adjust accordingly.

Processing the Activity

- Processing refers to the overall discussion about the activity to help the participants understand the activity's purpose and distill the key learning points and applications. This is where real learning takes place. Plan on using about as much time to process an activity as it took to conduct it.
- To ensure an effective discussion, prepare questions using the following format: What? So what? Now what?

- Begin by asking participants *what* they experienced during the activity:
  What went on during the activity?
  What was your reaction?
  What did you observe?
  How did you feel?
- Next ask questions that address *so what?* What insights did you gain from the experience?
  What did you learn about yourself?
  What did you learn from the experience?
  What similar experiences have you had? How does this relate to anything you have experienced on the job?
  How did this experience help you?
  What are the implications of the behaviors you experienced or observed?
- Finally, ask the participants to answer questions dealing with *now what?*
  Now what are you going to do with this information and/or learning?
  How can you apply what you learned through this activity on the job?
  What might you do differently?
  How can this experience help you in the future?
- Capture the key points on the flip chart. You might ask one participant to serve as a scribe so that you can concentrate on facilitating the discussion.
- Sometimes, no matter how well you prepare and present the processing questions, some groups will not get it. It's your job to help the participants make the connection between the activity and their own situations as well as the learning objectives.
- Complete the discussion by asking a few general processing questions to elicit feedback and reactions to the activity itself.
  What did you like about the activity?
  What did you dislike about the activity?
  What changes would you make?
  What suggestions do you have to make this a more meaningful experience?

PRACTICAL APPLICATION

The following case illustrates how active training can be applied to a program that focuses solely on cognitive learning. In this case the session was a 6-hour leadership development program based on the Ken Blanchard's situational leadership model, using three primary active-training designs.

Each of the three designs was 50 to 60 minutes long, spread throughout the day, and incorporated the four basic elements of every active training or cooperative learning activity: positive interdependence, face-to-face student interaction, individual accountability, and interpersonal collaborative skills. The three activities were used to help the participants learn new material rather than review previously introduced information.

The first major cooperative learning design was group inquiry. To introduce the concept of situational leadership, the participants were put into pairs and were given a diagram of the situational leadership model developed by Blanchard. The diagram shows in four quadrants the four leadership behaviors of directing, coaching, supporting, and delegating along with the followers' development level continuum. The participant pairs were asked to study the model and place question marks and notations on the items they did not understand. After about 10 minutes the trainer reconvened the entire group, solicited questions, and facilitated a discussion about the model. The primary questions raised by the participants focused on the relationship between the continuum and the four styles; the meaning of terms in the diagram, such as *commitment, competence, supportive,* and *directive;* and the significance of the bell-shaped curve superimposed on the quadrants.

In this program the jigsaw design was used to help the participants learn the four stages of group development: forming, storming, norming, and performing. Four subgroups were formed, and each subgroup was given a sheet with one of the stages described in detail. Each group was given approximately 20 minutes to discuss and learn the assigned development stage. New learning groups were then created with a member from each of the original subgroups, who then explained, demonstrated, or in some way communicated the characteristics of each of the stages of group development.

The final active training activity was the learning tournament, which was used near the end of the day as a method of helping the participants learn how to recognize which of the four leadership styles or behaviors would be appropriate in a given situation. The group was divided into three teams. The teams were given 10 minutes to study, discuss, and coach each other, using all the material they had been given throughout the day. This included the material used in the group inquiry and the jigsaw design as well as other information, including Blanchard's article "Situational Leadership II" and self-assessment instrument "Leader Behavior Analysis II" that was used earlier in the day. At the end of the period the trainer reconvened the entire group and distributed a handout with five situations or scenarios to each person to read and identify which of the four leadership styles would be the best approach. After the participants were finished, the correct or most preferred responses along with point values were shared and the rationale for the preferred choices was discussed with the group. The "most preferred" response was assigned 5 points, followed by 3 points for the next best answer and 1 point for the third best choice. No points were assigned to the least preferred choice. After individual scores were totaled, each team computed a team average, which was posted on a flip chart page. This process was repeated twice more for a total of three rounds and 15 different situational questions. At the end of the three rounds, each team's score was totaled and prizes were awarded to the winning team.

To measure the success of these active-training techniques, the trainer administered a questionnaire and conducted individual interviews to elicit participants' reactions according to the first level (reaction) and, to a limited degree, the second level (learning) of Kirkpatrick's four levels of evaluation. The results support the research in adult learning that has shown that people learn better by doing than by being told. One hundred percent of the participants indicated that they enjoyed the session, and 94 percent responded that they enjoyed working in groups. These results support the findings of earlier cooperative-learning studies that show that cooperative-learning produces more positive relationships among students and increases the enjoyment of the learning process. The positive reactions of the participants underscore the benefits of involving participants as much as possible in their own learning.

GLOSSARY

Active Training   An approach to learning in which the participants are actively engaged in the learning process through activities and structured experiences facilitated by the trainer.

Card Sort   An activity in which teams learn content by identifying and sorting pieces of information into appropriate categories.

Cooperative Learning   An approach to learning in which the participants learn from each other in pairs or small groups.

Group Inquiry   A technique in which participants work in pairs or small groups to generate questions about a piece of learning material.

Guided Discussion   The process of conveying content and information to participants by asking them questions about their knowledge of, opinions on, or assumptions about a topic.

Jigsaw Design   A training technique in which participants learn different pieces of information about a topic and then come together to share that information with each other.

Learning Tournament   An activity that combines individual accountability, cooperative learning, and team competition.

Processing   The discussion of an activity after its completion for the purpose of identifying key learning points and relating them to the participants' experiences.

Role Play   A learning activity in which the participants act out a scenario through assigned roles to practice the skills learned in the session. A role play can be scripted (prepared) or spontaneous.

CHAPTER 4

Rapid Instructional Development

Sivasailam Thiagarajan

Objectives

After reading this chapter, you will be able to:

- Explain the key features of the rapid instructional development (RID) technique and explain how it supplements the conventional instructional systems development (ISD) model.
- Improve the effectiveness of instructional development by focusing on accomplishment, performance, and learning.
- Speed the instructional development process by simplifying, combining, resequencing, and skipping steps.
- Speed the instructional development process by incorporating existing materials and job aids.
- Speed the instructional development process by using high-tech equipment and appropriate templates.
- Speed the instructional development process by redefining the roles and functions of subject-matter experts and trainees.

OVERVIEW

Rapid instructional development (RID) is a collection of strategies for quickly producing instructional packages that enable a specific group of learners to achieve a set of specific instructional objectives. RID involves alternatives, enhancements, and modifications to the instructional systems development (ISD) model, which in its common forms prescribes the steps of analysis, design, development, evaluation, and implementation.

WHY RID?

For more than three decades the ISD model has been used for the development of instructional packages. Thousands of instructional developers have mastered and applied nearly 60 variants of the original model. During the past 10 years several practitioners have suggested that the traditional ISD model be upgraded to keep pace with changing demands and resources. Critics have pointed out that the conventional ISD model is based on an outmoded top-down approach driven by subject-matter experts. The ISD model uses a rational step-by-step approach and assumes that the content area is stable. Newer realities, especially in the business world, include drastic changes in the characteristics and preferences of learners, rapid changes in skills and knowledge, increased availability of high-tech resources, and the demand for cheaper, faster, and better instructional design. RID techniques were created to meet those demands.

WHAT IS THE BASIC FRAMEWORK OF RID?

The traditional ISD model is an effective approach, but it is only one approach. RID represents an eclectic approach with a flexible choice of techniques based on the nature of the instructional objective, the characteristics of the trainees, and context of training.

The selection of appropriate instructional development techniques depends on two types of trade-offs. The first is between the *design* and *delivery* of instruction. Design involves all the activities undertaken before learners interact with the instructional package in a real-world training situation; delivery is what happens subsequently. An important principle in RID is that one can trade off the resources allocated to these two phases. For example, if you have a high resource level for delivery (subject-matter experts as instructors, ample time for instruction, small groups of learners, and alternative instructional materials), you can skimp on the design. By contrast, if you have extremely limited resources for the delivery of instruction (nonspecialist instructors, a tight learning schedule, and large groups of learners), you need to allocate extra time and other resources to the design process. The basic idea is that you pay now or pay later. Depending on the context, you can and should select the optimum allocation of resources between design and delivery. It would be inefficient (and unnecessary) to produce trainerproof instructional packages for all situations without carefully taking into consideration the resources available for the delivery of instruction.

The second trade-off is between the *content* (the materials) and the *process* (the method) of instruction. When instructional developers falsely assume that one of these two components is sufficient, the result is false economy and faulty instruction. Focusing on just the content or the process results in incomplete learning.

A basic principle in RID is that one can develop instructional content and process independently of each other. For example, you can rapidly videotape a subject-matter expert explaining the subtleties of a complex concept. You can develop appropriate activities to facilitate the learners' mastery of the concepts. As long as you integrate the content and the process in the final package, you produce effective instruction.

WHAT RID IS NOT

Rapid instructional development is not accelerated learning (AL). The focus of RID is the design of instruction, while the focus of AL is the delivery. RID does not result in faster learning by trainees. In most cases, the opposite is true because RID frequently shifts some instructional development responsibilities to the learner.

As was suggested earlier, RID is not a replacement for the traditional ISD model. In certain conditions application of the ISD model is likely to result in more effective instruction without requiring additional time. RID provides a preferred alternative when you are working with tight deadlines, limited budgets, and constantly shifting instructional content.

RID STRATEGIES

Human Performance Technology

Our paradigm recently shifted from instruction to improving performance through performance consulting. By shifting the focus from instruction to performance, you can avoid unnecessary training and help people learn on their own. You can apply different types of performance technology interventions to improve participants' learning: You can design appropriate physical facilities, provide tools and equipment, and supply job aids to help participants become better learners and reward them with powerful incentives.

Guideline 1: Focus on Accomplishment and Performance

The best way to speed instructional development is not to do it unless it is essential. To quickly determine whether instruction is essential, begin with the business goal and the individual accomplishments required for achieving that goal.

If the gap between the desired performance and the actual performance is not due to a lack of skills or knowledge, there is no need for instruction. Use one or more of the following alternative interventions to encourage and help people accomplish the goal: assign the job to the right person, outsource the task, clearly communicate the goal, give constructive feedback, encourage teamwork, modify the work process, reorganize physical facilities, provide tools and equipment, reduce excessive workloads, and reward appropriate performance.

Even if the gap is due to a lack of skills and knowledge, consider alternative interventions such as hiring new employees, simplifying the work flow, and installing an electronic support system.

Even if instruction is essential, increase the probability of performance improvement by ensuring organizational support for the new performance.

Guideline 2: Develop a Learning System Instead of an Instructional System

The fact that different people learn differently prevents us from developing the perfect instructional package for all participants. However, by providing instructional alternatives and flexible structures, you can demonstrate respect for diversity and save instructional development funds and time. Here are some suggestions for setting up a learning system:

- Conduct appropriate analyses to specify instructional objectives. Rewrite the objectives in the language of the novice learner and include a rationale that explains what is in it for the learner.
- Construct a criterion test that is based on these objectives. Prepare parallel versions of this test so that the learners can take them repeatedly.
- Collect all available materials in the relevant subject area, including textbooks, manuals, reprints, audiotapes, videotapes, and computer-based training (CBT) courseware.
- Prepare a list of resources for each instructional objective. Make specific references to different materials.
- If some instructional objectives are not covered by any available material, prepare your own handouts, audiotapes, or videotapes.
- Store copies of the materials in a convenient resource room, along with the necessary media equipment and computers.
- Develop an administrative system for tracking the learners, testing them, and certifying them. Prepare a handout explaining how learners can work through the system.

Guideline 3: Use Suitable Incentives to Reward Learning

Because of impossible deadlines for implementing a mandated course in one of my client organizations, we were forced to try an innovative approach: We took the funds allotted to the instructional development project and used them to reward employees who passed the certification test on their own. This approach to instructional incentives can drastically reduce the development time. Here are some suggestions for developing a suitable instructional incentive system:

- Conduct an analysis to identify different rewards that motivate members of the target population. Prepare a menu of suitable rewards. Don't limit yourself to monetary rewards; try creative alternatives such as lunch with the president and a prestigious parking space.
- Specify instructional objectives and procedures for demonstrating mastery. Construct several intermediate tests rather than a single final test.
- Match each level of mastery with the appropriate incentives. Offer alternative rewards at each level.
- Work with the personnel department to link mastery of the instructional objectives to pay increases, promotions, and other job-related rewards. Create suitable disincentives for the nonmastery of important instructional objectives.

Process Improvement

As long as you treat the conventional ISD model as a flexible framework (not as compulsory commandments), you can avoid wasting time. With this type of a flexible approach, you can use shortcut techniques during different steps of the process, combine different steps, proceed rapidly to implementation, and skip some of the steps.

Guideline 4: Use Shortcuts

You can save significant amounts of time and resources by employing shortcuts within the conventional ISD procedure. Every step of the instructional development process can benefit from these shortcuts. Here are some examples of various shortcuts by step.

Needs Analysis To confirm or reject an apparent need, use existing records (for example, reports of employee accidents or copies of customer complaints) instead of conducting extensive interviews.

Task Analysis To identify the various steps of a process, check the corporate procedures manual. Ask employees to describe exceptions to this procedure.

Production Ask a subject-matter expert to demonstrate an activity and make a videotape recording. Use this approach to bypass the elaborate ritual of preparing a treatment, writing a rough script, formatting a shooting script, preparing a storyboard, and producing an instructional video.

Expert Reviews   Instead of sending out review copies to experts and waiting for their feedback, conduct a focus group session. Give copies of the material to the selected group and walk its members through a structured discussion. This approach saves time by requiring experts to reconcile differences of opinion and provide specific prescriptions.

Evaluation and Revision   Test the instructional package individually with four or five representative learners, making on-the-spot revisions during the tryout session. Improvements resulting from this procedure are comparable to those from elaborate field tests with stratified random samples of several learners, control groups, batteries of pretests and posttests, and statistical analyses.

Guideline 5: Combine Different Steps of the Instructional Development Process

The steps in the instructional development process are not discrete activities. For example, you cannot declare that all your analyses will be completed at a specific time and that you will not do any more analysis later. Also, you do not have to specify the instructional objectives before beginning the development process. You can combine different steps to save time. Here are some examples:

Analysis and Development   Instead of completing a comprehensive analysis of an entire course, you can begin designing the course materials and do analyses as needed. The act of writing the materials will help you come up with the right questions for further analysis.

Analysis and Evaluation   Most valid evaluation strategies accurately reflect the results of analyses. For example, final tests should be based on the task analysis and the final impact of the instructional package should be evaluated against the need analysis. You can save instructional development time by reporting the results of different analyses in the form of evaluation questions.

Evaluation and Design   A standard operating procedure in instructional development is to specify behavioral objectives and use them as the basis for constructing criterion tests. You can bypass the step of specifying instructional objectives by using criterion test items to provide operational definitions of the objectives.

Concurrent Development   The ultimate application of this guideline is to combine all steps into one. You can begin by delivering instruction by making heavy use of subject-matter experts. During the training session you can videotape the presentation, conduct an instructional analysis that is based on what is being delivered, try out modifications with the next group of learners, and gradually replace the subject-matter expert with mediated materials.

Guideline 6: Implement the Instructional Package Immediately and Improve It Continuously

This is a special application of the fifth guideline. In the conventional ISD process the obsession with doing it right the first time through painstaking analysis and planning, pleasing all the people all the time by incorporating everyone's input and feedback, and attempting to achieve perfection through several rounds of testing and revision is unnecessary, especially in dealing with quickly changing content. Much time and other resources can be saved by focusing on critical content and key steps and producing a lean instructional package. Improvements to this core package can be added gradually, after it is implemented. Here are some specific suggestions:

Classify Content Areas in Terms of Importance   Separate the nice-to-know elements from the absolutely essential ones. Ignore the former and spend your time and resources developing instruction for the latter.

Identify Subgroups and Focus on the Majority   Design the package for use by the subgroup to which most of the learners belong. You can temporarily ignore the advantaged minority and make special provisions for tutoring the disadvantaged minority.

Guideline 7: Skip Steps in the Instructional Development Process

Most instructional developers feel guilty if they skip any step in the conventional ISD process. This results in an unnecessary waste of time and other resources. You can improve the efficiency of instructional development by recognizing and avoiding superfluous activities. Here are some examples.

Needs Analysis   If the client is convinced that there is a training need, avoid challenging this belief and conducting your own front-end analysis, needs analysis, performance analysis, and so on. Assume that the client is intelligent and that his or her conclusion is legitimate. After all, perceptions are as important as reality, and you are not going to establish rapport with a client by beginning the project with an apparently unnecessary activity.

Summative Evaluation   Instructional developers frequently attempt to conduct a final field test under controlled conditions to validate the cost-effectiveness of the instructional package. While this can be an important and worthwhile undertaking, ask yourself, Who cares? and So what? Unless you are working on a doctoral dissertation, there is no special advantage to collecting data and writing reports when nobody reads them and no useful improvements result.

Meetings and Report Writing An enormous amount of time and money is spent having people attend meetings and write reports before, during, and after each step in the instructional development process. Significant savings can be achieved by eliminating unnecessary meetings, having meetings attended by only the essential decision makers, increasing the productivity of meetings with a specific agenda and time limits, replacing information-dissemination meetings with memorandums and voice-mail messages, eliminating unnecessary reports, and limiting the essential reports to a single page.

Materials Production

All instructional packages consist of materials and methods. More than half a billion instructional and educational materials of various types exist in the English language. Millions more are ready to be downloaded from cyberspace. In spite of this, every instructional developer creates brand-new material. Here are some suggestions for avoiding and streamlining the development of instructional materials.

Guideline 8: Incorporate Existing Instructional Materials

The not-invented-here reaction to existing instructional materials is expensive and time-consuming. Even if an off-the-shelf instructional material does not meet your requirements exactly, it is usually cheaper and faster to modify it than to develop material from scratch. Even when there are no available materials, it is possible to adapt instructional packages that deal with a related product or procedure.

Here are some suggestions for incorporating an existing instructional material into a new instructional package.

- Begin with a quick analysis of the new problem, task, content, learner, language, and delivery variables. Look for existing instructional materials related to the results of these analyses.
- Modify the contents and activities in the existing materials to better suit your training needs. Specific modifications may include deleting portions of the material that deal with unnecessary objectives, adding new objectives and content, simplifying the language, and modifying the activities.
- Try out the existing instructional material in its current form with a representative group of trainees. On the basis of the feedback, make appropriate modifications to the material to better meet the needs and preferences of the trainees.

Guideline 9: Incorporate Noninstructional Materials

If you accept the division of an instructional package into content and activities, you can integrate noninstructional materials to present the basic content. For example, in training technical advisers for a project in western Africa, you can have them read a collection of short stories about life in Ghanaian villages to provide basic background information about the cultural values of the people they will be working with. To provide an opportunity to process this information, create an activity that requires the participants to list major cultural differences between themselves and the villagers. You can ask the participants to compare their lists with a list developed by cultural anthropologists.

Here are some additional examples of noninstructional materials being integrated into instructional packages.

- A course on public speaking uses videotapes of professional speakers. Trainees are provided with a checklist for evaluating key elements of each speaker's performance as a prelude to videotaping their own presentations and critiquing them.

- A new employee orientation package includes the policy manual and the annual report of a corporation. Trainees spend an hour reviewing these documents and coming up with the answers to 20 questions.

- An in-house management training package contains excerpts from television sitcoms. The facilitator uses the excerpts as examples of different management styles. Later, trainee teams create their own sitcom segments to illustrate a new type of manager for the next decade.

- A workshop package on change management uses reprints of articles from *Popular Mechanics* from the 1940s. Participants read glowing reports of technological breakthroughs and figure out why those innovations did not live up to their promise. This module explore factors that enhance and inhibit the adoption of novel ideas.

Guideline 10: Develop Instructional Packages around Job Aids

Job aids include checklists, decision tables, worksheets, flowcharts, and other devices that improve the performance of a person. Printed job aids are being supplanted and supplemented by electronic performance support systems such as help screens and wizards. Instructional packages for most technical and procedural tasks can be developed efficiently by incorporating existing job aids.

Here is a simple two-step procedure for using this strategy.

- Conduct a task analysis to identify the activities and decisions in a procedure. Prepare a set of job aids that will enable a typical learner to complete the procedure. Coach a person through the job aids to collect feedback. Modify the job aids to make them more effective and user-friendly.

- Analyze the job aids to identify the basic skills required for using them. Prepare an instructional package to teach trainees how to use the job aids. Test the package on representative learners and modify it on the basis of their feedback.

The basic idea is to develop an instructional package that teaches trainees to use a job aid rather than how to perform the job.

Guideline 11: Develop Generic Instructional Materials for Local Finish

This technique is especially useful in large organizations with policies and procedures that are adapted to suit local conditions, cultures, and resources. The generic version is produced rapidly at the headquarters, and local variations are developed in branch locations. The success of this approach depends on using flexible development principles to create the original package. Here are some suggestions.

- Modularize the instructional package by objectives to permit local developers to delete modules and rearrange them to suit local needs, resources, and constraints.
- Use media that are easy to revise. Printed materials are easier to modify than are multimedia productions. Within print, pages formatted with word processing software are easier to modify than are those which are typeset. Simple illustrations are easier to revise than are photographs.
- Whenever possible, build the training package around a set of job aids. By modifying the job aids to suit the local needs and constraints, you can rapidly modify the instructional package.
- Make the structure and organization of the training package clearly visible through the use of appropriate headings. Provide a detailed table of contents and indexes that refer to sectional page numbers.
- Keep the illustrations, examples, and exercises culturally neutral. This guideline is especially important for global organizations with local employees.
- Include a collection of alternative examples and exercises in the generic instructional package. Provide keyword indexes to these items to permit local developers to choose the most appropriate ones.

Tools and Templates

The development and production of instructional materials can be speeded through by the use of high-tech tools and instructional-design templates. These tools and templates can be used during different steps in the instructional development process.

Guideline 12: Use Software Tools

Computer programs can significantly increase instructional development productivity. Learning how to use different computer programs and standardizing their use among the members of the ID team can speed the steps in the development process. Here are some examples of useful software programs.

Analysis

- Questionnaire construction programs for designing, administering, and scoring surveys
- Flowcharting programs for rapidly preparing flowcharts to summarize task analyses
- Spreadsheets and statistical packages for analyzing, summarizing, and charting quantitative data
- Information management systems for sorting and analyzing qualitative responses to open-ended questions

Design

- Creativity tools for designing the instructional package
- CBT authoring systems to identify the use of appropriate instructional strategies and tactics
- Outliners for systematically building up from analysis data through criterion test items to instructional content
- Word processors for producing initial drafts and revisions
- Grammar checkers for cleaning up the draft version and maintaining an appropriate reading level
- Desktop publishing software for the rapid layout of finished pages
- Graphic packages for producing charts and illustrations
- Presentation packages for the rapid production of slides and transparencies

Evaluation

- Groupware for collaborative review and editing of the instructional material
- Test-construction programs for the design, administration, and scoring of tests
- Statistical packages for data analysis

Guideline 13: Use Recording Equipment

In recent years, digital audio- and video-recording devices have become cheaper, smaller, lighter, friendlier, and more powerful. They provide a powerful set of tools for automating and speeding different aspects of the instructional development process. Here are some examples.

- During task analysis you can videotape an expert demonstration of a complex technical task. By replaying, pausing, slowing down, and freezing this videotape, you can complete a thorough task analysis without wasting the expert's time.
- During instructional design you can record an interview with a subject-matter expert and edit the tape to present the basic instructional content. You also can create a prototype rapidly by recording a lecture.
- During evaluation you can videotape a focus group session and analyze the comments later.

Guideline 14: Use Internet and E-Mail Tools

Input from a variety of people is an essential component of the instructional development process. Unfortunately, however, the usual techniques used for obtaining such inputs—meetings, telephone calls, and letters—waste a lot of valuable time, especially when members of the instructional design team are dispersed around the globe. The solution to this problem is to use E-mail and the Internet. Here are some suggestions.

- You can send questionnaires and survey instruments to several people by E-mail. Electronically copy their responses and paste them to your word processor for immediate processing.
- Subject-matter experts and others can send you computer files as attachments to E-mail messages. With this approach you don't have to wait for a document or retype it into your computer.
- Instead of conducting face-to-face or telephone conference-call meetings, you can use a listserv arrangement in which people discuss various topics during instructional analysis. This approach enables each team member to participate at his or her convenience.
- You can display draft copies of instructional materials and reports on your Web site for review and feedback.
- You can save time on library research during instructional analysis by using search engines on the Internet. This enables you to obtain a lot of relevant (and often irrelevant) content in a short period.

Guideline 15: Use Templates for Presenting Instructional Content

Instructional objectives can be classified into different learning domains. Although there is no single best strategy for each learning domain, there are preferred strategies based on empirical principles of learning. Effective CBT authoring systems frequently include templates for designing instruction for specific learning domains. These templates also can be used for non-computer-based instruction. Here are some guidelines.

- Use a convenient scheme to classify instructional objectives into domains such as factual information, concepts, processes, procedures, and principles. For each type of information use a standard format to organize the instructional content.
- For teaching factual information, use this structure: Present the information in suitable chunks, emphasize logical links, provide mnemonics to facilitate recall, require trainees to process the information, provide suitable feedback, review the information, repeat the information in different configurations, and summarize the information.
- For teaching concepts, use this structure: Present clear-cut examples, present matched nonexamples to emphasize critical features of the concept, present divergent examples to emphasize variable features, require the trainees to generalize to new examples and differentiate nonexamples, provide feedback, and test for the ability to generalize and discriminate.
- For teaching procedures, use this structure: Provide an overview of the entire procedure, demonstrate each step and identify its critical elements, coach trainees as they practice each step, require trainees to demonstrate mastery of each step, integrate all steps, and provide systematic practice toward fluent application.

Guideline 16: Use Standard Procedures for Designing Instructional Activities

You can use different templates and shells to speed the design of interactive, experiential activities. Here are some examples.

- *Framegames* are training games that are designed to permit the easy loading of new instructional content. Different framegames are available for use with different types of learning and different types of learners.
- *Computer game shells* are a special type of framegame in which the computer acts as the timekeeper and scorekeeper. These shells permit the rapid insertion of new content and questions. The resulting activities can be used by individuals working at a computer or by large groups interacting with projected images.

- *Interactive lectures* involve participants in the learning process while giving complete control to the instructor. These templates permit a quick and easy conversion of a typical presentation into an interactive exercise. Different types of interactive lectures involve built-in quizzes, interspersed tasks, and teamwork interludes.
- *Read-me games* superimpose a training game on a reading assignment. The participants read a handout and play a game that uses peer support to encourage recall and transfer of what they have read.
- *Metaphorical simulation games* reflect real-world processes in an abstract, simplified fashion. These templates are useful for designing instruction in interpersonal skills and concepts.

Managing Human Resources

In spite of all the advances in instructional technology, training is ultimately an interaction between a subject-matter expert (SME) and a learner. Rather than attempting to beat this system, why not make it more efficient? Here are some guidelines for improving the efficiency of the expert and the novice.

Guideline 17: Train and Support Subject-Matter Experts

Most SMEs train the way they were trained: with a focus on transmitting the details of everything they know. Here are some suggestions for shifting an SME's focus from covering the curriculum to increasing trainees' competencies.

- Involve SME trainers in the development of the instructional package. Emphasize that the materials are geared toward changing the trainees' behavior.
- Support SME-based training with accurate handouts and manuals. Reassure trainers that these materials will ensure high levels of technical quality.
- In train-the-trainer sessions, practice what you preach. For example, don't lecture on the importance of interactive activities.
- Use behavior modeling. Ask SME trainers to observe an expert trainer in action. Stress how the trainer focuses on learning rather than lecturing.
- Videotape practice training sessions and provide specific feedback to improve SMEs' training techniques.
- Provide lesson plans to structure and support SMEs' training activity. Instead of a content outline in the lesson plan, list a series of questions the trainee should be able to answer at the end of the lesson.

Guideline 18: Change the Role of Subject-Matter Experts

An effective approach for shifting SME trainers away from lecturing and toward performance improvement is to give them a different job title. Here are a few suggestions on how to change the role of the SME trainer.

- Make the SMEs coaches instead of trainers. Explain that their task is to improve the job performance of the members of a team.
- Involve the SMEs in developing job aids. Later, have the SMEs coach the trainees in using those job aids.
- Stress the importance of guided practice. Provide a detailed set of practice exercises for use by SME coaches.
- Stress the importance of giving feedback to the performer. Provide a job aid to SME coaches on how to give specific and timely feedback.
- Make SMEs play the role of consultants. Explain that their task is to help their clients perform better on the job.
- Train SMEs to function as consultants and train participants to function as clients. Organize the instructional session as individual and small-group consulting activities.

Guideline 19: Shift Instructional Development Responsibilities to Trainees

Trainees are an important and often ignored resource in instruction. You can tap this valuable resource by using adjunct activities to reinforce the instructional content presented through different methods and media. Here are some examples of adjunct games.

- The *press conference game* begins with trainees brainstorming a list of critical questions related to a specific topic. Teams of trainees edit those questions and take turns interviewing the subject-matter expert for a specified period. At the conclusion of each segment of this press conference teams prepare and present a brief summary of major learning points. The game is repeated, with every team getting a turn to question the experts.
- The *team quiz game* uses the SME to present relevant information in the form of a short lecture. After each lecture different teams spend 5 minutes comparing their notes and preparing a set of questions. Later, teams take turns quizzing each other to win points.
- The *question game* is used as a follow-up activity to a videotape presentation. After viewing the presentation, each trainee prepares 10 cards with a question on one side and the correct answer on the other. Trainees are

divided into groups of four or five, and each group shuffles its cards and exchanges them with another group. Using the new cards, the trainees in each group play a game with players taking turns reading the question on the top card and coming up with an answer. Other trainees in the group may challenge the answer. Depending on the original answer, the challenge, and the correct answer, trainees earn different numbers of score points.

Guideline 20: Use Peer Coaching Techniques

Current field studies confirm the truth of the ancient Latin advice *doce ut discas*: ("teach in order to learn"). From an instructional development point of view, peer coaching enables you to spend less time on development by utilizing the trainees as a valuable resource. Here are some suggestions for maximizing the effectiveness of this approach.

- To initiate the peer coaching process, teach the basic skills and knowledge to an initial set of trainees. Use any medium and method to teach different knowledge and skill elements to different trainees so that everyone has to (and is able to) teach and learn from the others.

- Self-managed learning teams increase the efficiency of peer learning. Use a blend of cooperation and competition by requiring teams to coach and support each other during collaborative learning periods and fight with the members of other teams for points during competitive tournaments.

- One-on-one coaching is effective with training objectives such as conversing in a foreign language and mastering a motor skill. By coaching, testing, and certifying a few representative trainees and dividing them into two teams, you can initiate an effective peer learning format: Certified tutors coach other trainees on an individual basis. Then, the trainee is tested by a certified member of the other team. If this is successful, the trainee becomes a certified coach. This process is continued until all the trainees are certified.

A SUMMARY JOB AID

Here is a checklist that summarizes the guidelines presented earlier. Each item begins with a prescription, which is followed by a set of suggestions. Use this checklist to guide your activities during your next instructional development project.

1. *Focus on accomplishment and performance.* Confirm a lack of skills and knowledge. Use alternative human performance technology interventions (assigning the job to the right person, outsourcing the task, clearly communicating the goal, giving constructive feedback, encouraging teamwork, modifying the work process, reorganizing the physical facilities, providing tools and equipment, reducing excessive workloads, and rewarding appropriate performance) to achieve performance goals. Reinforce instruction with these interventions.

2. *Develop a learning system instead of an instructional system.* Develop a combination of instructional objectives, criterion tests, and alternative instructional materials. Create an administrative system for tracking the progress of learners and certifying them for their mastery of the objectives.

3. *Use suitable incentives to reward learning.* Specify the instructional objectives and procedures for demonstrating mastery. Match each level of mastery with appropriate incentives. Link the mastery of instructional objectives to pay increases, promotions, and other job-related rewards.

4. *Use shortcuts.* Use existing records to identify needs. Check with procedure manuals to conduct a task analysis. Videotape a demonstration by an SME. Conduct a focus-group session to review the prototype version of the instructional package. Test the instructional package with four or five learners.

5. *Combine different steps of the instructional development process.* Undertake analyses as needed during the design of instruction. Make sure evaluation strategies accurately reflect various analyses. Bypass the writing of instructional objectives and use criterion test items instead. Combine the field test with the initial implementation of the training program.

6. *Implement the instructional package immediately and improve it continuously.* Produce a lean instructional package by focusing on critical content and typical learners. Gradually improve and expand this basic package through repeated implementation.

7. *Skip steps in the instructional development process.* Skip needs analysis if the client provides details of a training need. Skip final evaluation if nobody is going to read the report or use the data. Skip meetings and the writing of reports that don't add value to the instructional development process.

8. *Incorporate existing instructional materials.* Conduct a quick analysis of the performance problem. Locate existing instructional materials related to the results of this analysis. Add, delete, and modify the content and activities in the materials. Collect feedback from a tryout group and make more modifications.

9. *Incorporate noninstructional materials.* Use a variety of noninstructional materials (books, articles, movies, and videotapes) to provide the basic content. Add activities and exercises to encourage participants to process the content and apply the new skills and knowledge.

10. *Develop instructional packages around job aids.* Create one or more job aids that enable a beginner to complete a specific procedure. Coach a learner through these job aids and make them more effective and user-friendly. Analyze the job aids to identify the basic skills required for using them. Prepare an instructional package to teach trainees how to use the job aids.

11. *Develop generic instructional materials for local finish.* Modularize the instructional package by objectives to permit local developers to delete and rearrange the content. Use media that are easy to revise. Make the structure of the training package clearly visible through the use of appropriate headings. Use culturally neutral illustrations, examples, and exercises. Include alternative examples and exercises and permit the local developers to select the most appropriate ones.

12. *Use software tools.* Use word processors, spreadsheets, graphics packages, desktop publishers, and presentation tools to prepare instructional materials. Use specialized programs for questionnaire design, test construction, flowcharting, data analysis, and design templates. Standardize the use of software among the ID team members.

13. *Use recording equipment.* Videotape expert demonstrations of complex technical tasks for detailed analysis and incorporation in the training package. Videotape focus-group sessions and analyze the comments later.

14. *Use Internet and E-mail tools.* Send questionnaires and survey instruments by E-mail. Electronically copy the responses and paste them to your word processor. Transfer computer files as attachments. Use a listserv arrangement for discussion among SMEs. Use your Web site to circulate draft copies of reports and instructional materials for review and feedback. Conduct instructional analyses by using search engines on the Internet.

15. *Use templates for presenting instructional content.* Classify instructional objectives into appropriate learning domains. Use a standard format for designing suitable content sequences. For teaching factual information, present the information in suitable chunks, emphasize logical links, provide mnemonics to facilitate recall, require trainees to process the information, provide suitable feedback, and review the information. For teaching procedures, provide an overview of the entire procedure, demonstrate each step and identify its critical elements, coach the trainees as they practice each step, require the trainees to demonstrate mastery of each step, integrate all the steps, and provide systematic practice toward fluent application.

16. *Use standard procedures for designing instructional activities.* Use different templates and shells to design interactive, experiential activities. Framegames can be loaded with new content. Computer game shells permit the rapid insertion of new content and questions. Interactive lectures involve participants in the learning process while giving complete control to the instructor. Read-me games superimpose a training game on a reading assignment. Metaphorical simulation games reflect real-world processes in an abstract, simplified fashion.

17. *Train and support subject-matter experts.* Involve SMEs in the development of the instructional package. Support them with accurate handouts and manuals.

Ask SMEs to observe an expert trainer in action. Videotape training sessions and provide specific feedback to improve SMEs' training techniques.

18. *Change the role of subject-matter experts.* Make SMEs play the role of coaches instead of trainers. Explain that their task is to improve the job performance of teams. Encourage SMEs to implement practice exercises and provide expert feedback. Train SMEs to function as consultants and train participants to function as clients.

19. *Shift instructional development responsibilities to trainees.* Use adjunct games to reinforce the instructional content presented through different methods and media. Use a press conference format to provide control of the instructional content and sequence to trainees.

20. *Use peer coaching techniques.* Teach different knowledge and skill elements to different trainees so that everyone has to (and is able to) teach and learn from the others. Organize self-managed learning teams to increase the efficiency of peer learning. Blend cooperative and competitive activities that require team members to coach and support each other during learning periods and fight for points with contestants from other teams during tournaments.

TWO PRACTICAL APPLICATIONS

Here are two case studies from my RID activities during the past 5 years. They are examples from a hard-skill area involving technical training and a soft-skill area involving leadership principles. I have modified the nature and the sequence of the activities slightly to shift the focus from this-is-how-I-did-it narratives to this-is-how-you-can-do-it suggestions. Use these case studies as instructional materials by matching their content against the 20 items in the preceding checklist.

Telephone Switching Equipment

The trainees for this instructional package were engineers working on telephone networks. The training objective involved complex programming activities to expand the capabilities of the network using sophisticated switching equipment manufactured by my client.

Instructional Analysis
The project lasted 5 days. On the first day we assembled a group of field engineers who regularly perform these activities. We added a few SMEs and trainers to this group. We used a series of structured activities to brainstorm tasks performed by master performers as a part of programming the switching equipment. Using a technique called affinity diagramming, participants clustered the tasks into com-

petency groups. The items and clusters were inputted into a computer, and the lists were projected onto a large screen. At the conclusion of the activity, the printouts of key tasks were reviewed by three SMEs for accuracy.

Performance-Test Construction

On the second day we worked with SMEs to construct a series of performance tests to check mastery of the key competencies. This test closely resembled workplace conditions and involved actual programming on a simulator. We constructed several parallel versions of the test items. We asked a master performer to coach a typical trainee through these performance test items at the simulator. We recorded this session on videotape and debriefed the trainee to identify difficult procedures that required more explanation. We analyzed the videotape to identify critical content for the instructional package. We assembled reference materials, job aids, videotape demonstrations, and audiotape walk-throughs related to the different procedures.

Design and Evaluation

On the third day we assembled eight typical trainees, organized them into two teams, and briefed them about the daylong training session. Each team received $10,000 in play money and a copy of the performance test items. Each team was told that every one of its members would be required to pass a parallel version of the performance test. They could learn all the necessary procedures and principles through a variety of approaches:

- *Trial-and-error learning.* Each team has access to a workstation. Team members can decide to learn on their own, using intuition, previous knowledge of similar procedures, and help screens. This learning resource is available free to all teams.
- *Job aids.* A packet of printed reference materials is available at $100 per copy.
- *Audiotape walk-through.* An audiotape cassette walks the trainees through each procedure in a step-by-step fashion. This tape (along with a cassette player) can be rented for $200 per 15 minutes.
- *Videotape demonstration.* A videotape demonstrates each procedure. This videotape (along with a video cassette recorder and television monitor) can be rented for $500 for 15 minutes.
- *Coach-consultant.* Two SMEs can provide specific answers to any technical question and demonstrate different procedures. The consulting fee is $2000 per 15 minutes.
- *Practice test.* The team can take a practice version of the final performance test. The facilitator will administer the test for $2000.

Scoring System

We explained to the participants that whenever a team was ready to demonstrate its mastery of the procedure, all its members would assemble at a workstation and one randomly selected team member would sit at the keyboard. This member would be given the performance test and would begin the procedure while the other team members silently observed. From time to time, the facilitator would randomly replace the team member at the keyboard with another team member who would continue the procedure. The team's score would be based on the time taken to complete the procedure correctly.

In addition to the performance test score, each team would receive three other scores:

- *Learning speed.* This is the time taken by the team to report for the performance test.
- *Budget management.* Team scores reflect how effectively the members used their learning budget.
- *Collaborative learning strategies.* Throughout the game period, the facilitator will observe the learning procedure used by different teams and score how collaboratively they help each other in the learning process. The team will receive a score from 1 to 5 to indicate the efficiency of team learning.

We left the participants to their own devices, assigning an observer to each team. We took copious notes about how each instructional resource was used. We made on-the-spot modifications in the process and incorporated them in a master copy of the facilitator's guide.

Final Production

We spent the final 2 days of the project making suitable modifications based on the feedback from the participants. We also expanded our procedural outline into a facilitator's guide. We prepared multiple copies of the materials for the next level of testing.

Leadership Principles

The trainees for this instructional package were managers in a large utility company. The training objective was to increase their leadership potential by exploring principles and the associated procedures.

We developed and produced the 2-day course in 7 days. The key to our productivity was the availability of two experienced facilitators who were also SMEs.

Days 1 and 2
We assembled a team of managers and with their help identified job-relevant training objectives for the course. The two experienced facilitators then took turns conducting experiential activities related to those objectives. For example, one of the objectives required risk taking. Each facilitator independently conducted an activity that involved prudent decision making in risky situations. While the managers were participating in the activity, an instructional developer took copious notes on the process, using a notebook computer. The manager-participants made real-time suggestions for improving the activity and the debriefing discussion. We selected the better activity between the two. In some cases we combined the two activities into a new version.

Days 3 and 4
The instructional developer expanded the notes into a prototype facilitator's guide. The two facilitators created a prototype workbook for the participants. A project manager assembled and packaged materials and supplies that were required for conducting the activities.

Days 5 and 6
The two facilitators conducted a 2-day workshop for 12 new managers, using the facilitator's guide for the basic structure but improvising as needed. The instructional developer made changes in the document in the notebook computer. Four additional facilitators observed the workshop and made suggestions to the instructional developer.

Day 7
The facilitators and the instructional developers reviewed the course and made final changes. Two of the additional facilitators were selected to conduct the next offering of the course in a different location.

CHAPTER 5

Basic Training: Getting Ready to Present

Bill Withers

Objectives

After reading this chapter, you will be able to:

- Design your own learning plan to help you not only survive the training assignment but knock their socks off.
- Find the tools you need to get the job done.

OVERVIEW

This chapter will help you get yourself or someone else ready for a training assignment. If you are a beginner, read it from beginning to end. If you have some experience, skim the headings and use the chapter as a checklist.

As you read, take notes about what you need to work on to improve your skills. At the end of the chapter there is a knowledge and skill survey to help you put what you have learned into action.

THE BASICS

There was a football coach whose team was doing so poorly that he decided to go back to basics. "This," he said, holding up a football for the team, "is a football." One player looked up from his notebook and said, "Coach, could you slow down just a bit?"

We're going to get almost that basic here: Skip what you know and learn what you don't. Even some experienced trainers avoid techniques they are not familiar with. I'm not particularly fond of overhead projectors. You might not like role playing. One friend of mine with a powerful voice turns up her nose at microphones. However, there is a time and place for all these tools, and we'll look at some dos and don'ts for them.

AUDIOVISUAL AIDS

Technology. There is no better way to invite Murphy's law to a presentation than to use a lot of equipment, especially if you haven't tested it or practiced with it. A colleague and I lived our own trainer's nightmare a few years ago at an international conference for training executives. Every single piece of equipment malfunctioned during the workshop. The presentation was a good one that we had made several times before. There were 100 to 200 people in the room, and we had designed quite a show for them. We had music to set the mood when they walked in and during various periods, videotaped examples of what we were talking about, computer-driven overheads, and several microphones for questions and answers. The conference hotel had received our request for equipment several weeks in advance, and we arrived in the room an hour early to make sure everything worked. Imagine our surprise when we found that nothing was set up or even scheduled for the room. When people filed in and took their seats, the equipment was not ready. Picture several hundred training executives waiting expectantly while a crew of harried technicians crawled between the chairs with wires and plugs.

"Pay no attention to the men behind the curtain," I said, and we began. Five minutes into the presentation, the microphones cut out, and we spent the rest of the 2 hours bellowing. There were no videos, and so my colleague paraphrased the content while I acted it out. The overhead projector finally came on. The first slide was about planning for changes in the marketplace. "What Can Go Wrong?" it said, answering its own question by being upside down. "We meant to do that," I said, smiling bravely.

The first rule of using equipment is: *Check everything to be sure it works and have a backup plan in case it doesn't.* This includes extra bulbs for projectors, extra batteries for portable microphones, and extra ideas for just in case. We had filled out all the forms and talked to all the right people, but when we got to the workshop, nothing had been set up.

The second rule for using audiovisual (A/V) equipment is, Less is more. Don't fall in love with all the bells and whistles. Just because you have figured out how to make PowerPoint simulate Epcot Center doesn't mean you have to use it every time.

So when should you use A/V? When it will help people learn. We'll look a little later at learning styles, and some of the other chapters in this book deal with design in more depth. Since we're concentrating on presentation here, let's just say that you should use A/V based on what you need to do so that people will see what you are doing. For me, this means using flip charts or a white board for groups of 20 or less unless other technology is part of the lesson.

Even though they don't need bulbs and batteries, it's possible to screw up flip charts. The number one flip chart rule works great with anything you are using to show people information in a workshop: Get out of the way.

Be sure that your carefully prepared flip charts can be seen by everyone. When talking, stand next to the chart or screen. If the room is cramped and you have no choice but to block the view, move occasionally so that people can see. When setting up your flip charts, projection screens, or televisions, check the sight lines. Before your people come in, sit all over the room and be sure that none of your materials will be blocked or turned so that they can't be seen.

Overhead Projections

Whether you are writing on blank overheads, projecting from a laptop, or turning transparencies by hand, keep the overheads uncluttered. A rule of thumb is that there should be no more than six lines (I like four) and that people should be able to read a slide from the back of the room. Avoid putting up complex tables or whole pages of text. These "eye charts" will be illegible to most of the people in the room. Consider handing out a hard copy of the form or chart instead.

If your overheads are driven from a laptop computer, be sure you know how the laptop works. And turn off the screen saver. I saw a chief information officer making a presentation on leadership to a bunch of new managers. As he talked, the computer switched to his Gary Larsen screen saver. The poor guy couldn't figure out why people in the audience were nudging one another and giggling during his very passionate presentation. If he had turned around, he would have seen the *Far Side* cows floating across the giant projection screen (and perhaps enjoyed the joke).

Some presenters use their overheads as speaking notes. While this can work for many people, be sure you are prepared enough so that the next slide doesn't take you by surprise. Avoid turning your back on the group. While it is a good idea to check the screen from time to time, look instead at the image on the laptop or the transparency on the projector for reference. This way you will stay facing the group, and you and they will be able to hear and see one another better.

Use a Pointer on the Projector

Walking up to the screen and pointing at it turns you away from the group and may cast a shadow or otherwise block what you need the group to see. Use a pointer or set a pen or pencil on the projector to indicate what is being stressed. If you are projecting from a laptop, use the cursor arrow as a pointer.

Always Have a Backup

If you are projecting from a computer, have a hard copy of the presentation handy on transparencies and a projector that can show them, just in case.

Overhead projections can help visual learners focus on specific points without the distraction of a lot of peripheral information. Most presentation software will let you highlight or bring in information on a slide one line at a time. If you are projecting from hand-turned transparencies, you can cover parts of the slide with a piece of paper and expose sections of the slide as you go. You may not need to use a pointer or these other techniques if you keep slides uncluttered. Remember to avoid putting too much information up at one time. Simply designed flip charts and overheads ensure that people will see what you need them to see when you need them to see it.

Using Audiotapes and Videotapes

Like any learning tool, audiotapes and videotapes should be carefully selected to support learning. Be sure all your equipment is in working order and have backup equipment or a backup plan just in case. Cue up your tapes before the class so that you don't lose the group's interest by fumbling around trying to find the right spot.

Microphones

A word about microphones: When in doubt, use one. You may have a voice that can fill Carnegie Hall, but most hotel ballrooms and other training sites have terrible acoustics. Both you and your participants will be grateful for the mike, especially in a multiday session. It is safe to go mikeless with groups of 25 or fewer. With more people than that, consider using one. If you can't get a microphone and have a big group, move into the second or third row when speaking. It will take some practice to get used to this "training in the round" approach, but people will be able to hear you and you won't end up straining your voice.

Microphones are attached to a stand or podium, designed to be held in the hand, or worn by the user. The hand-held mike has a built-in drawback for the presenter. Using one may require some juggling if you are trying to flip pages, run an overhead, or hand out materials.

When you pretest a microphone, figure out how far to place it from your mouth. You don't want to be right on top of most mikes. If you are wearing a clip-on or lavaliere mike, be sure you have backup batteries. Practice talking while moving around the room to check for dead spots or places where you get feedback—that awful whistling sound. If you want to be cool when talking to a hotel A/V crew, refer to your wireless lavaliere microphone as a "lav." But don't sustain the urban myth by wearing your lav into the lavatory, or at least be sure it is turned off.

Printed Material

Handouts, including manuals and workbooks, are an often neglected visual aid, maybe because so many people drawn to training like to communicate by talking. Be sure that your handouts support the major points of the presentation, that they are clear and can be used as job aids or as references to refresh people's memories in the future. Color-code information on the handouts or assign graphics to certain facts and figures to make them easier for people to remember or to find certain sections again. The number one rule for handouts fits all your other audio and visual aids as well: People are more accepting of information when it is presented attractively and professionally. You have worked hard on your presentation. Don't turn people off because of typos, dirty photocopies, or illegible or confusing materials.

A/V QUICK CHECK

1. Check everything to be sure it works and have a backup plan in case it doesn't.

2. Less is more.

3. Get out of the way. Be sure you are not blocking screens, flip charts, and the like.

4. Check sight lines. Place visuals so that they can be seen from every seat in the room.

5. Keep prepared flip charts and overheads uncluttered. Use six lines of text at a maximum.

6. Turn off the screen saver.

7. Microphones: When in doubt, use one. When offstage, turn it off.

8. Cue up audiotapes and videotapes before the workshop begins.

9. People are more accepting of information when it is presented attractively and in a professional manner.

SPEAKING

As trainers, we have to do a lot of talking and we need to be sure that people understand us, we hold people's interest, and we don't become hoarse halfway through class.

Save Your Voice

Take it easy. Don't kill yourself. Some rooms have better acoustics than others. Remember, if you find yourself shouting or if it hurts your throat to speak loudly enough to be heard, use a microphone. If more than 25 people need to hear, consider using a mike.

Here are a few tricks used by speakers to be sure they are heard.

- *Speak slowly.* Pause after main points and then repeat them so that they sink in. Ask frequently for questions to be sure the learners are with you.
- *Breathe easy.* Practice lying on your back with a book on your stomach just below the rib cage. As you breathe naturally, the book will move up and down. What you are seeing is your diaphragm at work. When it is up, your lungs fill with air; when it is down, it pushes air out of the lungs. Sit or stand up straight in a relaxed manner. Breathe in deeply while keeping your shoulders absolutely still. Now that you have felt where it is, tighten your diaphragm and let the air out in a slow, steady stream. Time yourself to see if you can let it out over longer and longer times.

Frank Sinatra used to swim laps underwater to build lung capacity. He wanted to be able to hold a note singing as long as Tommy Dorsey could hold a note on his trumpet. Demosthenes practiced speaking with his mouth full of pebbles over the roar of the surf. You may or may not be that fanatical, but get creative with ways to practice. Check yourself for power and clarity. Are you as clear and strong at the end of a sentence as at the beginning?

Try the following:

- Read two pages from a novel aloud through clenched teeth. Although you can't open your mouth, shape each sound carefully with your lips. Be sure you are speaking clearly enough to be understood.
- Read two pages from a novel aloud to someone sitting at the other end of a large room. Don't worry about being a great actor; just get the words across.
- Pretend you are James Earl Jones when you are practicing. You don't need to become the voice of Darth Vader, but think of how Jones speaks: clearly, carefully, and crisply.

- Warm up before training. Stretch out as if you were about to go for a run. Nobody's watching, and so you can do as much or as little as works for you. The idea is to relax all your muscles, but concentrate especially on the head, throat, and shoulders.
- Either standing or lying on your back, practice breathing from the diaphragm. Read aloud clearly and slowly. Sing a song.
- Have a cuppa. A little warm tea with lemon and/or honey is a way many trainers warm up their pipes and keep them clear. If you find that you continually need to clear your throat when speaking, avoid gooey sweets or dairy products before training.

Use Your Voice to Keep Them Interested

Do you know what you sound like? Audiotape or videotape yourself while you are training. The sound quality won't be wonderful and you may not have Hollywood looks, but what you are listening for is intonation and phrasing.

It is easy for our voices to become monotonous if we are tired, have led a particular workshop many times, or are lost in thought. Practice using your voice for emphasis: Change volume and pace to underline a particular point. What does it mean if you suddenly whisper or raise your voice? What does it mean if you speed up or slow down?

While reading aloud, sing the words on the page. Alternate between very high and very low notes. Now go back and read it again. This time exaggerate inflections, volume, and pace. Be the worst actor you can be. With regular practice, you will begin to hear your own voice and learn how to use it to your advantage.

Working with Stage Fright

Anguish is a wonderful thing that lets us know we are about to do something new and different. Anguish happens when our actions are going to exceed the boundaries we have grown to accept. The throat goes dry, the voice trembles, the palms sweat, the knees knock, and the stomach feels queasy. What we are about to do is going to change where we are and who we are, and we'll never be able to go back again. Anguish is the signal that an adventure is about to begin.

When we feel anguish before getting up in front of a group of people, we call it stage fright. Stage fright is a good set of signals, but we don't really want anybody else to notice that we're going through it. There are a lot of ways to control the outward manifestations: the shakes, the tics, the tremors. Being well prepared can help, and you'll read later how you can be prepared even if you're called on to speak off the cuff. Other ways to work through stage fright are to control your body, your environment, and your material.

Controlling Your Body

Even if your mind is settled, sometimes your body refuses to follow suit. One bit of good news: Sometimes even the most experienced people get a case of nerves, but not once in my 20-plus years of getting up in front of people has anyone ever noticed me shaking like a leaf. Some experienced trainers need to work through the jitters every time, standing there convinced that what is a slight tremor is making them look like a palm tree in a hurricane. The thing to bear in mind is that nobody else can tell that you are shaking. Here are a few things to do if you have the shakes:

1. *Smile.* Remember that nobody but you can tell if you are trembling.
2. *Keep your hands out of your pockets.* Jingling keys or coins is a dead giveaway. (I have the bad habit of putting my hands in my pockets when I am very relaxed. This is probably okay in casual settings. I often make sure my pockets are empty before I begin.)
3. *If you are using notes, put them down* on a table or podium. If your hand is shaking, the paper will shake and make noise.
4. *Anchor yourself.* Stand still. Pacing or shifting from one foot to another makes it worse. Rest one hand lightly (don't lean) on the corner of the podium, table, projector, or flip chart easel. A little anchor goes a long way.
5. *Drop the fig leaf.* Avoid standing with your hands clasped in front of you. Let them hang comfortably at your sides.
6. *Use your hands to express yourself.* In private, try practicing talking with your hands. Exaggerate your movements. Put on some music and practice moving your body, especially your arms. Dance, jump, shout, conduct the orchestra. It doesn't have to be pretty, just fun. You not only will give the neighbors something to talk about, you will over time become more comfortable in your own skin.
7. *Shift the spotlight to the group.* Open with a question. This gives you something to do—listening, writing down their responses—and gets you into the swing of things while the audience members focus on one another.

Owning the Space

You need to realize that you have power in the training situation. You are the expert. People have come to work with you so that they can learn. Even resistant members of the group will give you the benefit of the doubt for a while. They may think they don't need training, but most will assume that you have some level of expertise or you wouldn't be there.

Try interacting with the group members as if they were in your living room at home. They are your guests. This means that you strive to please them but that you also own the place. I might be a little nervous having the chief executive officer and the board of directors in my living room, but my ownership requires that they be on their good behavior. It is your space, and you can set it up to your advantage.

How do you like to train? The chapters on program design in this book will go into more detail, but think about which elements of the workshop design will make both the learners and you more comfortable. Build a space—with the seating arrangement, music, peripheral information, handouts, and so on—that puts you at ease, and the learners will no doubt relax as well.

Be Prepared

The better you know your material, the more relaxed you will be. I tell trainers, "If you are teaching addition and subtraction, know calculus." That way, little will throw you for a loop and you can adjust your material to the level of the group. If you don't know calculus and need to teach addition and subtraction anyway, be sure you know the material backward and forward.

We fear what we don't know. To the extent that we don't know how to move our bodies, don't "own" the space, and feel unready, we give ourselves a chance to suffer from stage fright. What if you're ready, you're calm, and you feel comfortable in the environment and someone throws you a curve? Then what?

Speaking Off the Cuff

The vice president of human resources smiles sweetly and says to you, "Tell us about the new sales training program."

You came to the meeting fully prepared to discuss the plans for the company picnic. Take a breath. Remember that she is asking because you know and she doesn't. That makes you the expert. Ask a question: "Would you like to know about the program design process, the course content, or the whole thing from soup to nuts?"

This gives you time, and while she is answering, you can write down her response. Her answer may give you an outline: "I'd like to hear about your needs analysis, the decision to use a consultant for some of the content design, and how the course is being received."

If she isn't forthcoming and says, "The whole thing," you need to think in a very straight line. Think of your presentation as a history. Start at the beginning and proceed in orderly steps to the end. Before you begin, tell your listeners what you will cover and check how much time you have: "I'll start with the needs analysis, then go on to our consultant relationship, a quick outline of the learning experience itself, and some of our first feedback. Should take about 5 or 10 minutes. Okay?"

Your audience will now let you know whether your outline is what it wants. Be brief and stick to the outline. Avoid anything that doesn't reinforce the message. Finish 5 minutes early and ask for questions.

USING THE WORKSHOP DESIGN AS A PRESENTATION TOOL

Other chapters in this book deal with designing a program. Here we will look at what to do with the design elements. The more your learners are actively involved in what is going on, the easier it is for you to hold their interest. Role plays and discussions are more than rest stops for the trainer or "recess" for the group. Use these powerful tools to keep people engaged, underline major points, and check for understanding.

As a presenter, you need to know why a particular exercise is being used. Always discuss the learning purpose of the exercise with the learners. Never forget that these people are adults and will resist being manipulated. A good question to ask the group is, "Now, why in the world did we just do that? What relevance can it possibly have to business?" Then listen while the group members build a bridge from the exercise to their particular applications.

It can be fun for a trainer to observe and comment on what the group does in order to work through an exercise. Occasionally trainers get carried away by the exercise and forget its purpose. Avoid using problem-solving exercises or games to stump the group. Your job is to help learning happen, not to make the learners dependent on you for answers.

Facilitating a Discussion

They talk, you listen. Not a bad start when it comes to facilitating discussions, but there is more to it than that. Facilitating a discussion is one part science and three parts art. The science part is your awareness of what else is going on in and around the discussion. Two of the art parts are about knowing yourself and winging it.

What else is going on in and around the discussion is called the context. It may be helpful to think of the context as the box the discussion comes in. It can be helpful for you to know who the boss is, for example, or to know if a particular group has had this discussion before. You may want to know whether this is a group that usually works together and if people generally join in. You certainly want to know what the group expects to get out of the discussion and if that is an achievable goal.

When you are aware of the context, it helps you direct the flow of the discussion and referee a bit. The specific context will shift as the discussion moves forward. People will support positions, take sides, join in, or clam up depending on what's going on in the room at any particular moment. Check to see whether a person or group is being excluded. If you think they are, check in with them: "Did you have something to say about this?"

If someone is dominating the discussion, knowing the context will help you guess why. Your guess can help you determine how to get others involved. Is the dominant party the boss, does she or he have seniority, is she or he older, younger, smarter, louder, scarier, better connected, or more knowledgeable? Whatever the case, your job is to be sure that everyone feels that he or she has been heard.

Interrupting works with many dominant participants. They usually don't mind because it is part of their normal discussion pattern. A compliment never hurts, either: "Thanks, Lou. We have a very clear idea of your position now. Let's hear from somebody else."

If there are people who don't seem to be participating, resist the temptation to call on them. Give them an opportunity to respond, and when they do, thank them and tell them how important it is for the group to hear their input. Some people will not speak up because of the context, especially if the topic is sensitive or they feel there may be repercussions. Others may not be comfortable expressing their views in public for cultural or personal reasons. These people need to feel safe participating at whatever level is comfortable for them. Catch up to them on a break and speak to them about what you are trying to accomplish, why their verbal participation will be supported, and so on.

You need to know about yourself to be good at facilitating discussions. What are your hot buttons? Are you aware of your style of interaction? Try as we may, none of us can be entirely neutral. Does a certain style or type of person set you off or annoy you? Do you feel the need to take the side of the underdog? Do you feel obligated to defend company policy? Do you feel that the members of a certain group (accountants, women, minorities, managers) need special support or need to be controlled when speaking? You have your reasons for each of your biases, and they may not be particularly bad or good. Just know what they are and check in with yourself from time to time.

FACILITATOR'S SELF-CHECK

1. Am I giving people equal time?
2. Am I helping people feel safe in participating?
3. Am I helping people who tend to dominate give other people a chance?
4. Am I avoiding taking sides?

When you check in with yourself, if you feel that you can answer a reasonable yes to each of these four questions, you're probably doing okay. It's good to check with a trusted and supportive group member or a colleague. Ask individuals on a break how they think it's going. Ask the group after a break (they'll have had time to talk about the meeting with each other) how they think it's going and if everyone feels he or she is being heard.

Sometimes you have to adjust what you are doing in midstream. The best preparation for this is experience. While you are getting experience, watch facilitators whose style you like. Talk with them after their meetings about the things they did that you found particularly effective.

Here are a few things most good group facilitators do:

- *Be a good listener.* A big part of facilitating is listening. Stay focused and take notes if you have to.
- *Control the pace.* Don't let the meeting run away from you. If it is going too fast for you to keep up, call a break, interject a comment at a different pace, or call on someone who will slow it down for you. As you become more experienced, you will use this technique less and less.
- *Admit ignorance.* It's their meeting and their topic, after all. If you need clarification, ask a question. If you need to go back and pick up something that was skipped or change direction, go ahead. Just don't let yourself get lost too often. The reason you are there is to keep them on track.
- *Check in.* It is vital to check in with the group all the time. "Are we on track?" is a great question. "Before we move on, is there anything else on this topic?" is another. If you are taking notes on a flip chart and condensing someone's long statement into a word or two, be sure to ask the speaker if you got it right and change it if you didn't.
- *Avoid making judgmental comments even if they are complimentary.* If you are going around the circle and say "Good comment," or "Excellent observation" to the first three people, what are you going to say when the fourth person says something you don't agree with? Or what if you just forget to say "Attaboy" to one group member after saying it to the rest? A simple "thank you" is great after a comment and can keep you out of trouble.
- *Support the process.* Know what the desired outcome of the meeting is and keep the group focused on the task. Do they want to come away with a list, action items, a plan? There is no need to apologize for keeping the group focused, but you can duck a few brickbats by reminding them why you are there: "This is a great discussion, but we're getting away from what we have scheduled. Shall we jot this down for another meeting, or do you think this is important for the strategic plan?"

• *Smile.* Some people become very solemn-looking while listening intently. Some may even furrow their brows or scowl. This can unintentionally send a message of disagreement or disapproval. Be aware of how you look while listening. Practice a welcoming expression or at least a gentle poker face.

Building on Participants' Knowledge

All the skills you have read about so far will help you adjust the presentation as you go. Flexibility is the hallmark of an expert presenter. Flexibility not only demonstrates interest in the immediate needs of the learners but supports the idea that adults know best about what and how they need to learn. After all, if the group only needs to learn Chapter 3, why make it suffer through Chapters 1 and 2?

You may need to have a few sessions under your belt before you are comfortable tweaking the workshop design as you go to suit the audience. If you know the subject matter and understand your strengths and weaknesses as a presenter, you will be able to shift your approach to better serve the learners.

Learning Styles and Multiple Intelligences

The chapters on program design in this book cover different types of learners in detail, but there is one thing we need to be aware of about people from a presentation standpoint: They are all different.

Be sure you know what the session's top three or four main points are that must be communicated. Then make sure that the people in the workshop will have an opportunity to experience the main points by observation, reflection, action, and emotional involvement. Each main point must be demonstrated to the class. There needs to be time for people to think about each point by reading a section to themselves, writing their response to it, or participating in a discussion. People need to practice applying what they have learned: Role playing, simulations, and games come into play here. Some learners need to become emotionally involved with the material. This can happen during practice and discussions, but probably will not happen if you limit interaction or stifle objections or other forms of vocal resistance.

Even if you have to cut something else out, be sure there is time for people to manipulate the information you are sharing in all the ways we just discussed.

Culture

Know about the culture of the people in the class. There are national, regional, ethnic, departmental, and corporate cultures that influence how people are used to learning. If you are going to come at them from a new direction, be sure that they know it and are on board.

Style

There are a lot of different ways for people to be smart. We refer to Baryshnikov and Michael Jordan as geniuses, but we don't know if they can balance their own checkbooks. Stories abound about Einstein forgetting to tie his shoes or overlooking other details that were not important to him. The stereotypical computer whiz is brilliant with numbers and not so good with people. The stereotypical trainer is often the opposite.

Get creative. Be flexible. Try and fail and try again. But don't give up flexing your approach to fit the styles of the learners you are working with. After all, they are your customers. Without learners, there would be no trainers.

Learning As You Go

Even the most experienced trainers slip up from time to time. It isn't an exact science, and making mistakes and trying new things is how we learn. As you develop your own style, you will make mistakes. Make a note of what didn't work and what you will try next time. Have other trainers watch and give you honest feedback. Talk to trusted people who attend your classes about how to improve your approach. Include questions about your presentation style in the evaluation sheets.

Every trainer, no matter how experienced, can get better. Most of the best ones solicit feedback no matter how many times they have presented a particular piece.

Documents, Job Aids, and Other Helpful Hints

Finding a Mentor

The best job aid is an experienced learning partner. The instantaneous and continuous feedback of a good coach or mentor is priceless. If we could all learn this way, we wouldn't need training. The problem for some people is finding such a person.

Start by looking close to home. Do you belong to a training department? Take turns with your colleagues watching one another and offering feedback. If feedback isn't offered, ask for it. Don't let one another get away with "It was good." Get details. Get picky. Improve.

If you feel you need more than that, find other presenters in the organization—sales people, marketing people, and so on—who are particularly polished. Trade expertise with them. They can help you with your presentation skills, and you can help them learn about the ways adults learn, listening skills, and the like.

One of the best ways to learn presentation skills is to attend as many presentations as possible. Join ASTD and/or other human resources and training groups at both the local and national levels. National conferences give you a chance to observe and learn from the leaders in your field. Local meetings let you talk with more experienced people and learn with them.

Trainers are generally nice people who are excited about helping other people learn new things in order to grow. If you ask a trainer for help, you'll always get *something.*

In asking someone to be your mentor or coach, be very specific about what you want. Have an idea about how you will learn best, the amount of time you are looking for, and what you want to accomplish.

Be ready with something like: "I would like to meet with you at lunch once a month to talk about my presentation skills. I'll bring my evals and other feedback with me and pick your brain about ways to improve. If you could come and watch me work once or twice, that would be great." That's going to get you a lot more help than: "Will you be my mentor?"

Measurement and Evaluation Basics

Other chapters in this book will help you measure important things such as training transfer and behavioral change. You also should measure how well you are being received. It is easy to include questions about your presentation in the "smile sheets" at the end of the session. Like any measurement, it will be more valuable if you track these responses over time. Check for patterns or areas that need improvement. Also check to see if things you are working on are improving. Here are some presentation-related questions pulled from a workshop evaluation sheet created for one of my clients.

In evaluating the **entire workshop,** please respond to each question by circling one rating (1 = Low/Needs Improvement; 3 = Average/Adequate; 5 = High/Superior) and adding relevant comments.

I. Presentation

1. Content clarity	1	2	3	4	5
2. Delivery	1	2	3	4	5
3. Audiovisual	1	2	3	4	5
4. Pace/flow	1	2	3	4	5
5. Open learning environment	1	2	3	4	5
6. Small group activities	1	2	3	4	5
7. Use of rowing as a team-building tool	1	2	3	4	5

II. MATERIALS

8. Relevant to content	1	2	3	4	5
9. Helpful during presentation	1	2	3	4	5
10. Useful for future application	1	2	3	4	5
11. Appearance	1	2	3	4	5

Learning Styles Inventory

The more you know about your learners and the more they know about themselves, the better prepared you will be. Several inexpensive instruments can help people identify the ways in which they learn best. Think about using an instrument at the beginning of the session or send it out as prework. While every good workshop should be accessible to all styles, knowing who you are working with can help you adjust. One very good instrument is Kolb's Learning-Style Inventory. This self-scoring booklet is available in quantity from McBer & Company, 116 Huntington Ave., Boston, MA 02116. Phone orders are accepted at 800-729-8074. A very good leaders' guide is also available.

Fun and Games
Whether you want to create your own exercises or adapt something that someone else has designed, a couple of good places to go for ideas are a series of books that start with *The Games Trainers Play* (McGraw-Hill) and Bob Pike's *Creative Training Techniques Newsletter* (Lakewood Publications).

ASTD
The American Society for Training and Development is a great reservoir of information for its member trainers at any level of experience. The society publishes a monthly magazine, has local chapter meetings for learning and networking, and provides many other services. If you are not a member or if you are a member and have not availed yourself of the society's resources for a while, get more information by calling 800-628-2783 or visit the ASTD Web site at www.astd.org.

Lakewood Publications
Lakewood Publications publishes several valuable periodicals including *Training*, a monthly magazine, and *The Training Directors' Forum Newsletter*. Lakewood sponsors several conferences each year targeted at specific areas of training and development. You can check out Lakewood's products at www.trainingsupersite.com.

Linkage, Inc.

Many human resources and training professionals have told me,"If it's a Linkage conference, it's going to be good." Linkage assembles best-practice practitioners for conferences on specific business topics. When you are ready for in-depth information and practical applications, this is the place to go. To find out more, visit its Web site at www.linkageinc.com or call 781-862-3157.

International Alliance for Learning

You will read a lot in this book and elsewhere about "accelerated" or "accelerative" learning, "transfer of training," and "brain science." A good source for both the history of and the newest thinking in these approaches is the International Alliance for Learning. Call 800-426-2989 or visit the Web site at www.ialearn.org.

Basic Needs Analysis

Other chapters deal with this topic in more detail, but needs analysis is included here as a presentation aid. You need to know what your learners need or you will not be able to present to them well. A simple way to find out what people want to learn is to ask them. There are some good samples of forms and formats for needs analysis in the ASTD's *Needs Assessment Instruments*. This collection of articles and sample survey instruments is a good place to start or to use as a refresher.

Academic and Business Publications

Remember that if you are going to teach addition and subtraction, you should know calculus. Read about your company's or client companies' industries. Be not just a training person but a businessperson. This will contribute not only to your own expertise as you present but to your credibility and the credibility of the training profession.

There are many excellent sources of business information that may apply directly to what you need to know. Check them out at a library or bookstore before subscribing so that you can choose the ones that work best for you.

Your local newspaper business section. If you work for a big company, it will be in there. If you work for a small company, read about your local business environment.

The Wall Street Journal. Not only will you look cool on the train on the way to work, there are special sections and reports about workplace issues. You can use the index in every issue to look for specific companies whose cultures or practices interest you.

Inc. This is a great source of lists for companies you may want to benchmark as well as current reporting and insights into the world of business.

Fast Company, Inc. This publication often focuses on new ideas, mavericks, and innovation.

Wired. You should be conducting training in classrooms because it is the best way for a specific audience to learn specific content. If you are training in classrooms because you don't know what computers can do, pick up a copy of *Wired* and imagine new ways of interacting with learners.

Harvard Business Review and *Sloan Management Review.* Don't be intimidated by the lofty sources of these journals. They vary slightly in style, but most of the articles are written clearly and with a minimum of jargon. Many new ideas about organizational learning appear here months or even years before they appear anywhere else.

The Systems Thinker. No list would be complete without this relative newcomer. Monthly newsletters address "systems thinking" ways to approach complex problems. Individual and organizational learning challenges are often addressed. For more information, call Pegasus Communications at 781-398-9700.

Junk Mail

Once you subscribe to any of the services or publications mentioned above, you will begin to receive unsolicited information about workshops, books, societies, and CD-ROMs from all over. Don't automatically discard these items. Some of your best ideas may come from reading advertising material, even if you aren't going to buy anything. By following what is going on out there, you will be able to stay abreast of all the new tools and approaches and pick what works best for you.

YOUR PRESENTATION CHECKLIST

When Ethan Allen, the backwoods hero of the American Revolution, was asked why his guerrilla fighters were always successful, he said, "We don't forget nothin'." The following list is a compilation of lists used by many experienced trainers. Use it, add to it, and adapt it to your needs.

PRESENTATION CHECKLIST

Will people get a chance to learn the main points of the workshop by
——— Acting   ——— Thinking
——— Watching   ——— Feeling

Equipment

——— Has everything been ordered?   ——— Are there backup bulbs and
                                                     batteries?
——— Has setup and practice time been scheduled?
If using a laptop for overheads:
        ——— Does it work with the projector?
        ——— Do I have backup transparencies and projector?
        ——— Is my screen saver turned off?

Me

_____ Have I scheduled myself so that I will be as well rested as possible?
_____ Have I scheduled warm-up/rehearsal time for myself?
_____ Have I arranged for someone to give me feedback about the workshop?

Space

_____ Is the space set up to support the activities of the day?
_____ Do I know where rest rooms, phones, and food are?

BREAKING THE RULES

As you become knowledgeable about the dos and don'ts listed in this chapter and feel more comfortable with your technique, you will develop your own style. Some of the basics in this chapter may come to be irrelevant to the way you work. Good. Just remember, as you pace through the audience with your hands in your pockets or shoot paint balls at the projection screen, what rules you are breaking and exactly how breaking them will support learning. Have fun.

CHAPTER 6

Technology in the Classroom: Velcro for the Mind

W. Wayne Turmel

Objectives

After reading this chapter, you will be able to:

- Identify many of the training tools available to classroom facilitators.
- Choose the appropriate media for any training situation.
- Recognize the potential and limits of each one.
- Realize that you'll be denied the budget for much of it.

No matter who we are or what skill we are teaching, all trainers have one thing in common: We want the audience to learn and remember what we share with. them. Since experts say that most people forget most of what they hear within 12 hours, this seems like a large task. What we need is an edge, something to increase their retention, to make the information "stick" to their minds like Velcro.

GETTING STARTED

Just as a hammer is not appropriate for working on a computer (although it can be both tempting and temporarily satisfying), not all tools are appropriate for every facilitation opportunity.

Among the things you need to consider are the following:

- How many people are in the total target audience? (Budget considerations are made on this basis.)

- How many people are in each class? (Can everyone see and hear the message, and what will be the cost per student?)
- How much information do you have to convey?
- What is the most appropriate way to reinforce that message? (For example, in language training, audio is more powerful than an easel chart.)
- What is your comfort level with classroom technology? (Do you know how to operate this stuff and maintain your credibility?)
- What is the budget?

This chapter examines the different types of media and evaluates them using three criteria: audience size, cost, and ease of use.

RULES OF THUMB

In implementing any facilitation strategy, it is important to have a set of guidelines to work from. That's what this chapter is intended to be: None of these suggestions are inviolate. They are subject to multiple forces, including your flair for graphics, how much time you have to prepare, what the budget is, and, most important, your own judgment.

Here are some commonsense rules for choosing appropriate media.

Use a Mixed Strategy

Media are used to give participants a break from hearing lectures and stimulate the other senses. One of the most overlooked ways to stimulate the brain is to give it something new to look at. Even the most well-prepared and professional visuals can become routine if they are presented one after the other; the participants' brains seek novelty.

The mind becomes more alert at anything that strays from the familiar. Obviously, you want to use a wide spectrum of color and a mix of visual and kinesthetic stimuli. Less obvious—but almost as effective—can be placing media in a variety of places around the room and using distinctive music to emphasize a point. Use your imagination.

Use the "Burning Building" Test

The building is on fire, and you can save only the tools that are *absolutely* necessary to your message. That's how to evaluate whether to invest in a particular medium. This will reduce instances where you have 105 transparencies for a 4-hour class, saving time, money, and sanity.

Avoid Unhealthy Relationships with Your Media

This is not as silly or unusual as it sounds. We all have preferences when it comes to classroom tools, and the temptation is to utilize the same ones over and over at the expense of the learning objective. If there is a powerful tool that will increase the transfer of learning to your participants, it is incumbent on you as a facilitator to get comfortable with it.

However, it is easy to become so enamored of the new computer-aided technology that it can become addictive, resulting in overuse and cluttered, ineffective visuals.

Whenever Possible, Use the Least Expensive Method

Use the least expensive method that will accomplish the learning objective. The obvious accomplishment will be to keep costs down, an important consideration whether you are an outside consultant or an "internal" training person. In addition, this usually means using a less complicated method, freeing your concentration for the matter at hand. It is much easier to listen to the learners' questions and comments when you are not worried about the batteries in the remote mouse.

TYPES OF MEDIA

Easy to Use, Find, and Afford

Some of the most effective media used in the classroom cost very little and are amazingly powerful. These media have been around seemingly since the dawn of time. It is believed that the cave paintings in Lascaux, France, were actually done as a form of prehunt instruction. This is borne out by the fact that next to pictures of the animals they stalked was a list of names and objectives for the training.

There is a reason the tradition of writing down key learning points continues: It is very successful. The act of seeing a picture of the topic discussed or a new word, definition, or concept in print stimulates receptors in the brain of the participant. The phrase "A picture is worth a thousand words" was never truer than in the classroom.

For our purposes, we will use the following admittedly subjective criterion: A low level of technical skill is required on the part of the instructor, the medium is commonly available, and it is relatively inexpensive. Among the media included in this category are:

- *Blackboards and whiteboards.* These are the twentieth-century equivalent of writing on cave walls. They offer flexibility inasmuch as the participant or instructor can make spontaneous decisions about what is recorded on them. Anything written on them is by nature temporary.

- *Easel Charts, also known as flip charts, rip charts, newsprint, and chart pads.* These media offer the spontaneity of a whiteboard with the added feature that individual sheets of paper can be posted in the classroom for reference throughout the session. They can be prepared beforehand and saved for later use.
- *Props and pictures.* By some estimates, 80 percent of information is absorbed visually. It thus makes sense that a learner finds it invaluable to be able to see and even touch the item being discussed.
- *Handouts and manuals.* These are printed materials that are used as a reference and to reinforce the key learning points. They range from the simple (photocopies of a single page) to the complex (entire textbooks). They range in price but offer little other than reference.
- *Workbooks.* For our purposes these vary from handouts and manuals because while they provide information for later reference, they have one feature not found in other printed materials: interactivity. Whether simply filling in blanks with terminology or solving complex problems, the learner activates parts of the brain that too often are not involved in classroom learning. These media can range in complexity and cost from hole-punched photocopies to elaborate binding and custom printed materials.

Before you get too complacent about these old tools, keep in mind that time marches on. Electronic easel charts can take the handwritten results of a brainstorming session and instantly generate a computer printout. So-called smart boards can take the instructor's scribbling and relay it through phone lines to identical boards in other locations. This medium has magnified the interactivity level of distance learning and increased the need for a whiteboard with a spell check.

Familiar but More Complex

Murphy said, "If it can go wrong, it will." A wiser man added, "Murphy was an optimist." The first level of technology was pretty simple: The only piece of equipment needed was a writing instrument and something to write on. It doesn't get much easier, although anyone who has written on a whiteboard with the wrong kind of marker can tell you that that is enough of a challenge on a Monday morning.

The next tier of classroom technology requires the use of projectors or audio equipment, a step up the complexity scale but nothing most trainers are not familiar with. Teachers have been using projectors since the Lumière brothers first displayed photographs in Paris at the turn of the century. Why? Because they are incredibly effective. Projection allows material to be seen more clearly and by larger groups of people.

Bright light can make colors more vivid and interesting, thus increasing retention. Music and other audio stimuli are powerful teaching media. User-friendly computer applications such as PowerPoint and Corel have allowed even people born graphically challenged to create colorful, attractive transparencies and handouts.

Many of these media are being replaced over time. Scanners and color photocopying are eliminating the need for opaque projectors. The videocassette player has displaced filmstrips and 8-mm film. Overhead projectors now show objects as they are; unlike in the past, when objects had to be presented upside down and backward. The fans are infinitely quieter, and the bulbs are longer lasting. Audiocassettes and compact discs can be played on small, portable, but powerful "boom boxes" rather than huge reel-to-reel players.

We are talking only about presenting finished material in this chapter: equipment actually used by a classroom trainer during a class session. There is no assumption that the facilitators have to create the media themselves. Many trainers use only "canned" presentations.

As technology has marched inexorably onward, two things have happened: These tools have become less expensive and easier to use, and the participants' expectations have increased with familiarity. In other words, unless one is instructing raccoons, shiny lights on a wall will not by themselves awe the participants. There are definite industry standards of appearance and competency with the tools. The good news is that they are relatively simple to achieve.

This relatively inexpensive and easy-to-use equipment includes the following:

- *Audio recordings.* These can be used as background music or can contain lesson material; they include both audiocassettes and compact discs. The quality of the recording and the clarity of playback are the main concerns. Audio stimulation is a very effective teaching tool but is used less frequently than it should be.
- *35-mm slides.* This technology is not used frequently in the classroom and is being replaced by computer-based presentation tools (see the next section). It offers the ability to show photographs larger than life and is effective with large audiences. Anyone who has had to listen to an annoying clicker or seen a carousel jam will not mourn its passing.
- *Filmstrips.* This is another dying technology. These are individual frames of 35-mm film joined together in a loop and advanced one by one.
- *Opaque projector.* This is a large device used to project images from nontransparent sources such as the pages of a book. This type of machinery is becoming obsolete as scanners and digital cameras become commonplace.
- *Overhead projector.* This is perhaps the most common electrical tool in today's classroom. It is a simple, relatively inexpensive projector that

displays transparencies (images on clear film such as acetate). Simply photocopying text or images in black and white or using desktop tools such as inkjet printers to create colored visuals can create these transparencies. Just as rings tell the age of a tree, you can tell the age of a facilitator by whether he or she calls them slides (the latest term, derived from PowerPoint), foils, or viewgraphs. Advances in these projectors have made them lighter and more durable. The new bulbs generate less heat, although they still burn out regularly and must be replaced.

- *Videocassette recorders and players (VCRs).* Just as they have in most homes, VCRs have become ubiquitous in training facilities. The images can be viewed on a regular television, a special monitor system, or a rear-screen system similar to big-screen televisions. Off-the-shelf tapes are cost-effective, and you may decide to produce your own if sufficiently large numbers of people will be trained. They offer a refreshing change of pace for learners. However, anyone who has dozed off in front of the television will recognize the downside.

Newer and More Complicated

So far we've covered technology which is effective, relatively inexpensive to create, and easy to use. Why mess with a good thing?

Rapid advances in computer technology and communication have allowed trainers to increase their capabilities greatly. Static transparencies are being supplanted by computer-generated presentations with animated text, bright colors, and video and music clips. Imagine the reaction in the participant's brain to all that stimulation.

The trainer does not even have to be in the same room—or country—as the participants, thanks to videoconferencing and satellite technology. Think of how that broadens the potential audience and lowers travel costs.

Many otherwise rational trainers have a deep suspicion and even outright fear of electronic media. Will it take the "humanity" out of training? Does learning really transfer effectively? If I can't program my VCR, how do you expect me to use a remote mouse?

Remember, the first overhead projectors weighed 40 pounds and displayed things upside down and backward with a bulb life less than 5 hours. Remember too that video was never supposed to match the quality of 8-mm or 16-mm film. Above all, remember the first universal law of computer presentations: The odds of a presentation going awry are directly proportional to the importance of the presentation and inversely proportional to the training and the precautions taken.

In other words, get used to the technology. One of the keys to good adult learning is to focus on the *learners' needs*, not your own phobias. Find out what your comfort level is and raise it. Take a class. Rumor has it there are good trainers out there. Know any?

The most commonly used forms of advanced media are the following:

- *Computer-based presentations.* These differ from transparencies created in a computer application such as Microsoft's PowerPoint and Corel in that they emanate directly from a computer, usually a laptop hooked to a projection device. This allows for a full range of animation, hyperlinks to other presentations, displays of Web sites live from the Internet, and generally more powerful presentations. They are usually displayed through one of the following projector types:

   LCD panels. These were the first generation of projectors used to display computer-generated images. They worked by forcing light through liquid crystal display (LCD) panels of red, blue, and green. Some used the light from an overhead projector. Unfortunately, so much light was diffused that the room needed to be completely dark, making training conditions less than ideal.

   LCD projectors. Eventually engineers came up with an LCD panel that provided its own light. The first few needed very low ambient light to be seen clearly and were extremely heavy and difficult to use. The latest projectors weigh less than 10 pounds and can be used easily in full daylight.

   LMD projectors. These devices represent the latest step forward. These lose almost no light as the image is bounced off tiny mirrors, as opposed to passing through a colored filter. The result is incredibly bright, clear pictures and easy troubleshooting. While they are still expensive, their brightness allows classroom training in full light, making facilitation more successful.

- *Video conferencing.* This is where many people leave their comfort zone. How can they do serious instruction when they are miles away from the students? While there is no doubt that some degree of interactivity is lost, many companies feel that the savings in time and travel and the ability to deliver information "just in time" outweigh such concerns. As we've already mentioned, changes in technology have allowed us to take familiar tools such as whiteboards and easel charts and incorporate them into distance learning, increasing the facilitator's comfort level.

One of our rules of thumb has been to use the least expensive tools to do the job, yet this type of conferencing can cost thousands of dollars per hour. How is that economical? Well, how much do 60 airfares to Chicago cost? If the session is of relatively short duration and there are numerous people involved in a training intervention, this can be a very cost-effective way to deliver training. Advances in technology have made it easier to watch and more reliable to use.

There are two types of videoconferencing. Both can include video and music as well as the instructor's face and voice. In addition, the students can ask questions in real time via video feed or computer linkup, which feeds questions back to the instructor in text form so that she or he can answer them live.

- *Telephone lines.* The instructor's image is broadcast over telephone lines. While it can be extremely reliable, it is expensive and subject to all manner of technical problems stemming from the "bandwidth," or capability, of the lines. (Think of it as a water pipe. The larger the pipe—the bandwidth—the more stuff flows through it.) New technology such as Picture-Tel allows individual learners in multiple locations to participate cost-effectively. The drawback is the tiny camera, which allows mostly for "talking heads" rather than classroom-size pictures.
- *Satellite link-ups.* Now we're talking cool stuff. While instruction can be delivered just as it is in a classroom, the potential is immense. Imagine being able to do a class from anywhere on earth or even from an orbiting space station. The picture quality can be excellent, but this technology is in its infancy. Unlike the smaller scope of phone lines, full studio-quality broadcasting is possible. The cost is as big as the potential. The good news for companies that lack the resources to set up their own satellite networks is that there are rental facilities, such as Caliber centers and Kinko's that provide both broadcast facilities and classrooms.

Other Tools

The new technology raises an interesting question: What is a classroom? The old definition of any room with chairs, learners, and a facilitator no longer applies, since the instructor does not need to be in the same room or even the same country as the learners. In fact, even mundane tools such as whiteboards have been electronically enhanced and pressed into service for distance learning.

New technology in computer networking allows instructor-led distance learning over the Internet or a company's Intranet. A streaming video picture of the instructor appears on their desktop computer. Audio, video, and text responses can be sent back and forth instantly. This is a supervisor's dream come true: sending people to training while keeping them at their desks.

This is not a distant dream. The technology exists. What isn't in place yet is the infrastructure to support it. The viability of the technology is dependent on bandwidth (the amount of information that can be carried by a company's internal wiring) and other technical considerations that seem to be overcome the minute someone says they can't be. It is incumbent on educators and facilitators to use this new technology not for its own sake but to achieve the best end result for the learner.

PUTTING IT ALL TOGETHER

Workbooks, overheads, even satellites. How does a facilitator make sensible choices about the media that will offer the greatest opportunity for learning and meet the needs of both the participants and the payer?

Table 6–1 gives you a matrix of the factors we have discussed that are involved in making those decisions. Let's take a look at an example.

You are responsible for instructing 200 people in customer service. They are all in one location that has training facilities, and your budget is $175 per student day.

Now, using Table 6–2, let's analyze our choices.

We know there will be 10 classes that are identical in nature. We want media and materials that will be consistent throughout.

A relatively small class size means that we do not require elaborate projection systems or special audio equipment. An overhead projector or an LCD projector hooked up to a laptop will be sufficient.

The need for people to retain the information indicates that they should have some take-away material to refer to. Since we have a budget of $35,000 and want interactive learning, workbooks are appropriate. Brainstorming requires flexible media such as easel charts or a whiteboard. Perhaps a take-away card-size job aid would be appropriate.

TABLE 6–1

Giving Instruction in Customer Service

Total Number of Participants and Locations	Number of Participants per Class	What Would Ideal Media Accomplish?	What Is My Comfort Level?	Budget (Including Travel Expenses for Participants and Facilitator)
200 students at one site	20	Role play, brainstorming, retention of procedures	High	$175 per student No travel No facilities cost Total: $35,000

TABLE 6-2

Technology Options

Type of Medium	Optimum Number of Students	Type of Learning and/or Memory	Advantages	Disadvantages	Relative Cost	Appropriate
Blackboards and Whiteboards		Visual	Can be created spontaneously No maintenance Easy accessibility	Not permanent	Practically nil	
Props	Less than 30	Visual, kinetic	Tangible, close-up study	May be too expensive or large	?	
Photocopied handouts	All participants	Visual	Can be referred to over and over	May be distracting or let participants get ahead of lesson plan	Very low	
Printed manuals and texts	All participants	Visual	Reference; offers credibility	Reading can reduce interactivity	Usually low	
Workbooks	All participants	Visual, kinetic	Reference Interactivity	Must be well done or credibility suffers	Low	
Audio recordings (prerecorded)	Depends on equipment availability	Audio	A different form of stimuli Variety Good for interpersonal skills	Must be audible to all participants Can be unwieldy	Low to moderate	
35-mm slides	Depends on projector	Visual	Photographic quality Colorful	Machinery is unwieldy and often hard to operate smoothly	Initial cost moderate	
Filmstrips	Depends on projector	Visual, sometimes audio	Professional quality	Hard to replace now Dying technology	Initial cost low; replacement cost high	

Technology Options

Type of Medium	Optimum Number of Students	Type of Learning and/or Memory	Advantages	Disadvantages	Relative Cost	Appropriate
Opaque projector	Small to moderate-size groups	Visual	Allows almost any two-dimensional object to be magnified for all to see Choices can be made as the class dictates	Machinery is heavy, and picture quality mediocre	Low cost of operation	
Overhead projector transparencies	Small to moderate-size groups	Visual	Colorful, good quality, easy reproduction Very easy to use	Static Can be prone to dullness	Low	
Purchased video	Depends on projection equipment	Visual, audio	When done well, can be amazingly powerful Can lend credibility	Ever fall asleep in front of the TV? No interaction	Moderate	
Computer-generated (PowerPoint or similar software)	Depends on projection equipment	Visual, sometimes auditory	Can be colorful, using motion and special effects Can be updated easily	Current technology still a mystery to many Not very flexible once class begins	Low to produce Projection equipment is expensive	
Video conferencing	Large numbers of people in multiple locations	Visual, auditory	Participants can see and hear facilitator Some degree of interactivity	Full interactivity is not yet available Subject to technical glitches	Low cost to produce Satellite time and facilities relatively expensive	

There will be at least 10 classes, and so the investment in more permanent media such as overhead transparencies or PowerPoint slides (or similar presentation software) makes sense.

Since customer service is behavior-based, it would help to see examples of the desired behavior. Here we have some choices to make. Video is expensive to produce, and we have a limited budget. An off-the-shelf video from an outside vendor can run $800 or more, but divided over the 10 classes, this is well within our reach. You may decide that a good training video is worth the initial cost. If it is not or if you cannot locate one, you may wish to have a video camera and a VCR in the classroom to tape the participants as they role-play. This is a much less expensive option and a powerful teaching tool.

There are a lot of things you can do. The amount of time the participants can spend away from their work stations may dictate some prework or an assessment. This could be done by Internet or Intranet, but the technology is still more expensive than is warranted here, and so this remains a comparatively inexpensive form of training to conduct. You could conduct one giant training session using video in multiple classrooms, but the cost in terms of equipment and lost productivity of having everyone gone at once makes this impractical. Besides, customer service is behavior-based, and the facilitator should be able to interact with all the participants. Remember one of our rules of thumb: Choose the least expensive media to accomplish all your training objectives.

SUMMARY

We know what we want our students to learn, and we know how they will best remember it. With a comprehensive list of tools at our disposal and a good understanding of those media, we can make effective choices based on learner needs, budget considerations and our knowledge of and comfort level with the technology.

We now have what it takes to present the information to learners and help it truly stick. After all, that's what it's all about.

CHAPTER 7

Using Games to Energize Dry Material

Steve Sugar

This is how learning is meant to be—active, passionate, and personal.

Warren Bennis
On Becoming a Leader

Perhaps you have noticed it: There has been a surge in the use of training games, and more games are being displayed in major catalogues and at major training conferences. Games, which once were considered marginal to serious training, are now viewed in a much more positive light. Dr. Thiagarajan noted: "Twenty years ago, only one trainer in fifty had used training games. Today, it is more likely that only one trainer in fifty has not used training games."

A major reason trainers use learning games is the fun these games bring to learning. Participants seek to have fun whatever they do, especially in the accelerated-learning environment. Add a learning game that brings fun to even the driest material and you have a strong case for using games. Participants like to have fun while they learn, and trainers like to have happy participants.

Today's adult learner expects more information in less time, a more user-friendly training environment, and more of a focus on resource information. Learners don't want to hear you lecture, so how can you tell them what they need to know?

Recent studies tell us what we already knew: An adult learner learns best by doing, by interacting with and demonstrating knowledge of the topic. Learning games create an interactive learning experience by transforming participants into active players and translating inactive information into enjoyable learning episodes. Learning occurs at three levels:

1. Players interact with the content, demonstrating their knowledge and ability to apply the information.

2. Players observe their own behavior and that of others during game play. Post game debriefings give insights into those behaviors in thoughtful vignettes and examples observed during game play.

3. Discussion of newly acquired awareness guides the learner to the discovery of personal and work site applications.

WHAT ARE LEARNING GAMES?

A learning game is a contrived framework through which you present images of reality.

S. Sugar
Games That Teach

The five components of a learning game are as follows:

1. *It is a contest* (the play) involving competition between players and teams of players, or against an established standard such as time or quantity.

2. *Between adversaries* (players) who play as individuals or as teams.

3. *Operating under constraints* (rules) that indicate what you can do, what you can't do, and the status of play.

4. *For an outcome* (payoff or victory), that is, winning or successful completion of a task or event such as building a tower or crossing a path.

5. *While learning something of value* (instructional), that is, the demonstration of an understanding and/or the application of the topic material.

FEATURES OF AN EFFECTIVE GAME

Every learning game has its own format, pattern of play, and rules. A good learning game has a subtle balance of fun (game play) and skill (content questions) that provides a dynamic learning environment.

The features of good games are as follows:

- *User-friendly.* The game format is easily understood.
- *Easily adaptable.* The game accepts the content, can be scaled up or down to any audience, and can be made more or less competitive, depending on the audience.
- *Fun to play.* The game keeps the players' interest throughout the contest; it evokes a "smile quotient" among the players.
- *Portable.* The game can be modified to fit into almost any time schedule; it also can be carried into almost any training site.

CRITERIA FOR THE BEST GAMES

The best learning games promote player excitement and continued interest. This is done by capturing player involvement through a unique and intriguing pattern of play. After entry, the game should continue to promote involvement through a challenging balance of chance and skill.

Pattern of Play

This is the working format of a game: how it is structured, scored, and played. In tic-tac-toe, the pattern of play meets the four criteria of play, players, rules, and payoff by requiring the player to be the first to cover three squares in a row. To add the fifth component, we "adapt" this into a learning game by adding the element of knowledge in the form of questions. Instead of automatically acquiring the space, the player is required to solve a problem to "earn" the space. This painless adaptation allows the instructional designer to link training content to the playing of the game. Our tic-tac-toe model now meets the requirements of a learning game.

Balance

This is the appropriate mix of chance and skill. Too much chance makes the game boring and mindless; too much emphasis on knowledge and skill reduces the game to a test. Balance in play keeps player interest and guarantees continuity of the game experience. The usual "answer factor"—the target response rate for a learning game—is 50 to 80 percent. Achieving less than a 50 percent correct response rate discourages interest and creates disenfranchised players; achieving over 80 percent correct responses removes the element of risk and turns the game into a mindless dice roll.

TYPES OF LEARNING GAMES
Paper-and-Pencil Games

The playing materials involved in this group of games are limited to resource sheets, reproducible game sheets, and handouts. The advantage of this type of game is economy, ease of transfer of the material to a game format, instant involvement, and the creation of a source for personal take-home notes. Paper-and-pencil games range from simple play-and-learn activities to complex team consensus activities. Game formats are as varied as the designer or the desired learning outcome. One team learning game, *RAT Race*, uses group puzzles to challenge team assumptions. *Headlines*, one of a series of interactive lecture games, requires teams to read handouts and then apply them in a copywriting exercise. The bingo-style reinforcement game *QUIZO* is an open "frame" requiring instructor questions. Later in the chapter we will discuss the paper-and-pencil game *Deadlines.*

Board Games

These games are played on a board or special surface. Board games usually involve the use of accessories such as dice, chips, timers, pawns, and question cards. Given the additional expense of money and time, why invest in a board game? And why are board games still considered one of the "sexiest" training vehicles? The answer lies in the play. Board games often evoke a frenzy of play that demonstrates real time skills and behaviors. Because of this impact and high player involvement, there will always be room in the corporate curriculum for *Gold of the Desert Kings* and other "high-end" games.

The production of the game board can be expensive, especially if you prefer a folding board. The bifold requires a preprinted game sheet "wrapper," a back-wrap cloth, two pieces of cardboard, and specialized equipment. To gain economy of scale, folding game boards usually are produced in runs of 500 or more. Sometimes a local notebook bindery will make a "short" run of 50 to 100.

"Place-mat" game boards are more cost-efficient, especially with the availability of computer graphics and lamination. The game sheet is color printed, backed with a white cardboard sheet, and laminated on both sides. These game boards can be produced in a well-outfitted office, at a local photocopy or print shop, or at a large-format print house. *Stepping Stones* produces a large game board by ingeniously using a configuration of six 8.5-inch by 11-inch plastic sheets.

A *wall game* is a "vertical" board game in which an oversized game sheet is positioned on a vertical surface to show game play and scoring. A wall game keeps players focused on the status portrayed by one playing board. A "find someone who" icebreaker requires two teams to identify matches with team members and then inspect the opponent's chart for mistakes. A brainstorm game uses a vertical game sheet matrix to conduct a structured brainstorm. *A Question Of . . . "* scores responses to case studies in ethics and diversity on a vertical game sheet.

Card Games

These games use playing materials in the form of cards. The cards can contain all the learning material needed for play or can be supplemented by accessories or other written material. Production quality ranges from handwritten index card sets to laser printouts to professionally prepared decks.

Card games present an interesting range of activities. You can create an ice-breaker by distributing one or more cards to the participants and requiring them to meet and match. You can use the *Customer Service Action Plan* card sort to evaluate problems and develop action plans. You can use an "idea" pack to promote creativity, discussion, or retention. You can use flash cards to test and demonstrate learning.

Ordinary playing cards also can be used to create interesting simulations. Dr. Thiagarajan randomly distributes playing cards to create an instant icebreaker (find others with the same card) or an instant role play (think in terms of the characteristics represented by the suit). However, Thiagi is probably best known for his famous whist-style *BARNGA,* which provokes intense play and serious dialogue about personal assumptions.

Prop Games

In these games the play is centered on a specially designed prop. The prop can be something as simple as balloons or rope or as complex as an electrically wired carpet. Props do not always have to be associated with outdoor exercises. *Feeding the Zircon Gorilla* demonstrates a variety of activities that can be used in indoor training.

Props bring learning to the classroom in a variety of ways: players coaching blindfolded mates down a path using dinner bells, teams crossing a simulated minefield, teams moving a large egg to safety, teams tossing differently weighted objects in a relay race, players with letter cards scrambling to create word combinations, and teams building the tallest structure of balloons, newspapers, or straws. *GroupGrope* uses ordinary index cards to promote discussion on an endless variety of topics. *X-O Cise* uses special dice to create a differential scoring system. *Electric Maze* uses a grid carpet to create a minefield. *Team Building Blocks* uses ordinary wooden blocks to demonstrate a variety of team tactics.

A *floor game* is played on the floor and uses players as one of the props by requiring them to move around on squares or complete a journey or task. The props usually are limited to string, masking tape, and newspapers. One game requires two teams to pass through each other to the other side of a path; another requires a team to discover the secret path to the opposite side of a matrix. An important feature of these games is active player involvement along with ongoing communications and planning.

Computer Games

A computer game uses an electronic information-processing device to translate and portray a game package that is projected onto large screens or played at the computer terminal. Computer games are especially useful for review-type questions.

They add the dimension of acting both as the game master in delivering the structure of the game to the user and as the keeper of the time and score.

Computer game shells are a special type of framegame that is presented on a computer screen. The shells permit the loading of new content—usually in the form of questions—by the instructor. The three top-selling game shells are *Game Show Pro, Computer Game Shells,* and *Gamemill.* The shells permit those who are not computer programmers to convert documents into games by typing in questions and information.

On-line games are becoming ever more popular. Although Internet games are mostly recreational, they foretell an exciting educational experience. *Acrophobia* can be conducted only on a computer because of its imaginative play, instant feedback, and unusual scoring system. Like any other open format frame of play, these games can be translated into one's own instructional review game.

ADAPT YOUR OWN GAME

A frequently asked question is, "How do I create my own learning game?" The best answer is: "First adapt, then create." Learn the procedures and techniques for adapting an existing game with your content and then transfer that knowledge to your own design.

This section will take you through a seven-step model. The model will guide you through the process of selection, setup, play, and debriefing. This short apprenticeship should help you create your own learning game.

Have you checked your E-mail? There was an important message. Perhaps we can use this new training "challenge" to demonstrate the seven-step adaptation process.

> Pat Collins, the manager of Division 1A, feels her supervisors are time management—challenged. She wants a complete time management update in a half-day program. You are to deliver this program to 12 to 15 supervisors next Tuesday. The manager does not want any precourse reading. To standardize this training, incorporate items from our time management test file. We expect high participant feedback, at least 4.5 out of 5, and an imaginative, interactive lesson design. Good luck!
> Executive Branch

This has never happened to you, but let's pretend. This E-mail presents us with an opportunity to select and adapt an interactive learning game. For the pending time management class, we will adapt *Deadlines,* a game that scores teams on their ability to estimate and then match the number of correct responses to seven questions (Table 7–1). The game is played in rounds to allow for adjustments in game play as needed.

TABLE 7–1

Deadlines: Sample Time Management Set
We will answer _____ correctly.
Expected points _____.   Actual points received _____.

1. A to-do list helps keep you focused on your daily work load. Who is more likely to make and follow a daily to-do list, men or women?

   Answer: Women. Source: Priority Management Study.

2. In setting up your filing system for day-to-day use, what must be considered its most important feature?

   Answer: Being able to find or retrieve items quickly.

3. What is the standard size of paper crossing the American professional's desk?

   Answer: 8.5-inch by 11-inch (21.5 × 28 cm). This must be considered in plans for handling and storing of office papers.

4. Under normal conditions, what is the optimum number of people who should be involved in a decision?

   Answer: Five (accept three to six).
   Source: Executives at Motorola.

5. According to support staff, what is their most frequently performed activity?

   Answer: Answering the telephone. Is this the best use of their time?

6. What is the best time of day to plan your next workday: the evening before or the morning of the workday?

   Answer: The evening before gives you a clear picture of where you want to go and gets you off to a flying start the next morning.

7. Give one reason why eating lunch at your desk is a poor time management technique.

   Answer: The minutes you might save are lost to decreased energy and loss of focus.

Step 1. Game Selection: Deadlines

Consider the following in adapting the game for your learners.

Target Audience

The most important consideration is the audience. The game must reflect their knowledge, skills, abilities, and work environments.

Level of Play   This reflect's the audience's intellectual level and expectations in the quality of the rules, questions, and game experience. The questions here will be written at the high school literacy level.

Length   Games must be formatted to fit the length of the training session. Most facilitators prefer games whose rules are familiar and/or easily understood and that can be conducted in less than 50 minutes. The three parts of conducting a game are: setup (20 percent), to establish the game environment; play (60 percent), including the actual play and closure of the activity; and debriefing (20 percent), the process of game content and player conduct.

Number of Players   This is the total number of players involved in the game experience. In other games it includes all participants, including players, observers, coaches, and judges. Most games seem to be more effective with smaller groups of 6 to 15. Facilitator-controlled games may be able to handle larger groups, but learning impact is usually lost with each player above 25. To accommodate larger groups consider using a cofacilitator or assistant.

For this time management program, prepare for 20 and expect 14. Preparing for 20 allows you to deal with unexpected attendees, with the subsequent distribution of handouts and game materials, on the day of class.

Learning Outcomes

What do you want the audience to learn or demonstrate while playing the game? *Deadlines* will be adapted to update our audience on the latest information and techniques in time management. This information will be supplemented by handouts distributed at the beginning of the program. The topic area will be time management, as requested by Division 1A.

Game Features

Deadlines will have the following features:

- Played in rounds.
- Displays written material in a test or problem statement format.
- Team contract. A team's score is based on its ability to match its estimated score.
- Competitive. Teams compete against their own estimates and against other teams.
- Can be played in less than 50 minutes.
- Facilitator-run. The facilitator collects estimates, records scores, and provides the correct responses.
- Ordinary accessories. Uses photocopied question sheets, overhead transparencies, paper and pencil, and a flip chart.

Game Settings

Time of Play   The time for each round is 20 minutes: 5 minutes to respond to the questions and 15 minutes to deliver answers, a rationale, and scoring. The program time allows for three rounds of play.

Plan for three rounds of play, with a fourth set of questions in case of continued interest or a tie breaker.

Questions   Prepare 7 questions per round for 4 rounds, for a total of 28 questions. The first round should focus on easier recall information as presented in the introductory lecture. Using easier questions in the first round allows players to become familiar with the rules, game environment, and information. After the first round players should be ready to deal with more difficult problem statements.

Variations
The following variations can be used:

- Expand or decrease the time allowed for responses.
- Vary the question format to include problem statements requiring seven examples.
- Vary the rounds of play. Expand rounds of play for lengthy topics.
- Vary the number of questions. Award points using the same scoring mechanism.

Step 2. Game Content: Research and Development
Information on the topic is developed and fitted into the game.

Demonstration of Learning
The outcome for this training is to update the supervisors in time management information and skills. *Deadlines* has demonstrated that it generates energy, is competitive, and can bring information to the audience.

Placing Content into the Game
Develop a set of questions based on the test item file and the latest materials. Prepare a list of 40 questions that will be culled to 28 for the program. Create a conceptual flow of easier items for the first round of play, items of moderate difficulty for the second round, and the most challenging items for the third round.

Develop a supplementary handout containing ideas, applications, and readings that underscore the entire learning experience. Handouts may range from a thoughtful expansion of the question material to an in-depth reference manual. Handouts traditionally are distributed at the beginning of class to be used as study and note guides.

Step 3. Game Accessories

These materials create an appropriate game learning environment.

Game Sheets

Deadlines requires one question sheet per player per round. Prepare 20 copies of each round's question sheets times four rounds for a total of 80 pages. Question sheets should be collated into sets of five sheets per team that will be distributed on a round-by-round basis. Prepare one set of master (answer) sheets for use during the debriefing part of each round, perhaps with a copy for the overhead transparency.

Audiovisual Equipment

Use the following equipment:

- *Flip chart* to reinforce lecture, display game objectives and rules of play, keep score, and list comments and reactions
- *Overhead projector* to show sample game sheet (optional), rules of play, scoring matrix, and answer sheets (optional)
- *Audiotape player* to play background music and introduce audio information from speeches or sound tracks

Special Props and Accessories

Use the following props and accessories:

- *Felt-tip markers* to list responses and fill out name cards
- *Masking tape* to post charts, mend paper, and secure electrical wires
- *Timer* to time the 10-minute response period and the entire round of play
- *Noisemaker* to alert teams to start and stop
- *Name cards and tent folds* to create an informal networking environment, allowing teams to create their own identity
- *In box* to simulate the work environment in delivering game sheets
- *Prizes* to stimulate the players

Step 4. Pregame Setup: The Golden Hour

This is the critical time to ready the classroom and yourself.

Room Inspection and Setup

Do the following:

- Conduct a room inspection, checking wall outlets, audiovisual equipment, and so on. Set up conference tables, chairs, and name cards.

- Place posters, banners, or wall charts containing time management quotations. Post rules of play and other materials (optional).

Instructor's Table

This is your resource area. Take time to organize the following:

- Four rounds of *Deadline* question sheets (20 per round)
- Four master (answer) sheets
- Four master sheets on overhead transparencies (optional)
- Overhead transparencies, rules of play, and scoring matrix
- Felt-tip markers and masking tape
- Timer and noisemakers (optional)
- Prizes (optional)

Conference Tables

Deadlines is best played at separate tables to allow for team planning (estimating scores) and problem solving (answering questions). Set up six chairs at each table.

Step 5. Game Preliminaries

In-class procedures discussed before game play establish the structure and environment of the game.

Divide the class into teams of four to five players and do the following:

- Seat each team at its own table.
- Have team members fill out name cards (optional).
- Have teams select team names and print them out on name cards (optional).

Display the game information by showing the objective and player instructions on an overhead.

DEADLINES

Game objective: to score as many points as possible
Player instructions:

- Your team must estimate how many correct responses it will provide to seven questions about time management.
- After posting its estimates, your team will receive a game sheet of seven questions. (All teams receive the same sheet.)

continued

concluded

- Each team will have 5 minutes to respond to the questions.
- The facilitator will go over the set of questions.
- Teams will compute their scores based on their correct responses, as shown on the scoring matrix.
- The facilitator will post each team's score.
- Play is the same for each round.
- At the end of the game the team with the most points is declared the winner.

The introduction should acquaint the players with the game rules and create a positive learning environment.

Sample Introduction

Use your version of the following introduction:

Good morning. I want to briefly go over the game *Deadlines*. This game is played in rounds. Each round consists of your team estimating how many correct responses you will provide to seven questions. Then your team will receive a set of questions. After we stop play, we will go over the correct responses. Your score will be determined by the scoring matrix. You will have 5 minutes to answer as many of the questions as you can.

Display the scoring matrix.

SCORING MATRIX

Estimated Correct	Expected Score
1	1
2	4
3	9
4	16
5	25
6	36
7	49

If a team does not accomplish its estimate, it receives only 2 points for each correct answer. If a team exceeds its estimate, it receives an additional 2 points for every correct answer above the estimate.

Step 6. Game Play

The game is conducted as follows.

Preliminaries
Collect the team estimates and then do the following:

- Poll each team for its estimate before answering the question sheet.
- Post the estimate on the flip chart.

Start Game Play
Do the following:

- Distribute the first set of question sheets, one per player, to each team.
- After all the players have received a copy of the question sheet, start play.
- Call time after 5 minutes.
- Poll the participants about their responses to each question. Indicate and discuss the correct answers, as needed.
- Help the teams compute their scores according to the scoring matrix.
- Record each team's points on the flip chart.

Round 2 to End of Game
Do the following:

- Continue each round of play in the same manner for three rounds.
- Conduct the fourth round as required.

End of Game
The team with the most points is declared the winner. Here is a scoring example:

1. Team A estimates five correct answers for a contract at 25 points.
    a. Team A provides six correct answers.
    b. Team A receives 25 points for meeting its estimate, plus 2 points for the additional correct answer beyond the estimate.
    c. Team A total: $25 + 2 = 27$ points.

2. Team B estimates six correct answers for a contract at 36 points.
    a. Team B provides four correct answers.
    b. Team B receives 2 points for each correct answer because it did not meet its contract, scoring = 2 points per correct answer.
    c. Team B total: $4 \times 2 = 8$ points.

Step 7. Closure and Debriefing

This step ends the game and brings the learning experience home.

For *closure,* total all team scores and declare the winner(s). Use this period to discuss problems with the game in terms of rules, questions, or team play. In the event of very competitive play, remind the players that it was just a game, a competitive exercise to underscore the topic; all competitive feelings should stay in the room.

Debriefing is the process of helping people reflect on their experiences to develop meaningful learning. It usually takes place immediately after the game experience. In guided debriefing, the facilitator initiates and moderates the discussion. The debriefing period can include venting, in which learners let off steam or share insights that can generate generalizations about the relationship of the game and its content to real life and applications of generalizations to the workplace.

Most instructors have their own methods of debriefing but may wish to follow a debriefing process of What? So what? And Now what?

What? What did you experience?

- How did you feel when you made your estimate?
- How did you feel when you did not make or exceeded your estimate?
- What happened when your team was ahead in points? Behind in points?
- How did the score affect the way your team functioned?
- What happened chronologically?

So What? What learning happened?

- What critical incidents in the game led to an insight?
- What did you learn from the readings or lecture?
- What major idea or concept did you learn?
- What things does this relate to or remind you of?

Now What? What applications can be made to the real-life workplace?

- How does this relate to real life?
- How does the risk factor relate to real life? To the workplace?
- From your experiences here, what behaviors would you show at the next group problem-solving meeting?
- What if different people from your organization were present?

CHAPTER 8

On-The-Job Training

David A. Gallup,
Ed.D.

Katherine V. Beauchemin,
Ed.D.

Objectives

After reading this chapter, you will be able to:

- Define on-the-job training (OJT).
- Differentiate between formal and informal OJT.
- Know when to consider implementing OJT programs.
- Describe challenges to OJT.
- Identify two criteria for selecting OJT trainers.
- List four qualities OJT trainers must possess.

OVERVIEW

One of the oldest forms of training, on-the-job training (OJT) has its roots in the apprentice systems of ancient cultures, giving it a long and distinguished history among instructional methodologies. Even today OJT is often associated with training in the crafts and is especially well suited to craft or technical skill training, where it has been used for centuries to help a novice move through increasing levels of skills and knowledge. However, OJT has uses beyond developing cognitive and psychomotor skills. Teacher and new manager mentoring programs are also forms of OJT. In these programs a mentor may serve as a role model and guide for a new employee, who can benefit from the wisdom and expertise of a more experienced employee.

At the most basic level OJT occurs whenever one person conveys to another person the skills or knowledge needed to do a task while both are on the job. By this definition, informal versions of OJT occur whenever one employee is involved in training another one in some aspect of work.

Informal OJT interactions are a fact of life in virtually every organization. Who has not been the beneficiary of a more experienced employee sharing his or her knowledge of how to do something, from explaining the steps involved in using a new telephone system to locating the best office supply center? These impromptu "training sessions" are likely to occur on an as-needed basis, without benefit of training materials, evaluation instruments, or records.

WHY A FORMAL OJT PROGRAM?

If what is being taught is easy to do, easy to explain, or of little significance to the job, informal OJT may be acceptable. Problems arise when the skills and/or knowledge being conveyed are complex and critical to a job and require evidence that the employee can do the task. In these cases informal or unstructured OJT will not do, and a more systematic approach is in order.

Consider a new employee whose OJT consists primarily of shadowing an experienced employee for a few days or weeks to learn how to do a job. This frequently is described as the "following Joe around" method of training, and the outcomes associated with it are haphazard at best. Although the new hire may be considered trained after the specified period is up, no evidence exists that the new employee is competent to perform the job. Suppose Joe is not a high communicator or resents having to do the training. Perhaps he has ignored the trainee or neglected to explain important parts of the process. Or maybe Joe's idea of training is to talk the trainee through a process without allowing him or her to practice new skills.

Although some organizations may consider this informal instruction OJT, this sort of training has a number of drawbacks. Learning may occur during the interaction, but no evaluation exists to verify what was conveyed or point out areas requiring remediation. Without the key components of sound training program design—learning and performance objectives, targeted training materials, and evaluation instruments—informal or unstructured OJT cannot be relied on to convey the skills and knowledge needed to do a job.

For the purposes of this discussion, we consider OJT to be a *systematically developed solution to a training challenge*, not an informal or off-the-cuff method of transmitting skills or knowledge. The rest of this chapter will examine when to use OJT and how to ensure that OJT programs are effective.

WHEN TO USE OJT

Its early origins in craft training suggest that OJT works well when the training objective is linked to developing cognitive and psychomotor skills through repetition and under supervision. This includes training conducted in simulators or on a shop or plant floor during equipment downtime.

OJT is also useful in situations where role modeling is beneficial, such as mentoring programs for new professionals. These OJT encounters may be scheduled to occur at specified intervals, during which the mentor talks with and provides behavior modeling for the trainee. OJT can be combined with other methodologies to enhance a learner's skills and knowledge. It is not unusual for OJT to be used as a supplement to classroom training in manufacturing or plant setup or as an adjunct to self-instructional training in sales and other professional situations.

Virtually any type of training can be designed to occur on the job. In practice, though, OJT applications usually are limited by the training situation and the program budget. In regard to the training situation, since OJT by definition is conducted in a one-on-one setting, it is unsuitable for training large groups of people at one time. If an organization is concerned with training many new hires at once, OJT does not make sense as a training solution. However, if an organization hires only a few people a year, OJT may be a good way to deliver some or all of the training.

Other aspects of the training situation also affect the decision to implement OJT. For instance, is management concerned with sending trainees a consistent message that is not subject to the interpretation of an individual trainer? In that case OJT may not be the best method. Are experienced employees available to serve as trainers and still maintain production goals? Will trainers be given the time needed to present the program effectively? Does the training budget allow for the expense of OJT?

In regard to the budget, the one-on-one nature of OJT, combined with the time lost in taking experienced employees away from the job, shows why OJT often is cited as the most expensive approach to training. This is true whether OJT is conducted formally or informally, but when it is conducted informally, the costs are frequently untracked and therefore overlooked. A challenge in developing a systematic OJT program is that when managers begin to assess the associated costs, they may be surprised at the time and expense of developing and implementing instructionally sound OJT. This is one reason why it is important to justify OJT as the method of choice.

REAL-WORLD CHALLENGES TO OJT

Like any method of training, OJT can be successful when it is well designed and well presented. However, OJT faces some real-world challenges. The first challenge involves the time required to prepare for the program. Leading an OJT program requires that an experienced employee serve as a trainer, which in turn calls for that employee to devote considerable time and effort to preparing the program. This preparation extends to learning the material, developing skill in presenting the program, adapting to individual learning styles, conducting evaluations, and possibly dealing with hostile trainees. Add up the time involved—which is time lost from work duties—and you can see that to be successful, OJT requires a considerable commitment from the organization to provide release time for employees.

Taking experienced employees away from work may interfere with production, quality, and other important goals. One significant challenge OJT trainers and trainees often face is the reluctance of supervisors and managers to provide release for formal OJT training. When production takes precedence over training, trainers and trainees find that training sessions are postponed or canceled altogether. To be successful, OJT requires the strong support of all levels of management and supervision, who should be aware at the start of the time and commitment involved in the training. One way to do this is provide written estimates of the time that will be involved before beginning to develop an OJT program.

DEVELOPING OJT PROGRAMS

Developing an OJT program is like developing any other type of training. It involves following an instructional system design model that includes the components related to sound training. Typically, those components include the following:

Needs analysis. This involves comparing what is with what is desired to ensure that the problem can be solved through a training intervention.

Situation analysis. This involves assessing the training audience and analyzing the resources available to design and implement the training.

Job inventory and task analysis. This involves identifying the skills and knowledge employees must obtain to perform the job competently.

Behavioral objective specification. This involves writing measurable performance standards and specifying the conditions under which the performance will occur.

Training material selection, design, and production. This involves selecting, designing, and producing the methods and media that will be used in the training program.

Evaluation material selection, design, and production. This involves selecting, designing, and producing the instruments to use in determining whether the behavioral objectives have been attained.

WHO DESIGNS THE TRAINING?

Following a model of this kind almost always requires enlisting the services of an experienced training program designer. This is an important point because in some organizations the idea persists that the employees who are designated as OJT instructors also should develop the training program. However, experienced employees are rarely the best persons to design a training program that is consistent with the elements of sound training program design. Designing training programs involves considerable expertise and effort, and few OJT trainers have the background or the time required to develop a solid training program.

OJT is better served when instructors serve not as program designers but as subject-matter experts (SMEs) working with designers to develop content for the program. SMEs consult with the program designer to ensure accuracy at every step in the instructional systems design model. This takes considerably less time away from an SME's job than does serving as an instructional designer and uses the SME's expertise in the most effective way.

One of the jobs of the training program designer is to develop two essential components that should be part of any effective OJT program: a trainer's guide and a trainee's guide.

The Trainer's Guide

Because OJT usually is facilitated by an experienced employee, some designers feel that OJT materials need not be as detailed as those developed for classroom or self-instructional training. In fact, materials for OJT need to be as detailed and easy to follow as materials developed for other types of training. OJT instructors may be experienced in their jobs, but they are not necessarily experienced in training others. What if the most experienced employee is not available to lead the program? The OJT trainer's guide needs to be as easy to use as possible for anyone facilitating the training.

The Trainee's Guide

Trainees' guides vary in OJT. Some are detailed, almost duplicating the trainer's guide; others may read like a reference manual. The guide may consist primarily of checklists or note-taking guides. No hard-and-fast rules exist for developing trainees' guides, but at the very least they should contain the objectives for the training and an area for note taking.

SELECTING OJT TRAINERS

Who should conduct OJT training? Most training experts agree that an OJT trainer should possess the following characteristics.

In-Depth Knowledge of the Subject

This is the first and perhaps most important prerequisite. The adage that it is easier to turn an SME into a trainer than it is to turn a trainer into an SME is especially true of OJT, where the one-on-one setting is conducive to probing questions from the trainee.

Enlisting SMEs as trainers may have one drawback: They may not be well versed in presenting structured training programs. Two ways to address this are to make sure training materials are explicit and easy to use, with step-by-step instructions for the trainer and the trainee, and to conduct a thorough train-the-trainer session.

A Willingness to Serve As a Trainer

Training takes time and energy; beyond that, it can exact an emotional toll on trainers. Reluctant or unwilling trainers may not devote the time and effort needed to make the training a success. Serving as an OJT trainer can significantly enhance an employee's work experience. Choose OJT trainers wisely and you will be rewarded with employees who bring more expertise than ever to their jobs.

TRAINING OJT TRAINERS

Once trainers are selected, they need to be trained. OJT trainers do not usually arrive at the training task with formal training skills. The following skills should be provided to all OJT trainers if they are to be successful in implementing an OJT program.

Basic Adult Learning Principles

OJT trainees should be provided with the following adult learning principles and practices.

1. Adults bring experience to the learning situation.
2. Adults prefer variety.
3. Adults want to learn.
4. Adults learn best by doing.
5. Treat adults as adults.
6. Ensure practicality of the training.

General Training Skills

OJT trainers should be made aware of the following general training skills.

1. **Physical presence**
   a. Face the trainee and make eye contact as much as possible.
   b. Avoid distracting behavior that may interfere with the training message.

2. **Observing**
   a. Look at the trainee's body language.
   b. Look at the trainee's face.
3. **Listening**
   a. Listen to what the trainee says.
   b. Repeat what the trainee says to check for understanding.
4. **Questioning**
   a. Group.   An open-ended question asked of the whole group. Group questions such as "What do you do when . . . ?" give everyone a chance to talk.
   b. Direct.   A question directed to a specific member of the group. Direct questions can be used to elicit specific information or involve a group member who has not participated.
   c. Redirect. A question asked by one participant that the facilitator redirects to another participant. This technique involves participants in the discussion. It also can be used when the facilitator does not wish to offer an opinion.
   d. Return. A question asked by a participant that the facilitator refers back to the same participant. Return questions such as "There are several answers to that question; what answers occur to you?" encourage the participant to think, bring out opinions, and help the facilitator avoid giving an opinion.

One-on-One Training Skills

For an OJT trainer to be successful, three one-on-one training skills must be used in implementing the program: planning, preparing, and presenting.

Planning
In the planning step, the trainer should review both the trainer's and trainee's guides so that he or she can deliver the program effectively. It is imperative that the trainer be familiar with the program objectives and the methodology used for presenting each portion or module of the program. Listed below are a number of methods trainers may use to present the training program:

- Lectures
- Readings assigned to the trainee, with time provided for questions and answers
- Demonstration to show a trainee how to perform a given task or job

- Discussion to allow a trainee to share information and experience
- Simulation and role play, which involves assigning a role to the trainee and asking him or her to show how to solve a problem or reach an understanding

Preparing
In this step the OJT trainer should review the training materials one last time, meet the trainee, and set a time and place to begin training. This is also a time to rehearse the presentation and select a time and place to meet the trainee on the day training begins.

Presenting
Presenting information or demonstrating skills to a trainee can follow this pattern:

- *Tell.* The trainer prepares the trainee for what is about to happen, explaining what is being done and why.
- *Show.* The trainer demonstrates specific skills to the trainee.
- *Practice.* The trainee practices the task or skill under careful supervision.

Handling Problem Situations

OJT trainers should be given guidance in handling problem situations they may encounter. Problem situations typically arise from

- Fear of failure
- Resentment toward the trainer
- Issues outside of training

SUMMARY

The decision whether to implement an OJT program involves a consideration of the training situation and the budget. OJT may be the solution of choice in training situations that call for training small numbers of people, provided that trainers or mentors will be available to lead the training. Effective OJT requires following a systematic approach to training program design and ensuring adequate preparation of trainers. Used properly, OJT can be a creative solution to a training challenge, one that enhances both the trainers' and trainees' working experience.

DOCUMENTS, JOB AIDS, AND HELPFUL HINTS

Use the following checklists for your program.

Job Aid for On-the-Job Training: Training Manager or Instructional Designer

1. **Developing OJT Training Materials**
   Did you
   _____ Follow an instructional design system model?
   _____ Create a trainer's guide?
   _____ Create a trainee's guide?

2. **Selecting OJT Trainers**
   Did you
   _____ Consider the trainer's knowledge of the subject?
   _____ Consider the trainer's willingness to train?

3. **Training OJT Trainers**
   Did you provide
   _____ Basic adult learning theory?
   _____ General training skills?
   _____ One-on-one training skills?
   _____ Methods for handling difficult situations?

Job Aid for On-the-Job Training: Trainer

Before Training Did You
_____ Plan?
        _____ Review the trainer's guide?
        _____ Review the trainee's guide?
        _____ Decide on a training method?
_____ Prepare?
        _____ Review training materials?
        _____ Meet the trainee?
        _____ Set a time and place for the first training session?

During Training Presentation Did You
_____ **Tell.** What is about to happen?
_____ **Show.** Demonstrate specific skills?
_____ **Practice.** Observe the trainee perform the skill?

Sample Lesson: Trainer's Guide

LESSON 2: COMPENSATION AND BENEFITS

Purpose

In this lesson, the new part-time employee will learn his or her responsibilities regarding the Store Payroll Document. Part-time employee pay rates and benefits also will be discussed.

Time Needed

20 minutes

Materials Needed

1. Readings: Compensation/Benefits, pages R-1 to S-4
2. Current Store Payroll Document

Lesson Format

Discussion and Demonstration

Your Role in this Lesson

1. Demonstrate the proper procedure for entering time in and time out on the payroll document.
2. Meet with the new employee to discuss his or her rate of pay and opportunity for increases.
3. Meet with the new employee to discuss company benefits and part-time employees. The new employee will be prepared to complete the question guide on the next page.
4. Compare the employee's answers to the questions according to the responses shown on the question guide on the next page.

CASE STUDY: CONVENIENCE STORE CHAIN

This OJT program was aimed at training part-time employees at a convenience store chain with 500 stores. High turnover in the part-time positions, combined with the hands-on nature of the job, made classroom training a less acceptable option than OJT.

Sample Lesson: Trainer's Guide

QUESTION AND OBSERVATION GUIDE: COMPENSATION AND BENEFITS

Questions

1. What must you do when reporting to or leaving work regarding the payroll document? Why?

   YOU MUST POST THE EXACT TIME YOU START AND FINISH (TO THE MINUTE). THIS ASSUMES THAT YOU ARE CORRECTLY COMPENSATED FOR ALL TIME WORKED.

2. What do we mean by premium hours?

   PREMIUM HOURS ARE HOURS IN WHICH AN ADDITIONAL 50 CENTS PER HOUR IS ADDED TO THE NORMAL HOURLY RATE FOR THE EMPLOYEE. PREMIUM HOURS ARE PAID FOR WORKING SATURDAY, SUNDAY, AND HOLIDAYS.

3. List all days eligible for premium hours.

   PREMIUM HOURS ARE PAID FOR SATURDAYS, SUNDAYS, AND HOLIDAYS. THE ELIGIBLE HOLIDAYS ARE NEW YEAR'S DAY, MEMORIAL DAY, JULY 4th, LABOR DAY, THANKSGIVING, CHRISTMAS EVE, AND NEW YEAR'S EVE.

4. What are the guidelines used for determining if a part-time employee is eligible for vacations?

   A PART-TIME EMPLOYEE MUST WORK FOR A MINIMUM OF 1000 HOURS PER CALENDAR YEAR TO BE ELIGIBLE FOR THESE BENEFITS. A CALENDAR YEAR RUNS FROM JANUARY TO DECEMBER.

5. What day do paychecks arrive at your store?

   TELL THE EMPLOYEE WHEN CHECKS ARRIVE AT THE STORE AND WHEN THEY CAN BE OBTAINED BY THE EMPLOYEE.

Training was conducted by store managers and associate store managers, who served as role models and mentors for employees. The program included readings and activities along with performance demonstrations to convey the skills and knowledge needed to do the job.

GLOSSARY

Cognitive   The area of behavior change that deals with imparting knowledge.

Instructional Designer   The person responsible for designing training programs. Typically has background and experience in instructional systems design. Works with an SME to develop program content.

On-the-Job Training   A systematically developed solution to a training challenge.

Psychomotor   The area of behavior change that deals with body movement.

Subject Matter Expert   The person responsible for providing training program content. May present the training program. Works with an instructional designer.

CHAPTER 9

Evaluating Training Programs: The Four Levels

Donald L. Kirkpatrick

I developed this four-level model to clarify the elusive term *evaluation*. Some training and development professionals believe that evaluation means measuring changes in behavior that occur as a result of training programs. Others maintain that evaluation lies in determining the final results that have occurred because of training programs. Still others think only in terms of the comment sheets that participants complete at the end of a program. Still others are concerned with the learning that takes place in the classroom, as measured by increased knowledge, improved skills, and changes in attitude. They are all right—and wrong, because they fail to recognize that all four approaches are parts of what is meant by evaluating.

These four levels are all important and should be understood by all professionals in education, training, and development, whether they plan, coordinate, or teach; whether the content of the program is technical or managerial; whether the participants are or are not managers; and whether the programs are conducted in education, business, or industry. In some cases, especially in academic institutions, there is no attempt to change behavior; the goal is to increase knowledge, improve skills, and change attitudes. In these cases, only the first two levels apply. However, if the purpose of the training is to get better results by changing behavior, all four levels apply. In human resource development circles, these four levels are recognized widely, often cited, and often used as a basis for research and articles dealing with techniques for applying one or more of the levels.

EVALUATING: PART OF A TEN-STEP PROCESS

The reason for evaluating is to determine the effectiveness of a training program. When the evaluation is done, one can hope that the results are positive and gratifying both for those responsible for the program and for upper-level managers who will base decisions on their evaluation of the program. Therefore, much thought and planning need to be given to the program to make sure it is effective. This chapter contains suggestions for planning and implementing a program to ensure its effectiveness.

Each of the following factors should be considered in planning and implementing an effective training program:

1. Determining needs
2. Setting objectives
3. Determining subject content
4. Selecting participants
5. Determining the best schedule
6. Selecting appropriate facilities
7. Selecting appropriate instructors
8. Selecting and preparing audiovisual aids
9. Coordinating the program
10. Evaluating the program

REASONS FOR EVALUATING

There is an old saying among training directors: When there are cutbacks in an organization, training people are the first to go. This isn't always true, but whenever downsizing occurs, top management looks for people and departments that can be eliminated with the fewest negative results. Early in their decision they look at overhead departments such as human resources. This department typically includes people responsible for employment, salary administration, benefits, labor relations (if there is a union), and training. In some organizations top management feels that all these functions except training are necessary. From this perspective, training is optional and its value to the organization depends on top executives' view of its effectiveness. In other words, trainers must justify their existence. If they don't and downsizing occurs, they may be terminated, and the training function will be relegated to the human resources manager, who already wears many other hats.

The second reason for evaluating is to determine whether to continue to offer a program. Some programs are offered as a pilot in hopes that they will bring about the desired results. These programs should be evaluated to determine whether they should be continued. If the cost outweighs the benefits, a program should be discontinued or modified.

The most common reason for evaluation is to determine the effectiveness of a program and the ways in which it can be improved. Usually, the decision to continue it has already been made. The question is how it can be improved. In looking for the answer to this question, one should consider these eight factors:

1. To what extent does the content meet the needs of those attending?
2. Is the leader the one best qualified to teach?
3. Does the leader use the most effective methods for maintaining interest and teaching the desired attitudes, knowledge, and skills?
4. Are the facilities satisfactory?
5. Is the schedule appropriate for the participants?
6. Are the aids effective in improving communication and maintaining interest?
7. Was the coordination of the program satisfactory?
8. What else can be done to improve the program?

A careful analysis of the answers to these questions can identify ways and means of improving future offerings of the program.

Most companies use reaction sheets of one kind or another. Most are thinking about doing more. They have not gone further for one or more of the following reasons:

- They don't give it a lot of importance or urgency.
- They don't know what to do or how to do it.
- There is no pressure from higher management to do more.
- They feel secure in their jobs and do not see a need to do more.
- They have too many other things that are more important or that they prefer to do.

In most organizations, both large and small, there is little pressure from top management to prove that the benefits of training outweigh the cost.

There are three reasons for evaluating training programs. The most common is that evaluation can indicate how to improve future programs. The second is to determine whether a program should be continued or dropped. The third is to justify the existence of the training department. By demonstrating to top management that training has tangible, positive results, trainers will find that their jobs are secure even if downsizing occurs. If top-level managers need to cut back, their impression of the need for a training department will determine whether they say,

"That's one department we need to keep" or "That's a department we can eliminate without hurting us." Their impression can be greatly influenced by trainers
who evaluate at all levels and communicate the results to them.

THE FOUR LEVELS: OVERVIEW

The four levels represent a sequence of ways to evaluate programs. Each level is
important. As one moves from one level to the next, the process becomes more difficult and time-consuming but also provides more valuable information.

None of the levels should be bypassed simply to get to the level the trainer
considers the most important. The four levels are

Level 1: reaction
Level 2: learning
Level 3: behavior
Level 4: results

Level 1: Reaction

As the word *reaction* implies, evaluation on this level measures how those who participate in the program react to it. I call it a measure of customer satisfaction. For
many years I conducted seminars, institutes, and conferences at the University of
Wisconsin Management Institute. Organizations paid a fee to send their people to
those public programs. It is obvious that the reaction of the participants was a
measure of customer satisfaction. It is also obvious that the reaction had to be favorable if we were to stay in business, attract new customers, and get current customers to return to future programs.

It isn't quite so obvious that reaction to in-house programs is also a measure
of customer satisfaction. In many in-house programs the participants are required to attend whether they want to or not. However, they are customers even
if they don't pay, and their reactions can make or break a training program. What
they say to their bosses often gets to high-level managers, who make decisions
about the future of training programs. Thus, positive reactions are just as important for trainers who run in-house programs as they are for those who offer public programs.

It is important to get not only a reaction but a positive reaction. As was just
described, the future of a program depends on a positive reaction. In addition, if
the participants do not react favorably, they probably will not be motivated to
learn. A positive reaction may not ensure learning, but a negative reaction almost
certainly will reduce the possibility of its occurring.

Evaluating reaction is the same as measuring customer satisfaction. If training is going to be effective, it is important that trainees react favorably to it. Otherwise, they will not be motivated to learn. Also, they will tell others about their reactions, and decisions to reduce or eliminate the program may be based on what they say. Some trainers call the forms used for the evaluation of reaction *happiness sheets*. Although they say this in a critical or even cynical way, they are correct. These forms really are happiness sheets, but they are not worthless. They help us determine how effective the program is and learn how it can be improved.

Measuring reaction is important for several reasons. First, it provides valuable feedback that helps us evaluate the program as well as comments and suggestions for improving future programs. Second, it tells trainees that the trainers are there to help them do their job better and need feedback to determine how effective they are. If we do not ask for reaction, we tell trainees that we know what they want and need and can judge the effectiveness of the program without their feedback. Third, reaction sheets can provide quantitative information that can be given to managers and others concerned about the program. Finally, reaction sheets can provide trainers with quantitative information that can be used to establish standards of performance for future programs.

Evaluating reaction is not only important but also easy to do effectively. Most trainers use reaction sheets. I have seen dozens of forms and various ways of using them. Some are effective, and some are not. Here are some guidelines to help trainers get the maximum benefit from reaction sheets:

Guidelines for Evaluating Reaction
1. Determine what you want to find out.
2. Design a form that will quantify reactions.
3. Encourage written comments and suggestions.
4. Get a 100 percent immediate response.
5. Get honest responses.
6. Develop acceptable standards.
7. Measure reactions against standards and take the appropriate action.
8. Communicate reactions as appropriate.

Level 2: Learning

Learning can be defined as the extent to which participants change attitudes, increase knowledge, and/or increase skill as a result of attending a program.

Those are the three things a training program can accomplish. Programs dealing with topics such as diversity in the work force aim primarily at changing attitudes.

Technical programs aim at improving skills. Programs on topics such as leadership, motivation, and communication can aim at all three objectives. To evaluate learning, the specific objectives must be determined.

Some trainers say that no learning has taken place unless a change in behavior occurs. In the four levels described in this chapter, learning has taken place when one or more of the following occur: Attitudes are changed, knowledge is increased, or skill is improved. Change in behavior is the next level.

There are three things instructors in a training program can teach: knowledge, skills, and attitudes. Measuring learning therefore means determining one or more of the following:

What knowledge was learned?

What skills were developed or improved?

What attitudes were changed?

It is important to measure learning because no change in behavior can be expected unless one or more of these learning objectives have been accomplished. Moreover, if we measured behavior change (level 3) instead of learning and found no change in behavior, the likely conclusion would be that no learning took place. This conclusion may be erroneous. The reason no change in behavior was observed may be that the climate was preventing or discouraging. In these situations, learning may have taken place and the learner may even have been eager to change his or her behavior. However, because the boss prevented or discouraged the trainee from applying the new learning on the job, no change in behavior took place.

The measurement of learning is more difficult and time-consuming than the measurement of reaction. These guidelines are helpful:

Guidelines for Evaluating Learning

1. Use a control group if that is practical.
2. Evaluate knowledge, skills, and/or attitudes both before and after the program. Use a paper-and-pencil test to measure knowledge and attitudes and use a performance test to measure skills. Employ E-mail if you have the capability.
3. Get a 100 percent response.
4. Use the results of the evaluation to take appropriate action.

Level 3: Behavior

Behavior can be defined as the extent to which a change in behavior has occurred because the participants attended the training program. Some trainers want to bypass levels 1 and 2—reaction and learning—in order to measure behavior, but that is a mistake. For example, suppose no change in behavior is discovered. The obvious conclusion is that the program was ineffective and should be discontinued. This conclusion may or may not be accurate. The reaction may have been favorable and the learning objectives may have been accomplished, but the level 3 or level 4 conditions may not have been present. For change to occur, four conditions are necessary:

1. The person must have a desire to change.
2. The person must know what to do and how to do it.
3. The person must work in the right climate.
4. The person must be rewarded for changing.

The training program can accomplish the first two requirements by creating a positive attitude toward the desired change and teaching the necessary knowledge and skills. The third condition—the right climate—refers to the participant's immediate supervisor. Five different kinds of climate can be described:

1. *Preventing.* The boss forbids the participant from doing what he or she has been taught to do in the training program. The boss may be influenced by the organizational culture established by top management, or the boss's leadership style may conflict with what was taught.

2. *Discouraging.* The boss doesn't say, "You can't do it," but he or she makes it clear that the participant should not change his or her behavior because that would make the boss unhappy. Or the boss may not model the behavior taught in the program, and this negative example discourages the subordinate from changing.

3. *Neutral.* The boss ignores the fact that the participant has attended a training program. It is business as usual. If the subordinate wants to change, the boss has no objection as long as the job gets done. If negative results occur because behavior has changed, the boss may create a discouraging or even preventing climate.

4. *Encouraging.* The boss encourages the participant to learn and to apply his or her learning on the job. Ideally, the boss discussed the program with the subordinate beforehand and stated that they would discuss its application as soon as the program was over. The boss basically says, "I am interested in knowing what you learned and how I can help you transfer the learning to the job."

5. *Requiring.* The boss knows what the subordinate learns and makes sure the learning transfers to the job. In some cases a learning contract is prepared that states what the subordinate agrees to do. This contract can be prepared at the end of the training session, and a copy can be given to the boss. The boss sees to it that the contract is implemented. Malcolm Knowles's book *Using Learning Contracts* describes this process.

The fourth condition—rewards—can be intrinsic (from within), extrinsic (from without), or both. Intrinsic rewards include the feelings of satisfaction, pride, and achievement that can occur when a change in behavior has positive results. Extrinsic rewards include praise from the boss, recognition from others, and monetary rewards such as merit pay increases and bonuses.

It is obvious that there is little or no chance that training will transfer to job behavior if the climate is preventing or discouraging. If the climate is neutral, a change in behavior will depend on the other conditions that were just described. If the climate is encouraging or requiring, the amount of change that occurs depends on the first and second conditions.

As was stated earlier, it is important to evaluate both reaction and learning in case no change in behavior occurs. Then it can be determined whether the lack of change resulted from an ineffective training program or the wrong job climate and lack of rewards.

It is important for trainers to know the type of climate the participants will face when they return from a training program. It is also important for them to do everything they can to make sure the climate is neutral or better. Otherwise there is little or no chance that the program will accomplish the behavior and results objectives, because the participants will not even try to use what they have learned. Not only will no change occur, those who attended the program will be frustrated with the boss, the training program, or both for teaching them things they can't apply.

One way to create a positive job climate is to involve bosses in the development of the program by asking them to help determine the needs of subordinates. Such involvement helps ensure that a program teaches practical concepts, principles, and techniques. Another approach is to present the training program, or at least a condensed version of it, to the bosses before the supervisors are trained.

A number of years ago I was asked by Dave Harris, a personnel manager, to present an 18-hour training program to 240 supervisors at A. O. Smith Corporation in Milwaukee. I asked Harris if he could arrange for me to present a condensed, 3- to 6-hour version to the company's top management. He arranged for the condensed version to be offered at the Milwaukee Athletic Club. After the 6-hour program, the eight upper-level managers were asked for opinions and suggestions. They not only liked the program but told us to present the entire program first to the 35 general supervisors and superintendents who were the bosses for 240 supervisors. We did what they suggested. We asked the bosses for their comments and encouraged them to provide an encouraging climate when the supervisors had completed the program. I am not sure to what extent this increased the change in behavior over the level that we would have seen if the top managers had not attended or even known the content of the program, but I am confident it made a big difference. We told the supervisors that their bosses had already attended the program. This increased their motivation to learn and desire to apply the learning on the job.

What happens when trainees leave the classroom and return to their jobs? How much transfer of knowledge, skills, and attitudes occurs? This is what level 3 attempts to evaluate. In other words, what change in job behavior occurred because people attended a training program?

This question is more complicated and difficult than evaluating at the first two levels. First, trainees cannot change their behavior until they have an opportunity to do so. For example, if you decide to use some of the principles and techniques described here, you must wait until you have a training program to evaluate. Similarly, if the training program is designed to teach a person how to conduct an effective performance appraisal interview, the trainee cannot apply the learning until an interview is held.

Second, it is impossible to predict when a change in behavior will occur. Even if a trainee has an opportunity to apply the learning, he or she may not do that immediately. In fact, change in behavior may occur at any time after the first opportunity, or it may never occur.

Third, the trainee may apply the learning to the job and come to one of the following conclusions: "I like what happened, and I plan to continue to use the new behavior," "I don't like what happened, and I will go back to my old behavior," "I like what happened, but the boss and/or time restraints prevent me from continuing it." We all hope the rewards for changing behavior will cause the trainee to come to the first conclusion. It therefore is important to provide help, encouragement, and rewards when a trainee returns to the job from a training class. One type of reward is intrinsic. This refers to the inward feelings of satisfaction, pride, achievement, and happiness that can occur when a new behavior is used. Extrinsic rewards are also important. They include praise, increased freedom and empowerment, merit pay increases, and other forms of recognition that come as a result of a change in behavior.

In regard to reaction and learning, the evaluation can and should take place immediately. When you evaluate a change in behavior, you have to make some important decisions: when to evaluate, how often to evaluate, and how to evaluate. This makes it more time-consuming and difficult to do than are levels 1 and 2. Here are some guidelines to follow when evaluating at level 3.

Guidelines for Evaluating Behavior
1. Use a control group if that is practical.
2. Allow time for a change in behavior to take place.
3. Evaluate both before and after the program if that is practical.

4. Survey and/or interview one or more of the following: trainees, their immediate supervisors, their subordinates, and others who often observe their behavior.
5. Get a 100 percent response.
6. Repeat the evaluation at appropriate times.
7. Consider cost versus benefits.

Level 4: Results

Results can be defined as the final results that occurred because the participants attended the program. The final results can include increased production, improved quality, decreased costs, reduced frequency and/or severity of accidents, increased sales, reduced turnover, and higher profits and return on investment. It is important to recognize that results like these are the reason for having some training programs. Therefore, the final objectives of the training program must be stated in these terms.

Some programs have these things in mind on what can be called a far-out basis. For example, one major objective of the popular program on diversity in the work force is to change the attitudes of supervisors and managers toward minority group members in their departments. We want supervisors to treat all people fairly, show no discrimination, and so on. These are not tangible results that can be measured in terms of dollars and cents, but it is hoped that tangible results will follow. Similarly, it is difficult if not impossible to measure final results for programs on topics such as leadership, communication, motivation, time management, empowerment, decision making, and managing change. We can state and evaluate desired behaviors, but the final results have to be measured in terms of improved morale or other nonfinancial terms. It is hoped that things such as higher morale and improved quality of work life will result in the tangible results just described.

Now comes the most important difficult task of all: determining what final results occurred because of attendance and participation in a training program. Trainers ask questions like the following:

- How much did quality improve because of the training program on total quality improvement we have presented to all supervisors and managers, and how much has it contributed to profits?
- How much did productivity increase because we conducted a program on diversity in the work force for all supervisors and managers?
- What reduction did we get in turnover and scrap rate because we taught our supervisors to orient and train new employees?
- How much has management, by walking around, improved the quality of work life?

- What has been the result of all our programs on interpersonal communication and human relations?
- How much has productivity increased and how much have costs been reduced because we have trained our employees to work in self-directed work teams?
- What tangible benefits have we received for all the money we have spent on programs on leadership, time management, and decision making?
- How much have sales increased as a result of teaching our salespeople things such as market research, overcoming objections, and closing a sale?
- What is the return on investment for all the money we have spent on training?

All these and many more questions usually remain unanswered for two reasons. First, trainers don't know how to measure the results and compare them with the cost of the program. Second, even if they know how, the findings probably provide evidence but not clear proof that the positive results have come from the training program. There are expectations, of course. Increases in sales may be found to be directly related to a sales training program, and a program aimed specifically at reducing accidents or improving quality can be evaluated to show direct results from the training program.

A number of years ago Jack Jenness at Consolidated Edison in New York was asked by his boss to show results in terms of dollars and cents from an expensive program on leadership that Con Ed was giving to middle- and upper-level managers. The company had hired consultants from St. Louis at a very high fee to conduct the program. I told Jenness, "There is no way it can be done." He said, "That's what I told my boss." Jenness then asked me to come to his organization to do two things: conduct a workshop with its trainers on the four levels of evaluation and tell his boss that it couldn't be done. I did the first. I didn't get a chance to do the second because the boss had been convinced and didn't see the need or didn't have the time or desire to hear what I had to say.

This example is unusual at this point, but it might not be too unusual in the future. Whenever I get together with trainers, I ask, "How much pressure are you getting from top management to prove the value of your training programs in results such as dollars and cents?" Only a few times have they said they were feeling such pressure, but many trainers have told me that the day isn't far off when they will be asked to provide such proof.

When we look at the objectives of training programs, we find that almost all of them aim at accomplishing a worthy result. Often it is improved quality, productivity, or safety. In other programs the objective is improved morale or better teamwork, which, it is hoped, will lead to better quality, productivity, safety, and profits. Therefore, trainers look at the desired end result and say to themselves and others, "What behavior on the part of supervisors and managers will achieve these results?" Then they decide what knowledge, skills, and attitude supervisors need in order to behave in that way. Finally, they determine the training needs and proceed. In so doing, they hope the trainees will like the program; learn the knowledge, skills, and attitudes taught; and transfer them to the job. The first three levels of evaluation attempt to determine the degree to which these three things have been accomplished.

Now we have arrived at the final level: What final results were accomplished because of the training program? Here are some guidelines that will be helpful:

Guidelines for Evaluating Results
1. Use a control group if that is practical.
2. Allow time for results to be achieved.
3. Measure both before and after the program if that is practical.
4. Repeat the measurement at appropriate times.
5. Consider cost versus benefits.
6. Be satisfied with evidence if proof is not possible.

Evaluating results (level 4) provides the greatest challenge to training professionals. After all, that is why we train, and we ought to be able to show tangible results that more than pay for the cost of training. In some cases such evaluation can be done easily. Programs that aim at increasing sales and reducing accidents, turnover, and scrap rates often can be evaluated in terms of results, and the cost of a program isn't too difficult to determine. A comparison can readily show that training pays off.

IMPLEMENTING THE FOUR LEVELS

Everybody talks about it, but nobody does anything about it. When Mark Twain said this, he was talking about the weather. It also applies to evaluation—well, almost. My contacts with training professionals indicate that most use some form of reaction, "smile," or "happiness" sheets. Some of these things provide helpful information that measures customer satisfaction, but others do not. And many trainers ignore critical comments by saying, "Well, you can't please everybody" or "I know who said that, and I am not surprised."

Where do I start? What do I do first? These are typical questions from trainers who are interested in evaluation and have done little of it.

My suggestion is to start at level 1 and proceed through the other levels as time and opportunity allow. Some trainers are eager to get to level 3 or level 4 right away because they think the first two levels aren't as important. Don't do that. Suppose, for example, you evaluate at level 3 and discover that little or no change in behavior has occurred. What conclusions can you draw? The first conclusion is probably that the training program was no good and we had better discontinue or at least modify it. This conclusion may be entirely wrong. The reason for a lack of change in job behavior may be that the climate prevents it. Supervisors may have gone back to the job with the necessary knowledge, skills, and attitudes, but the boss wouldn't allow change to take place. Therefore, it is important to evaluate at level 2 so that you can determine whether the reason for a lack of change in behavior was lack of learning or a negative job climate.

The first step to take in implementing the evaluation concepts, theories, and techniques described in the preceding chapters is to understand the guidelines of level 1 and apply them in every program. Use a philosophy that states, "If my customers are unhappy, it is my fault, and my challenge is to please them." If you don't, the entire training program is in trouble. It is true that one seldom pleases everyone. For example, it is a rare occasion when everyone in my training classes grades me excellent. Nearly always some participants are critical of my sense of humor, the content presented, or the quality of the audiovisual aids. I often find myself justifying what I did and ignoring their comments, but I shouldn't do that. My style of humor, for example, is to embarrass participants. I do that in a pleasant way so that they don't resent it. That happens to be my style, and most people enjoy and appreciate it. If I get only one critical comment from a group of 25, I ignore it and continue as I did in the past. However, if the reaction is fairly common because I have overdone it, I take the comment seriously and change my approach.

I used to tell a funny story in class. It was neither dirty nor ethnic. Nearly everyone else thought it was funny too, and I heard no objections to it. One day I conducted a training class with social workers. I told the story at the beginning of the class and proceeded to do the training. After 40 minutes I asked whether anyone had a comment or question. One lady raised her hand and said, "I was offended by the joke you told at the beginning of the session, and I didn't listen to anything you said after that."

I couldn't believe it. I was sure she was the only one who felt that way, so I asked if any of the others felt the same way. Seven other women raised their hands. There were about 45 people in the class, and so the percentage was very much in my favor. But I decided that that joke had no place in future meetings. If she had been the only one, I probably would still be telling it.

The point is this: Look over all the reaction sheets and read the comments. Consider each one. Is there a suggestion that will improve future programs? If the answer is yes, use it. If it is an isolated comment that will not improve future programs, appreciate it but ignore it.

Evaluating at level 2 isn't that difficult. All you need to do is decide what knowledge, skills, and attitudes you want the participants to have at the end of the program. If there is a possibility that one or more of these three things already exist, a pretest is necessary. If you are presenting something entirely new, no pretest is necessary. You can use a standardized test if you can find one that covers the things you are teaching, or you can develop your own test to cover the knowledge and attitudes you are teaching.

Levels 3 and 4 are not easy. A lot of time is required to decide on an evaluation design. A knowledge of statistics to determine the level of significance may be desirable. Check with the research people in your organization for help in the design. You may have to call in an outside consultant to help you or even do the evaluation for you. Remember the principle that the possible benefits from an evaluation should exceed the cost of doing the evaluation and be satisfied with evidence if proof is not available.

There is another important principle that applies to all four levels: One can borrow evaluation forms, designs, and procedures from others, but one cannot borrow evaluation results.

Learn all you can about evaluation. Find out what others have done. Look for forms, methods, techniques, and designs you can copy or adapt. Ignore the results of these and other evaluations except out of curiosity.

Trainers must begin with desired results and then determine what behavior is needed to accomplish them. Then trainers must determine the attitudes, knowledge, and skills that are necessary to bring about the desired behavior. The final challenge is to present the training program in a way that enables the participants not only to learn what they need to know but also to react favorably to the program and apply what they learned in the workplace.

CHAPTER 10

Measuring Training's Return on Investment: A Case in Point

Scott B. Parry

Training doesn't cost; it pays. Human resources development (HRD) is an investment, not an expense.

It is a rare trainer who doesn't believe this. Far more common is the trainer who doesn't believe that return on the training investment can or even should be calculated.

Should all training programs be required to show a return on investment (ROI)? Not at all. However, courses of 3 days or more that are offered many times to reach a large number of trainees (say, 100 or more) represent a significant expense. A professional trainer should justify this expense by calculating the return on this investment.

We're talking about level 4 (results) in Kirkpatrick's evaluation model (Chap. 9), and it's the most difficult level to measure. Level 1 (reaction) and level 2 (learning) can be measured with relative ease in class, using paper-and-pencil instruments and simulations. Level 3 (application at work) is more difficult because it requires measuring performance on the job, where many variables affect the performance of the graduates. Level 4 (results) is usually shown as ROI: the dollar value of the benefits of training over and above the cost of the training.

There's the rub. Many factors make this level of measurement the most difficult by far. Here are some of the common difficulties that are cited as reasons for not doing a level 4 evaluation:

- The costs of training are known and expressed in dollars, but the benefits are often soft, subjective, and difficult to quantify and convert to dollars.
- It is difficult enough to get managers to send people to training without imposing requirements to collect data to document the impact.

- Costs are known up front, before training, but benefits may accrue slowly over time. At what point after training should one attempt to measure impact?
- Trainers lack the time and accounting skills to do a cost-benefit analysis. Besides, requests for data disrupt productivity.
- We probably will continue to run most of our popular training programs even if costs exceed benefits, so why bother? We're not a profit center.
- The outcomes could be damaging to the HRD staff and to budget support from top management. We may be better off not knowing.
- People at work perform the way they do for many reasons, only one of which relates to training. How can we take credit or blame for their performance?
- The act of collecting data on the dollar value of performance tends to bias the information we get, making it hard to present a true picture.

If you've been looking for reasons not to evaluate the ROI of your training efforts, read no further. This list should enable you to persuade the most insistent believer that any attempt to prove that training pays for itself is sheer folly. Let sleeping dogs lie. What we don't know can't hurt us. Right?

Wrong. Let's give equal time to a list of reasons why one should take the time and effort to calculate the costs and benefits of major training programs. Here are some supporting reasons:

- HRD budgets can be justified and even expanded when training contributes to profit and is not seen as an act of faith or a cost of doing business.
- Course objectives and content will become more lean, relevant, and behavioral with a focus on monetary results rather than on the acquisition of information.
- There will be better commitment from trainees and their managers, who become responsible for follow-up and ROI, not just for filling seats.
- Action plans, individual development plans, and managers' briefings will be taken seriously, strengthening the trainee-manager partnership.
- There will be better performance by the HRD staff in containing costs and maximizing benefits. They will become performance managers, not just instructors.
- The HRD staff has solid data about where training is effective and where it is weak, and so courses can be revised and fine-tuned to produce the best returns.

- The curriculum of courses offered can be determined on a financial basis, not just on the basis of popularity, the rank of the manager requesting it, and so forth.
- The trainees will be aware of the expectations that follow graduation. We'll get the right faces in the right places at the right times.
- By calculating ROI on the courses where it is possible, we are more apt to be trusted on the ones we can't evaluate at level 4.

Now that we have examined the pros and cons of calculating the ROI of a training program, let's look at a case history to better understand how costs and benefits can in fact be calculated.

Instructions

1. Read the case study that follows.
2. Use the costs and benefits templates to input your figures and calculations.
3. Compare your approach with the calculations explanation and the costs and benefits templates that follow.

CASE STUDY

WORKSHOP ON "RUNNING EFFECTIVE MEETINGS" AT SOUTHWEST INDUSTRIES

Southwest Industries was no different from other organizations its size (about 900 employees) when it came to time spent in meetings. Their managers felt that time was wasted, key players were often absent, and agendas were not followed (or in some cases even established). B. J. Lewis, the training manager, decided to do something about it. Using a questionnaire and group interview with managers in each department, she came up with the design for a half-day workshop to meet the following objectives:

1. *Reduced length of meetings.* Managers estimated that the average meeting ran about 75 minutes and hoped this could be reduced to under an hour.
2. *Reduced frequency of meetings.* Managers attended an average of 8.6 meetings per week and hoped to reduce this to 5 or fewer.
3. *Better follow-up and execution.* Many decisions reached at meetings didn't get acted on until the next meeting or after a reminder.
4. *Appropriate participants attending.* Time was wasted because key people were absent and unnecessary people were present.
5. *Better decisions and stronger commitment.* Through teaching the use of a decision matrix, decisions could be more effective.

Lewis sent these objectives and a cover memo to the company's 95 managers and supervisors, who approved them and added the two shown on the next page. They also suggested that a workshop on how to run meetings shouldn't be restricted to managers since about 250 employees were members of work teams of 8 to 10 persons each. These teams typically held 1-hour meetings once a week to address problems and improve quality. Here are the two additional training objectives:

6. *Effective problem solving.* The process would be taught and applied to typical work-related problems.

7. *Timely minutes for follow-up.* Minutes were often distributed too late to be effective and were unclear about the actions to be taken.

During her development of the workshop's methods and materials, Lewis realized that a half-day workshop would not have the desired impact. For example, the ability to prepare results-oriented and measurable objectives for a meeting is important to its success. This meant preparing an exercise in which the participants would evaluate and rewrite a dozen typical meeting objectives. Similarly, Lewis designed two forms (a meeting announcement form and a recap form) that required time for participants to get hands-on practice in using them.

"Running Effective Meetings" ended up as a 1-day workshop (6.5 hours). Other than one learning exercise that was different for the 95 managers and supervisors than for the 250 team members, the workshop was the same for both groups.

COSTS

The workshop was offered 15 times, with an average enrollment of 21 participants. Lewis ran it off-site to get participants away from interruptions at the plant. She was able to get a nearby motel to give her a cost per person of $20 to cover coffee break, lunch buffet, and afternoon soda and snack. The room cost $100 per day.

The other costs were minimal. The biggest expense was Lewis's time in preparing the objective and getting feedback (1 day), preparing course material (5 days), and running the program (15 days). The 22 pages of handouts took 3 days for Lewis's administrative assistant to type and lay out (desktop publishing). The cost of reproducing, collating, and inserting handouts in folders came to about $2 per participant. The set of 12 colored overhead transparencies cost about $150.

Lewis felt that it would not be appropriate to consider the salaries of the participants during their day at the workshop to be a cost of training, and her manager agreed. Similarly, the cost of any productivity lost as a result of attendance was not seen as a cost of training. However, her administrative assistant did spend a total of 2 hours on each of the 15 workshops to schedule participants and send out invitations.

BENEFITS

The workshop handouts included a log that participants were asked to make entries on after each meeting during the 3 months after the workshop. Lewis's analysis of the entries on the 264 logs that were returned to her indicated the following data (listed in the same sequence as the seven objectives presented earlier):

1. The average length of a management meeting was 55 minutes, a saving of 20 minutes from the preworkshop average of 75 minutes. The length of work team meetings remained the same at about an hour.

2. Fewer meetings took place. During the 3 months after the workshop managers attended an average of 5.6 meetings per week, down from the pretraining average of 8.6. (These figures came from the 65 managers who returned their logs. The change in the frequency of meetings among members of work teams was not significant, since most teams continued to meet once a week.)

3. All the respondents reported that execution and follow-up had improved. No figures were asked for on this question on the log.

4. The responses indicated that three managers who had run their weekly departmental meetings with everyone present (a "command performance") were now making participation voluntary on a need-to-know basis. As a result, over the 39 meetings held during the 3 months, 87 hours were freed up for people who previously had been required to attend.

5. The respondents were asked to estimate the dollar value of better decision making and problem solving. Although the participants indicated that they were using the processes taught in the workshop, only eight indicated a dollar value. Their estimates ranged from $50 to $10,000. Lewis decided not to use these data in her cost-benefit analysis.

6. During her workshop Lewis introduced a recap form that the participants were taught how to use during a meeting to record any decisions, actions, and assignments. This made the writing and distributing of minutes unnecessary, which meant a savings of 45 minutes on average per meeting on the part of the participant who served as the recorder.

Given this information, Lewis was ready to calculate the dollar value of the time savings (on objectives 1, 2, 4, and 7) the workshop had made possible. The improved performance reported in response to objectives 3, 5, and 6 was a qualitative estimate and hard to quantify, and so Lewis ignored it in her calculations.

Before doing the cost-benefit analysis, Lewis made the following assumptions and verified them by checking with her boss (the vice president of HRD) and several other managers.

- The average annual salary of managers and supervisors at Southwest Industries is $52,000, which amounts to $1000 per week, $200 per day, or $25 per hour.

- The average annual salary of team members is $36,000, which amounts to $692 per week, $138 per day, or $17 per hour.

- The cost of employee benefits at Southwest Industries (insurance, medical, etc.) is figured at 30 percent of salary. In other words, every employee costs the company 130 percent of his or her gross salary.

- The meetings held by managers typically have about five persons in attendance, compared with the team meetings, where nine members typically attend.

- The meetings included in the cost-benefit analysis are held at Southwest Industries and have no significant expense other than the salaries of the participants. (Seminars, conventions, trade shows, and other meetings are excluded from the calculations.)

Now it's your turn. Put yourself in Lewis's shoes. Calculate the cost of the workshop and the benefits (Figs. 10–1 and 10–2). You have all the information you need to estimate costs and benefits. You are working with benefits (savings) for the 3 months after the workshop, which can be entered on Fig. 10–2 as savings per participant per month (last column).

1. Did costs exceed benefits or vice versa?
2. By what amount? What ratio?
3. Is a year too long, too short, or about right as the payoff period?
4. What was the cost per student-hour of this workshop?
5. Is that high, low, or about average for company-run training?

The cost-benefit analysis worksheet that Lewis used is shown in Figs. 10–1 and 10–2. It is a standard (generic) form, and so many of the categories will not apply. Make entries only where they apply.

THE CALCULATIONS AT SOUTHWEST INDUSTRIES

Costs

The costs of researching, developing, and delivering 15 one-day workshops on "Running Effective Meetings" are relatively easy to calculate. Lewis spends 1 day on research and 5 days on the design and writing of the course material, for a total of 6 days. Since Lewis is a manager, we can assume that her salary is about $200 per day, and the cost of benefits adds 30 percent to her salary. Thus, we enter $260 and $1300 under "Course Development" on Fig. 10–1.

An administrative assistant took 3 days to type and lay out the materials. Assuming the salary to be about the same as that of a team member, we have 3 × $138, or $414. Again, benefits add 30 percent to this amount, and so we enter $538 as the cost of production (typesetting and layout).

In "Instructional Materials," each participant received a presentation folder with handouts. This item cost about $2 to reproduce and collate, which we enter as the cost of participant materials.

There are two costs for the instructor: the $150 for the 12 overhead transparencies, which we enter under "One-Time Costs," and the $20 for Lewis's lunch and breaks, which we enter under "Costs per Offering."

Since the only equipment needed was an overhead projector, which the motel provided, there was no cost for equipment. (If Lewis had purchased a projector or if the course had required a major use of existing equipment, it would be appropriate to add a cost for this course's "fair share" of the equipment.)

The next entry is for facilities. Since the room cost $100 per day, we enter $100 under "Costs per Offering."

COST/BENEFIT ANALYSIS

COSTS

	One-Time Costs	Costs per Offering	Costs per Participant
1. Course Development (time) **or Selection** (price, fees)			
• needs analysis and research			
• design and creation of blueprint			
• writing and validating and revising			
• producing (typesetting, illustrating, ready for reproducing)			
2. Instructional Materials			
• per participant (expendables: notebooks, handouts, tests, etc.)			
• per instructor (durables: videotape, film, PC software, overheads) . .			
3. Equipment (Hardware)			
• projectors, VHS, computers, flip charts, training aids			
4. Facilities			
• rental or allocated "fair share" usage of classrooms, etc.			
5. Off-Site Expenses (if applicable)			
• travel, hotel overnights, meals, breaks			
• shipping of materials, rental of AV equipment, etc.			
6. Salary			
• participants (no. hrs. instruction × aver. hourly rate)			
• instructor, course administrator, program manager, etc.			
• fees to consultants or outside instructors			
• support staff (audiovisual, administrative, etc.)			
7. Lost Productivity (if applicable)			
• production rate losses or material losses			
A. Total of all one-time "up front" costs			
B. Total of all costs incurred each time course is offered			
C. This sum (Box B) × no. times course is run (——)			
D. Total of all costs incurred for each participant			
E. This sum (Box D) × no. participants (——) over life of course			
F. Total costs (sum of Boxes A, C and E)			

FIGURE 10–2

Cost-Benefit Analysis: Benefits

BENEFITS	One Time over Payback Period	One Time per Participant	Per Participant per Month
1. Time Savings			
• shorter lead time to reach proficiency (hrs. saved × $)			
• less time required to perform an operation (hrs. saved × $)			
• less supervision needed (supvsry. hrs. saved × supvsry. $).			
• better time management (hrs. freed up × $)			
2. Better Productivity (Quantity)			
• faster work rate ($ value of addl. units, sales, etc.)			
• time saved by not having to wait for help (hrs. saved × $)			
• less down time ($ value of reduced nonproductive time)			
3. Improved Quality of Output			
• fewer rejects (scrap, lost sales, returns, etc. ... $ value)			
• value added to output (bigger sales, smoother castings ... $)			
• reduced accidents ($ value of savings on claims, lost work)			
• reduced legal costs (EEO, OSHA, WC settlements ... $)			
• improved competitiveness (change in market share ... $)			
4. Better Personnel Performance (attributable to training)			
• less absenteeism/tardiness (self or subordinates ... $ saved)			
• improved health ($ saved on medical and lost time)			
• reduced grievances, claims, job actions ($ saved)			
• same output with fewer employees ($ on jobs eliminated)			
A. Total of all one-time benefits			
B. Total of all benefits occurring once per participant			
C. Total value of all improvements per participant per month			
D. Length of payback period in months			
E. Number of employees affected during this period (D)			
F. Total of B times E			
G. Total of C times D times E			
H. Total Benefits (sum of A plus F plus G)			

As for "Off-Site Expenses," Southwest Industries was billed $20 per person to cover refreshments and lunch for each participant. Thus, we enter $20 under "Costs per Participant."

Under "Salary," Lewis and her boss had agreed not to include the salary of participants or lost productivity as costs of training. However, the salary category that does apply is the instructor's time. Lewis costs $200 per day for salary. Adding 30 percent for employee benefits gives us $260, which we enter under "Costs per Offering." Similarly, her administrative assistant spent 2 hours on each workshop to schedule participants and send out invitations. At $17 per hour, this comes to $34, which becomes $44 when we add 30 percent for benefits, and so we enter $44 as a support staff cost under "Costs per Offering."

If we add up the costs just itemized and multiply by the number of offerings (15) and the number of participants (315), we get a total of $15,538. This is the sum of all the costs of producing and running the 1-day workshop 15 times.

Benefits

Now let's look at the benefits of training: the payoff that Southwest Industries realized as a result of the workshop. This was calculated as the value of the time saved in addressing objectives 1, 2, 4, and 7.

On objective 1, the participants reported a saving of 20 minutes per meeting on average. This applied to meetings attended by managers, since the meetings of work teams did not change significantly. The company's 95 managers reported an average of 5.6 meetings per week, which converts ($\times$ 4.33) to 24.25 meetings per month. One-third of an hour is saved at each meeting, for a total of 8.08 hours saved per manager (0.33 $\times$ 24.25). At $25 per hour, this savings amounts to $202, which we enter under "Time Savings" as in Fig. 10–2 as "better time management."

On objective 2, a major benefit was realized by reducing the number of meetings from 8.6 to 5.6, a savings of 3 meetings per week, or 13 meetings per month. Since the time managers spent at meetings had been averaging 75 minutes, or 1.25 hours, the monthly savings is 13 $\times$ 1.25, or 16.25 hours at $25 per hour, or $406. We can enter this under "Better Productivity" as "less downtime" (value of reduced nonproductive time).

On objective 4, three respondents to Lewis's log and questionnaire reported a savings of 87 hours over the 3 months, for an average of 29 hours per month. Lewis didn't know whether managers or nonmanagers accounted for this saving. To be conservative, she assumed they were nonmanagerial, and so the salary figures for team members were applied: 29 hours $\times$ $17 for savings of $493 per month. However, this is not a "per participant" saving, and so none of the three column headings in Fig. 10–2 apply. The nearest heading is the first column's "One Time" if we decide to make the length of the payoff period 1 year (i.e., the 12 months after the workshop). Thus, we multiply $493 by 12 to get a one-time saving of $5916, which we enter under "Better Personnel Performance" as "same output with fewer employees."

On objective 7, by having participants make their own notes ("minute") during meetings, there were savings of 45 minutes on average per meeting on the part of the recorder. To calculate this saving, Lewis had to determine how many meetings were held during the 3 months after the workshop. This number is different for managers and for work teams. Let's look at each.

Managers

Ninety-five managers attend 5.6 meetings per week, for a total of 532 attendees. However, the average number of managers at a meeting is 5, and so 532 ÷ 5 comes to an average of 106 meetings per week × 45 minutes saved at each, for savings of 79.5 hours per week, or 344 hours per month. This converts to 8.6 weeks (344 ÷ 40) of a recorder's time saved each month. At $1000 per week, managers freed from serving as recorders have saved $8600 per month. This belongs under "Time Savings" as "less time required to perform an operation." None of the headings apply, and so we divide by 95 managers so that we can enter it in the last column as a per participant saving: $8600 ÷ 95 = $91.

Team Meetings

We know that 250 employees are team members. Teams have an average of nine members. Thus, 250 ÷ 9 gives a total of 27.8 teams. They meet once a week, or 4.33 times per month, for a total of 27.8 × 4.33, or 120 meetings per month × 45 minutes for the recorder to prepare minutes. This is a savings of 90 hours, or 2.25 weeks, of recorders at $692 per week, for total monthly savings of $1557. Now we can convert this to a per participant saving by dividing $1557 by 250. We enter the result—$6—in the last column, just as we did for managers in the last entry.

Because our per participant savings are listed for two different populations (managers and team members), we have to keep these figures separate when we multiply by the number of persons in each population. Lewis did this by inserting a diagonal line in the calculation boxes at the bottom of the page.

Now we are ready to do the calculations at the bottom of the benefits columns so that the savings per month and per participant are extended over the total number of months (payoff period) and the total number of employees effected. In Lewis's case this is 95 and 250, a figure greater than the 315 participants, since the savings at meetings were realized by everyone who attended them, not just by the 315 participants in her workshops.

SUMMARY

Recall that the total cost was $15,538. Compared with the total projected benefit in the first year of $820,776, we can see that the value of the benefits is 53 times greater than the costs. We have no reason to assume that the ability of managers to run shorter and fewer meetings will end after the first year, but Lewis was quite content using the figures for 1 year as her payoff period.

As to the cost per student-hour, 315 employees attended the 6.5-hour workshop for a total of 2047.5 student-hours. Dividing the total cost by the total number of student-hours gives us a cost per student-hour of $7.59. This is well below the published ASTD student-hour figure of $22 as the 1994 average cost of formal training in U.S. organizations with 500 or more employees.

Note that the total population to be trained included 95 managers and 250 employees. All those persons attend meetings. However, they did not all attend the 1-day workshop. Thus, the costs of training are based on the total number who attended (15 × 21, or 315), whereas the benefits of training were realized by all those who attend meetings (95 + 250, or 345). There were undoubtedly other employees who also spend time in meetings, since Southwest Industries has about 900 employees, but they were not surveyed by Lewis since their participation in meetings was seen as being much less frequent.

CHAPTER 11

How to Plan for Technology-Based Training

Lance Dublin

Objectives

In an impressive bit of prediction, the Mad Hatter in *Alice in Wonderland* warned turn-of-the-twenty-first-century companies against jumping into the use of technology-based training before having an effective strategy in place. He said, "If you don't know where you're going, any road will take you there."Clearly, the Hatter was concerned that companies would be tempted to jump into using technology for training on the basis of the technologies they liked best instead of on the technologies that best supported the directions they wanted to go in, the amount of growth they wanted, and the degree of change they could handle. The Hatter feared that these companies would treat technology as a collection of children's toys instead of a set of serious and powerful business tools.

It's easy to tell which companies don't heed the Hatter. They're the ones with a Web course, a satellite course, a CD-ROM course—and no plan. They're the companies that train a lot and never get anywhere. This chapter is about training a lot and getting somewhere by building a cohesive, coherent strategy for using technology-based training that is linked to a company's goals, consistent with its culture, and appropriate to its resources.

OVERVIEW

This chapter examines the effectiveness and efficiency of technology-based training when its purpose is shaped by thoughtful planning and ongoing learning.

An important characteristic of a planned approach to implementing technology-based training is that financial benefits in both the short term and the long term can be increased, by accelerating the return on an organization's initial capital investment.

Short-term profitability can be achieved by reducing nonproductive time and the costs associated with traditional instructor-led delivery while increasing the level of usable knowledge in the workplace. Long-term profitability can be achieved by training more people and training them more quickly and effectively. As employees begin to behave like independent learners and can count on a technology-based infrastructure to support them, they will begin developing and applying new skills without the need for a costly trainer to prompt them or expensive classrooms and facilities to support them. In this way technology not only makes training more efficient and effective but, most important, transforms the business process, making each employee more valuable.

Achieving these long-term benefits, however, often requires that companies make broader investments in their people than those prescribed by the introduction of technology-based training. Once employee stakeholder groups reach what might be considered critical mass—in other words, when they are large and skilled enough to represent the broad spectrum of the company's people authentically—the benefits of true ownership can be realized as internal experts displace external consultants.

Until recently the art and science of applying strategic planning to the use of technology-based training did not fit conveniently into conventional market definitions. However, the rise of large consulting firms that incorporate technology-based training and performance support as an integral part of their work has demonstrated that the expertise, flexibility, and speed such consulting firms offer are invaluable to businesses competing in an environment of seemingly constant change.

If you don't think technology-based training constitutes a critical competitive advantage, consider the following questions: "What if everybody in our company could know enough about every product we make or every service we offer to sell one or the other to the next customer who called or walked in the door? What would our business be like then?" Better yet, "What if everybody in our company could perform to his or her highest potential whenever needed and all the time? Then what would our business be like?"

A DESCRIPTION OF THE BASIC TECHNIQUES

In its purest form a business strategy is a thorough yet flexible plan whose purpose is to increase the chances for success, stated in terms of measurable results, by establishing a direction in which to proceed and a framework within which to increase profits. Technology-based training and learning strategies are not written for trainers, however, or for learning experts. They are written for companies concerned with increasing performance and achieving a better bottom line. Whether a strategy is judged to be successful, therefore, is determined by the extent to which achieved (or perceived) business goals meet company expectations.

In consequence, training and learning strategies are more effective when

- They are applied to help a company whose culture is supportive, whose tools are good, whose information flow is sufficient, and whose management systems and structures are whole and functioning well.
- They are based on input from all the major organizations in a company, including information systems and information technology (IS/IT), sales, marketing, finance, manufacturing, customer service, and human resources.
- They are undertaken with an understanding of the general business environment. The general business environment today, for example, can be described as one where fewer people do more work in shorter periods of time by using increasingly powerful technologies that require frequently changing procedures.

The development of such a strategy can be divided into the following nine steps.

Step 1: Understand the Company's Business and Culture

Based on assessment and evaluation techniques such as interviews, focus groups, and surveys, ascertain and describe the company's business in terms of its characteristics (values, disciplines, technology, goals), business drivers (cost reduction, innovation, service), and corporate culture (human purposes, points of pride, motivational factors, idiosyncrasies, habits).

The characteristics that constitute a company's culture act as accelerators and inhibitors of change and influence performance and behavior to such an extent that no technology can entirely overcome their effects. Law firms, for example, were slow to adopt technology because their cultural concept that people (i.e., secretaries), not technology, support people (i.e., lawyers) was central to how those firms thought of themselves and what made them tick. No matter how flexible a company may think its culture is, the specific characteristics that make it tick — whether loyalty, perseverance, or respect for authority— can result in an aversion to technology.

Simply put, the success of a strategy for applying technology-based training and learning depends largely on whether the company as a whole, including the individual performers and/or workers, are ready, willing, and able.

Step 2: Speculate on the Future

Albert Einstein said: "Speculation is more important than fact. And imagination is more important than knowledge." He would have predicted that the process of unleashing a company's ability to speculate and imagine is where training strategies derive their power.

Asking, Where are we today? Where do we want to be in the future? What size will we be? How many people will we eventually employ? What will our competition look like? and other questions that relate to a company's characteristics, business drivers, and corporate culture increases a company's ability to withstand external forces and maximizes its chances of getting where it wants to go.

However, strategy is more than making sure that a desired future will happen. It is also a matter of making sure that a company will excel when the future it is planning for actually arrives. Typically, successful business executives look ahead 3 years or more. Thus, unless a strategy is based on speculating about the future, business executives who know the importance of such speculation will spot a strategy that is stuck in the present. They will say, correctly, that this strategy is not forward-thinking enough.

Step 3: Create a Picture of a High-Performing Work Force

The purpose of this step is to ensure thinking from a performance, not a technology, perspective. When a vision of how a company wants to perform (usually a written description based on assessment and evaluation techniques) is created, a picture of an appropriately high-performing work force emerges. This type of work force might be described in a phrase such as "optimal performance of all employees all the time."

When the vision is bold and compelling, it will provide direction for the training and learning strategy. Design decisions can be made about what role technology will play in the actual training and how its application will ensure that a project's scope is defined and targeted accurately.

For example, a new software system may dictate new ways in which the business is going to run by providing, perhaps for the first time, organizationwide access to global inventory figures. If one of the components of the company's vision is to provide a high level of customer satisfaction, its people will have to be taught a new way of dealing with customers who will expect information at the new, higher level.

Step 4: Focus on Performance Enablers

Although they may comprehensively unite and coordinate skills and knowledge, technology-based training and learning are not the only variables that affect business performance. Accordingly, considering that each individual worker must perform highly for a business to reach its goals, make sure that technology is significantly enhancing (enabling) each worker's ability to do the following:

1. Develop tools that facilitate performance
2. Provide information that is critical to job success
3. Provide advice and support systems that direct and help workers when needed
4. Provide technology-based training and learning that refine existing skills and develop new ones
5. Share knowledge across the company in ways that create competitive advantages

Step 5: Review Current Constraints

Even the most optimistic companies must deploy their training and learning strategies within constraints posed by technology and a company's politics (a subset of its culture), resources, and vision.

Obviously, the amount of technology to which a company has access will determine the directions in which technology-based training and learning can go. Despite an increasing awareness of what they can do for a company, training and learning are not heavy business drivers. There is no point, for example, laying out a technology-based strategy that is totally dependent on satellite delivery lines if the IT department has no plans to implement that technology.

Therefore, in the current business climate in which senior management is faced with competing and complex strategic decisions, proposals for technology-based training and learning are more likely to be adopted if they are made in partnership with the IT department. Between now and any foreseeable future reliant on technology, strategic plans cannot be developed without the close cooperation of IT. In other words, there is no way to get dollars for technologies that do not fit into the corporate IT strategy and that IT does not approve of.

Political pressures represent an important constraint as well as a potential force for change. A company with a huge instructional, educational, and training organization, for example, may not respond positively to the idea of replacing it with a technology-based training and learning program. However, the move to E-commerce means that companies are adopting Intranets as an integral part of business operations, opening the door for the use of Intranets to deliver training and learning.

Overall, the necessary human, financial, technical, and physical resources can be constrained in amount or type. Today's organizations are run "lean and mean" in nearly all aspects of their operations, and so there will always be a struggle over the allocation of what is available. The greater constraint therefore may be whether the right resources—including instructional designers, project managers, and technical experts—are available. In fact, this constraint may need to be addressed in regard to the architecture as a critical success factor.

There is also the matter of vision. If a compelling vision can be the key to creating an effective companywide strategy, a less than compelling vision can be an important constraint. As a result, special care should be taken to ensure that the vision creates an appropriate picture of a future state in the company, one that might require, for example, the effective use of technology for training and learning.

Step 6: Develop a Scalable Architecture

Based on the analysis of a company's operations, goals, and constraints, the development of a scalable architecture whose components include leadership, communications, training and learning, performance support, evaluation, and future organizational considerations is an essential step.

A scalable architecture's flexibility means that it is easy to build on and that single or multiple components can be added as needed without losing the overall coherence and momentum. This flexibility also minimizes the time and money spent on misjudged directions, unrelated activities, and technologies that turn out to be usable in the short term rather than for the life of the project.

A scalable architecture, its characteristics, and its components constitute a foundation on which training and learning strategy can be based and a direction in which training and learning can move confidently forward.

Step 7: Develop a Business Case

Since the operation of most businesses is governed by the notion of a healthy bottom line, a business case must be made to demonstrate how technology-based training and learning further a company's business strategy, produce measurable business results, create or sustain competitive advantages, and equate to a positive return on investment (ROI).

Unless these questions can be answered persuasively, there will be no strategy for the technology-based training and learning, only a wish list of satellites, CD-ROMs, and Web sites. The truth is that in and of itself, technology-based training and learning are not very useful. To be valuable to a company, they must be tied to questions such as, How do they increase customer satisfaction? How do they affect product innovation? How do they lower costs? How do they enable us to compete more effectively?

Finding the answers to these questions and in the process linking the strategy to an improved business result can guide the identification and selection of the measurements and measuring tools that help make the case.

For example, measuring improved performance requires the identification of specific business performance criteria. Measuring customer satisfaction requires specially designed surveys. Although it is not yet clear how to measure some key parameters, such as the huge amounts of funds a company must invest from the time a person is hired to the time when that person can minimally perform his or her job, in looking for an answer, the appropriate measurement criteria and measuring tools will become obvious.

In regard to ROI, there is good news and bad news. Although ROI has become one of the most widely referred to business indicators, there is not one standard formula to measure it. In fact, ROI is largely in the eye of the beholder. Put another way, ROI is a matter of opinion, and everyone is entitled to his or hers.

There are so many variables involved in calculating ROI that it behaves more like a financial calculation than a discrete measuring tool. As with most financial calculations, the numbers can be made to prove anything. This becomes apparent when a company tries to calculate the value of a person starting a job earlier than anticipated. If ROI were calculated as a function of that person's percentage of contribution to the total profit of the company, for example, the almost complete lack of hard numbers available for the calculation would allow for a very wide range of interpretation.

The corollary to this is that a company generally will respond positively to an interpretation of ROI that reflects the values of its culture. Therefore, a formula for ROI that is developed in accordance with a knowledge and appreciation of that culture will help make a better overall case for technology-based training and learning.

Step 8: Develop and Implement an Internal Marketing Plan

In recognition of the cultural issues that arise when new operational practices or procedures are introduced into a company, a strategy that is accompanied by an implementation or marketing plan has a better chance of succeeding.

This type of marketing plan has to address all the company's stakeholder or interest groups (including, in addition to end users, corporate, IT, operations, sales, and human resources) and lay out the action steps through which the changes are going to proceed.

Like conventional marketing plans aimed at promoting a product or service, an internal marketing plan must tell all the groups it addresses how their jobs will be affected and what they will receive in terms of benefits, and why, in forms they can easily access and in language they will not only be able to understand but also find compelling. Creating such a plan also presents an excellent opportunity to provide an overall view of how each department or division fits into the context of the companywide changes.

A strategy will work best if the company starts "selling" it throughout the organization even before the strategy is ready to be rolled out, literally as soon as it goes into development. It is easier to gain people's acceptance and commitment if they feel involved.

While people feel threatened by anything new, they feel especially threatened by technology-based training and learning. The massive infusions of organization-wide technology systems are causing both training and learning to be reexamined. The learners are threatened because they are being asked to learn in a new way. The trainers are threatened because they worry that they may be out of a job either immediately or in the near future. The instructional designers are threatened because they sense a challenge to their authority and competence. The managers are threatened because they have never managed anybody who is learning with technology-based training.

When training and learning classes were primarily instructor-led, managers would know when employees were in training: They didn't see them. These days employees can be in training while in place at their computers, but the managers don't know this unless an employee has put a sign up on the computer saying, "Don't bother me. I'm learning."

This manager-specific problem, a consequence of the fact that managers generally have not been taught how to manage properly, makes the development of an implementation or marketing plan involving managers and all key stakeholders of critical importance.

Step 9: Evaluate, Communicate, and Iterate

The evaluation process, based on data collection, provides an opportunity to benchmark measurable business results and compare them with goals and results as well as to find out what is and what is not working. It also presents an opportunity to share with and sell strategy to the people in the trenches. In talking to people, note that communicating a genuine interest in and respect for their input and a commitment to making use of it will yield the best results.

As part of an overall marketing plan, it is important to keep people informed on an ongoing basis about the status of a project and the milestones and new discoveries that affect the plan. As such information is communicated to each stakeholder group, it forms the basis for determining how to make improvements and adjustments.

In addition, it is important to be open to expert input from specialists in all the many aspects of technology-based training. In building a house, for example, electricians, plumbers, structural engineers, interior decorators, landscape architects, and many other experts are involved. Each of these specialists has an equivalent in building a technology-based training and learning strategy.

When properly equipped and informed, a team of experts can help a company plan and implement a strategy for using technology-based training and learning that is linked to that company's business goals and resources and is flexible enough to respond to opportunity and reality.

Keep in mind that it is performance that links the purpose and technology of training and learning to the business strategy. Remember what the training and learning intervention is intended to achieve. Examine the technology-based solutions that are possible and consistent with the company's culture. Make sure that the strategy is not engraved in stone. Above all, separate out purpose from tactics and technology. In the end, that's what strategy is all about.

A READINESS CHECKLIST

The following checklist (a modified version of Brandon Hall's original list; see chap. 15) will help determine whether a company is prepared to take steps 1 through 9:

1. All stakeholder groups have made a commitment to moving toward a technology-based strategy for training and learning.
2. A business case has been built, and the ROI has been clearly established.
3. Visible sponsorship of the project has been established.
4. Leadership has aligned itself in support of the business case.
5. A strategic and tactical plan for preparing the training department to support technology-based training and learning has been put in place.
6. A process has been developed to prepare the learners and ensure that they are willing to support technology-based training and learning.
7. A process has been established to ensure that the necessary hardware and software are in place to design and implement the technology-based training and learning programs.
8. A process has been established to determine how to match the learning content to the technology and to ensure that the course content and design meet the needs of the learners.
9. A process has been developed to ensure that high-quality programs will be created by following proven design principles, processes, and tools and using experienced developers.
10. A system is in place for the ongoing evaluation of the results and for making changes to the strategy as they become necessary.

TEN GUIDELINES FOR USING PERFORMANCE TECHNOLOGY SUCCESSFULLY

Organizations today look, act, and compete like never before. The work force is shrinking, tasks are becoming more complex, and business processes are changing constantly. This situation has created a tremendous opportunity for using technology-based tools to support organizationwide learning and performance initiatives. Paying attention to the following 10 guidelines will increase the chances for success.

1. *Adopt new mental models.* In the industrial age, the training and learning paradigm was characterized by fixed attributes such as one size fits all, teacher-centered, and available when ready. Today, technology-based tools can be used to implement a new training and learning paradigm characterized by customizable attributes such as one size fits one, performance-centered, and available when needed.

2. *Solve the right problem.* Technology-based tools can provide impactful learning, effective information access, and outstanding support for on-the-job performance. They cannot, however, correct inadequate business processes, ineffective management structures and systems, inappropriate jobs and roles, and out-of-sync values and beliefs.

3. *Apply appropriate solutions.* Technology-based learning tools are most effective at providing foundational skills. Technology-based information and performance support tools are most effective at providing just-in-time skills. Combined, they can ensure on-time performance.

4. *Ensure quality.* Well-designed or well-developed tools will always leave a lasting positive legacy, beginning with each user's first impression.

5. *Focus on results.* To meet the organization's goals, stay focused on the business results to be produced (e.g., less rework, higher customer satisfaction), not on the activities to be accomplished (e.g., number of learning hours, screens of information). At their best, technology-based learning tools are only a means to an end.

6. *Work from the top down and from the bottom up.* Success requires active support from all the levels in an organization, including senior management, middle management, front-line supervisors, and the work force.

7. *Apply "high-tech–high-touch" thinking.* The use of technology-based "high-tech" tools will benefit when people enjoy easy, "high-touch" access to them. In fact, human-to-human contact through hotlines, voice mail, and E-mail systems is a critical element in overcoming resistance and gaining acceptance.

8. *Keep in mind that the whole is greater than the sum of its parts.* Make full use of all available learning and performance support resources and integrate each one into a system that supports on-time performance and continuous learning. Older technology-based tools such as print (job aids), multimedia (audio and video), and people (coaches) can play a critical role in the success of any solution.

9. *Address the whole system.* To achieve defined business results, understand and address the processes, technologies, management structures and systems, jobs and roles, and values and beliefs that make up the business system. Technology tools typically represent just one part of a total solution. Intangibles often offer even greater leverage.

10. *Be ready, willing, and able.* Implementation is the key to success. A wonderful technology-based learning and performance tool is good only if it is used and used properly. To be effective, an implementation approach must ensure that the organization and its target audience have the right processes and structures in the right culture, equipped with the right capabilities.

A PRACTICAL APPLICATION

Overview

The client was a large restaurant chain with a strong focus on cleanliness, quality, customer service, and growth. Many of its management's administrative functions, however, were handled manually.

Approaching the new century, therefore, the client decided to provide its restaurants with new tools (point-of-sale hardware and software and back-office technology, including cash management, scheduling, and inventory) to make the operation more efficient and reduce administrative tasks. This would give restaurant managers more time to work with staff and customers, helping them reach business goals such as increased sales.

The client was also looking for a customized training solution that would help the company move to a technology-based infrastructure in line with a vision of the future linked both to its industry and to the use of training and learning in the whole company.

The client was aware of a possible conflict between its vision of the future and its cultural constraints (averse to both technology and risk). This led it to request a dynamic strategy that would act as a catalyst for change within the company, helping to ensure that the training and learning would be used aggressively to form the basis of further change and the next steps. In other words, the request was not for a fixed strategy and a predetermined number of training and learning hours; it was for an approach to a solution.

Business Challenge

The client had already selected a hardware provider for both point-of-sale and back-office functions, a software provider able to customize its product, and a business partner to deploy hardware and software and provide help-desk services. The client still required a business partner to help create a companywide commitment ("buy-in") to the new solution, create training, and perhaps supply supplemental on-the-job support.

Employee training and learning already had a strong tradition in the company in terms of both resource allocation and an ongoing focus. However, the company had never implemented an initiative that required employees to be trained in new ways of managing operations, and all prior training had been instructor-led and video-based.

The client's business drivers included increasing the amount of revenue per restaurant, improving customer service, maintaining consistency, maximizing longevity, minimizing sales disruption, and improving the employees' quality of life. An additional driver was the client's corporate training department's desire to use training and learning as catalysts for the possible conversion of instructor-led and video-based training to multimedia.

Business Solution

The solution was to design, develop, and implement training and learning while providing necessary change management and on-the-job performance support.

Based on extensive corporate and field interviews and focus group work, a new training and support paradigm consisting of computer-based training (CBT) and an on-line extended help facility was developed. This paradigm was accompanied by a strategy to ensure that people would be ready, willing, and able to perform at a high level in the new environment.

The strategy for ensuring that people would be ready, willing, and able was based on two major determinations:

1. A determination that the organization and structure of the existing field management could be used to accelerate people's buy-in and commitment. A strong hierarchy-based leadership tradition in the company made it possible to make field management feel that it "owned" the implementation. Core programs included intensive briefings on the paradigm's historical, business, and technical aspects. Work sessions required that each level of management make tactical decisions for its own area. The communications strategy emphasized sending key messages by using vehicles designed to engage management and providing accessible venues for asking questions.

2. A determination that the existing training and on-the-job performance support methods would not work for this project. After it was determined that traditional instructor-led training and learning would take too long and cost too much and that it would be less expensive to develop CBT and an extended on-line help facility, it was demonstrated that CBT would provide better retention.

An additional finding, based on IT plans for the installation of a client-server architecture in the restaurants, was that the new infrastructure could provide both CBT and an on-line help facility in the short term and the downloading of new learning modules from the company's Intranet or by satellite in the future.

This new paradigm therefore met the requirements of achieving consistency and longevity. Since the learning would be self-paced and individual, it could be scheduled in time frames that would not compete with the accomplishment of ongoing business targets.

Activities

Phase I

An architecture and strategy document was prepared that defined a range of viable options for ensuring that people would be ready, willing, and able to make the transition to the new restaurant environment. This document identified critical success factors for the project as well as a recommended approach. Upon its acceptance, a more detailed design was prepared for the next phase of work.

Phase II

An implementation master plan was presented that consisted of "blueprints" for developing, delivering, supporting, and evaluating the program defined and approved in phase I. This implementation master plan included the following components:

1. A leadership plan described events that would build and share knowledge about the project throughout field management. These events included working sessions and briefings using supporting materials.
2. A communications plan focused on sending key messages to audiences affected by the project. The plan leveraged existing vehicles as well as creating new means of delivering messages needed for a clear understanding of the project.
3. A training curriculum design served as a high level "blueprint" for the CBT components that described audiences, training modules, topics, tasks, and learning tracks for all the identified audiences. The plan specified who was to receive what kind of training, how it would be delivered, and in what sequence it would be delivered. The plan also described learner certification requirements.
4. A performance support design served as a high-level blueprint for "day 1" and ongoing on-the-job support components and activities. This design also described an extended on-line help facility; outlined requirements for

selecting, training, and deploying an on-site coaching network; and began to define the roles of and relationships among individuals on the help desk.

5. A resource plan described the preliminary resources needed to complete development. The resource plan also described the development methodology; the roles and responsibilities of development team members; a development timeline; learning area requirements; reproduction, duplication, and distribution requirements; and information on learner scheduling and tracking requirements.

In conjunction with the development of the implementation master plan, a project identity critical to the success of the project was created. A project vision, mission, icon, and tag line to be used in all communications about the project were developed, providing a clear focus and common understanding of the project. The project identity was used in the training and performance support components to strengthen the project's focus.

Phases III and IV

Leadership materials such as leader guides and participant guides were developed for the delivery of working sessions and briefings. Communication components were developed, including a project newsletter, briefing kit materials, and communications audits. Run-time versions of approximately 50 unique learning hours of CBT were developed. The performance support system was developed as defined in the implementation master plan.

Phase V

After all the components were tested, piloted, and delivered, a thorough evaluation was made in partnership with the client. Then all documentation of the work, both in hard copy and in electronic files, was handed off to the client for future use.

GLOSSARY

Business Case A demonstration of how technology-based training and learning further a company's business strategy, produce measurable business results, create or sustain competitive advantages, and equate to a positive return on investment.

Change Management The process of moving people affected by change from awareness through engagement to commitment to the change.

Communications Plan A plan for the use of communication and conversation as the starting point for engaging people and gaining their commitment to change.

Culture The qualities and characteristics that define an organization and make it tick.

Implementation Master Plan A synthesis of all the subplans (learning, performance support, change management, communications, and resources) required to ensure the success of a project or strategy.

Leadership Plan   A plan that ensures that sufficient leadership will be demonstrated so that everyone affected by the change will understand its implications, be able to talk about its various aspects, and have confidence in it.

Measurement   A way of assessing a strategy's or project's success at moving toward its goals.

Mission Statement   An extension of the vision statement that reflects and examines a project's purpose, expresses its sense of value, inspires its people, guides its leaders, and answers the question, Why are we doing this?

Performance Support Plan   A plan that ensures that ongoing on-the-job support components and activities are in place, including but not limited to printed user manuals and job aids, on-line help and reference, and help desks.

Ready, Willing, and Able   *Ready* refers to ensuring that an organization is ready for change. *Willing* refers to creating the values, behaviors, and norms that are necessary for success. *Able* refers to the knowledge, skills, and abilities people need to perform in the new environment.

Resource Plan   A description of the preliminary resources and methodologies required to complete the project.

Scalable Architecture   A foundation on which a strategy can be based and added to and a direction in which that strategy can move confidently forward into the future.

Strategy   A thorough yet flexible plan whose purpose is to increase the chances for success, stated in terms of measurable results. Strategy establishes a direction in which to proceed and a framework within which to increase profits.

Training and Curriculum Design   A high-level blueprint for the training components that describes audiences, training modules and topics, and learning tracks. It specifies who receives what kind of training, how it is delivered, and in what sequence it is delivered as well as information such as learner certification requirements.

Vision Statement   A picture of what the future can look like and what a company aspires to become, achieve, and create. A vision requires significant change and progress to attain, and becomes real for people through communication and conversation.

Design and Delivery of Technology-Based Training

Brandon Hall, PhD

In 1969, as a young college student, I was handed a book that was an example of programmed instruction. On each page there was one short concept or fact consisting of no more than one to three sentences. When the learner turned the page, there was a brief quiz, usually a similar statement with a key piece of information left blank for the user to fill in. When I turned the page, the answer was provided, along with a new factoid to begin the process again.

Back then, the dream was to put this type of instruction on a computer, one of those huge, glass-enclosed mysterious devices that only college administrators had access to.

Although it seemed like science fiction at the time, in the 1970s instruction did make it to the computer and computer-based training (CBT) was born. See Gloria Gery's classic *Making CBT Happen* for a full description.

The 1980s saw the advent of the personal computer and the videodisc, and interactive training was born. Although it included full-screen, high-quality video, the development and delivery of this type of training proved to be too expensive.

In the early 1990s, Apple Computer tested several terms for the delivery of audio and video via computer-based CD-ROMs. The original term *hypermedia* did not do well with focus groups, but the term *multimedia* did. A new industry was born: multimedia for learning, games (Broderbund's Myst), and information (Microsoft's Encarta).

Professional trainers were warming to the idea of using this technology to deliver instruction. The authoring tools were very effective, such as Macromedia's Authorware and Allen Communication's Quest. The CD-ROM was becoming more popular on employees' desktop computers, and organizations were building

173

learning centers replete with multimedia personal computers and lots of learning programs on topics ranging from safety to word processing to sexual harassment.

Just when trainers were getting accustomed to the idea of using CD-ROMs, the game changed again. The Internet took off, and Web-based training with it. While bandwidth limitations and authoring tools still keep the design of Web-based training about 18 months behind the best design for CD-ROMs, things are now getting better. Over the next 18 months, bandwidth will improve, more tools for creating training on-line will emerge, and more trainers will see the value of using technology to supplement (not replace) instructor-led training.

The chapters in this section provide a comprehensive view of the state of the art of on-line learning. The lineup of authors and their topics will provide the information you need to begin or accelerate your work with technology. Good luck, and stay informed of new developments in the field by visiting resource center Web sites dedicated to the field, such as ours at www.brandon-hall.com or trainingsupersite.com.

BRIEF OVERVIEW OF CHAPTERS AND AUTHORS

If you want to learn the best approaches to implementing a change process or need to sell upper management on the idea of technology for learning, Lance Dublin, the author of Chapter 11, is an expert teacher and implementer. He is a rarity in training:someone who has the bottom-line sensibilities of a senior executive but the intellectual experience of an intervention specialist and human resources professional.

Having developed and used technology to advantage, off-the-shelf programs seem to provide ready-made solutions. Dorman Woodall challenges us in Chapter 12 with some advise on how to make sure we don't fall for the "technology will drive the learning" thesis.

In the mid 1980s only the dedicated were figuring out how to apply computers to training. Robert Steinmetz, the author of Chapter 13, was one of them. An instructional designer by profession, he founded and developed Learning System Sciences into one of the premier custom development houses in the country. His coauthor here, Ann Kwinn, has worked on over a dozen projects, applying her specialty of instructional design.

The best interactive training in the world does not matter if it is not funded and implemented. Dr. Jack Phillips, the author of Chapter 14, is the premier expert on return on investment (ROI) for training. Along with his colleague, J. Patrick Whalen, he provides an overview of the ROI process.

Brandon Hall, the author of Chapter 15, has been in training for over 20 years and has been researching and writing about technology for training full-time since

1993. His firm conducts research studies on u8sing the Internet for training and publishes white papers and research reports.

Jim goldsmith, the author of Chapter 16, has been working on technology delivery longer than most, first at Aetna and now at Anderson Consulting, He is a thoughtful practitioner and is willing to document and share his ideas about the development process with his colleagues in training.

In Chapter 17, Robert Zielinski, Michael Allen, Lynn Misselt, and Steve Lee of Allen Interactions, along with Joan Busch of United HealthCare Serves Inc., document an advanced yet simplified approach to the development of interactive design. Their technique has helped dozens of companies implement technology-based training using the intuitive Savvy process instead of the more linear approach of traditional instructional design.

David Metcalf, the author of Chapter 18, is a pioneer in the use of the Internet for training. His work at NASA's Cape Canaveral was the basis for his doctoral work and was highlighted in his Web-Based Training Cookbook of 1997.

In Chapter 19, Carol Gunther-Mohr and cowriters, Sam Field and Geoffrey Frank, write about the use of virtual reality for training. While the early interest in virtual reality has been replaced by the use of on-screen three-dimensional images, there are still benefits to be gained from using either approach.

In Chapter 20, Deborah Stone and John Endicott describe advances in the use of performance support. They are both part of the DLS Group, one of the foremost development firms for custom performance support projects.

Harvi Singh, the author of Chapter 21, is one of the brightest people in the area of technology-based training. Every time I talk to Harvi, I learn something. His firm, Empower, does state-of-the-art development of on-line training and the design of architectures for enterprisewide deployment of on-line learning.

When you complete this section, you will have a good grasp of the major issues in designing and developing technology for learning. Then comes the hard part: taking the lead for advancing the use of on-line learning in your organization.

CHAPTER 12

Selecting Off-the-Shelf Courseware and Suppliers: CD-ROM, LAN, and Web

Dorman Woodall

Life is short, the art long, opportunity fleeting, experience treacherous, judgment difficult.

Hippocrates

And the training is urgent.

Dorman Woodall

Objectives

After reading this chapter, you will be able to:

- Distinguish between sizzle, subject-matter, and skills-based courses.
- Develop a set of questions for off-the-shelf suppliers that best fit your training needs.

If you have read anything about using multimedia or technology-based training in a training program, you probably think it is cost-prohibitive. You probably have been told that moving from classroom to technology-based training is a wonderful and exciting but very expensive venture. This is true if you must develop your own courses using a highly skilled and talented staff. However, if your training needs can be satisfied by a high-quality generic course, you can obtain the same great return on investment that you would from custom-developed courses for only a fraction of the outlay. You can do this simply by securing the right off-the-shelf training materials. Using generic courses to improve your organization makes good business sense and can become a viable method for expanding the skills of a business team.

Training professionals need to think about how to make better buying decisions since the task of obtaining off-the-shelf courseware is becoming an ongoing and essential activity for every training manager. With the increased demand placed on you by the growth of the training audience and the speed of technical change, you cannot fulfill all your training needs by developing every course yourself or afford to teach every course in a classroom environment. You have no choice but to learn how to buy good off-the-shelf courses.

There seems to be sufficient advice and expertise within the training industry about how to select custom multimedia developers, authoring languages, and courseware templates and how to build in-house media development staffs. If you need assistance with the choice of authoring packages or don't know how to create a custom development course, refer to Brandon Hall's *The Web-Based Training Cookbook* or check out his web site at *www.multimediatraining.com*. However, little information is available to guide your selection of off-the-shelf training materials. For the most part, supplier sales representatives, marketing materials, and Websites are the only sources of information for selecting off-the-shelf courseware. These are not always the most reliable or objective resources. You are in luck if the salesperson is a solutions-based seller, has a good product, knows a great deal about training, and demonstrates a high degree of integrity. Still, you must be prepared to make the best decision for your organization.

This chapter will assist you in avoiding the pitfalls of buying inferior technology-based training products that will distract from the important work you have to do in providing your organization with the best return for the training dollar. The first part focuses on how to identify and categorize technology-based courseware into three major course groupings: *sizzle, subject matter, and skills-based.* The second part reloads your fact-finding arsenal with several questions that will help narrow your selection of the best courseware supplier.

SELECTING THE RIGHT COURSEWARE
The Three Major Courseware Categories

One of the first things you need to learn in buying off-the-shelf courses is how to categorize the various types of technology-based training available. This section will give you some practical insights that will save time and reduce your risks during the selection process. The overwhelming task of sorting out true substance from sizzle in training products can be made simpler even if you are doing it for the very first time. With some good advice, the process can become much clearer.

Because off-the-shelf training courses offer so many options for a training program, there are several features to review. Therefore, you must be diligent since serious business results depend on the outcome of your evaluation. Some courseware is simply ineffective and poorly designed, resulting in a lot of wasted time and money. Even worse, bad courses will thwart first-time efforts and prevent you from devising alternative methods of training for you and your organization. Usually courseware falls into one of three general categories.

Sizzle

This term describes flashy courseware designed solely to appeal to your sense of fun and concern for making learners comfortable with technology-based training. The biggest problem with sizzle is that the suppliers are interested only in getting you to buy their superficially designed courses by providing media glitz and glitter in place of meaningful content and teaching techniques. Lots of "flashy trash" is the main ingredient in most sizzle courses, which focus mostly on neat technical features and cool media (look for talking heads, nice wrappers, cute cartoons, and childish humor and perhaps a black box to make it all work).

Subject Matter

These quickly developed, passive page-turners focus on your desire to get the most content for your money. Subject-matter suppliers try to dump a wide range of concepts and content while providing little in the way of engaging media or learner interactions. Subject-matter courses are usually boring page-turners. This approach to training requires much more learner time than is necessary since it attempts to cover everything the learner may ever want to know (encyclopedia philosophy). Expect a low return on your learning investment since the learner is typically not ready to apply skills immediately after finishing the course.

Skills-Based

This description refers to courses that use good instructional design and have sufficient course content to increase the job performance of learners. These courseware suppliers are the ones who seek to provide the right balance of engaging instruction with performance-oriented course content and the appropriate media to engage learners; in other words, the best balance for an adult learner. Look for an increased application of skills since performance-based instruction is designed to make the training widely available within an organization. Also, the architecture of a skills-based course makes training available on all platforms. Look for the supplier to provide delivery over the local area network (LAN) and Intranet in addition to CD-ROM without sacrificing the benefits of the multimedia features.

You will know a skills-based course when you see it. It can be as simple as trying out the course or seeing a well-structured demo version. More in-depth evaluations will include feedback from subject-matter experts (SMEs), learners, and instructional designers who carefully considered the factors of accurate content, technical requirements, deployment, and instructional design.

Distinguishing among these courseware types requires some experience with courseware and careful thought about your audience and its needs. Some training managers already know the sizzle and subject-matter distinction. They learned the hard way: by buying the products and later discarding them. Lost time and money is a hard way to build training management experience. Still, some trainers feel they must continue to buy a few sizzle products for a small portion of the training audience so that they have something to attract the professional "training tourist" into the learning center. Some good trainers, feeling they have no other choice, buy boring subject-matter courses because they have to get something in a hurry. Most trainers can identify good skills-based courseware and seek to give it to serious learners whenever and wherever they can.

Sizzle: Is Entertainment Really Training?

The person who says they are too old to learn new things probably always was.

G. B. Shaw

What Do Some Learners Say about Sizzle Courses?

A typical learner's reaction to a sizzle course is, "I don't remember exactly what the course was about, but I sure enjoyed it." This is a very telling statement , since the purpose of sizzle courseware is to entertain the learners, not necessarily to train them. The use of multimedia features in technology-based training is very important. However, these features are only the supporting players. The stars should be good course content and sound instructional design. The most common justification for obtaining sizzle courses comes from harried, overworked, and confused trainers who feel that using these courses is the only way to get people to show up at a learning center for training. Unfortunately, it's the wrong group of learners who always show up: the ones who expect to be entertained, not educated.

The Training Game to Sizzle Suppliers Is Simply That: A Game

The hallmark of sizzle courses is their focus on gratuitous media and games with little or no consideration of practical course design or sufficient course content. Here are some examples:

- In a Windows 95 course a morphing cartoon character explaining the process of changing wallpaper on the desktop leads the first practice. The learners then are instructed to take this action by toggling to the real software since interactive simulation is not provided. Nothing of any great business consequence follows this cute piece of instruction.
- In a Word 97 course a video segment shows a clown spinning plates, dropping them one by one. He says, "Oh, you wanted to learn about

templates? Sorry, I thought you said *ten* plates." There is no escape. Each time you enter the course to refresh your knowledge of templates, you get another dose of this sophomoric humor.

Many Are Called, but Few Really Learn via Sizzle

Although many people start sizzle courses, few finish them. Wily marketeers must know this because they generally place the flash in the front of the course or in its wrapper. They expect you to conduct only a superficial evaluation. "Flash for cash" is their prime directive. Marketing (as opposed to training) companies that truly believe a PowerPoint sales presentation married to a Nintendo game is the highest form of training usually develop sizzle-based products. As a rule, the supplier relies heavily on outside custom houses to build its courses. The partnering of smart marketers with highly creative media experts is destined to create a lot of creative sparks. The problem is the apparent absence of training leadership or significant involvement from good instructional designers. Since the media is the focus of the course, the developers naturally tend to dominate in this type of arrangement. They make more money if they can fill the course with media bells and whistles.

Subject-Matter Courseware: Is Information Really Training?

> The great aim of education is not knowledge, but action.
>
> *Herbert Spencer*

Getting Ready to Get Ready

Subject-matter courses focus on course content over all else and thus are almost the opposite of sizzle courses. The subject-matter approach assumes that the more the learner can read, the more the learner will remember, and then somehow the learner will be able to find a place to apply all this knowledge later. A typical learner response to this type of training is, "I think that maybe I understand this topic, but I'm not sure I can do it yet. I need a bit more time." This is a classic training case of getting ready to get ready. In this courseware, the learners spend more time than necessary in training because they are overwhelmed by the huge amount of nonperformance content they must experience first.

I Need More for My Training Dollar

As a training manager, you may buy subject-matter courses because you want all the content you can get for your money. It is natural to want more bang for your buck. However, without effective interaction, the course becomes a highly didactic page-turner and a very boring waste of time. Even though the course may contain rich graphics, a spot or two of fancy simulation, and the occasional use of cute cartoon characters, the deadly lack of learning interaction remains. The course forces the poor learners into reading page after page until they fall into a Dilbert-like semicatatonic state. Subject-matter courseware has a lot of content, very little media use, and nothing in the way of interactive teaching.

My Learners Will Like Whatever I Give Them

Generally, organizations that select subject-matter courses tend to be bureaucratic in nature and traditional in their approach to training. This is the case because the style of training they practice is based on a child learning model as opposed to an enriched adult learning model. The resulting view is a teachercentric one which professes that the students are always passive and that you have to teach them everything before they are allowed out of the room. This is a self-fulfilling prophecy. What these organizations fail to realize is the time wasted in training that covers far too many topics without engaging the learner.

Something Is Better Than Nothing, Right?

The suppliers who build subject-matter courses try to minimize the use of media and learner interaction in their courses because it takes more development time and resources to include these features. Their objective is to provide content (conceptual or otherwise) as quickly and cheaply as possible. To these suppliers it's a time-to-market issue, a case of quantity over quality. Adding engaging features and simulations simply reduces the time spent getting their courseware onto the market (and reduces their profits). By getting to the market first, the supplier can ensure a continued customer base, even though these customers may not be satisfied.

Skills-Based Courseware: Is Increasing Job Skills Our Objective?

Life is either a daring adventure or nothing at all.

Helen Keller

Winning isn't everything, it's the only thing.

Vince Lombardi

Increased Job Performance Is the Goal of Training

The goal of training should be to deliver performance-based instruction. The learners need to apply the right amount of information to close their current skills gap so that they can improve job performance. Therefore, a skills-based course must ensure that the learners have the desired skill so that they can quickly leave the training and return to more productive work. The fundamental design seeks to move the learner from training to real-life application as quickly as possible. This is a basic practice of all accepted theories on adult learning. Proper selection and use of these courses will provide a clear return on the dollars your organization invests in training. This is not a novel idea, but it is one that will ensure your ongoing popularity in your organization.

Adults Learn Best by Doing

Typically, learners who complete skills-based training say, "I have learned what I need to know; now I'm ready to use it in my job." The primary reason for using technology to deliver the training is so that the learners can control their access to the information. Learners are able to obtain the training when they need it or use it to refresh their knowledge. This approach to training depends on good instructional design and a wide range of training deployment options. Good courses and effective deployment are both necessary for a successful technology-based training program. You can't have one without the other. Deployment means getting the right training to the learners where and when they need it. It is a key factor in the success of this training approach.

Mastering a Skill Is a Great Motivator

Mastery of skills through testing is the true measure of how effectively skills-based training has accomplished its objectives. Pretesting filters out the learner's prior knowledge and adjusts the course instruction to focus on the skills and knowledge the learner does not possess. Mastery testing at the completion of a portion of the course will provide evidence of the learner's skills. Unlike the temporary fun of a sizzle course, the feeling of accomplishment a learner gets by mastering a skills-based test is significant and intrinsically gratifying.

Continuous Improvement Always Requires New Skills

Skills-based courses work for a wide range of organizations, from traditional environments to high-performance work groups. Typically, the skills-based approach is best received in dynamic, fast-paced organizations that value continuous improvement. These organizations tend to foster respect-oriented, collaborative, open relationships with their employees. In most cases it is assumed that the learner is motivated to perform and is capable of self-direction. Some organizations have policies that link learning to job orientation and to the individual learner's career path.

One More Tip

The more you follow these guidelines when evaluating courses, the more you will be able to distinguish between the various types of courseware: the good (skills-based), the bad (subject matter), and the pretty (sizzle). Resolve now to not waste your time dealing with sizzle or subject-matter suppliers. Remember, if the courses you are buying do not teach, nothing else matters. Most courseware suppliers have sample versions of their courses available from their Web sites. You can download the courses and perform your own evaluation before seeing a sales representative.

WHEN TALKING TO SUPPLIERS, WHY DO YOU NEED QUESTIONS?

Most buyers are poorly prepared to seek out information about off-the-shelf suppliers. A well-thought-out series of open-ended questions can be a valuable tool. The following series of 60 probing and open-ended questions has been developed to ensure that you choose the best training partner for your organization. These questions can be modified, increased, or even placed in a request for a proposal. Use them to your advantage. The intent of this section is to present questions and specific requests you can make to a supplier's sales representative so that you can evaluate whether the supplier will fulfill its role as an effective partner and a provider of high-quality training products.

The questions appear in the order of their importance for you. Since your first priority is the training provided by the courseware, the questions dealing with your needs are placed first, with general information about the supplier placed last. You obviously need to know whether the course can teach and has the right amount of content before you become serious about a relationship.

Remember, there are a lot of very good salespeople with great products. These people are professionals, and they like to be asked direct and meaningful questions. This process gives them an opportunity to respond to you, bringing out the more important features and functions of their products. This is good for you too. Good sales professionals tend to stay focused on your needs and can clearly explain how using their products will best serve you and your training audience.

By contrast, if salespeople don't have a good product or don't know how to answer your questions, they will resort to all sorts of nasty sales tactics. These could include negative selling, indifference to your questions, outright arrogance, an overemphasis on minor features, and other ploys. Therefore, when a supplier resorts to these tactics, be suspicious. Consider acting like Sergeant Friday on *Dragnet* and ask them to just stick to the facts.

What Is Your Training Vision?

Before proceeding with a series of in-depth questions for your supplier, perhaps you should take a moment to verify your vision, beliefs, and values concerning your mission as a training leader. This exercise will allow you to think through the larger context of your training program. Without agreement on some of the following points, you may become distracted by all the possibilities off-the-shelf courseware may provide.

The following are some assumptions being made about your training vision:

- *You respect your learners.* You show respect by following valid adult
  learning principles. This commitment causes you to recognize the value of

your learners' time, knowledge, and experiences. You know that your learners have very little time, and you want to focus the training on their skill gaps so that they can complete the learning as effectively as possible.

- *Your training is learnercentric versus instructorcentric.* This means that you design your programs around what is best for the training audience, not around the ego of the instructor.

- *You want to see an increase in skills and knowledge in the work environment.* To you, training is not measured solely on a stack of smile sheets. You want the skills to provide behavioral change and business results (measured at Kirkpatrick's level 3 or 4). Therefore, your focus is on producing solid business outcomes rather than getting favorable reactions from learners.

- *You prefer meaningful interactions in courses and avoid page-turners.* You recognize that if only passive information or concepts are being delivered, methods other than technology-based training are far more useful and in some cases cheaper (such as books, audio, video, and the classroom).

- *Instructional design and course content are both important to you.* This is almost like the old chicken and egg debate since both are so important and interdependent. The course must teach (for example, the learning objectives must be linked to intelligent practices, which are linked to valid testing) or it has no value to your organization. The content of the course must be performance-oriented and deal with real-life topics that are covered in sufficient depth to meet your learning objectives.

- *You are not easily fooled by clever pricing schemes.* You seek the highest value for your training dollar. You steer clear of suppliers that manipulate course titles by reducing the content within a course so that you must purchase multiple courses in order to equal the content coverage of a single, better course.

- *You want training deployed so that learners can take it anytime, anywhere.* You envision the "training mountain" going directly to the learners wherever or whenever they need it, not requiring the learner to come to a specific location at a certain time. You want the training delivered via CD-ROM, LAN, or the Web, and these courses also should mix well with your current classroom courses.

Instructional Effectiveness Questions

If you tell me, I will listen.
If you show me, I will see.
If you let me experience, I will learn.

Lao Tzu

1. *How do your courses make use of sound instructional design principles?* If the salesperson gives you a blank or dazed look and begins to stammer the moment you ask this question, resolve to end the interview immediately. If you decide to continue, the following questions in this section will help pinpoint this bigger question. If they do respond, listen for common sense (objectives, practices, pretesting, posttesting, interaction, proper use of media, learner control, ease of deployment, simulation, learner tracking, etc.). Take notes on the supplier's strengths so that you can test its integrity when you evaluate the products later. See if the salesperson sticks with solid instructional design explanations, showing evidence of proven theories and practices. Look for methods from experienced instructional design (ID) masters such as Mager, Bloom, Gagne, Merrill, and Keller. Disregard references to new age experts or training fad of the week celebrities. You may want to review instructional design issues or involve an instructional designer in the interview. Better yet, allow an instructional designer to review the course before the interview. Usually you can do this by downloading a course from the supplier's Web site.

2. *What are the navigational features available to assist my learners in taking your course?* Your learners need to be free to control the pace of the course, review the material, go forward or backward, and look at help information or learning objectives as desired. Look for several basic features. These must include a how-to-take-the-course tutorial, a course menu, a course map, bookmarking features, help functions, allowance for nonsequential processing, a notepad option, exit options, and flexible control over learner features. These are common elements expected in each of the supplier's courses no matter how they are deployed. These features are available to enhance the learning and provide the learner with great flexibility. If any of these functions is missing, it will be too difficult for your learners to navigate the course.

3. *How do your courses help my learners achieve certification status?* Try to determine if the supplier used the learning objectives from the certification program to develop its courses. Hopefully, the supplier has linked its training practices and course testing to the certification exams. If the supplier has done so, your learners will have a better chance of becoming certified. Request some credible evidence from the supplier to prove this point. Otherwise, there is no way to be certain that this criterion has been met.

4. *Does your courseware offer both pretesting and mastery posttesting?* If they do not have testing, then this becomes a show stopper. Consider ending the interview immediately and returning all the sales materials. Testing is necessary to confirm that the learner has mastered the course materials. Pretesting allows the course to filter out prior learning so that learners who may already know the material require less time. The goal of this part of the training is to train for the skills gap only. Posttesting verifies the overall mastery of an entire set of skills. The course should regularly quiz the learners during the practices to assist their understanding of the material, particularly during the more complex parts of the instruction. Additionally, ask if the learner is regularly quizzed during the instruction.

5. *How important is testing to you? Describe your testing philosophy.* Additional questions to ask include: When a learner retakes a test, does it look the same as it did when he or she took it previously? How can I be sure that your test questions reflect the same level of objectives as the instruction? Do you use true-false questions only? If the course does test but only provides a simple, repeatable quiz, consider ending the interview. The best testing philosophy is to have a random series of test questions that ensure that the learner understands and can demonstrate the skills being taught. However, if the test is repeated verbatim, it's very easy for a learner to record answers and obtain a high score without retaking the course. Perhaps someone you know got through college using this method. If this is done, testing is of little value and you cannot be assured that the training has been effective. The use of random questions means that the learner takes a different test each time, eliminating memorization of the answers. This forces the learner to be "skills-smart" (good) versus "test-smart" (bad). Avoid true-false questions and you will eliminate mastery by guessing. Look for multiple-choice questions instead; simulation questions (step-based) are even better. Testing should be done at the level of the instruction. The lesson objectives should have one or more test items linked to each objective. If they do not, the testing may be causal, arbitrary, or superficial.

6. *I just hate page-turners; don't you? Tell me about interactivity in your courses.* It's time for a definition. In some courses *interactivity* is a euphemism for a lot of mouse clicking or page turning. Real interactivity in any course means that the learner is fully engaged with the skills-based instruction by doing something meaningful, such as opening a file, entering some data, moving something around, or answering a question directly tied to a real-life business situation. Getting lost in the course or in the software or having fun with cartoons and games does not count as interaction; it is wasted time. A rule of thumb is that at least one-third of the instruction should engage the learner in a learning activity before the course can truly be called interactive. It is very difficult to have real learner interaction unless simulation is built into the course. Therefore, simulation equals interaction and no simulation equals no interaction. This also applies if the course content is mostly conceptual because there is little content to engage the learner.

7. *In your course, what is the ratio of skills taught to concepts explained?* Since skills training allows the learner to apply the learning sooner, concepts should prepare the learner to move into the skills training. If the course has too many concepts and too few skills, the learner will need additional training (maybe in a classroom) to become productive, increasing training costs and time. If the course is mostly concepts, consider using an alternative approach (videotape may be a cheaper medium). The percentage of the mix is the key. A smaller percentage of concept instruction versus skill instruction is needed. The general rule of 80 to 20 applies here. At least 80 percent of the courses should focus on skills, and no more than 20 percent should focus on concepts.

8. *When training on the actual content, do you rely on the real software to teach?* This is a "gotcha" question. Relying on the real software is not a good training method. If the course supplier does, the course is a tutorial, not a skill-based course. Requiring the learner to return to the real software means the learner is on his or her own and can't obtain important feedback. Simulations will control the instruction for the learner and give immediate feedback. Some suppliers place a token amount of simulations in their courseware so that they can make misleading claims. If this is the case, the amount of simulation in the course is the key question, not the type of simulation. Subject-matter course suppliers usually do this to retrofit their products to compete with skills-based courses. Training on the application without the application software allows you to do a better job of migration training. You should also expect to see simulation used heavily in the testing segments. Remember, if they are selling a tutorial, the true cost of your training includes the course *plus* the software for each learner. If control is also an issue, they now have the software in place before they are trained in the use of it.

9. *How is the training organized? Describe how you break up the instruction.* The word for which you are looking is *chunking.* If the course is chunked, it provides training in learning bites and can be delivered to your learners easily in smaller amounts of time. Since smaller amounts of learner time are available, the training must serve the learners' needs by teaching only a single objective in each chunk or learning object. If the learner must take in large amounts of data, training and time to learn are both lengthened and compromised. Chunking also aids the deployment and customization of training. It allows the objects to quickly transfer to the learner and allows you to modify the objects.

10. *Do all your courses have a consistent look and feel?* You save a lot of time and money if the courses look the same to everyone. If a different look is used for one group of courseware and not the other, support and assistance could be compromised. The same look across the supplier's courses means that it has engineered the same instructional design and methods into all of its courses. A different look indicates that two or more completely different development groups probably were involved and you are actually dealing with a broker.

11. *Are workbooks required for your courses?* This is another "gotcha" question. If the courses are interactive, why does the supplier provide workbooks? In addition, if the workbook is optional (which is okay), is it provided free of charge? Is it in electronic form so that it can be modified and printed only if you decide to use it? If not, can you make copies free of charge? Remember that if you have to pay for a new workbook for each learner, it will increase the cost of the training.

12. *Can I customize the course?* You may desire this option. A good guideline for any off-the-shelf course is that it meet at least 80 percent of your training needs.

Suppliers generally build their courses to fit a broad audience, and yours may not need all the available course topics. In some cases you may need to add a unique topic. If the course is good, the likelihood is that you will have too much content. Therefore, removing some of the course content is an option you might want so that your learners do not waste time learning skills they will not use.

13. *Can you give me a short demonstration of the course?* This is a fundamental request. You can learn a lot from looking at the course. You need to see the actual product from the salesperson's point of view. This step will get the supplier off the sales pitch and force him or her to explain how the product is appropriate for you. Be prepared to listen closely and take notes. View the demo or an actual course during the first meeting with the salesperson. If this meets your criteria for success, you are justified in continuing the relationship. If it does not, no amount of discussion will improve the product. It will also be enlightening to see if the salesperson can present an effective explanation of the product as it meets your needs. It may pay to have someone who has instructional design experience in attendance also. Do not allow a demo using a supplier's sampler or demo course. Samplers are built to show the best side of a course. You can't train with the demo version; ask to see the real thing.

14. *How does the training perform when operating from a LAN or on an Intranet?* You need to determine how well the network version works in an environment similar to yours. Ask the supplier to provide a reference you can visit or at least call. You also need to know if the help desk can assist you with any problems you may experience while running the courses on your network.

Course Content Questions

Computers are useless. They can only give you answers.

Pablo Picasso

15. *What content coverage do you have in your catalogue?* Expect the supplier to have a full range of technical, desktop, and professional courses. For example, if the training is for software, all the major software providers for the information technology (IT) professional and for the desktop user should be addressed. These include Microsoft, Novell, Oracle, Lotus, Netscape, SAP, client-server, and networking topics. If professional certification is your goal, the courses should be mapped to each of the exams. Expect the supplier to have comparative data about its coverage of the certification exam and ask the supplier to show you how it compares to its competitors. Since the use of Microsoft Office desktop applications is growing in popularity, look for courses mapping to MOUS (Microsoft Office User Specialist).

16. *Do your courses have the depth of training my audience needs?* Your chief concern is whether the course content is accurate and up-to-date. It is best to have one or more of your subject-matter experts involved in this process. Ask the salesperson to show you and the SME the contents of preselected topics; this should reassure you that the supplier has both the depth and the currency of content. If not, you may want the SME to take the entire course.

17. *Do you codevelop courses with your larger technical providers?* Development alliances with large software developers (e.g., Microsoft, Oracle, Novell, Cisco) are extremely important. These alliances ensure robust, accurate courses with comprehensive content treatment and optimum time to market. Check for the highest level of certification and relationship.

18. *Do these providers use your courseware to train or certify their own people?* Usually, marketing agreements create partnership statements about the supplier's courses that sound appealing, but this question seeks to discover whether the developer uses the supplier's products to train its own internal people for certification. This is a powerful endorsement. Be sure to get a specific reference to call. Because of marketing connections, it is difficult to discover the truth regarding the relationship between the provider and the supplier of the training.

19. *Do you understand my training requirements? Please explain them to me.* This is a process question that seeks to verify the supplier's understanding of your needs. In other words, have the supplier repeat back to you what it understands your needs to be. Obviously, the supplier's sales representative is concerned about making a sale. Therefore, you should ensure that they are listening to you and matching their products to your needs. Otherwise, you will be accommodating their needs, not yours. Be sure to ask if the sale includes implementation support and ask for references about the supplier's postsale support.

20. *Will there be any charge for assisting us in a short-term pilot of the courses?* This is only a test. In fact, it is a willingness test. This question is posed to determine the supplier's eagerness to assist you in performing an objective evaluation of its products regardless of whether you intend to go forward. If they provide the materials and the support, you have a good candidate for a future partnership. If they want you to pay the full amount up front, you have found out early on that their talk of a partnership may be untrue. Of course, if your evaluation process is substantial, expect to pay for a portion of the effort; that is only fair.

21. *Do you provide "live" courses for evaluation, or do you have demo versions?* Here's an alternative to the above question: It's better to evaluate the "live" or full course than to make your decision after viewing a demo or sampler version. The demo version selects the best portions of the course (the "sweet spots") and, while truthful, can be misleading. Expect the supplier to lend you the courses for a short evaluation process. The supplier may teach you to set up the course prior to releasing it to you. This is understandable and very appropriate since they want you to be successful. If they don't want to lend their courses to you, maybe there is something they don't want you to see.

22. *Have your courses been transferred from an older medium to a new medium?* This is a big "gotcha" question. What you are looking for is "repurposed" content. This means they have moved some older content (video) to multimedia and perhaps enhanced it with some sound or animation before placing it on a CD-ROM. If it was bad then, it will be bad now. It's called "shovelware, " a collection of old repurposed material used to quickly build up an impressive set of multimedia titles for the catalogue.

23. *Can my learners earn college credits for completing your courses?* This is a very positive feature for your organization and learners. It indicates that the supplier understands the need for academic accreditation as a motivator to the learner and has taken the trouble to obtain certification.

Deployment and Installation Questions

Armies can be resisted, but nothing can stop an idea whose time has come.

Victor Hugo

24. *Do you offer training on multiple platforms? If yes, which ones? If not, why not?* If you have learners at remote locations, you will need to look ahead to other options since you will grow in the deployment of training. At a minimum, look for CD-ROM, LAN, and Intranet deployment options for the courses. It is best if the supplier has consistent course architecture (look and feel) across the various platforms. Expect them to explain when it is best to use the various options. If they have not planned for multiple platforms, you may be dealing with a supplier with a huge investment in CD-ROM-only courses that is unable to make the shift to network-deliverable methods. Thank them for their time and move on.

25. *How compatible are your courses with my current platform?* You can use your current equipment if it isn't too old. Avoid buying high-end or state-of-the-art equipment just to run the courses. If you must upgrade, you need to know the total cost of the training so that you can factor it into your budget. You should also spot the true cost of special features (video, etc.) built into the courseware and determine if you are willing to pay for them.

26. *How do you deliver Web-based training (Intranet)?* If they don't deliver over the Web, you will have a deployment problem very soon. Most suppliers can at least download courses using a lengthy file transfer method. This is risky, but it can be done. Some use plug-ins or software to work with the Web. It is best to choose sophisticated suppliers who use either learning object download or a browser playable from the Web, which saves time and in some cases can be platform-independent (meaning that you can train using those Mac and Unix workstations).

27. *How easy is it to set up and use your courses?* This test is to ensure that you can install and use the products with little overhead and trouble. Try to install the course without the assistance of the salesperson.

28. *Can you deliver audio and text? Can you deliver it over my network?* Both text and sound increase the learning methods (modalities) for the learners. Both are effective and should be available.

29. *Do you have local support to assist me with the implementation of this training program?* Expect to receive a yes to this question. Choose a supplier willing to come to your site to help with the implementation and help train your staff to use the products.

Training Administration Questions

Things won are done; joy's soul lies in the doing.

Shakespeare

To be or not to be, that is the question.

Shakespeare

To do is to be.

Sigmund Freud

To be is to do.

Immanuel Kant

30. *Do you provide a data management system to track training delivered to my learners?* Technology-based training suppliers must provide a system to do this; there is no other choice. Launching and tracking courses require an open administration system that will handle courses developed by multiple suppliers. If the supplier's system handles only its own products, it is trying to restrict your choices. It is not likely that a single supplier has the answers to all your training needs.

31. *Could I have a short demonstration of your data management system?* This is a fundamental request. You need to see the package working in conjunction with the courses. The system should be feature-rich for the administrator and simple to use for the learner. See enough of the system to be sure it is rigorous enough for your demands.

32. *Does your data management system track training on the LAN? On the Intranet?* This is an important feature. Most courses have an administration system for a single desktop that covers CD-ROM courses. However, since more and more training is being delivered remotely, via LAN or an intranet, you will need a package that can operate and look the same over the different platforms.

33. *Can your system import information from my existing system?* You want to eliminate all the unnecessary conversion work possible. The ability to take existing data into the supplier's system is essential and should be one of the fundamental features of the system.

34. *Does your system provide a customized reporting system?* You will need feedback from your learners about their reaction to the supplier's courses. In addition, you need the ability to compose the questions you expect them to answer when they complete the course. As you go forward with your program, you probably will need some important marketing and financial information too. Custom reports will let you keep track of the groups taking training. The system needs to tell you quickly if you are missing your target with some of your market segments. Sooner or later you will have to prove your business impact and utilization to those concerned with the financial impact of the training. Data proving that people are really taking the training can be vital.

Product Development Questions

Decide what you want;
decide what you are willing to exchange for it.
Establish your priorities and go to work.

H.L. Hunt

35. *Do you have a quality process to ensure that your products will be problem-free?* Nobody is perfect; however, requiring the supplier to describe its quality process to you is essential. If they have made an investment in the testing process, you can expect a relatively error-free product.

36. *How many professionals do you have on your product development staff?* Evaluate the number of full-time professionals on the development staff just as you would examine a doctor's diploma before an operation. A number of people with doctorates in instructional design is a good indicator of a quality product. You want to guarantee that the supplier is committed to its development plans, and a highly qualified staff is a good sign.

37. *How much are you investing in new course development?* It is important that the supplier invest heavily in new course development. The size of the development budget is a good indicator of its commitment to its training philosophy and customers. The larger the investment, the better for you. A good rule of thumb is to look at an investment ranging from 10 to 20 percent of gross revenue. You should be wary if you find that they are not building new products. What plans do they have for their future, which is also your future?

38. *How well do you meet your forecasts for developing new products?* Again, nobody is perfect, but you need to determine if the supplier has a good track record in meeting his or her course development plans. Typically, the supplier may not have the course you need on the shelf right now, but if it will be produced according to the development plan, it may be worth the wait. Things don't always go as planned, but you need to know whether they have a serious commitment to meeting their plans or if they are using a plan as a "bait and switch" sales technique.

39. *Have you localized your courses into other languages? If so, which ones?* An affirmative answer to this question means you are dealing with a serious global training supplier. If you are also in a global business, this is very important. In addition to English, the standard languages to look for include Spanish, French, German, and Japanese. Be sure the course operates similarly and has the same look and feel.

40. *How do your courses integrate with my classroom training?* You will always need classrooms. In several cases you will need to integrate your training into a classroom program. Be sure the course fits comfortably into a well-designed classroom delivery system. Ask for examples and ask whether the supplier is working with classroom providers.

Pricing and Contracting Questions

41. *What pricing models do you provide?* The supplier should provide you with a variety of models from which to choose. The first option is a single-user license that allows you to provide training to a specific individual at the lowest possible price. The next option is a multiple-user license that gives you the right to allow as many learners as you wish to take the course. The price for this is usually much higher. Other possibilities include network-only, enterprisewide, and pay-as-you-use options. It is beneficial to be aware of the pricing models early in the sales relationship.

42. *How does your pricing compare to the market?* Additional questions are: Are discounts available for larger purchases? And does the discount rate increase as the contract term increases? Expect that with increased purchases and an extended contract period, you will receive increased discounts. Ask the supplier to compare its prices with those of other suppliers. Determine if they are willing to be flexible with those prices to assist you in meeting your goals or if they are rigid and insist on doing business their way. Remember to get what you want for the best price, but don't buy sizzle or subject-matter courses simply because you got a good deal. You always pay too much for what you don't need.

43. *Do you offer a simple license agreement?* Demand that they be easy to do business with and provide a simple agreement along with the option to return the product if it doesn't meet your expectations. Subject-matter suppliers usually try to lock you in to their products. If a better skills-based course is released later, you must be able to get out of the agreement.

44. *Do you have proof that they are not splitting up your courses into smaller course titles and increasing the overall prices?* Expose "title inflation" by asking them to compare their courses to those of the leading competitor. Look for the same content in a curriculum and compare the total price.

Customer Service Questions

45. *Do you provide toll-free support?* A toll-free number is essential. You do not want to pay extra for service when you have difficulty with the courseware.

46. *What are your support hours?* The more hours available, the better. Seven days with 24-hour service is the best option, particularly if you have learners training around the clock. Test the service by calling them several times at regular and odd hours. Better yet, call the support center before you speak with the salesperson.

47. *What expertise is available to me?* Expect them to offer expert advice and help you with a wide range of problems. Also, expect to have friendly, helpful people at the other end of the telephone. You deserve it.

Sales and Marketing Questions

Victory belongs to the most persevering.

Napoleon

48 . *Who is your primary competitor, and what does it do best?* This is a true test of character for any salesperson. Check out the competition in advance. Whether or not you shop around is not the point; you want to know how they will respond (positively or negatively) to the question. Expect them to give you at least one competitor's name and one of that supplier's strengths. However, don't expect the salesperson to promote the competitor. If they reply that they have no competition, they are afraid to let you know about the competition, or perhaps they are too arrogant for their own good. Either way, you know they are withholding information. If they make a big deal and put down the competition, they probably are engaged in negative selling. Negative selling is a mudslinging technique used to compare their features with the features of their closest competitor and force you to choose. If you get pulled into deciding which is the better organization, you probably will forget about your original objectives.

49. *What additional resources do you have to assist me in implementing my training program?* You may be buying more than electronic media and manuals; in most cases you are building a strategic training solution. Make sure the supplier offers not only a solid product but also a support team that can assist you in making the solution work. Ask to meet some members of the team so that you know their skills.

50. *Do you have global office locations with local technical support?* Be sure to obtain a listing of international locations and call to verify the level of support they will provide for your training sites.

Customer-Base Questions

Imagination is more important than knowledge.

Albert Einstein

51. *What organizations make up your customer base?* Look for corporate, industry, or academic organizations similar to yours. In all cases, the existing customer base should be from the Fortune 1000 with a good representation from the top 100. If they have a global business, ask for international references. If their primary market segment is consumer or retail sales, their courses may appeal more to the teenager than to the adult corporate learner.

52. *When can I meet some of your more established and loyal customers?* Long-term customer relationships are a true indicator of consistent quality service and industry leadership. Call two or more of the references that seem close to your training environment. Ask for a site visit with one or more customers who are using the supplier's courses.

53. *When can I meet some customers who left you and then returned?* It is great to meet the customers who stayed around; better yet, look for those who left and came back. These customers may have a story you would like to hear.

54. *Do you include customers in your strategic planning process? How?* Determine if the supplier conducts regular ongoing partnerships or customer meetings at which it discusses how to increase the productive use of its courses. Learn if they truly listen to what the customers say they want and need. Most suppliers need to be customer-driven and aligned with your training future as much as possible.

Financial and Organizational Questions

Lack of money is the root of all evil.

G. B . Shaw

55. *How many years have you been in business?* The more years they have been in business, the better. You want a long-term relationship with a supplier who has a good reputation and will continue to develop more courseware. Start-up companies tend to disappear very quickly. The market can be very fickle.

56. *Are you currently experiencing business growth or decline?* It is important for the supplier to be in a growth mode. Since the training business is booming, something is very wrong with their products or their leadership if they are not making money. Business vision and the ongoing development of high-quality courseware are essential to the supplier's organization.

57. *Are any active class-action lawsuits being filed against your company? Why?* Do your homework first and check the Internet before you ask this question. You can find out about the supplier's public dirty laundry by checking with the Yahoo search site at http://biz.yahoo.com. If the lawsuit is frivolous, the salesperson should fill in the blanks for you. Maybe the lawsuit has some validity. If the supplier has a serious integrity issue, that could well be reflected in what the salesperson is telling you.

58. *Who owns your company?* Determine if the company is owned by a parent that is as interested in developing courseware or is interested in industry-related acquisitions and growth only in nontraining areas.

59. *What is your company's mission statement?* Determine if they are primarily committed to their training mission. Ask what percentage of their business is dedicated to providing high-quality technology-based training.

60. *How secure is your organization financially?* It's acceptable if the supplier has had some ups and downs in the past, but you need to know that it can pay its bills and is not likely to be going out of business soon.

CHAPTER 13

Converting Your Curriculum: How to Choose the Right Course

Robert A. Steinmetz, MA, PhD
Ann Kwinn, PhD

Objectives

After reading this chapter, you will be able to:

- Identify the complete range of variables to consider in choosing the "best" course or courses to convert.
- Use the provided guidelines to evaluate the specific courses in your curriculum.
- Select the best candidates for successful conversion.
- Justify your choices to others in the organization.

You have been asked to evaluate a relatively complete curriculum and select the courses you are going to convert to technology-based training. You can't convert them all, and you probably shouldn't. The question, then, is which ones should you convert, and probably equally important, which ones should you convert first?

It would be great if the answer were simple. Unfortunately, like most issues in a technological age, the decision is not clear-cut. Also, the consequences of failure are too costly and damaging to your credibility for you to embark on a "hit and miss" adventure. This chapter explores the numerous factors you should consider in your quest to choose the right courses, presents some case studies illustrating what others have done when faced with this challenge, and provides some job aids you may be able to use in your own unique environment.

MONEY, POLITICS, AND OTHER CONSIDERATIONS

There are several categories of variables to consider in deciding which courses to convert to mediated delivery methods (Table 13–1). The common tendency is simply to look at the types of instruction involved and then select one on the basis of its inherent "transferability" to technology-based training. You do a great disservice to yourself and to your sponsoring organization by taking such a myopic or single-focus perspective. The truth is that you should consider a host of factors, including not just the objective or instructional aspects but the political and economic aspects as well.

The economic considerations are dealt with quite extensively in Chapter 14. This chapter explores the other equally critical decision criteria.

Babies Don't Buy Baby Food

Political or subjective criteria often are ignored or disparaged in the academic and professional training worlds. In the noble mission to impart knowledge and skills to the audiences we serve, we tend to discount the inclinations of others on the corporate and administrative ladders. In so doing, we can easily ignore the fact that the success of all our course conversion efforts is dependent on multiple audiences.

We all recognize that when a course fails to meet the needs of the targeted students, it means we have failed and the likelihood or ease of future success is threatened or at least brought into question. Equally crucial in the success or failure equation are the desires of those who provide access to the resources we need for development. If executives, administrators, field management, our peers, and others who directly or indirectly influence our access to resources do not realize a significant benefit from our conversion efforts, we will fail. It will only be a matter of time before we hear a chorus of comments such as "You know, that multimedia stuff just doesn't work in our environment."

Remember that babies don't buy baby food. Just because one has designed a nutritious product, it doesn't mean parents will buy it off the shelves. The subjective aspects are just as important as the objective ones. If we are to build skills and knowledge into the repertoires of our end users, we must clearly satisfy the needs and wants of the high-level "influencers" and decision makers, whether they are local managers, corporate managers, administrators, information technology (IT) support groups, executives, or oversight boards.

TABLE 13-1

How to Choose the Right Course for Conversion

For each statement, rank its appropriateness to the course you have in mind.

	Politics				
Statement	**Strongly Disagree 1**	**Disagree 2**	**Neutral 3**	**Agree 4**	**Strongly Agree 5**
Will this course be welcomed by the end-user group as a computer-based training (CBT) course?	☐	☐	☐	☐	☐
Will this course be welcomed by the supervisors of the end users?	☐	☐	☐	☐	☐
Will the current instructors support the conversion of this course?	☐	☐	☐	☐	☐
Will this course dramatically affect the mission of others in the organization?	☐	☐	☐	☐	☐
Can the course be presented or "packaged" in a way that makes it appealing to higher-ups?	☐	☐	☐	☐	☐
Does the existing course need improvement (spicing up)?	☐	☐	☐	☐	☐
Is the course in high demand?	☐	☐	☐	☐	☐
Is standardization or consistency especially important?	☐	☐	☐	☐	☐
Sponsor					
Do you have a sponsor for this course conversion who is influential at multiple levels in the organization?	☐	☐	☐	☐	☐
Do you have a sponsor who is likely to remain in his or her current position for at least 6 months after program rollout?	☐	☐	☐	☐	☐
Logistics					
Is the student population of this course geographically dispersed?	☐	☐	☐	☐	☐
Might the trainees need the material before the scheduled class times?	☐	☐	☐	☐	☐
Is there a sense that the current training is taking students away for too long?	☐	☐	☐	☐	☐

Statement	Strongly Disagree 1	Disagree 2	Neutral 3	Agree 4	Strongly Agree 5
Are the students complaining that the course is too long?	☐	☐	☐	☐	☐
Is the turnover among trainees high?	☐	☐	☐	☐	☐
Is there a benefit to reviewing the course material after it is taught?	☐	☐	☐	☐	☐
Must large numbers of students be trained in a short period?	☐	☐	☐	☐	☐
Will large numbers of students (over 100) be trained eventually?	☐	☐	☐	☐	☐

Resources

Statement	Strongly Disagree 1	Disagree 2	Neutral 3	Agree 4	Strongly Agree 5
Is there ready access to similar types of computers among the target audience for this course?	☐	☐	☐	☐	☐
Can the equipment and development costs be capitalized?	☐	☐	☐	☐	☐
Are qualified instructors for this course hard to find?	☐	☐	☐	☐	☐
Is the transportation and housing of trainees becoming cost-prohibitive?	☐	☐	☐	☐	☐
Does the current course use equipment that could be used elsewhere?	☐	☐	☐	☐	☐

Instructional Objectives

Statement	Strongly Disagree 1	Disagree 2	Neutral 3	Agree 4	Strongly Agree 5
Does this course have strong "cognitive" components?	☐	☐	☐	☐	☐
Does the training seek to evoke strong emotions or motivation or create a sense of camaraderie?	☐	☐	☐	☐	☐
Is hands-on equipment required?	☐	☐	☐	☐	☐
Is the course content suited to simulation?	☐	☐	☐	☐	☐
Is there important material that students should practice frequently?	☐	☐	☐	☐	☐
Are you training people in software skills?	☐	☐	☐	☐	☐

Feasibility of Alternative Approaches

Statement	Strongly Disagree 1	Disagree 2	Neutral 3	Agree 4	Strongly Agree 5
Are there behaviors you would like to model in this course that would be hard to re-create in a classroom setting?	☐	☐	☐	☐	☐

Statement	Strongly Disagree 1	Disagree 2	Neutral 3	Agree 4	Strongly Agree 5
Have the course objectives been difficult to achieve with conventional methods?	☐	☐	☐	☐	☐
Do you have activities in mind, such as games, drill and practice, and problem solving, that could be re-created on a computer?	☐	☐	☐	☐	☐
Is damage to equipment, environment, or personnel likely in training with actual equipment?	☐	☐	☐	☐	☐
Does the necessary equipment or software exist? Or, is it hard to acquire?	☐	☐	☐	☐	☐
Are there at least 6 months for course development before rollout?	☐	☐	☐	☐	☐
Is the subject matter reasonably stable?	☐	☐	☐	☐	☐

Learner Characteristics

Statement	Strongly Disagree 1	Disagree 2	Neutral 3	Agree 4	Strongly Agree 5
Do the students for this course vary widely in ability?	☐	☐	☐	☐	☐
Do the students vary widely in job responsibilities?	☐	☐	☐	☐	☐
Does this course target entry-level employees?	☐	☐	☐	☐	☐
Will the students for this course benefit from individualized instruction?	☐	☐	☐	☐	☐

Record Keeping

Statement	Strongly Disagree 1	Disagree 2	Neutral 3	Agree 4	Strongly Agree 5
Are reports of individual, group, and course progress required periodically?	☐	☐	☐	☐	☐
Is there a desire to automate student record information and perhaps integrate it with other human resources data?	☐	☐	☐	☐	☐
Is annual recertification required?	☐	☐	☐	☐	☐
Would it be beneficial to track the time it takes students to complete segments of the course?	☐	☐	☐	☐	☐
Is there a need for course security (blocking some students' access to a course)?	☐	☐	☐	☐	☐

Sum your responses. If you have a score of 157 to 225, your course is an excellent candidate for conversion. If you have a score of 112 to 156, your course is a good candidate, but it may not take advantage of all of the benefits of CBT. If you have a score of 0 to 111, technology-based training may not be appropriate for your course.

When you consider a course for conversion, don't forget to ask yourself the following questions:

- How big a "splash" will it make?
- To what extent will it be welcomed by the end-user group?
- To what extent will it be welcomed by the supervisors of the end users?
- Am I taking away a course people like to teach in its current mode?
- Which of the courses under consideration will most dramatically affect the mission of others in the organization?
- Can it be packaged in a way that makes it appealing to higher-ups?

Do You Believe in Angels?

Closely related to the subjective or political criteria is the notion of a sponsoring angel. The potential viability of a course for conversion is one thing; success in executing that conversion effort is another thing altogether. Without successful execution, the results are obvious: failure to achieve your instructional objectives and questionable support for subsequent conversions.

If the course you are considering for conversion is not championed by an influential and dynamic supporter high up in the organization, you will encounter obstacles all along the way that will distract you from your design and development activities and threaten your ultimate success. In fact, in an informal survey of project managers in the middle of conversion efforts, the need for an "angel" was cited as the greatest single determinant of success.

The course or courses you choose for conversion should have a strong and natural connection to the right kind of angel: one who

- Is influential at multiple levels in the organization
- Is very likely to remain in his or her current position for at least 6 months after program rollout
- Believes wholeheartedly in the program's goals
- Believes wholeheartedly in the media and methodology you plan to employ
- Is willing to support you without controlling every aspect of your effort (not a bottleneck)
- Is decisive

THE OTHER SIX THINGS TO CONSIDER

Now that we have addressed the more subjective aspects of the decision equation, let's turn to the variables educators and trainers find a bit more comfortable: the objective or more concrete aspects of the existing course being considered for conversion.

Logistics

One of the greatest benefits of technology-based training is the ability to deliver training where you need it and when you need it. When is this aspect of training most valuable? When the targeted students are distributed over a large geographic territory and need to be trained at different points in time.

Live training is a very acceptable form of administration when there is a relatively large population concentrated in one fairly centralized location and the students in that population need the training at the same time. While this may be the state of affairs in an academic environment, it is rarely the case in most industrial environments. In most organizations new individuals who need training are coming in all the time. If the organization is of significant size, those individuals are scattered around the country, if not internationally. What does this tell us in terms of the criteria for choosing the best course or courses? When you look at the courses up for consideration, ask yourself the following:

- Is it difficult or costly to assemble the audience in a centralized or region-alized classroom setting?
- Do the trainees need the course materials at a particular point during their tenure with the organization, or can they wait until a class is scheduled?
- Is the turnover among trainees (or the inflow of new people) such that a class has to be scheduled almost every couple of months?
- Is there a benefit to some sort of follow-up, remediation, recertification, or other requirement to "reach out and touch" trainees after they have left the classroom setting?

If the answer to these questions is yes, you have a good candidate for delivery where and when the trainees need it: on their desktops.

Available Resources

Technology-based instruction can be a very expensive proposition. How many times have we all heard the lament, "We just don't have the resources"? This is especially the case if you are just embarking on the path to conversion. While the issue is addressed more thoroughly in Chap. 14, consider for a moment the following simplified example.

The mission is to train 1800 cashiers at 120 stores (Washington, Oregon, and California) in the operation of a new electronic point-of-sale system. The costs of two types of training are shown here.

Live Instruction		Multimedia	
12 Trainers (28K/year)	$336,000	Equipment	$288,000
Travel and living	$ 25,000	Setup and transportation	$ 42,000
Student time (8 hours)	$144,000	Student time (4 hours)	$ 72,000
Material development costs	$ 25,000	Development costs	$190,000
Total	$530,000	Total	$592,000

Obviously, if the equipment is taken out of the equation, the resources required to convert the live training into technology-based training will be reduced dramatically. Similarly, if the equipment and development costs can be capitalized, the annual expenses for the conversion effort will be far more tolerable.

What does this mean when you are evaluating your own curriculum to select a candidate for conversion? It means that some courses may represent a better starting point than do others. For example, if one of the courses under consideration is intended for people with the technology already on their desktops, you have a lot of the necessary resources at hand. This makes it a far less costly undertaking than a course aimed at people with no access to the technology.

On the other side of the equation are the resources required for the live training you are considering converting. Often there is a shortage of people qualified to teach a particular topic or set of objectives. If there is such a shortage, once again you have an excellent candidate for conversion.

An interesting and often overlooked aspect of the resources issue involves the hardware requirements associated with the live training approach. Take, for example, computer skills training. In a workshop mode one obvious requirement is to have a workstation for each student. In the case of special-purpose technology, tools such as electronic cash registers, hand-held scanners, and electronic test equipment are needed for each student, but the tools sit idle between classes. It is not unusual for very costly equipment to sit idle 3 to 6 months out of the year; reserved and in place for the next live training session. By converting such a course to technology-based simulation training, you can become a hero to your chief financial officer. You will be converting a "resource utilization" figure from zero (i.e., not available for productive work) to something approaching 100 percent.

Instructional Objectives

What you are trying to teach should dictate the media and the methods you employ. Choosing a course for conversion to technology-based media is no exception. The instructional objectives should and do play a major role.

In considering which types of instructional objectives are most appropriate for conversion, one must consider three issues:

1. Which objectives are best left in "live" mode?
2. Which objectives are best for CDs or fast Intranets?
3. Which objectives are best for the Web or slower Intranets?

Live Isn't Necessarily Bad

While technology-based instruction can be beneficial to educators, it is not a panacea. Some training objectives are best left within the four walls of a classroom.

Technology-based training is a relatively cold format. While it can be engaging, it is not nearly as immersive as a live experience. There are exceptions, of course, such as state-of-the-art virtual reality. However, such exceptions tend to be cost-prohibitive for most training applications. For the most part, live instruction provides a greater opportunity to adequately address objectives that require a strong emotional ingredient. When you are confronted with objectives that embody things such as the following, you might want to leave the course in its live format:

- Esprit de corps, camaraderie, or networking
- Motivation to excel
- Encouragement to act and feel like part of a "larger" effort or group
- Emotional identification or empathy
- Insight into oneself

In general, when you are looking to achieve "experiential" or emotional types of outcomes, you probably should rely on a well-designed live experience.

Many people proffer the notion that the list of what works best in live training should also include just about every "soft skill." While the term *soft skill* is open to interpretation, it seems safe to conclude that a large contingent believes that technology-based training is not conducive to teaching things such as negotiating, teamwork, selling, and other skills with a strong behavioral component. These individuals could not be more wrong. While some sort of live interaction may be a very valuable adjunct (e.g., evaluation of the student as he or she executes the skills), there is no reason why the cognitive aspects of these skills cannot be addressed in a mediated program.

Good for Just about Everything

If instructional objectives in what one might call the "affective" domain do not lend themselves to easy conversion, which ones do? The answer for all intents and purposes is just about everything else. This includes rules, principles of behavior, the application of rules and principles, facts, concepts, and almost any type of objective from any pedagogue's taxonomy. In lay terms, this includes

- Interview techniques
- New hire orientations
- Selling skills
- Public speaking
- Computer software training
- Math skills
- Reading
- Report writing
- Business principles
- Management skills
- Negotiation
- Counseling
- Team building
- Customer service
- History
- Geography
- Safety
- Product knowledge
- Presentation techniques
- Nursing and patient care
- Medical diagnostics
- Crisis management
- Equipment and tools operation
- Equipment maintenance and repair

Although this list seems extensive, it could be argued that it is not extensive enough. If your candidates for conversion are in the "effective" realm and involve objectives with operational terms such as *identify, name, cite, compare and contrast, apply,* and *execute,* you probably have a viable candidate for successful transfer to technology-based training, all things being equal.

Unfortunately, in the world of technology, all things are not equal. As we all know, the capabilities available over the Web are significantly different from those available via personal computer (PC) resident programs. In relegating instructional objectives to these two forms of technology, you therefore should take the following position: *If the primary objectives do not require significant amounts of video, extensive animation, or any more than three or four of the following instructional devices, it is best to take advantage of the benefits available via the Web:*

- A prescribed set of experiences to be completed in a prescribed sequence (i.e., open architecture is not desired)
- Significant levels of remediation based on individual performance
- High levels of "redundancy" using alternative modes
- Rich graphics
- Large amounts of voice-over narration
- Significant branching based on user mastery and/or entry level
- Complex answer analysis
- Complex simulations

If your objectives involve rapidly changing information, "just-in-time" information, or a heavy dependency on text, the Web can be an ideal medium.

Feasibility of Alternative Approaches

Quite simply, this translates into "Do it right."

When you look at your curriculum, there are going to be a number of courses that just "pop out" as better if approached in a technology-based mode. By that I mean that the attainment of your true instructional or behavioral objectives is more feasible with the capabilities inherent in today's technology. Think about a workshop in which you wanted to represent a particular experience but were unable to, an experience that should be an integral part of your training strategy. Consider, for example, a course on handling distraught employees. It is obviously not completely feasible to realistically re-create a true crisis in the confines of a classroom. At best, one can attempt a role play using the more imaginative participants. Even with an innocuous topic such as customer service, it is not really feasible to re-create the full gamut of customer scenarios. Trainers often try to replicate these experiences through role-playing activities, skits, and group exercises, but these usually are a poor substitute for the richness of real-world experiences. While it may be feasible to bring media into the classroom to represent these situations, it is much more effective to immerse the trainees in the experience through technology.

Conversely, many live experiences cannot feasibly be converted into a technology-based approach. As was noted earlier, when a course is designed to provide insight or something akin to an "ah ha" phenomenon, is designed to build camaraderie, or is primarily affective in nature, it is not feasible to think it will translate into technology-based training.

In addition to "the experience," time is an important factor to consider in selecting courses for conversion. Time comes into play in two ways: time to develop and time to change. It takes a substantial amount of time to develop a good computer-based course, and often that time is not available. While many developers claim very aggressive schedules, it is not unreasonable to expect a development cycle of 6.5 to 9 months for a relatively rich and robust computer-based course. In contrast, an excellent workshop can be put together in a substantially shorter time frame.

When it comes to change, one of the best features of live training is that you can change it the night before or right in the middle of the workshop itself. If policies change or if the software being taught changes, you can adapt the live training experience almost instantaneously. It may not be pretty, but it is feasible.

Obviously, technology-based training requires a more involved change cycle. While the Web can reduce cycle time significantly through the elimination of media duplication and distribution efforts, it still takes far longer to change Web-delivered programs compared with live ones.

Before leaving this topic, I would like to rebut a common myth. More than once I have heard the claim, "We can't do technology-based training for this new software tool because the software is still under development." It is foolish to think it is not feasible to develop training for a software application until the underlying code is solidified. Software does not need to be operational for it to be taught on a technology platform. All you really need are the basic screen layouts and an understanding of how the screens will react to selected user inputs. In most instances it is quite feasible merely to mimic selected and limited aspects of the underlying programming. No "real" processing is needed in the "simulated" version used for instruction. The student will be taking a predictable and prescribed path through the screens, and the training program will rely on its own code to handle entry processing. Remember, this is simulation, not emulation. It is all smoke and mirrors, so why wait for the real thing?

In fact, technology-based training for software under development can be even more feasible than live training. The live training *is* truly dependent on the working application. An instructor cannot step the student through nonexistent software; only technology can do that.

Learner Characteristics: One Size Rarely Fits All

The area of learner characteristics probably represents one of the most compelling reasons for selecting a course for conversion. Perhaps the greatest single feature of technology-based delivery is its ability to take different learners on different instructional paths. Human beings do not necessarily all learn at exactly the same rate or in exactly the same manner. If you are a classroom instructor, you know from experience how frustrating a class composed of a very heterogeneous audience can be. You have seen those who sit at the front and try to dominate. You have seen those who sit in the rear and merely nod their heads. You have seen those who don't just nod but nod off. While good instructors try to adapt their presentations to the unique dynamics of the class makeup, there is only so much one can do. You generally have to aim for the mean, median, or mode. As a result, some people really get it, most of them sort of get it, and some never get it. With technology, you can ensure that everybody gets it. When is this most critical? When you have a very diverse audience. When the bell curve describing your students' entry levels is relatively flat. When

- Information-processing abilities, learning speed, and intelligence vary greatly
- Mastery of prerequisite facts, concepts, or skills is important and highly variable
- Different students have different needs and interests regarding the course content[1]

So, when you look at your curriculum, examine the audiences for which each course is targeted. Have you heard requests that courses be broken up to accommodate different entry levels? Are there subject areas that ideally should be treated differently for managers vs line workers? All these points of diversity are strong justification for moving a course to technology-based delivery.

In automated courseware you can assess entry levels, present different menus based on those levels, and use different tactics for feedback and remediation. You can have fast paths, medium paths, and slow paths. You can achieve the near equivalent of completely individualized instruction.

When the audience is widely divergent and the skills are essential, you have an excellent candidate for conversion.

The Dog Ate My Homework

Another important learner characteristic is preclass preparation. A good number of live classes require some sort of prework. This may include prereading, gathering materials, completing surveys or assignments, and/or case study preparation. How many times have you started a class only to find that too many students "just didn't have the time"? You've probably heard every excuse imaginable. If a class requires critical prework and the students aren't doing it, you should seriously consider offloading that portion to the Web. If one of your courses is more dependent than others on prework, you may have a good conversion candidate.

With the ability to instantaneously assess the status of your students, check their materials, and communicate with them before class, you are going to con-

---

[1]For example, in a course on safety, the relevant portions for someone in shipping may be quite different from those for someone in production.

dense the bell curve and skew it in a more positive direction. You may be able to reduce course length and ensure that students derive even greater benefit.

Some People Need Extra Help

Courses oriented toward entry-level trainees are ideal candidates for technology-based instruction. People who have trouble processing information of the type presented in classroom courses are probably the greatest beneficiaries of the features available with today's technology. These are the people who did not do very well in school. They do not look on the "classroom" as an attractive place to be, and the anxiety they feel in class interferes with their ability to learn and pick up new information. Conversion to computer-based training is one of the nicest things you can do for these trainees.

Technology-based instruction can be extremely friendly. It can significantly reduce the levels of anxiety students feel when they are called on. Technology-based instruction removes the pressure of sitting in a classroom feeling like everyone is watching and "you better get it" or "you better contribute."

Technology-based instruction can provide a much more sensitive form of remediation. It can put individuals through their own special learning paths without ever knowing they are receiving extra help. Fast learners can breeze through, and slow learners can take it one step at a time without any stigma.

Look at your courses and compare the complexity of the instructional objectives with the information-processing abilities of the student population.

- Is there a significant segment of the population for which the course is a bit tough?
- Are too few people passing the class test?
- Has the course been designed to "go slow" and a significant number of high achievers are complaining?

Closely associated with audience characteristics are what we might call delivery constraints. By this we mean hardships associated with getting to the classroom.

In many work environments it is difficult to put aside one's day-to-day responsibilities and dedicate a large block of time to attend a live class. Is the audience for a particular class in this situation? Do you have a class targeted at a group that for one reason or another has a high "no show" rate? You might be more successful in achieving the objectives for this class by making the instruction available in small chunks. If it is converted to technology-based delivery, the trainees can access it according to *their* schedule. They can take portions, leave, come back and review, and complete the course while handling other critical demands.

Record Keeping and Tracking Considerations

You are in a meeting, and your boss's boss asks, "So what are we getting for all those new training courses you worked on?" Conversion to technology-based training may give you the words he or she needs and wants to hear.

Technology-based instruction is naturally (or, more accurately, automatically) productive of excellent record keeping. You can measure just about anything you want to measure. In looking at your live classes, ask yourself, Are there things I would like to know about student performance that I can't easily derive from the live environment? Do you want to know how well students can apply what they are learning in a realistic simulation? Do you want to know how long it is taking to master a specific concept? These data points and almost any others you can imagine are very easily derived from technology-based courses. If any of your live courses suffers from a lack of good record keeping, conversion to technology may be the solution.

Let's explore these various record keeping issues in order, from pretraining, to the actual learning effort, to posttraining.

Preinstruction

One of the top 10 complaints of those who do stand-up instruction is that students arrive without the assigned prework or prerequisite skills. But what are you going to do? You can't send them home. Instead, examine your courses and look for those in which there has been a significant problem. As was noted earlier, you may want to use the Web as a "competency gate." You may want to convert a course or a portion of a course so that you can upload detailed records.

During Training

Within the actual training experience, technology-based instruction provides an opportunity to collect a host of data points, including things such as length of time in any particular segment, test scores, number of attempts at a test until mastery is achieved, specific problem areas, and user comments. With technology you can pinpoint concepts that are not being mastered, and your assessments can be instantaneous. You can accelerate people, route around concepts, and in general increase efficiency and mastery.

When you look at your live courses, if you see ones that obviously would benefit from more data about how the students are progressing, you can earmark those courses as conversion candidates.

After the Fact

Some of the courses in your curriculum invariably involve critical issues: those which need annual recertification or another sort of follow-up. Technology is great for this. Live courses on things such as safety, sexual harassment, hazardous material handling, and first aid often lack adequate means for assessing that post-training events are executed. If there is a course like this in your curriculum, you may want to move to technology-based delivery. Then you will be able to take advantage of its impressive review, assessment, and tracking capabilities. You will be more able to show "compliance" in sensitive and "high-exposure" issues.

SUMMARY

There are a wide range of factors to consider in deciding which courses to convert to technology-based instruction. Probably the best pieces of advice are the following:

1. Look for courses that are going to have the most impact and the quickest development schedule and that clearly benefit from the features and capabilities of technology.

2. Keep it simple. There is a tendency on the first conversion effort to "stuff the goose." This will bog you down. Remember that the first effort is going to pave the way for the second, third, and all subsequent efforts. If you pack the first one with every bell and whistle, where are you going to go after that? Start modestly and build from there.

3. Learn from the pros. Technology-based instruction has been around for quite a while. There are a lot of people out there who have worked with this technology from its inception. They have made a lot of mistakes and learned from their errors. Don't use your first conversion effort to relearn their mistakes.[2]

4. Sell, sell, sell. Do not assume that just because you do it right, everyone will welcome it with open arms. People resist change. No matter how well proven it is that computer-based training works and no matter how good your individual conversion effort is, some factions will disparage the results. To head this off at the pass, you need to involve the field at every key milestone during the development process. Get their concurrence on the courses to be converted, the scope of the training, the instructional strategies, and the plans for the rollout.

If you choose the right courses for the right reasons and then build them the right way, you will be a hero in your organization. Good luck.

The following case studies illustrate some of the authors' experience converting courses to technology-based training.

---

[2]The way you design a live course is very different from the way you design technology-based instruction. While both draw on creativity, a sense of pacing, knowledge of learning principles, and so on, technology-based instruction requires knowledge of a whole new net of factors. These include navigation conventions, screen layout, and answer analysis strategies, among a host of related variables.

CARTER HAWLEY HALE STORES:
A SOLUTION IN SEARCH OF A PROBLEM

In the days when technology-based training was the domain of the "early adopters," IBM asked Learning Systems Sciences to analyze the training requirements of one of its clients, Carter Hawley Hale (CHH) Department Stores. The top executives of CHH were intrigued by the capabilities of IBM's adventure into its version of technology-based training, which was called *Infowindow*. Those executives were willing to support a "proof of concept" project. They felt a fair degree of confidence in the features and capabilities of the IBM system. They believed that this technology might be a very viable solution in the retail arena. No one was sure, however, exactly where to begin.

Each of the key areas in the retail organization was examined for conversion candidates. Among the most promising were point-of-sale (i.e., register) training, sales training, and distribution center employee training. All these areas had diverse entry-level audiences, were geographically dispersed, and evidenced high turnover. The technology was very appropriate for the types of objectives to be mastered, and the subject matters were heavily directed toward skills and concepts.

While there were a number of reasons to support each candidate, they all had a couple of drawbacks. Each candidate course represented a fairly large and lengthy undertaking. This is not necessarily ideal for a proof of concept. In addition, the reception in each of the targeted areas was only moderate or lukewarm.

The search finally ended in the loss prevention area, where several critical factors indicated an ideal opportunity for conversion to technology-based training.

The subject was detecting and apprehending shoplifters. This appeared to be an ideal candidate from almost every perspective except one: The population of store detectives, while distributed geographically, was comparatively small in number. Under most circumstances this could have weakened the business case. What compensated for the reduced audience size was the magnitude of the impact on the organization. Store detectives can expose a company to tremendous liability claims: Each wrong detention of a suspected shoplifter exposed the company to tens of thousands of dollars in potential litigation. Thus, the potential payback was quite high. Training in this area was considered critical and suffered especially from the following drawbacks:

- Classes could be offered only a couple of times a year.
- New hires had to be put out on the floor fairly shortly after coming on board.
- Consistancy in training and in applying the store's rules and policies was essential.
- Variances between instructors were not acceptable.

The head of the loss prevention area, Ed Wolfe, was in many respects the ideal "angel." He wholeheartedly believed in the technology, was influential in the organization, and was able to pave the way for access to all the necessary resources. When all was said and done, we had found an excellent candidate for the first conversion to technology-based instruction. The only significant obstacle was the scope of the effort and the length of development it required.

Since this was a proof of concept, the ideal candidate should have been one with high impact and fast delivery. To deal with this issue, it was decided to develop a limited portion or subset of the overall materials. We would begin with the segment of the training that had the highest impact and utilize the key features of the technology. Specifically, we would develop interactive simulations that covered the 10 most troublesome situations in which new detectives find themselves. The student would observe scenarios as they unfolded and, without overt prompting, be free to watch the scenario unfold or use a variety of on-screen tools (e.g., handcuffs to stop and detain, a walkie-talkie to call for backup, feet to change position relative to the suspect) to control the sequence of events and the ultimate outcomes.

The instructional methods employed were "discovery" methods with substantial record keeping. The system kept track of all the decisions and actions (or lack of actions) initiated by the student as he or she traveled through the unfolding scenarios. That data then were used to identify detectives who needed individual counseling, assess the exposure of the parent corporation, and justify development of the longer follow-on course.

The program was a resounding success. It was well received by the field and garnered industry awards. Perhaps the greatest testimonial to the wisdom of the selection, however, is the fact that over 10 years later the program is still in use. Federated Department Stores, which acquired CHH, still employs the program as it was originally built in all its divisions across the United States.

NOVATIONS: SOME THINGS JUST DO NOT TRANSLATE

Novations Group, a Provo, Utah, company, provides for its clients, among other things, a professional development workshop. This workshop focuses on the "Four Stages" of professional development through which one may progress during a career in business. With the fervor over Web development in full swing, several of Novations' clients had asked for delivery of the Four Stages materials over Intranets and the Internet.

On first examination this did not seem to present significant obstacles to conversion. The program had a sponsoring angel, was eagerly awaited by the field, served a very heterogeneous audience, and in general met many of the criteria for a successful conversion. As one of the first steps in the design and development effort, a team of three instructional designers analyzed the existing materials and attended the live workshop.

Many of us in the instructional design and human resources field have attended more professional development workshops than we can remember. In most instances these experiences are not overwhelmingly unique or complex. Their content is primarily cognitive in nature, with a dose of motivation thrown in. They often translate well into other media.

Our team found the Novations workshop to be a notable exception. At the core of the success of the Four Stages session is a progressive series of insights that move one from being a passive recipient of career-changing decisions to an active "controller" responsible for one's own direction and strategy for fulfillment.

One leaves the workshop with new insights and awareness. It is truly an eye-opening experience rather than a set of facts, rules, concepts, and the like. Truthfully, no conceivable small-screen image, set of interactive exercises, animations, or dramatizations could achieve what people experience in the live workshop. All was not lost, however. Web-based delivery could be of some benefit.

As prerequisites to the workshop, students are supposed to complete selected reading assignments and a number of probing surveys. The Web represents an excellent means for providing easy access to these materials, simplifying distribution, facilitating data collection by the workshop administrators, and instantly ascertaining the status of all the scheduled attendees.

While significant and successful efforts were undertaken to make the Web-based preworkshop materials congruent and consistent with the themes presented in the workshop, everyone concluded that some things are best done face to face. Not all human experiences can be handled by technology.

GLOSSARY

Affective Domain   The area of human learning dealing with attitudes, beliefs, and values, such as a desire to achieve.

Branching   In computer-based training (CBT), the program's taking the student down an instructional path based on his or her selections. The student may or may not be aware of the branching.

Cognitive Domain   The area of human learning associated with intellectual skills such as mathematics.

Design   A phase in the instructional systems design (ISD) process for creating an instructional program, whether or not it is computer-based. The phases are analysis, design, development, implementation, and evaluation. After needs analysis, the designer gathers information, completes a task analysis, writes objectives, assesses learner characteristics, and specifies learning activities and assessment methods. This process yields a "blueprint" of the course.

Development   The ISD phase that comes after design. The program is produced: Art, video, audio, programming, and so on, are created on the basis of the design document.

Individualized Instruction   Training given to a student by himself or herself. The goal is to give the student an experience tailored to his or her needs by letting the student guide himself or herself through the material. A computer-based training program can adapt itself to the user's inputs. CBT typically is administered in an individualized manner.

Input   The information the user communicates to the computer through the use of a device such as a keyboard, mouse, touch screen, or other peripheral connected to the computer, such as a magnetic stripe reader.

Interface   The place where the person meets the machine. This has come to mean the way the computer screen appears. It lets the user know what the options are, with the use of menus, toolbars, input fields, and so on.

Modeling   The representation of a process. This has been used in education to mean demonstration. In the world of CBT, it can have an interactive component, allowing the user to modify the system and see the effect. The is one of the modes of CBT.

Output   The information the computer communicates to the user through output devices such as the computer screen and the printer. It results from the computer carrying out an application program and responding to the user's input.

Peripheral Device   An electronic device that can be attached to a computer. Examples include printers, scanners, storage drives, keyboards, and mice.

Psychomotor Domain   The area of human learning related to physical movement, such as dance.

Simulation   A representation of a piece of equipment or a system that allows the user to give inputs and see the system's typical response. Simulation allows the "use" of the equipment without the potential of harming the equipment or person. Simulation is one of the modes of CBT.

Subject-Matter-Expert (SME)   The person on the design team who is there because of extensive knowledge of the subject matter to be taught. This person helps collect information and answer questions.

Tutorial   The most common mode of CBT. It is individually administered. The goal is to mimic the interaction between a tutor and a student, in which the tutor adapts the presentation in accordance with the student's apparent understanding.

CHAPTER 14

Return on Investment for Technology-Based Training: Building the Business Case

Jack J. Phillips
J. Patrick Whalen

There has been much debate about measuring the return on investment (ROI) in technology-based education and training. It is rare for a topic to stir up emotions to the degree that the ROI issue does. Some individuals characterize the concept of ROI as seriously flawed and inappropriate; others passionately characterize it as the answer to their accountability woes. The truth probably lies somewhere in between. The important thing is to understand the drivers of the ROI process and the inherent weaknesses and advantages of ROI. Then one can take a rational approach to the issue and implement an appropriate mix of evaluation strategies, including ROI. This chapter presents the basic issues concerning ROI and its use in technology-based training.

KEY ROI ISSUES

Paradigm Shift in Technology-Based Training

In recent years a significant paradigm shift has occurred that has dramatically affected the accountability of technology-based training. Organizations have begun to move from activity-based evaluation (number of participants, number of programs offered, equipment utilized) in favor of focusing on business results (value of a program to the organization). The paradigm shift from activity-based to results-based interventions includes several key elements that influence the way a program is designed, implemented, and measured. The factors of a true results-based technology intervention include the following:

- There is a linkage to specific identifiable business needs rather than to perceived needs and wish lists (i.e., implementing the newest and greatest technology).
- There is an accurate assessment of current versus expected performance of skills rather than the application of "blanket" technology and training for everyone regardless of current skill level.
- The program or intervention is designed to address specific objectives for behavior and business impact variables that will be measured after the intervention.
- Results expectations are communicated to the participants before and during the intervention.
- The job environment is prepared to support implementation of the technology: enhanced knowledge, skills, and behavior change (i.e., the participant is allowed time to practice the new system on the job before it goes live).
- Partnerships are established with key managers and clients to identify and implement strategies to enhance work performance and business measures utilizing technology.
- A process is in place to measure the business impact results and produce a cost-benefit analysis.
- Planning and reporting are thoroughly communicated on the basis of intended and actual outcomes of the intervention.

As organizations continue to experience increased competition and monitor costs more closely, technology is used to enhance skills and improve organizational performance. However, organizations are insisting that there be an adequate return on their investment in technology. The journey to increased accountability has forced training organizations to assess the competencies, skills, and readiness needed to be true partners in an organization. The results-based approach to technology interventions is characterized by measuring the appropriate returns and benefits resulting from a specific implementation. Measuring ROI for technology-based training programs is the ultimate measure of accountability. Figure 14–1 shows how to assess an organization's readiness for results-based technology.

ROI Will Not Go Away

ROI is not a fad. As long as there is a need for accountability for expenditures and an investment payoff is desired, ROI will be used to evaluate major investments in technology, education, and training. A fad is a new idea or approach or a new spin

F I G U R E   14–1

Activity-Based versus Results-Based Learning

This exercise provides an opportunity to assess the degree to which a paradigm shift has occurred. After each element, a scale from 1 to 5 is presented to judge the degree of the shift. In this scale, a score of 1 indicates that the focus is on implementing activity-based interventions. A score of 5 means that the issue has completely shifted to implementing interventions for results. The scores 2, 3, and 4 reflect the relative degree of the movement toward the complete shift at 5.

Circle the appropriate number for each of the issues and total the score.

	Activity-Based Interventions			Results-Based Interventions	
Linking to business needs	1	2	3	4	5
Assessment of current versus expected performance	1	2	3	4	5
Application and business impact objectives	1	2	3	4	5
Communicating expectations to participants	1	2	3	4	5
Work environment supports transfer of learning	1	2	3	4	5
Building partnerships with managers	1	2	3	4	5
Measuring results	1	2	3	4	5
Communicating results	1	2	3	4	5

Action items:_____

_____

Scoring

Use the following chart to insert your scores. Tally the score and compare it with the interpretation below. The absolute minimum score is 8, which means there has been no shift at all. The maximum score is 40, reflecting a complete shift on all eight elements. Most organizations will be in the middle range.

Issue	Issue Score
Linking to business needs	
Assessment of current versus expected performance	
Application and business impact objectives	
Communicating expectations to participants	
Work environment supports transfer of learning	
Building partnerships with managers	
Measuring results	
Communicating results	

Total Score	
Range	**Interpretation**
8–15	Virtually no paradigm shift has occurred on the vast majority, if not all, of the issues.
16–23	Some shift has occurred, at least for certain areas, but improvement is needed to focus more attention on results.
24–31	Significant progress has been made, with a major shift in several areas.
32–40	There has been a dramatic shift with a focus on results for most, if not all, of the issues.

An important part of this exercise is to identify specific areas where additional emphasis is needed. In addition to scoring the individual elements, it may be helpful to identify the two issues where the most progress has been made and the two where the least progress has been made. Appropriate consideration is needed for key issues where little progress has been made. After analysis and discussion, indicate the specific actions to be taken in the space provided after each issue.

on an old approach. The concept of ROI has been used for decades. The seventy-fifth anniversary issue of the *Harvard Business Review* (HBR) described the tools used to measure results in organizations.

In the early issues of HBR, during the 1920s, ROI was an emerging tool that could place a value on the payoff from investments. In more recent years the application of this concept has been expanded to all types of investments, including training and education, change initiatives, and technology. With increased adoption and use, it appears that ROI is here to stay. Today hundreds of organizations are routinely developing ROI calculations for education and training programs. Two casebooks have been developed to show specific applications.

Debating this issue is meaningless in an organization where there has been a mandate to show ROI by using monetary values. The question is not whether it should be pursued but how can it be accomplished with the current resources and the capabilities of the staff. To understand the application of the ROI process, it is helpful to understand the basic concepts and the reasons for its success.

The Ultimate Level of Evaluation: ROI

The ROI process adds a fifth level to the four levels of evaluation developed by Kirkpatrick almost 40 years ago to measure the success of training. The concept of different levels of evaluation is helpful and instructive in understanding how ROI is calculated. Table 14–1 shows the five-level framework used in this chapter.

At level 1—reaction and satisfaction—input from program participants is measured. In the context of technology implementation, this level measures the user's reaction to the technology-based program. Almost all organizations evaluate at level 1, usually by administering a generic end-of-program questionnaire. While this level of evaluation is important as a measure of customer satisfaction, a favorable reaction does not ensure that the participants have gained new skills or knowledge.

TABLE 14-1

Five Levels of Evaluation

Level	Measurement Focus
Reaction and satisfaction	Participant satisfaction with the program and technology
Learning	Changes in knowledge, skills, and attitudes
Implementation	Changes in job performance and application of technology
Business results	Changes in business impact variables
Return on investment	Comparison of program benefits to costs

At level 2—learning—measurements focus on what the participants learned during the program, using tests, skill practices, role plays, simulations, group evaluations, and other assessment tools. A learning check is helpful to ensure that the participants have absorbed the program material and know how to use it properly. However, a positive measure at this level is no guarantee that what was learned will be used on the job. For example, an employee who participates in an Intranet-based learning program on database management may have learned the new skills, but the old database system is still in place and is supported at the work site. The literature is laced with studies that show the failure of learning to be transferred to the job.

At level 3—implementation—a variety of follow-up methods are used to determine whether the participants have utilized the technology on the job. The frequency and use of skills are important measures at this level. While level 3 evaluations are important to gauge the success of program implementation, this still does not guarantee that there will be a positive business impact in the organization.

At level 4—business results—the measurement focuses on the actual results achieved by program participants as they successfully apply the program material by using the technology. Typical level 4 measures include output, quality, costs, time, and customer satisfaction. Although the program may produce a measurable business impact, there is still the concern that it may cost too much.

At level 5, the ultimate level of evaluation—return on investment—the measurement compares the monetary benefits from the program with the program costs. Although ROI can be expressed in several ways, it usually is presented as a percentage or cost-benefit ratio. The evaluation chain is not complete until the level 5 evaluation has been conducted.

While most organizations conduct evaluations to measure satisfaction, very few actually conduct evaluations at the ROI level. Perhaps the best explanation for this situation is that ROI evaluation often is characterized as a difficult and expensive process. When business results and ROI are desired, it is also very important to evaluate the other levels. A chain of impact should occur through the levels as the skills and knowledge learned (level 2) are applied on the job (level 3) to produce business results (level 4). If measurements are not taken at each level, it is difficult to conclude that the results achieved were actually caused by the program or intervention. Because of this, it is recommended that evaluation be conducted at all levels when a level 5 evaluation is planned. This practice is consistent with the practices of benchmarking forum members of the American Society for training and development. Figure 14–3 in the case study at the end of this chapter shows how the levels of evaluation are translated into objectives for the implementation of a software package on a pilot basis.

Why ROI for Technology-Based Training Interventions?

There are some good reasons why ROI has become a hot topic. Although the viewpoints and explanations may vary, some things are clear. First, in most organizations education and training budgets continue to grow every year. The technology portion of the training budget is growing very rapidly. Technology-based training interventions usually have high initial, if not long-term, costs associated with them. As expenditures grow, accountability becomes a critical issue. A growing budget makes a bigger target for internal critics, often prompting the use of ROI. Second, total quality management and continuous process improvement have focused increased attention on measurement issues.

Third, in the past, project sponsors often were burned by inappropriate and improperly designed technology implementations, particularly in the area of education and training. Today the situation has changed. Administrators and executives who fund new projects are asking for a process to demonstrate accountability so that they can measure ROI at different time frames after implementation. This situation has stimulated interest in accountability for any project that uses technology, particularly in education and training.

Fourth, the restructuring and reengineering experience and the threat of outsourcing have caused many education and training executives to focus more clearly and directly on bottom-line issues. Many education and training processes have been reengineered to utilize technology to ensure that programs are closely aligned with business needs and produce maximum efficiency. These processes have brought more attention to evaluation issues and resulted in the measurement of the contributions of specific programs. The threat of outsourcing has forced some education and training managers to align programs to organizational objectives more closely and measure successes so that management can understand their contributions to the organization.

Fifth, the business management mindset of many current education and training managers causes them to place more emphasis on economic issues. The education and training manager of the 1990s is more aware of bottom-line issues in the organization and more knowledgeable about the operational and financial areas. This new "enlightened" manager often takes a business approach to technology-based education and training, and ROI is a part of this strategy.

Sixth, there has been a persistent trend toward accountability in organizations all over the world. Every support function is attempting to show its worth by capturing the value it adds to the organization. From the accountability perspective, the education and training function should be no different from the other functions: It must show its contribution.

Seventh, top executives are now demanding ROI calculations in organizations where they previously were not required. For years training and education managers have tried to convince top executives that training cannot be measured, at least to the level desired by executives. Yet many executives are finding out that it can, and it is being measured in many organizations, thanks in part to articles in publications aimed at top executives. Having become aware that it can be done, top executives are demanding the same accountability in their organizations. In extreme cases organizations such as IBM are being asked to show the return or face significant budget cuts. Other organizations are just asking for results. The chief operating officer for a global telecommunications company described it this way: "For years we have evaluated training with variables such as number of participants, number of programs, length of programs, cost of programs, and content of programs. These are input-focused measures. Now we must show what these programs are doing for our company and speak in terms that we can understand. We need output-focused measures." These no-nonsense comments are being repeated throughout major organizations.

Eighth, technology-based training interventions have the potential for high exposure within the organization, with large numbers of participants and advanced learning opportunities.

BUILDING A FEASIBLE ROI PROCESS
Concerns with ROI

Although much progress has been made, the ROI process is not without problems and drawbacks. The mere presence of the process creates a dilemma for many organizations. When an organization embraces the concept and implements the process, the management team usually is waiting anxiously for results, only to be disappointed when they are not quantifiable. For an ROI process to be useful, it must balance many issues, such as feasibility, simplicity, credibility, and soundness. More specifically, three major audiences must be pleased with the ROI process to accept and use it.

Practitioners

For years education and training practitioners have assumed that ROI could not be measured. When they examined a typical process, they found long formulas, complicated equations, and complex models that made the ROI process confusing. With this perceived complexity, these practitioners could visualize the tremendous efforts required for data collection and analysis and, more important, the increased cost of making the process work. Because of these concerns, practitioners are seeking an ROI process that is simple and easy to understand so that they can implement the steps and strategies easily. Also, they need a process that will not take an excessive amount of time to implement and will not consume too many precious staff hours. Finally, practitioners need a process that is not too expensive. In the face of competition for financial resources, they need a process that will not command a significant portion of the budget.

Senior Managers, Sponsors, and Clients

Managers, who must approve education and training budgets, request programs, or cope with the results of programs, have a strong interest in developing ROI. They want a process that provides quantifiable results by using a method similar to the ROI formula applied to other types of investments. Senior managers have a never-ending desire to have it all come down to an ROI calculation expressed as a percentage. As do practitioners, they also want a process that is simple and easy to understand. The assumptions made in the calculation and the methodology used in the process must reflect their point of reference, experience, and level of understanding. They do not want or need a string of formulas, charts, and complicated models. Instead, they need a process that they can explain to others when necessary. More important, they need a process with which they can identify, one that is sound and realistic enough to earn their confidence.

Researchers

Finally, researchers will support only a process that measures up to their scrutiny and close examination. Researchers usually insist that models, formulas, assumptions, and theories be sound and based on commonly accepted practices. Also, they want a process that produces accurate values and consistent outcomes. If estimates are necessary, researchers want a process that provides the most accuracy within the constraints of the situation, recognizing that adjustments need to be made when there is uncertainty in the process.

The challenge is to develop acceptable requirements for an ROI process that will satisfy researchers and at the same time please practitioners and senior managers.

Criteria for an Effective ROI Process

To satisfy the needs of these three critical groups, the ROI process must meet several requirements. Ten essential criteria for an effective ROI process are outlined below. These criteria were developed with input from hundreds of education and training managers and technology specialists.

1. The ROI process must be simple, without complex formulas, lengthy equations, and complicated methodologies.
2. The ROI process must be economical, with the capacity to be implemented easily.
3. The assumptions, methodology, and outcomes must be credible.
4. From a research perspective, the ROI process must be theoretically sound and based on generally accepted practices.
5. The ROI process must account for other factors that have influenced output variables.
6. The ROI process must be appropriate to a variety of programs.
7. The ROI process must have the flexibility to be applied on a preprogram basis as well as a postprogram basis.
8. The ROI process must be applicable to all types of data, including hard data (output, quality, costs, and time) and soft data (job satisfaction, customer satisfaction, and complaints).
9. The ROI process must include the costs of the program.
10. The ROI process must have a successful track record in a variety of applications.

Because these criteria are considered essential, an ROI process should meet the vast majority, if not all of them. The bad news is that most ROI processes do not meet these criteria; the good news is that the ROI process presented below, does.

A PRACTICAL MODEL FOR THE ROI PROCESS

The ROI Process

The calculation of the ROI in technology-based education and training begins with the basic model shown in Fig. 14–2, where a potentially complicated process can be simplified through the use of sequential steps. The ROI process model provides a systematic approach to ROI calculations. A step-by-step approach helps keep the process manageable so that users can tackle one issue at a time. The model also emphasizes the fact that this is a logical, systematic process that flows from one step to another. Applying the model provides consistency from one ROI calculation to another. Each step of the model is described briefly here.

FIGURE 14–2

ROI Process Model

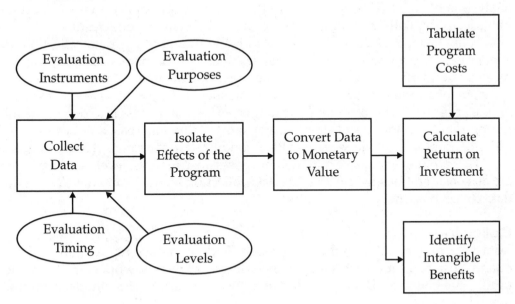

Preliminary Evaluation Information

The preliminary evaluation information is depicted in the figure as the circles surrounding "Collect Data." Several pieces of the evaluation puzzle must be explained in the process of developing the evaluation plan for an ROI calculation. Four specific elements are important to evaluation success, as outlined below.

Evaluation purposes should be considered before the development of the evaluation plan because these purposes often determine the scope of the evaluation, the types of instruments used, and the type of data collected. For example, when an ROI calculation is planned, one of the purposes is to compare the cost and benefits of the program. This purpose has implications for the type of data collected (hard type), the type of data collection method (performance monitoring), the type of analysis (thorough), and the communication medium for results (formal evaluation report). For most programs, multiple evaluation purposes are pursued.

A variety of instruments are used to collect data, and the appropriate instruments should be considered in the early stages of developing ROI. Questionnaires, on-line surveys, interviews, and focus groups are commonly used to collect data in an evaluation. The instruments most familiar to the culture of the organization and most appropriate for the setting and evaluation requirements should be used in the data collection process.

Technology-based training programs are evaluated at five different levels, as illustrated in the figure. Data should be collected at levels 1, 2, 3, and 4 if an ROI analysis is planned. This helps ensure that the chain of impact occurs as participants learn the skills, apply them on the job, and obtain business results.

A final aspect of the evaluation plan is the timing of the data collection. In some cases preprogram measurements are taken to compare with postprogram measures, and in some cases multiple measures are taken. In other situations, preprogram measurements are not available and specific follow-ups are still taken after the program. The important issue in this part of the process is to determine the timing for the follow-up evaluation. For most technology-based education and training programs, a follow-up usually is conducted in the range of 3 to 6 months.

These four elements—evaluation purposes, instruments, levels, and timing—are all considerations in selecting the data collection methods and developing the data collection plan.

Collecting Data

Data collection is central to the ROI process. Both hard data, representing output, quality, cost, and time, and soft data, including work habits, work climate, and attitudes, are collected. Data are collected by using a variety of methods, including the following:

- Follow-up surveys and questionnaires are administered to uncover specific applications of technology-based education and training. Participants provide responses to a variety of types of open-ended and forced-response questions. Questionnaires can be used to capture both level 3 and level 4 data.

- On-the-job observation captures actual skill application and use. Observations are particularly useful in technology-based training to determine skill application. The observations are more effective when the observer is invisible or transparent. Observations are appropriate for level 3 data.

- Postprogram interviews are conducted with participants to determine the extent to which learning has been utilized on the job. Interviews allow for probing to uncover specific applications and are appropriate for level 3 data.

- Focus groups are conducted to determine the degree to which a group of participants has applied the technology-based training to job situations. Focus groups are appropriate for level 3 data.

- Program assignments are useful for simple short-term projects. Participants complete the assignment on the job, utilizing skills or knowledge learned in the program. Completed assignments often contain both level 3 and level 4 data.

- Action plans are developed in programs and are implemented on the job after a program has been completed. A follow-up of the plan provides evidence of program success. Level 3 and level 4 data can be collected with action plans.
- Performance contracts are developed where the participant, the participant's supervisor, and the instructor all agree on specific outcomes from technology-based education and training. Performance contracts are appropriate for both level 3 and level 4 data.
- Performance monitoring is useful when various performance records and operational data are examined for improvement. This method is particularly useful for level 4 data.

The important challenge in this step is to select the data collection method or methods appropriate to the setting and the specific program within the time and budget constraints of the organization.

Isolating the Effects of the Program

A frequently overlooked issue in most evaluations is the process used to isolate the effects of technology-based education and training. In this step of the process, specific strategies are explored that determine the amount of output performance that is directly related to the program. This step is essential because many factors influence performance data after education and training programs have been conducted. The specific strategies at this step pinpoint the amount of improvement directly related to the program. The result is increased accuracy and credibility of the ROI calculation. The following strategies have been utilized by organizations to tackle this important issue:

- A control group arrangement may be used to isolate impact. With this strategy, one group participates in the program, while another, similar group does not. The difference in the performance of the two groups is attributed to the program. When properly set up and implemented, control group management is the most effective way to isolate the effects of education and training.
- Trend lines are used to project the level of the value-specific output variables if the program had not been undertaken. The projection is compared with the actual data after the program, and the difference represents the estimate of the impact. In certain conditions this strategy can be an accurate way to isolate the impact of technology-based education and training.
- When mathematical relationships between input and output variables are known, a forecasting model is used to isolate the effects of a program. With

this approach, the output variable is predicted by using the forecasting model, with the assumption that the program is not conducted. The actual performance of the variable after the program then is compared with the forecast value to estimate the impact of education and training.

- Participants estimate the amount of improvement related to education and training. With this approach, participants are provided with the total amount of improvement on a pre- and postprogram basis and are asked to indicate the percentage of the improvement that is actually related to the program.

- Supervisors of the participants estimate the impact of education and training on the output variables. With this approach the supervisors of participants are presented with the total amount of improvement and are asked to indicate the percentage related to the program.

- Senior managers estimate the impact of technology-based education and training. In these cases managers provide an estimate or "adjustment" to reflect the portion of the improvement that is related to the program. There are some advantages to having senior management involved in this process, such as senior management ownership.

- Experts provide estimates of the impact of technology-based education and training on the performance variable. Because the estimates are based on previous experience, the experts must be familiar with the type of program and the specific situation.

- When feasible, other influencing factors are identified and their impact is estimated or calculated, leaving the remaining unexplained improvement to be attributed to technology-based education and training. In this case, the influences of all the other factors are developed and the program remains the one variable that is not accounted for in the analysis. The unexplained portion of the output is then attributed to the program.

Collectively, these strategies provide a comprehensive set of tools to tackle the critical issue of isolating the effects of technology-based education and training.

Converting Data to Monetary Values

To calculate the return on investment, data collected in a level 4 evaluation are converted to monetary values to compare to program costs. This requires that a value be placed on each unit of data connected with the program. Ten strategies are available to convert data to monetary values; the specific strategy selected usually depends on the type of data and the situation.

1. Output data are converted to profit contributions or cost savings. With this strategy output increases are converted to monetary value on the

basis of their unit contribution to profit or the unit of cost reduction. These values are readily available in most organizations.

2. The cost of quality is calculated, and quality improvements are directly converted to cost savings. These values are available in many organizations.

3. For programs in which employee time is saved, participants' wages and benefits are used to calculate the value of time. Because a variety of programs focus on improving the time required to complete projects, processes, or daily activities, the value of time becomes an important and necessary issue.

4. Historical costs and current records are used when they are available for a specific variable. In this case organizational cost data are utilized to establish the specific value of an improvement.

5. When available, internal and external experts may be used to estimate the value of an improvement. In this situation the credibility of the estimate depends on the expertise and reputation of the expert.

6. External databases are sometimes available to estimate the value or cost of data items. Research, government, and industry databases can provide important information for calculating these values. The difficulty lies in finding a specific database related to the situation.

7. Participants estimate the value of the data item. For this approach to be effective, the participants must be capable of assigning a value to the improvement.

8. The supervisors of the participants provide estimates when they are willing and able to assign values to the improvement. This approach is especially useful when the participants are not fully capable of providing this input and in situations where supervisors need to confirm or adjust a participant's estimate.

9. Senior management provides estimates on the value of an improvement when it is willing to offer estimates. This approach is particularly helpful in establishing values for performance measures that are very important to senior management.

10. Education and training staff estimates may be used to determine the value of an output data item. In these cases it is essential for the estimates to be provided on an unbiased basis.

This step in the ROI model is absolutely necessary to determine the monetary benefits from education and training programs. The process is challenging, particularly with soft data, but can be accomplished by using one or more of these strategies.

Tabulating Program Costs

The other part of a cost-benefit analysis is the cost of the program. Tabulating the costs involves monitoring or developing all the related costs of the program targeted for the ROI calculation. Among the cost components that should be included are the following:

- The cost to design and develop the program, possibly prorated over the expected life of the program
- The cost of all program equipment, software, and hardware (prorated)
- The cost of the instructor-facilitator if appropriate, including preparation time as well as delivery time
- The cost of the facilities for the program if applicable
- Travel, lodging, and meal cost for the participants if applicable
- Salaries plus employee benefits of the participants for the time involved in the program
- Administrative and overhead costs of the education and training function allocated in a convenient way to the technology-based training program

In addition, specific costs related to the needs assessment and evaluation should be included if appropriate. The conservative approach is to include all these costs so that the total is fully loaded.

Calculating ROI

ROI is calculated by using program benefits and costs. The cost-benefit ratio is the program benefits divided by cost. In formulaic form it is

$$\frac{\text{Program benefits}}{\text{Program costs}}$$

ROI uses the net benefits divided by program costs. The net benefits are the program benefits minus the costs. In formulaic form, ROI becomes

$$\frac{\text{Net program benefits}}{\text{Program costs}}$$

This is the same basic formula used in evaluating other investments in which ROI is traditionally reported as earnings divided by investment.

Identifying Intangible Benefits

In addition to tangible monetary benefits, most technology-based education and training programs have intangible nonmonetary benefits. The ROI calculation is based on converting both hard and soft data to monetary values. Other data items are identified that are not converted to monetary values. These intangible benefits include items such as

- Increased job satisfaction
- Increased organizational commitment
- Improved teamwork
- Improved customer service
- Reduced complaints
- Reduced conflicts

During data analysis, every attempt is made to convert all data to monetary values. All hard data, such as output, quality, and time, are converted to monetary values. The conversion of soft data is attempted for each data item. However, if the process used for conversion is too subjective or inaccurate and the resulting values lose credibility in the process, the data are listed as an intangible benefit with the appropriate explanation. For some programs, intangible nonmonetary benefits are extremely valuable, often carrying as much influence as do the hard data items. The second part of the case study at the end of this chapter shows the ROI process model applied to a specific case.

CONCLUSION

ROI calculations are being developed by hundreds of organizations to meet the demands of a variety of influential stakeholders. The result is a process that shows the value-added contribution of technology-based education and training in a format desired by many senior administrators and executives. However, this chapter has demonstrated that the ROI process represents a significant and challenging dilemma for most organizations. While there are many drivers for the tremendous interest in and need for the ROI process, some question its appropriateness, accuracy, and necessity. The important point is that ROI calculations can be developed reliably and accurately for almost any type of technology-based education and training program. To accomplish this, the process must be approached with careful planning, methodical procedures, and logical and practical analyses. Above all, the steps, techniques, assumptions, and issues must follow a conservative approach to build the credibility needed for acceptance of the process.

GLOBAL FINANCIAL SERVICES, INC.
Linking Evaluation with Needs

Global Financial Services, Inc. (GFS), provides a variety of services to clients with a specific need to manage sales relationships in a more effective way. A task force composed of representatives from field sales, marketing, financial consulting, information technology, and education and training examined several financial solutions to improve relationships, including a review of several software packages. The following decision was made to implement software called ACT! This software, which was developed by Symantec, is designed to turn contacts into relationships and relationships into results. It has a flexible customer database, easy contact entry, a calendar, and a to-do list. It enables quick and effective customer communication and is designed to use with customized reports. It also has built-in contact and calendar sharing and is Internet-ready.

Instead of purchasing the software and teaching each of the 4000 relationship managers, GFS examined the success of the software on a pilot basis using three groups of 20 relationship managers. A 1-day workshop was designed to teach the relationship managers how to use the software to manage customer communication. The software was distributed and utilized in the workshop. If the program proved successful, yielding the appropriate return on investment, GFS planned to implement the program with all relationship managers. Because of the focus on results, detailed objectives were developed for the implementation of ACT!

FIGURE 14–3

Objectives of GFS

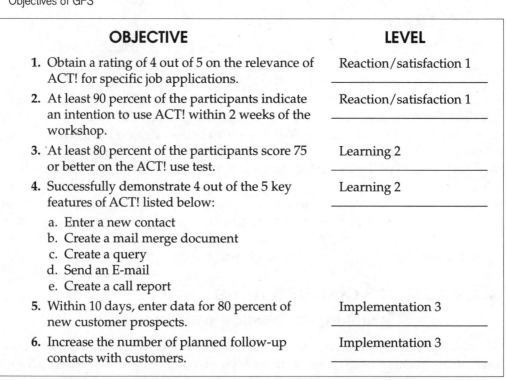

OBJECTIVE	LEVEL
1. Obtain a rating of 4 out of 5 on the relevance of ACT! for specific job applications.	Reaction/satisfaction 1
2. At least 90 percent of the participants indicate an intention to use ACT! within 2 weeks of the workshop.	Reaction/satisfaction 1
3. At least 80 percent of the participants score 75 or better on the ACT! use test.	Learning 2
4. Successfully demonstrate 4 out of the 5 key features of ACT! listed below: a. Enter a new contact b. Create a mail merge document c. Create a query d. Send an E-mail e. Create a call report	Learning 2
5. Within 10 days, enter data for 80 percent of new customer prospects.	Implementation 3
6. Increase the number of planned follow-up contacts with customers.	Implementation 3

7. Utilize ACT! daily as reflected in an 80 percent score on an unscheduled audit of use.	Implementation 3
8. Reduce the number of customer complaints regarding missed deadlines, late responses, and failure to complete transactions.	Impact 4
9. Reduce the time to respond to customer inquiries and requests.	Impact 4
10. Increase sales for existing customers.	Impact 4
11. Increase the customer satisfaction composite survey index by 20 percent on the next survey.	Impact 4
12. Achieve a 25 percent return on investment using first-year benefits.	ROI 5

This comprehensive set of objectives provided the appropriate direction and information for workshop designers, facilitators, participants, senior management team, and task force.

Data Analysis and Results

A data collection plan was designed to capture data for all five levels of analysis and evaluation. During the workshop data were collected for levels 1 and 2. A follow-up questionnaire was administered 2 months later to capture level 3 and level 4 data. A skill use audit was conducted within 2 months. For 3 months records were monitored for level 4 data. Here is a summary of the data.

Level 1
- Rating of 4.23 out of 5 achieved on the relevance of the ACT! for specific job applications.
- 92.5 percent of the participants indicated an intention to use ACT! within 2 weeks of the workshop.

Level 2
- 83 percent of the participants scored 75 or better on the ACT! use test.
- Participants successfully demonstrated an average of 4.2 of the five key features of ACT! listed here:
  1. Enter a new contact
  2. Create a mail merge document
  3. Create a query

4. Send an E-mail

5. Create a call report

Level 3

- Participants indicated that within 10 days, 92 percent of new customer prospects are entered into the system.
- Participants report an increase in the number of planned follow-up contacts with customers.
- An unscheduled audit of daily use resulted in a score of 76 percent out of a possible 100 percent.

Level 4

Business Impact Measure	Average Monthly Change	Contribution of ACT!, %	Annual Value
Customer complaints	−24.2	43	$575,660
Customer response	18 minutes per customer	72	NA
Sales to existing customers	+$321,000	14	$539,280
Customer satisfaction	+26%	49	NA
			$1,114,940

An important part of this process was to isolate the effects of the use of the new software combined with the training. Preprogram and postprogram differences could not be used, as other influences could have an impact on an increase or decrease in customer complaints, customer response time, sales, and customer satisfaction. This is usually the case with technology implementation. A control group arrangement could have been established to compare the performance of the three groups being trained with a carefully matched group of relationship managers without the training. However, it was decided to use input from the participants as an isolation technique and have them indicate the percentage of improvement related directly to the application of ACT! These estimates were adjusted by the error of the estimate taken from the participants. The results are shown as the contribution factor in the table above. The amount of actual change in each of the business measures is adjusted (factored) by this percentage to recognize that other factors have influenced the measure.

Level 5

To obtain the cost versus the benefits, the business improvement must be converted to monetary value. This conversion is shown in the table above as the annual value of the improvement. A standard value of $ 4,610 was used as the cost of a complaint. This value was developed after an analysis of the time involved in resolving complaints, the value of services and adjustments to the complaining party, and the potential lost business because of the complaint and the complaint situation. This value is multiplied by 24.2, which represents the monthly change for the three groups in training. Only 21 of the 58 participants who attended the program provided information on changes in monthly data, resulting in a total reduction of 24.2. Only the data provided by participants were used in the analysis. It was assumed that the remaining participants had no improvement in the reduction of customer complaints. This resulted in a monthly total improvement of $48,000, or an annual value of $575,660.

The improvement in customer response time came to a total of 18 minutes per customer, and there was no attempt to convert these data to a monetary value, although it should have an impact on customer satisfaction and sales. This item was listed as an intangible benefit. Also, customer satisfaction was not converted to monetary value.

Sales to existing customers increased $321,000, with 14 percent of that amount attributed to the use of the ACT! This resulted in an annual value of $539,280. The total annual improvement was $1,114,940.

In addition to converting data to monetary values, project costs were developed. The cost of developing the program and implementing it with 58 participants is shown here.

Development costs	$10,500
Materials and software	18,850
Equipment	6,000
Instructor, including expenses	7,200
Facilities, food and refreshments: 60 @ $58	3,480
Participants' time (lost opportunity): 58 @ $385	22,330
Coordination and evaluation	15,600
Total	$83,960

The ROI is calculated as follows:

$$\text{ROI (\%)} = \frac{\$1,114,940 - \$83,960}{\$83,960} \times 100 = 1228\%$$

Intangible Benefits

The following intangible benefits were reported:

1. Improvement in customer response time related directly to the use of ACT!
2. A 26 percent increase in customer satisfaction, with 49 percent related directly to the use of ACT!

3. Participants' reports indicating reduced stress as they addressed customer issues.
4. Participants' reports indicating a time saving (although considered minor)

Conclusion

The above presentation provides six types of data or analysis:

Reaction and satisfaction
Learning
Implementation
Business impact
Return on investment
Intangible benefits

This comprehensive profile of success with ACT! is reliable and accurate because steps were taken to isolate the effects of the project and conservative approaches were used in the data analysis. The decision was made to implement the software and training for all relationship managers.

CHAPTER 15

Training Management Systems: The Most Important Development in Training Since the Internet

Brandon Hall, PhD

Objectives

After reading this chapter, you will be able to:

- Define training management systems.
- Describe how training management systems are being used in organizations.
- List the major features of a training management system.
- Define the components of an enterprisewide system.

OVERVIEW

Training management systems are software packages that organize, deliver, and track training through a central interface over a local area network (LAN), Intranet, or the Internet. They can serve as a focal point for corporate training and can be used to deploy training within an office as well as in remote locations. There are a wide variety of training management systems with a range of capabilities to fill different niches. Some of the better known ones are Asymetrix Librarian, Knowl-edge*Soft*'s LOIS, Macromedia's Pathware, and Allen Communication's Manager's Edge.

Training management systems are the most important development in training since the Internet. These systems provide a way to automate registration, course delivery, competency management, assessment, and mass customization of training content. They also provide a way to demonstrate return on investment (ROI) to senior management and run training as a line of business.

237

Training management systems can be installed as a departmental or divisional way to manage training or as an enterprisewide and worldwide way to manage all employee and customer training. What PeopleSoft and SAP have done for human resources, training management systems will do for training, and much, much more.

TYPES OF TRAINING MANAGEMENT SYSTEMS

While many programs support the functions described above, many are set up only to handle courses that were authored in their own environment. The most useful training management systems can handle courseware from a variety of sources, but with varying degrees of success. Some training management systems just launch the material—"launch and forget," one vendor calls it. More sophisticated systems actually share information with the course and therefore can track individual fields to produce more meaningful output.

Other training management systems are capable of tracking only traditional instructor-led courses. Of course, in an instructor-led format, test scores and other information cannot be entered automatically into the training management system but must be entered manually, lessening some of the time-saving advantages of the system.

WHAT A TRAINING MANAGEMENT SYSTEM DOES

Learners can log on to the network from their desktops and launch courses that were assigned to them by the training administrator or enroll themselves in a course through on-line registration. Usually learners can be organized into groups based on geographic location, department, or other criteria. Different training requirements can be assigned to various groups, with any amount of crossover in the material.

Courses can be set up as prerequisites so that learners must complete them before they can move on to the next lesson. In addition, many training management systems feature precourse evaluations that allow learners to "test out" of subjects in which they demonstrate a minimum level of competence. This keeps users from losing interest as they cover material they already know and lets them skip ahead to more advanced sections.

Training administrators can access the records of each student to determine whether the courses were taken, when they were taken, and how long it took to complete them. Students can access their records to see how they've been progressing and determine their current status. Individual course histories are generated, and some training management systems allow you to export the information to programs such as Crystal Reports or a human resources database such as SAP.

BENEFITS AND PERSPECTIVE ON TRAINING MANAGEMENT SYSTEMS

A training management system automates registration and the administration of training. Administrators can directly track the effectiveness of the training, and since reports can be generated that identify exactly who, when, where, and for how long, administrators can focus their attention where it is needed. Tests directly reflect whether learners have command of the material and can even expose deficiencies in the courseware itself. If, for instance, a high percentage of students are unable to pass one section of the course, the administrator will be alerted to the problem and can ask: Are the instructions unclear? Is the information inaccurate? Do the learners need to complete a more basic course first?

Training management systems save resources by allowing the reuse of on-line course materials. When course content is updated or course requirements change, the system automatically applies the changes to everyone it affects. This allows even major restructuring in training to be implemented worldwide at once.

On-line training is changing the landscape of training, and training management systems are the engines that allow effective on-line training. The right system can save a company time and money and allow you to focus on the more valuable aspects of training instead of being distracted by the duties of administration.

The Past

Until a few years ago, if a company wanted to train its employees, there was one option: instructor-led training. If you managed training, your concerns were selecting and scheduling classes and instructors, managing resources, and registering students.

One of the problems with tracking this kind of training is that while a database can keep track of the who, what, and when of training as well as student scores and attendance, all this information must be entered manually.

On the upside, training management systems can check to make sure that resources are not double booked and act as a central place to track student information and progress.

Many of the training management systems described in this chapter were designed to handle instructor-led training, and many of them deal with every facet of that kind of training. As a company embraces the future, however, it may want to get more of its training on-line.

The Present

Corporate training is in a state of flux. New technologies are entering the arena, and others are becoming obsolete. Corporate training tends to be a mishmash of instructor-led, CD-ROM, Internet-based, LAN-based, asynchronous, and synchronous training. Although computer-based training (CBT) has been demonstrated to be an effective way to teach with a high ROI, it's not the best medium for every kind of training. A corporation probably will be seeking a training management system that can bridge the gap between past and future technologies and handle all its present needs.

With some CBT and web-based training already in place, a training management system that tracks only its own proprietary courses may not be the best option. A flexible, open-ended training management system better reflects the reality of the current state of training.

One of the pitfalls in shopping for such a product is that vendors tend to exaggerate the features of their products; they also like to couch their product descriptions in jargon. The buyer must go beyond asking if the product manages CBT.

The Future

At a certain point the rapid changes in training technology will inevitably have to stabilize. Technology training will not replace instructor-led training but will find its own niche. A variety of training methods will be used, and the long-term survivors will be the training management systems that have the flexibility to handle all the different types.

Standards will gain acceptance and become, well, standard whether they are the promising standards that are emerging now or something else altogether. For the sake of efficiency, the courseware and the training managers will need to be able to talk to each other.

As training management systems now can often "serve up" on-line training, it will be an easy shift in the future for training modules to be configured on the fly and for the application of reusable content.

JOB AIDS AND RESOURCE DOCUMENT

Top 10 Questions about Selecting a Training Management System

This list is based on the questions I have received from training professionals charged with selecting a system for an organization. This was never an easy task, and the job is harder now because of the sophistication of these products, the implications for the future, and the rapid development of features in these programs.

1. *How much should one expect to spend on a training management system?* This is a trick question. It depends on the complexity of your needs and the size of the organization. In addition to the software package and licensing, there are costs for installation, implementation (such as populating the database with your courses and employees), technical support, upgrades, training, and additional consulting to customize the program to meet your needs.

2. *Which training management system is best?* This is another trick question. It depends on your needs.

3. *Is it better to select a separate system for instructor-led training and another one for on-line training in order to have "best in class" in each one?* This is a tough call. The important point is the overall management of your training. If you decide on two separate systems—and this is the case for many organizations—ensure that they can exchange data with each other so that you do not have to keep duplicate sets of records.

4. *Why are training management systems becoming so important all of a sudden?* As on-line training becomes more popular, training organizations are realizing the need to manage it all. The Web has also led the way in regard to self-registration and other improvements in instructor-led training management programs. There is also a demand for enterprisewide reporting such as ROI for training and for managing competencies and knowledge within organizations.

5. *We use one vendor's authoring software. Therefore, should we buy its training management system too?* There is a good argument for doing that in terms of the compatibility of the systems and familiarity with the vendor. This issue will be less important as the AICC standard becomes more common for courseware and training management systems. It also depends on whether the system will do everything you want it to do.

6. *What is AICC compatibility, and why is it so important?* Without the octane standard for gasoline, you would have to go to a General Motors filling station for your GM car. With the octane rating standard, you can take any car to any filling station and get the right gas. With AICC compatibility you will be able to manage any on-line course with any on-line training management system.

7. *What about learning objects and the IMS standard?* "Learning Objects will Rule the Training World!" (headline from a recent editorial in the *Multimedia and Internet Training Newsletter*). Learning objects will change the game in training, but not for a while.

8. *What is an ERP, and what does it have to do with training management systems?* Enterprise resource planning (ERP) programs such as SAP, PeopleSoft,

and Oracle applications are being implemented in most large-scale organizations. Upper management is seeing the benefit of reengineering
and automating the function in finance, manufacturing, human resources, and other departments. Once senior management has seen the
cost savings of automating these other functions and centralizing the reporting enterprisewide, it becomes more receptive to using the same enterprisewide management system for training.

9. *Should we build or buy?* Buy. For the same reasons you don't want to build
your own word processor or accounting software, leave it to those who
focus on it full-time and can support it and provide feature and technology enhancements that stay up to date in this fast-improving area. (However, some organizations, such as JC Penney, have looked at many of the
commercial products included here and swear by a custom program they
are having built for them. But I don't recommend that.)

10. *If we choose the wrong system and everyone who has to use it is sending nasty E-
mails to our department, should we change our E-mail addresses or just change
companies?* Both. Unfortunately, choosing a training management system
is a highly visible decision. These decisions often have to be made in training departments, where there is not as much experience in selecting large-
scale software programs.

Table 15–1 will help you choose a training management system.

HOW TRAINING MANAGEMENT SYSTEMS ARE BEING USED

This section shows how training management systems are being used in organizations. Each of the four examples represents a different type of situation, from a few
training courses to a multinational firm with hundreds of courses.

Scenario 1

SIC, Inc., is a small industrial company with four courses on-line and is planning
to do more. So far the courses are available anytime to employees through the
company Intranet. There's no way to track who has access to the training, recording scores from the training, or determining who has completed the training. SIC
has 31 instructor-led courses, with about half provided by vendors who instruct
the classes and the other half being taught by trainers within the company.

Until now SIC has been using a simple program such as Registrar to manage
its instructor-led training. This is working well, but the company is interested in
shifting a number of its courses to the Intranet and needs to be able to manage them.

TABLE 15–1

Questionnaire for Screening Training Management System Vendors

Feature	Comments
Web-based training (WBT) features	
Can launch WBT	Yes or no; explain
Can track own WBT courses	Yes or no; explain
Can track others' WBT courses	Yes or no; explain
Is AICC-compatible now	Yes or no; explain to what extent
Future plans for AICC compatibility	Explain to what extent
Has browser for users	Yes or no
Has browser for administrators	Yes or no
Can support live WBT	Yes or no; explain to what extent
Can support discussion forums	Yes or no; explain to what extent
Instructor-led (ILT) features	
Capabilities	Explain
Database	
Which databases supported	
ODBC-compliant	Yes or no
Enterprisewide capability	
Largest implementation to date (number of users)	
Scalability	Explain
Worldwide architecture	Yes or no; explain
Skills-gap analysis and/or competency management	Yes or no; explain
Can check for prerequisites	
Curriculum management	Yes or no; explain
Certification management	Yes or no; explain
Administrator can customize	
Look and interface	Yes or no; explain
Fields	Yes or no; explain
Reports	Yes or no; explain
Number of full-scale implementations to date	
Year in which tool was developed	
Financial resources and stability of firm	
Other	
Have established links to other systems	Name them and describe link
Major competitive strengths	

SIC needs a straightforward training management system that costs $5,000 to $10,000 to purchase and install internally.

Once the system is in place, people will log on to the corporate Intranet and go to the training area. They will be able to see a training catalogue of all the courses, both on-line and instructor-led, and self-register for any of the courses.

When they register for one of the on-line courses and are approved for it, they will gain access to a new page with the URL for that particular course. When they click on the link, both the course and the training management system will be opened. A screen will appear requesting the name, employee identification number, and personal password. The training management system then will track whatever specifics the administrator chooses. For example, it can indicate who has started the course, who has completed the course, who is in progress, and what the scores were.

The training management system automatically provides reports to the administrator and the training manager on the information they want and at the frequency they want. Those reports are combined with the reports from the ILT management system to give them a complete picture of the training in their organization.

As SIC, Inc., adds any new courses, whether it is a prepackaged course or a custom-developed course, it can capture the information it needs from the course to integrate it into the reporting of its training management system.

Scenario 2

Izwix Enterprises is a software training company that has to be able to offer a training management system along with the courses it provides and installs on a customer's corporate Intranet. Each system will be stand-alone and will manage that curriculum internally for that customer organization. It also needs to be able to feed data, such as the licenses of current users, back into the company's main database to ensure accurate billing. It needs to have strong centralized components as well as a strong distributed computing component that will manage the flow of the information back and forth. Izwix also needs a system that is easy for the customers to maintain and that can work with a customer's existing system.

Scenario 3

MFC, Inc., is a manufacturing controls company that does as much customer training as employee training. Each year more than 150,000 students enroll in its courses. The company needs a program that is enterprisewide and can handle E-commerce so that when people register for a course from outside, they can pay with a credit card or through a company account. There has to be a way to track profiles of customers as well as those of employees who sign up for training so MCI can track the career paths they're on, what their skill gaps are, what the next learning opportunities are, what courses they've completed, when they've completed those courses, and so on. Because MFC offers more than 1000 courses a year, the company needs its training partners (i.e., the companies that provide instruction for its courses) to be able to maintain their portions of the course catalogue to reflect the descriptions of the courses, changes in instructors, scheduling, and the like. Administrators and users need to be able to access the system through a browser from anywhere in the world and go in and make changes in the specialized areas that are reserved for their use only.

Scenario 4

Worldwide Computers, Inc., has 110,000 employees and is interested in a training management system that can feed seamlessly into its existing large-scale, 3-year-old worldwide training management system. That system uses an Oracle database and manages training for all the company's employees. Worldwide Computers is also implementing SAP worldwide and needs a training management system that will integrate seamlessly with the SAP's human resources component, which currently tracks personnel information such as benefits and compensation. It also has a competency management system that defines competencies for different levels, and it needs to link that seamlessly with the training management system as well.

There is a mandate from upper management to shift 50 percent of all training on-line by the year 2000, including 100 percent of instructional technology training such as computer productivity skills, system administrator skills, and network specialist skills.

This company needs a very robust training management system that will grow with it and can manage an unlimited number of courses (it offers 2000 courses worldwide). Between the existing training management system and the new one, it needs to be able to manage ILT, on-line training, and self-study material such as CD-ROMs, books, videos, and outside development events.

Thus, Worldwide's system needs to be designed to deliver high performance with an Oracle database and has to be able to be hooked seamlessly with SAP and the existing training management system.

CHAPTER 16

Development Teams for Creating Technology-Based Training

James J. Goldsmith

Objectives

After reading this chapter, you will be able to:

- Understand the roles on a development team.
- Decide whether to use internal or external staff.
- Know where to find skilled professionals.

Assembling the right personnel can contribute significantly to a project's successful outcome. Assembling the wrong personnel can mean delays, confusion, internal strife, and any number of other career-threatening developments. As early as possible, and certainly before project design begins, it is important to give proper attention to staffing the project team with the right mix of talent and experience. Attention also needs to be paid when those people should join the team.

The principle is self-evident: Get the right people for the job. However, assembling a solid multimedia or Web team is not easy. The field of Web and multimedia development is growing rapidly, and the skilled professionals needed for a team can be difficult to find.

PROJECT TEAM FUNCTIONS

Who should be on the team? You need someone who will pay for the project and someone to run it. You need someone who knows the material well and another person who can write it all down. You need someone who can first figure out what the application should do and then determine how to do it. You need another person who can bring the material to life through illustration, animation, sound, music, and video. Finally, you need someone who can pull all this stuff together and package it so that it works.

In short, you need a team skilled in the following functions:

- Executive
- Content
- Design
- Media
- Technology

Of course, the level of skill required for each function varies with the project's length and complexity. Also, the application's goals will influence which functions will dominate. Nevertheless, all these functions are part of multimedia and Web development and must be properly staffed.

THE THREE TIERS OF THE PROJECT TEAM

The typical multimedia or Web project team logically falls into three groups. These groups, which serve different but complementary purposes, are

- Executive
- Core
- Transition

The executive group is composed of the client and management. These executives are involved in the project from beginning to end but, because they usually have other responsibilities, typically devote limited time to the project. In general, the team's infrequent interactions with the client and management tend to be both critical and brief.

The core group consists of the project manager, the lead designer, the lead programmer, the media manager, and the administrative assistant. For Web projects, the Webmaster may be part of this team. The core group has overall responsibility for the project and is intimately involved with it throughout the development cycle. Core group members may be asked to work on the project full-time through implementation, though core members with executive status may work only part-time because of other commitments.

The transition group is made up of the important role players who do most of the development work. These roles include the subject-matter expert, designer, programmer, scriptwriter, graphic artist, and media specialist. The transition group joins the project to fulfill specific roles at different times. These players may

FIGURE 16–1

The Project Team

Executive	
Client	Management

Core	
Project manager	Lead programmer
Webmaster	Media manager
Lead designer	Administrative assistant

Transition	
Subject-matter expert	Graphic artist
Designer	Media specialist
Programmer	Scriptwriter
Editor	

be required to work full-time on a project for long stretches but typically are not involved in all phases of the project cycle.

For a very small project (e.g., preparing a presentation that includes some multimedia elements) the core team (or even the entire project team) can consist of just one person. In this case a talented generalist could perform all the tasks. However, as projects become longer and more complex, more resources with specialized skills are required.

Figure 16–1 summarizes the personnel makeup of the project team.

THE ROLES

Let's examine these roles more closely. The descriptions that follow are detailed and some of the information may seem self-evident, but you can't be too explicit in defining a team role. The assumptions that one team member makes may not be shared by another, and this can lead to disastrous consequences ("I thought that was your job." "I didn't know you were going to do that."). Early in the project the team should discuss these roles and responsibilities in detail. This information should be recorded, published, distributed, digested, and revisited periodically.

For each role I have tried to address the following issues, though not always in this order:

- What they do
- What skills they need

- Issues associated with the position
- What motivates them

The Client

The client (or sponsor or any similar name) is the person who has agreed to enlist your services for a period of time and for a certain sum to do or provide something. Typically, you are helping the client solve a business problem or take advantage of an opportunity. Clients call you in because you can do something that they cannot do or lack the time or desire to do.

Your job is to understand their needs and then provide a product or service that addresses those needs. Your success will depend on your ability to

- Deliver the product or service as agreed to in the contract (with a level of quality that is acceptable or better and with a deliverable that is at least what was expected and maybe a little more)
- Deliver it on the targeted date (or sooner)
- Deliver it at the targeted cost (or less)

Clients like deliverables that are *predictable.* Interestingly, deliverables that are provided early and under budget can raise as many eyebrows as do ones that are late and over budget. The suspicion with early and/or cheap deliverables is that corners were cut.

Clients fund the project. They also

- Work with the core team to define the deliverable
- Provide subject-matter experts
- Review project work
- Sign off on interim deliverables at milestones
- Work with the core team to determine any adjustments to the deliverable during the development cycle (inevitably, with the passage of time, some early decisions give way to later, better-informed decisions)

Although there are exceptions, most clients are not "hands-on" players during product development either because they don't want to be or because they don't have the time. The team's job is to provide assurance that it is building or providing what the client has asked for and to address the inevitable production issues that arise during development. The team's infrequent but often intense discussions with the sponsor typically include the following topics:

1. Where the team said it would be
2. Where it actually is
3. If there are discrepancies between items 1 and 2 (and there will be), why this has happened and what the team will do about it

4. Where the team will be in the near future (generally by the next reporting period)

5. Any other news (especially bad news; it is in the team's best interest to relay bad news to the client as soon as possible and to address it before it gets worse)

Let's take a moment to examine the third item in more detail. Typically, as a project progresses, unanticipated issues surface. This is especially true for multimedia and Web development, which in general can be characterized as volatile and risky. As thorough as the most seasoned professionals try to be, unforeseen developments are inevitable, sometimes because of the changing nature of the business (e.g., a new version of a development tool is released after development is under way) or other variables (a significant change in content surfaces after the agreed-to content has been signed off). These developments are not necessarily bad; they may represent opportunities that have emerged over time. As was mentioned earlier, the point is that clients do not like to be surprised, and any changes, even for the good, have to be reviewed and negotiated. The sponsor's main concern is that the product be delivered as expected, and the team can maintain a good relationship with the sponsor by ensuring that this happens.

Whether a sponsor is internal (i.e., a member of your organization) or external, thinking of the sponsor as a member of the team will have a positive effect on your relationship, especially when you solve problems together.

To conclude, the sponsor's responsibilities are to

- Fund the project
- Provide overall goals and direction
- Provide visible high-level support
- Work with the executive group to address major project issues
- Sign off on deliverables

Management

Management includes the people the project manager reports to. It includes anyone other than the client who has executive responsibility for the course but is not on the core team. Independent producers may not have a management reporting relationship, but in a corporate environment management has considerable clout.

Like the client, management plays a key role in a project's success or failure. However, management has a focus different from that of the client. The client wants you to help it address a business need or opportunity. For management, the client *is* the opportunity. From management's perspective, your job is to meet or exceed the client's expectations while keeping within or below the contracted time and costs. The team's job is to make management happy by making the client happy. A satisfied client can lead to repeat business and positive referrals. The team represents the company, and the company wants to be perceived as a superior product or service provider.

Management has several needs, many of which overlap the client's needs. It also wants to know

1. Where the team said it would be
2. Where it actually is
3. Discrepancies between items 1 and 2
4. Where the team will be by the next reporting period
5. Any other news

However, unlike the sponsor, management's job is to help the team operationalize any issues associated with the project. It is management's job to

- Provide the team with the resources it needs, including time, money, people, and equipment (this sometimes means the painful process of requesting additional resources)
- Advocate and communicate to the team and any other interested parties company processes and procedures
- Approve the contract and project process
- Act as a liaison with the sponsor and an advocate for the team
- Work with the team and the client to establish success criteria
- Staff the project with the right mix of talent, skills, and experience
- Work with the client to identify subject-matter experts
- Explain how the team's project relates to other company projects
- Control any contingencies from other projects and let the team know how other company operations could have an impact
- Approve scope changes in the project (ones that add extra value to the final deliverable or ones that are approved by the client)
- Report the team's progress to upper management (if that reporting relationship exists)

Management establishes policies and guidelines and communicates them to the team. The team incorporates those policies and guidelines into the development process. In a large company the policies and guidelines may be detailed and exacting; in a small company they may be less formal. Companies of all sizes use standards to provide continuity from project to project, reuse process and procedures that work, and give a product or service an identifiable corporate stamp.

Also, the team relies on management to establish ground rules for success or failure. Besides understanding what has to be delivered, the team has to know how that will happen and what is expected of it. Focusing on the deliverable is not enough; management also must communicate clearly the processes that will enable creation of the deliverable and should do this early in the development cycle.

A primary responsibility of executives is to grow the staff. An effective way to do this is through coaching. Management should work with the team, especially the core team, to solve problems and exploit development opportunities. Stewardship is key to the long-term success of any team.

To conclude, management's role is to

- Communicate company policies and standards
- Outline success criteria
- Provide visible high-level support
- Provide resources
- Review and sign off at milestones
- Advocate for the deliverable
- Coach, mentor, and otherwise develop the team

The Webmaster

The Webmaster is the newest member of the team. Exactly what a Webmaster is or does is not quite clear. At a recent seminar, Ron Fernandez of NetObjects described a Webmaster as "anyone who was hired in a panic to put together a company's Web site."

Although the role is evolving and job descriptions vary from place to place (if they exist at all), Webmasters can be described as people who are responsible for developing, maintaining, and/or administering the hardware and software of a company's Web site. This site could be on the Internet, a specific Intranet, or both.

Webmasters have varied backgrounds, coming from film, publishing, graphics, training, advertising, multimedia, programming—in short, from anywhere. Initially, the Webmaster was a generalist who could set up the hardware, program the Web pages, and pack in the content. Now that Web sites have gotten more sophisticated and are big business, Webmasters have become more specialized, concentrating on hardware and software, site development, or content.

For a small project the Webmaster can absorb some of the other responsibilities for project development, such as graphics and media. For a large project he or she may concentrate solely on maintaining the Web site, allowing the designer to design the site, the subject-matter expert to supply the content, the graphic artist to create the graphics, the media specialists to supply the media, and the programmer to build the functionality. Any mix is possible, and the industry is still learning how best to apply the services of this new role.

The Lead Designer

Before discussing designers, let's briefly talk about design and try to put this elusive term into context. Design is the development of the means to address a need. It is the process of determining the format and, when appropriate, the associated activities that lead to the desired change. In multimedia and Web development, design is the process of devising formats and activities to support specific outcomes—the ones usually associated with information, learning, and/or entertainment.

Design is another critical-path role on the project team. An application's content can be solid, its programming can work well, and the project can be produced on time and on budget, but if the design is poor, the project will fail. The person who has overall responsibility for an application's design is the lead designer. On a small project the lead designer may be the only designer (and also may be the project manager, the graphic artist, the media specialist, etc.). On larger projects the lead designer may craft the design strategy and supervise one or more designers.

The lead designer has a great deal of responsibility because design drives every aspect of development. Although lead designers have much to think about, their responsibilities fall into three broad categories. They must be able to

- Develop the initial vision, although this sometimes is done at the highest level by the project sponsor or upper management. When this happens, the lead designer's job is to flesh out the vision.
- Determine the best way to implement the vision as it applies to the audience's needs.
- Articulate the vision and the plan to the project team (through a design document, functional specifications, an objectives matrix, and so on,) and then see the plan through.

The second point is the real test of design. Visions can be sweeping and profound (the vision of a car that uses seawater for fuel, for example), but figuring out how to make the vision work is the real trick. Thus, the best lead designers are both visionaries and pragmatists. They exploit possibilities but back them up with a realistic plan.

For a multimedia or Web project lead designers typically

- Work with the executive group and the project manager to articulate the training need and/or gap
- Work with the executive group and the project manager to identify deliverables, milestones, time frames, and budget and other project information
- Work with the core team to develop an appropriate approach to address the need
- Articulate the deliverable and the approach to the entire team
- Coordinate content, design, media, and technical development with the team
- Work with the team to implement the approach
- Test the approach and deliverable and make adjustments accordingly
- Review finished results and log lessons learned for the process and product
- Manage other designers (if they are needed for the project)

To fulfill these tasks, lead designers need many skills. Besides having a good understanding of general design theory, they need to know

- Software development
- Programming languages and authoring tools
- Graphics tools and techniques
- Audio, video, and animation production
- Storyboarding
- Screen design

Lead designers do not have to be expert programmers, but it helps. A lot of lead designers' time is spent imagining what could be done and then boiling that down to what is actually possible. Knowing what tools can and can't do makes this process much easier and adds credibility to a lead designer's decisions. This is true for media tools as well. The more a lead designer knows about the mechanics of graphics, animation, sound, and video development, the more informed the design decisions will be. Good lead designers are strong in all the basic project development functions, including management.

There's more. If lead designers are developing training and education applications, they also have to know

- Instructional design
- Adult learning theory
- Learning styles
- Motivation concepts
- Testing, evaluation, and validation processes
- Story development

What motivates lead designers to learn and continuously master so many skills? The answer varies from one person to the next, but many are driven by a need to develop something new, elegant, or unique. They like to create something that does not exist or improve something that does. They enjoy turning abstract thought into a workable solution. Lead designers are problem solvers. Although they may not build the application themselves, they are builders as well.

To conclude, the lead designer's job is to work with the team to develop, articulate, strategize, and implement the design vision.

The Designer

As we just discussed, the lead designer creates the "vision" of what a deliverable will be and how it will work. The designer may help in this process and then will spend a great deal of time developing the details that will make the vision work. Designers do much of the development work and work closely with the subject-matter experts (SMEs), graphic artists, media specialists, and programmer to create, integrate, test, and complete an application's components. Depending on the nature of the deliverable, the designer may develop

- Learning objectives
- Content (with the SME)
- Interfaces (with the media lead)
- Story (with the scriptwriter)
- Storyboards (with the graphic artist)
- Activities
- Exercises
- Glossaries
- Support materials
- Test scripts (for content)

Designers have many of the same skills as the lead designer, though typically they have less experience and spend more of their time on project details. Designers share goals with the lead designer with one notable exception: Many want to become lead designers themselves so that they can put their own stamp on the product.

The Lead Programmer

After an application has been designed, it has to be built. To a large extent this is the responsibility of the lead programmer and the programming staff. Programmers design an application's architecture and then write the code that enables its activities and usability components to function.

A distinction must be made between a programmer and an author. *Programmers* work with programming languages such as Visual Basic and C++. Program languages enable programmers to build routines and objects. These languages allow great flexibility but require considerable skill to use and generally entail more development time than do authoring systems. However, the extra effort pays off because projects that are programmed from scratch can be extremely efficient.

Authors work with authoring systems such as Macromedia's Authorware and Asymetrix's ToolBook. An authoring system offers precoded routines (built using a programming language) along with a metaphor of an icon, pages, or a timeline that is used to manipulate the routines. Authoring systems are easier to learn and use but offer less flexibility, and in general the finished product may be slower to complete than an application programmed from scratch. Instructional designers learn authoring systems so that they can build applications themselves. Hybrid systems such as Macromedia's Director offer the precoded routines of an authoring system along with base code (in this case the proprietary Lingo) to enable customization. As might be expected, the learning curve for hybrid systems is somewhere between that of authoring and that of programming.

Authoring systems are very good at what they were designed to do. If a system is designed to accommodate true-false questions and the application requires this, that system will meet the project's needs. However, if multiple-choice questions are required and the system does not provide them, building those questions from scratch with a programming language may be required. Thus, the trade-off is clear: Authoring is relatively easy to do and often does not require deep technical skills, but programming, though more difficult, provides the flexibility to address unique or demanding project requirements. The decision whether to program or author should be considered carefully and as early as possible.

Easy to use is a relative term. Authoring programs, especially ones with many options and features, require a significant investment of time and energy to learn and use. Additionally, complex routines require careful design and considerable development effort regardless of whether programming or authoring is used.

A summary of some of the advantages and disadvantages of programming languages and authoring systems appears in Table 16–1.

Because they are highly skilled and scarce, lead programmers are always in demand. [I was once at a convention where a human resources (HR) manager stood up at the end of a session and announced that he would provide an all-expenses-paid trip to Hawaii for two to anyone who could give him a lead on a C++ coder.] If the project's technical needs are specialized, there may be few in the pool who can fill the bill. When this happens, the lead programmer becomes a critical-path resource and extra effort must be applied to secure and retain this resource, generally with money. Befuddled project managers sometimes have to deal

TABLE 16–1

Advantages and Disadvantages of Programming Languages and Authoring Systems

	Programming Languages	**Authoring Systems**
Learning curve	Steep	Low to moderate
Resource availability	Scarce	Available (train yourself)
Flexibility	High	Low to moderate
Performance	Fast	Slow to moderate
Tool expense	Low	Moderate to high
Development expense	High	Low to moderate
Product support	Generally good	Variable, depending on vendor

with both the SME and the lead programmer as scarce resources and find themselves in the uncomfortable position of deciding how to divide up the budget to accommodate both.

Because their tools are constantly evolving, programmers have to be quick studies. Lead programmers in particular have to be adept with development tools because they have to determine how to use those tools to best meet the project's needs. Thus, the better lead programmers are flexible and versatile, with training and/or experience in

- Software development
- One or more programming languages or development formats (for multimedia, Visual Basic, C++, etc.; for Web-based development, HTML, Java, JavaScript, ActiveX, VRML, etc.)
- Technical architecture (in particular, object-oriented technology)
- Database construction and management
- Development and delivery hardware
- Unit, integration, concurrent, and regression testing

Because they work closely with the lead designer and others on the core team, the stronger lead programmers are familiar with

- Instructional design
- Audio, video, and animation production
- Storyboarding
- Screen design and usability

For projects that will be authored rather than programmed, authors need less technical competence but must be comfortable with software and should have training and experience in

- Authoring systems (for multimedia, some of the industry leaders include Authorware, ToolBook, and IconAuthor; for the Web, the ones just mentioned with plug-ins or specialized tools such as Dreamweaver Attain or hybrid systems such as Director)
- Instructional design (most authoring systems are built around instructional design metaphors)
- Database construction
- Screen design and usability

On a small project the lead programmer may be the only programmer. In that case he or she will be asked to design the technical architecture; prepare the technical specifications; write the application code; implement content, graphics, and media; test the application; roll out the completed product; archive the technology—in short, handle all the technical chores. On a larger project the lead programmer probably will have a staff of programmers to assist with the technical responsibilities. For these projects lead programmers concentrate on designing the technical architecture and setting the technical standards while overseeing the technical staff. Of course, the size of the staff and its level of specialization depend on the size and/or complexity of the deliverable.

Again, it varies with the individual, but lead programmers often are excited by the opportunity to design and build something "cool." Like lead designers, they want to create something new, elegant, or unique. They take pleasure in envisioning a technical architecture and then making it work. Lead designers also take pride in their mastery of programming languages and other technical development tools. These tools are their stock in trade, and the better lead programmers constantly polish their skills. Because of lead designers' enthusiasm for technical excellence and desire to master tools, project managers sometime have to review their work to check for scope creep.

For some programmers the act of programming is an end in itself. Authors, by contrast, tend to view authoring as a means to an end. Authors take pride in knowing how to use a tool (especially when they devise ways to circumnavigate its inherent limitations) but generally are more concerned with producing a deliverable. Authors typically wear more than one hat (and are often also designers), whereas programmers may concentrate all their energies on technical duties.

To conclude, lead programmers work closely with the core team to plan and build a project that meets client specifications as well as budget and schedule requirements. They

- Design the technical architecture
- Set the project's technical standards

- Set testing standards and oversee all phases of testing
- Monitor the development efforts of the technical staff (for larger projects)
- Program; integrate content, graphics and media; and test the application as needed (for smaller projects)

The Programmer

The programmer has many of the same responsibilities, skills, and interests as the lead programmer. Whereas the lead programmer is involved in the project from beginning to end, programmers typically are most involved during design and especially development.

On a multimedia or Web project the programmer may be asked to

- Help the lead programmer design the technical architecture
- Help the lead programmer prepare the technical specifications
- Write the application's code
- Implement content and media
- Write test scripts
- Test the application and amend it as needed

Not surprisingly, programmers often aspire to become lead programmers so that they can have a greater influence on a project's direction.

The Media Manager

Media are different formats that enable communication and expression. They include

- Text
- Graphics
- Video
- Sound
- Music
- Animation

On a large project the media manager coordinates all these formats to support the overall objectives of the application. The media manager works closely with the graphic artists to develop the look and interface; with the scriptwriters to develop the treatment and any media-related scripts; with the designers to coordinate the content and activities; with the media specialists to develop the video, audio, and animation (as needed); with the programmers to ensure that media elements are properly integrated into the application; and with the project manager to keep the project on time and on schedule. Media managers also coordinate the screening and scheduling of actors for video and audio productions. For Web projects the media manager also works closely with the Webmaster to make sure all media resources are properly deployed.

On a small project the media manager also may serve as the graphic artist, media specialist, Webmaster, and/or other roles. Media managers find satisfaction in helping create and implement the application's treatment and look.

Media managers need to be media generalists with training and skills in

- Design
- Graphic arts
- Graphic user interfaces and usability
- Media design and production (video, audio, animation)
- Media development tools such as Adobe PhotoShop, Adobe Premier, Microsoft, and FrontPage
- General management

To summarize, the media manager's job is to coordinate the design, development, and integration of all an application's media components.

The Media Specialist

Media specialists are the people who develop the media in multimedia. They work with the media manager to produce an application's

- Video
- Audio
- Animation
- Music

It is difficult to generalize about media specialists. Many concentrate on only one medium, though some handle multiple roles. Some aspire to become media managers, but others are content to stay in a supporting role so that they can hone their craft. Typically, media specialists work only briefly on a project, usually starting midway through production, after the scripts have been approved and the application has begun to take shape. Despite their limited involvement, media specialists' contributions are critical. As was indicated earlier, video often is regarded as an application's most powerful element. Ironically, even though their contribution is so vital, video specialists often don't have the "big picture" enjoyed by the core team because they are on the project so briefly. Today video is less prevalent in Web products because of slow transfer of video files on the Internet, but this will change as the Internet becomes more capable.

The Graphic Artist

A major aspect of an application's treatment is its "look." Graphic artists are responsible for designing and developing the look. They are also instrumental in creating the interface, working with the designer to make it complete, consistent, and easy to use. Graphic artists also spend a lot of time collaborating with other team members in various phases of development. They work closely with the designer to devise a treatment, with the scriptwriter to support the story line, with the programmer to integrate the visual elements, and with the media specialist to coordinate media development. Graphic artists provide the visual glue that holds a product together and gives it its defining characteristics.

Graphic artists need to be good at many things, especially if they work in multimedia and Web development. They must be skilled in

- Drawing, layout, and composition
- Design
- Graphic user interfaces (GUIs) and usability
- Media design and production
- Animation
- Media development tools such as Adobe PhotoShop and Macromedia Director

Graphic artists are creative individuals, and what often interests them is the chance to develop unique, powerful, or masterful images. Many also are interested in interface design and find satisfaction in creating elegant and usable GUIs. Creating a deliverable that is both professional and aesthetically pleasing is also a goal.

To conclude, the graphic artist's job is to

- Design and develop the application's graphic elements
- Help develop the treatment, logo, and other unifying elements
- Create the application's look

The Scriptwriter

In designing an application, a central concern of the core team is to develop a treatment. This treatment is a unifying device, an overall metaphor that gives an application its character and identity. Designers of video games spend a lot of time thinking about treatment, with results that range from the ordinary ("Doom") to the spectacular ("Myst"). Treatment deals with the who, what, when, where, how, and why of an application. It includes many elements, one of the most important of which is the story.

Many games and, increasingly, training applications are built around a story. Because stories are a part of our culture from childhood, the format is easily understood, and effective storytelling is very powerful. Audiences will overlook poor production values and even poor acting if the story is good (consider the original *Night of the Living Dead*), but good production values rarely compensate for a poor story (e.g., the most recent *Godzilla* movie).

Scriptwriters are hired because they are skilled with plot, character, and dialogue. Typically, designers have a good idea of what should be communicated but struggle to make the words and images natural and convincing. Also, they tend to try to insert too much content into the story line. A good scriptwriter can create a story that is believable and compelling while it supports the application's central premise. Much to the dismay of the design and programming staff, it is often the story that people think of first when they remember a multimedia application. The hours of exacting programming and design are ignored or forgotten.

Writing for Web and multimedia applications is a specialized skill. Traditional scripts for stage and television have a definite beginning, middle, and end. Multimedia scripts, in contrast, are nonlinear. A play proceeds exactly as the author intended, but how a multimedia or Web application unfolds is largely up to the user. A multimedia or Web scriptwriter must be able to write scenes that function independently but also can be grouped with other scenes in a different order while maintaining the integrity of the narrative line.

A large multimedia or Web production company may have its own in-house scriptwriters, but for many this skill is outsourced. Outsourcing makes sense because scriptwriters' involvement in a project is limited. They typically join the project during design (often working part-time) and stay until the last video is shot and okayed, roughly halfway through the development phase. Of course, their involvement is greater if the application requires a lot of video.

To summarize, scriptwriters must be able to

- Write and edit effectively in many styles, specifically for multimedia
- Understand the overall goals and purpose of the project
- Work with the designer to develop the treatment in support of those goals
- Develop the story line
- Write the scripts
- Update the story and scripts as needed
- Understand video production (including acting, directing, and editing)
- Deal effectively with change (because multimedia development is often an iterative process)

Scriptwriters in general are not hard to find, but skilled multimedia scriptwriters are. The art of multimedia and Web scripting is only a few years old, and unscrupulous amateurs sometimes pose as experts.

The Editor

We mentioned earlier that designers are often responsible for content development. We also mentioned that they are not always good storytellers, and so scriptwriters are brought in to help. Unfortunately, designers sometimes lack general writing skills as well. To address this need, the team hires an editor.

The editor has three principal responsibilities

- Editing for grammar, punctuation, and spelling
- Checking to make sure that what was meant to be communicated actually is communicated
- Checking for stylistic consistency (especially important when multiple authors are involved)

Editing multimedia and Web applications is a specialized skill. The nonlinear nature of the content can be confusing, and traditional editing techniques sometimes are not up to the task. Like the scriptwriter, the editor must be able to produce meaningful discrete chunks of information that can be ordered in any number of sequences. If this doesn't happen, the second point above can be in jeopardy.

Editors are great polishers. They enjoy taking sloppy phrasing and making it elegant and precise. Editors tend to be brought in on larger multimedia or Web projects and ones that have a lot of written content. The project manager or someone else on the team may double as the editor on a small project.

The Administrative Assistant

The logistics of running a Web or multimedia project can be enormous, and the administrative assistant (AA) is responsible for a lot of this. Among other things, AAs

- Schedule rooms for team meetings
- Document team meetings
- Maintain team calendars
- Order supplies
- Make travel arrangements
- Coordinate logistics for tests and other team events
- Transcribe video and audio
- Archive and maintain files
- Track down information (Net and library searches)
- Perform other clerical and administrative tasks

These tasks are not always glamorous, but they are very important. For a moderate to large project the team needs a dedicated AA from the first day through the end of the project. For a project to run smoothly, the administrative aspects have to be attended to throughout. The AA is particularly important for major events such as a pilot test. Pilot tests are very complex logistically, and many administrative chores must fall into place if they are to go well.

The best AAs on Web and multimedia teams have a good grasp of the development process. They understand the team's needs and are proactive in providing assistance. AAs like to bring order to chaos, and this is often needed.

AAs need to know

- Word processing (Microsoft Word)
- Presentation packages (Microsoft PowerPoint)
- Spreadsheets (Microsoft Excel)
- How to organize
- How to delegate

The Subject-Matter Expert

The subject-matter expert is the project's primary content resource. The best SMEs have deep knowledge or experience relative to the target deliverable and can communicate that knowledge effectively. They also are able to quickly understand the application's objectives and how to reach them. The value of an SME depends on his or her understanding of the topic and the number of other available SMEs in the field. From a project team's perspective, the best situation occurs when there are many experts and they all are available. More typical is a situation in which there are few experts and almost none are available. When this happens, the SME becomes *the* critical-path resource on the project.

The SME's job is to work with the team to supply or build the content. In some cases SMEs do this directly by writing the material themselves. In other cases they work with the team to develop the content through interviews. Sometimes the content is based on an article, book, or other source the SME has already developed. In this case the SME will work with the team to modify the existing materials.

The team's working relationship with SMEs depends on several factors, including whether the SMEs are

- Internal or external
- Full-time or part-time
- On-site or off-site
- From business or academia

As important as all these factors are, the most important factor concerning SMEs is motivation. Motivation is a key issue with all team members, but it is especially important with SMEs because from their point of view, the assignment and/or reporting relationship given to them may not be desirable. For some, participation on a multimedia or Web project may be a sideline, something they do between "real" projects. The assignment is not in their job description or development plan, and they are concerned that they will not be rewarded for their efforts. For others, participation in the project may be viewed as a distraction, something to be finished as quickly as possible so that "real" work can begin. In short, their perception could be that the assignment is trivial, transitory, and unrewarding. To avoid this situation, the team has several options:

- Compensate generously.
- Give the SME increased exposure for his or her work.
- Link the project to the SME's professional advancement.
- Establish a formal relationship.

Let's examine some of these points. Money is a great motivator, but some SMEs may be just as motivated by an opportunity to increase the audience for their work. In another scenario the team (specifically, management) could tie the success of the project to the SME's professional or career advancement. If the resource is internal, project participation could be added to the job description, with substantial benefits offered at the project's conclusion. If it is external, work on the course could become a significant résumé item. Another option is to make SMEs formal partners in a project, perhaps offering them a percentage of the profits or giving them an important reporting relationship on the team. Some creative thinking may be necessary to change an SME's negative attitude if these strategies do not work.

If it is lucky, the team may be able to find an SME who is already motivated. If the team is in the more typical situation of few experts with little availability, it needs to find out what the SMEs want and give it to them.

For a designer who will work with SMEs to be effective in that role, it is necessary to understand the application's content as quickly as possible. A good way to do this is to prepare all the written materials yourself. Interview the SME, ask a lot of questions, seek clarification, and, when ready, distill this information into the final written format. It is hard work, but your knowledge of the content will be both broader and deeper for your efforts, and it will mean less work for the SME, who may have limited time for the project.

SMEs sometimes downplay the importance of the design role, especially on training development projects. SMEs tend to be good communicators and sometimes mistake communication skills for instructional design skills. If this happens, work through the design with the SME and explain the thinking behind the instructional design.

To conclude, the subject-matter expert's role is to

- Provide expert testimony that can be translated into content
- Check the accuracy of all content developed for the application
- Work with the designer to ensure that the design and content are compatible

For more on the care and feeding of the SME, see my article "The Elusive SME" in the November–December 1992 edition of *CBT Directions*.

The Project Manager

Project managers will tell you that they are the most important people on the development team but, as was pointed out earlier, that distinction might apply better to the subject-matter expert, the lead programmer, or even the design manager. However, for anyone who has worked on a team that had a bad project manager, the importance of the role is quite clear.

Project management involves planning, implementing, and controlling an organized, temporary, and finite effort whose goal is to create a specific deliverable. Project managers are responsible for the overall welfare of a product and the project team. They have a lot to worry about, and so they tend to be generalists. Some of their responsibilities include

- Developing and maintaining project plans, time lines, and budgets
- Coordinating resources
- Working with the program manager to identify and address scope, time, money, resource, and quality issues
- Acting as a liaison to the sponsor and upper management
- Articulating the deliverable
- Providing status and budget reports on project progress
- Monitoring the quality of the deliverable
- Testing to ensure that the deliverable meets its overall objectives
- Facilitating team communication and addressing team issues
- Being resilient and adaptable
- Coaching the team and providing opportunities for professional development
- Assuming responsibility for the project
- In general, keeping the team on track to meet development milestones

For Web and multimedia projects they also have to

- Understand the unique design and technical issues associated with multimedia and Web development
- Maximize the potential of the multimedia or Web format for the product

- Keep current on technical, design, and media developments that can affect the project
- Coordinate and focus diverse creative, artistic, content, and technical resources to reach a common goal
- Work with the core team to ensure the integrity of the product
- Oversee the development of the application's treatment, especially the core activity, the interface, and the story
- Provide an atmosphere of stability
- Keep happy a unique group of professionals who have different talents, needs, and aspirations

Of course, with so much to worry about, multimedia and Web project managers are often grateful just to get through a project, but they also are driven by a desire to produce a good product and employ and develop good processes along the way. Some also are motivated by the opportunity to "grow" the team and see talents blossom. Others are motivated by money, power, and the opportunity to advance.

The roles described above are generic, and the specific titles can vary. For example, multimedia project managers also are called multimedia producers, and Web project managers sometimes are called Webmasters. Also, project teams can vary significantly in size from one person who does everything (common in early Web development) to 40 or more people developing a complex multimedia game or training simulation. Roles and role names will continue to evolve as the industry matures.

PROJECT TEAM DESIGN OPTIONS

Let's start at the top of Fig. 16–2 and consider the first dimension: internal versus external.

Internal resources are people currently employed by the organization. Some advantages of internal resources are that they

- Know the organization
- Know the project
- Are on-site
- Are a dedicated resource
- Have a long-term commitment
- Are under direct management control
- Don't say yes indiscriminately

External resources are consultants, vendors, and temporaries. Although they may have a long-term relationship with the organization, they typically do not receive the health insurance, pensions, profit sharing, and other "second paycheck" benefits of the internal staff.

F I G U R E   16–2

Dimensions of a Project Team

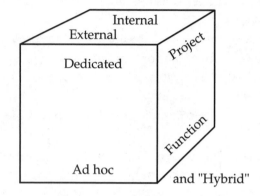

Some advantages of external resources are that they

- Have the skill set you need when you need it
- Have a broad perspective
- Incur lower overhead
- Are easy to expense to the project
- Can be disengaged quickly
- May be less involved in internal politics
- Are independent
- Can be objective
- Can serve as the fall guy (if the person who hired them is unscrupulous)

Unless a corporation has a sizable development department, it is unlikely that all the multimedia and Web team roles will be filled in-house. Also, it may not make sense to staff some of these roles unless there are several projects under way simultaneously. The specter of downtime is very real for the transition team members unless there are several projects for them to work on. Specialized tasks, such as acting and providing content expertise, are almost always contracted from outside, though in large companies content experts may be brought in from another part of the organization.

The next dimension to consider is dedicated versus ad hoc.

Dedicated project teams stay together from one project to the next. The advantages of a dedicated project team include

- Continuity
- Consistency

- Commitment
- Reduced start-up time
- Identification with the team
- High comfort level

Ad hoc project teams are formed to work on a specific project and then disbanded when the project is done. The advantages of an ad hoc team include

- Flexibility
- Variety
- Potential for better matching of skill to task
- Greater exposure to different ideas, procedures, and techniques
- Little downtime
- Less inbreeding
- Opportunity for a fresh start

If a group is essentially producing the same product from one project to the next, the dedicated team approach may be the right option. However, if the product is significantly different each time, different skills or experience will be needed and an ad hoc approach may make more sense. Of course, teams are always ad hoc to some degree because people retire, are transferred, leave to take another job, and so on.

Consider structuring your resources as a "SWAT team." A SWAT team in this context is a core team that stays together for several projects. The film director John Ford used this approach to casting. John Wayne, Ward Bond, Harry Carey, Jr., and Barry Fitzgerald appeared together in many of his films. Their success was due in no small part to fine ensemble acting brought about by the comfort that the team members felt working together.

The final dimension in organizing a team is function versus project. Design, programming, and media are all functions. When a team is organized by function, the team members report to their respective functional areas. Thus, a programmer would report to the technical manager, who would assign the work, review the employee's progress, recommend salary increases, and so on. When organized by project, the team members are accountable to the project manager. In this case the project manager assigns the work, reviews progress, and the like. Of course, a team could be organized by both function and project in a *matrixed* reporting relationship. Here the team member is accountable to both the functional area and the project manager. This may be the most equitable arrangement because the functional manager probably has the best perspective on the team members' skills and the project manager has the most knowledge about the actual work performed.

Teams rarely are staffed with only internal or external resources, organized purely as dedicated or ad hoc, or have reporting relationships that are exclusively functional or project. Instead, they have a mix of all these elements. These hybrid teams are the most common type found in multimedia and Web development because they are the most flexible.

STAFFING THE PROJECT (WHOM DO YOU NEED WHEN?)

Staffing is determined by several factors:

- The project's size
- The project's complexity
- Available resources
- The deadline
- Contingencies

This is a complex mix that has to be considered carefully. For example, if you have only a month to develop a Web site and estimate that the current team will be unable to handle all the content requirements, should you lobby for another resource to develop content or scale back the content for initial release and add to it later? Do you really need the sound engineer for the entire scheduled time?

The staffing profile shown in Table 16–2 illustrates the ebb and flow of resources on a representative project, in this case an 8-hour multimedia training course. The project will require about 6 months to complete and cost about $500,000. At about $62,500 per training hour, it is an application of moderate scope and complexity.

For a Web project the Webmaster would have a schedule similar to that of the project manager with one difference: Multimedia projects are close-ended. After a multimedia product is complete, it is assigned a version number and is not changed until a new development effort is approved. It then is revised and assigned a new version number. Web projects, by contrast, are open-ended and do not have version numbers. Because they are much easier to update and often are designed to be iterative, Web projects can continue indefinitely.

Several patterns emerge in Table 16–2. As was mentioned earlier, the executive group is involved in the project from beginning to end but only part-time, the core group is involved full-time for most of the project, and the transition team members come and go according to their roles. The project

- Begins modestly with the executive and core team doing most of the needs analysis
- Intensifies during the design phase, when the SMEs and designers begin their assignments

TABLE 16–2

A Staffing Profile

	Determine Needs	Design	Develop	Test	Implement	Evaluate
Time frame	2 weeks	6 weeks	12 weeks	6 weeks	2 weeks	Postproject
Expense	$20K	$120K	$240K	$100K	$10K	$10K
Client/sponsor	(X)	(X)	(X)	(X)	(X)	(X)
Management	(X)	(X)	(X)	(X)	(X)	(X)
Project manager	X	X	X	X	(X)	(X)
Administrative assistant	X	X	X	X	(X)	(X)
Lead designer	(X)	X	X	X	(X)	(X)
Designer 1		X	X	X		
Designer 2		X	X	X		
Lead programmer	(X)	(X)	X	X	(X)	(X)
Programmer 1			X	X		
Programmer 2			X	X		
Media manager	(X)	X	X	X	(X)	
Media specialist (video)		(X)	X	(X)		
Media specialist (animation)		(X)	X	(X)		
Graphic artist		X	X	(X)		
Script writer		(X)	X			
Editor			X	(X)		
Subject-matter expert 1		X	X	(X)		
Subject-matter expert 2		(X)	X	(X)		

Note: X = full-time; (X) = part-time.

- Intensifies again as development begins
- Peaks about halfway through development, when all the media efforts are under way
- Begins to taper off as development concludes and testing begins
- Drops off considerably when testing is complete
- Is represented only by a small part-time group through the final phase of implementation and evaluation

In the best of all possible worlds, the content determines the design and the design dictates the budget and work plan (Fig. 16–3). However, this is not always the case.

F I G U R E 16–3

Early Stages: I

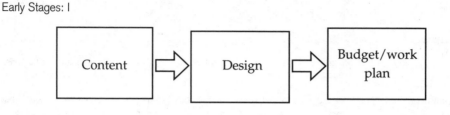

F I G U R E 16–4

Early Stages: II

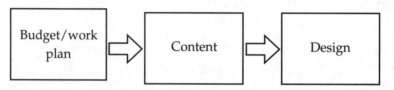

F I G U R E 16–5

Early Stages: III

Instead, what sometimes happens is that a budget is set and a tentative work plan is drawn up. At this point, the depth and breadth of the content are determined by the budget, which in turn influences the design (Fig. 16–4).

Of greater concern is the scenario where the budget and plan are drawn up, the design is set, and the content is then back-filled into the design (Fig. 16–5).

As these diagrams illustrate, the timing of staffing is critical. Designers can't design effectively if they don't know the content, yet they sometimes are forced to do this because content resources arrive too late in the design stage. Timing issues also affect other team members. Scripts completed after a scheduled video shoot date lead to significant cost overruns and delivery delays.

WHERE DO YOU FIND THE RIGHT PEOPLE?

If they don't already exist somewhere else in the organization, your best bet is referrals from friends or acquaintances who work in the industry. They may know someone who is looking for a job who might be a good fit. Another option is to network at conferences or professional society meetings. These events have many participants who may be suitable for a team role. Also, many people are there because they are looking for work. The third and least preferred method is to use an employment agency. This process is time-consuming and expensive and may not yield the results you want, but if friends and professional organizations fail you, it may be the only option.

Here is a sampling of professional societies to investigate:

- American Society for Training and Development (ASTD)
- Association for Computing Machinery (ACM) and SIGGRAPH, the association's special-interest group on computer graphics and animation
- Association of Proposal Management Professionals (APMP)
- Association for Project Management (APM)
- Center for International Project and Program Management (CIPPM)
- Institute of Electrical and Electronics Engineers (IEEE)
- International Interactive Communications Society (IICS)
- International Society for Performance Improvement (ISPI)
- Project Management Institute (PMI)
- Society for Technical Communications (STC)
- Software Publishers Association (SPA)

Some conferences to consider include the following:

- ASTD Technical Training Conference and Exposition
- Computer Game Developers Conference
- COMDEX
- InfoComm International
- Interactive Multimedia (ASTD)
- International Interactive Communications Society (IICS)
- Internet World (Mecklermedia)
- International Society for Performance Improvement (ISPI)
- Learning Technology Conference & Expo (Ziff-Davis)
- Macromedia Developers Conference (Reed)
- New Media Instructional Design Symposium (Influent)

- Online Developers Conference (Jupiter Communications)
- OnLine Learning Conference and Exposition
- Seybold Web Publisher Conference (Ziff-Davis)
- Society for Technical Communications (STC)
- Training IT Conference and Expo (Training/Inside Technology Training)
- VISCOMM

This list is not comprehensive, and by the time this chapter is published, some of these conferences may no longer be offered. Most active societies and conferences have a Web site, so check there for more information.

CONCLUSION

It's clear that having the right people on the team is essential to a project's success, but it is also clear that finding and keeping the right people is a challenging task. A good understanding of what they do, what they need to know, when you need them, and what they want is critical. So also is giving them an opportunity for continued growth and development. Applying your knowledge of team functions, roles, organization, and character will help ensure the successful conclusion of a project.

CHAPTER 17

How to Design and Develop Technology-Based Training Without Storyboards

Robert S. Zielinski, Dr. Michael Allen, Steve Lee, Dr. Lynn Misselt, and Joan Busch

Objectives

After reading this chapter, you will be able to:

- Design and develop interactive training.
- Describe the significant differences between the iterative SAVVY model and traditional instructional systems design (ISD) methodologies.
- List the benefits of using an iterative methodology.
- Use checklists to ensure that your project remains on track.
- Describe how this methodology worked in a case study.

Developing courses for delivery by CD-ROM or on-line requires a different approach from traditional instructional design. SAVVY is a unique process that includes early prototyping and quick iterations for the design, development, and evaluation of interactive multimedia. This process improves the results of course design regardless of the authoring or development tool used and restores sanity and inspiration to this challenging work (Allen 1993).

After completing this chapter, you will be equipped to design truly interactive multimedia for delivery by CD-ROM, the Internet, or an Intranet, using a process that is in sync with today's media and authoring tools.

OVERVIEW

Unlike instructional systems design (ISD), which is too linear for a computer environment in which random access and nonlinear progression carry the end user off in a wide variety of learning directions, SAVVY is a successive approximations approach that

FIGURE 17–1

The SAVVY Approach

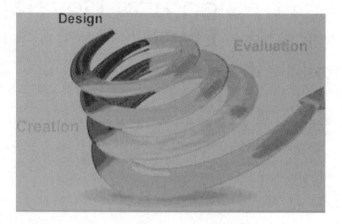

iterates design, creation, and evaluation activities in small steps (Fig. 17–1). This assures project stakeholders that the evolving designs are effective and desirable solutions. As a result, course corrections occur before significant resources have been invested.

KEY FEATURES

As you begin to use the SAVVY model of rapid prototypes and frequent iterations to design and develop interactive multimedia, you will recognize the following key differences between it and traditional ISD approaches.

Iterative Design

Design occurs in small steps and evolves through a controlled and creative "what if" process that includes frequent reviews and evaluations. Iterations commonly require only a few minutes to a few hours to complete. If you are spending more time than this to "complete an iteration," perhaps you are spending too much time.

Rapid Prototyping

Early prototypes are built to present "disposable ideas" for review and discussion. In exploring design opportunities for a specific content area, you should create multiple prototypes (i.e., ideas) for the same content. Then, taking the best of all those ideas, continue to develop prototypes that are more refined. If the parts of the content are quite dissimilar (heterogeneous), a greater number of prototypes will be necessary to explore each content area. You should always be willing to throw away a prototype once it has served its purpose.

End User Involvement

From a project's inception, design possibilities are tested by representative end users. In a traditional ISD approach, such involvement by the end user typically is feared because a significant investment has already been made in the analysis, design, and development of the project. Therefore, incorporating ideas generated by the end user could mean that much of that investment is wasted.

Model-Based Production

Finding cost-effective methods for creating interactive multimedia has led many organizations to use models. Unfortunately, these organizations commonly sacrifice instructional results in their attempts to reduce production costs or implement design standards. With SAVVY, designs, styles, and standards are built into high-productivity tools customized for the specific content. Because the models are based on the content, not acquired independently of the content, instructional integrity is maintained while development is conducted more cost-effectively.

Full Team Participation

In a traditional ISD project, the phases of analysis, design, development, implementation, and evaluation usually are conducted independently by different sets of individuals. In using SAVVY, all team members are involved in the project at an appropriate level from conception to completion.

Optimal Breadth versus Depth

There is no greater challenge to developing interactive multimedia than maintaining the delicate balance of human resources applied to the project. Critical to success is adherence to the plan of giving successive attention to all areas of content development. In other words, one must not delve too deeply into the perfection of one content area before giving attention to others. Doing so risks losing control of the budget, schedule, and quality consistency because too much has been invested in only one area.

These risks are not the only reasons for spreading successive layers of attention across the full body of content. Moving on to other areas of content almost always gives designers and developers insights that are valuable and applicable in multiple areas. If one area is "perfected" before these insights have been gained, project managers are then faced with only two alternative paths, both of which are objectionable: (1) Leave the "perfected" areas as they are, inconsistent and weaker than the rest of the project, or (2) toss out finished work, redevelop it, and let the budget and schedule slip.

COMMON MULTIMEDIA DEVELOPMENT PROBLEMS

In creating technology-based courses, it is important to be aware of the many frustrations experienced in developing interactive multimedia, including the following.

Poor Design

Despite the work of multimedia designers who have years of experience, powerful authoring tools, and the best intentions, too many interactive multimedia courses are mediocre at best. Fortunately, this is often a characteristic of the process, not the individuals involved in the creation of the design. Deal with the issues that lead to poor design in the ways shown below.

Design is often affected by politics.	A traditional approach to designing multimedia often results in an environment of political negotiation. Final design elements are implemented on the basis of the power of or sacrifices made by the individuals involved. Instead, allow designs to be created through end user validation. While the design team may provide a starting point, it is the project stakeholders' needs and responses that ultimately determine what the final program must contain.
Ineffective paper-based designs are a standard part of the process.	It is difficult to communicate the nonlinear random nature of an interactive multimedia application complete with time-based events such as animation and three-dimensional positioning by using a paper-based representation. Instead, use rapid prototypes displayed in the final medium to assess alternative designs and usability. This perspective facilitates the creative design process typically experienced in the writing of a document on a word processor or the composition of music on a piano keyboard.
Much multimedia design focuses on presentation.	Multimedia design typically focuses on the presentation of content. Instead, focus on the design of interactivity to create memorable experiences.
The inability to incorporate late-arriving design ideas results in mediocre applications.	The best design ideas arrive when one has the ability to experience the design in the intended medium. This explains the common phenomenon of design team members, subject-matter experts, clients, and end users

contributing ideas long after the design phase has been completed and development is under way or even finished. Instead, use an iterative approach in which such contributions are expected and acceptable because the design being experienced by the design team members and end users is an early prototype, not the final product.

Excessive design efforts lead to defensiveness.

The longer one works on something, the more resistant one is to throwing it away. However, if a better design idea evolves or is offered by a project stakeholder, the original idea should be discarded. For this reason, an iterative design model such as SAVVY uses small design steps with a great deal of review to promote objectivity and reduce resistance to holding on to an idea.

Time Overruns, Cost Overruns, and Missed Deadlines

Sophisticated project management tools have been developed to track each element of a project. Detailed graphs and statistical reports may be created to show a project's progress and its relationship to the proposed budget and schedule. With these sophisticated tools, however, it is estimated that over 70 percent of all projects are not completed within the proposed budget and time frame. An iterative approach to design, as shown below, can provide a solution.

Problems are discovered too late in the process.

In the typical ISD process, program design concepts are not seen in the actual delivery medium until after development. Therefore, problems with the design often are discovered too late. To modify the program, either the design must be compromised and the problem not rectified or costly rework must be undertaken. Instead, ensure that these design issues are discovered during the design process by employing functional prototypes, with only an insignificant amount of the budget used.

Creeping elegance affects the budget and schedules.

The development phase of the ISD process generally forces the production team to focus on production quality rather than the overriding objectives of the program. With the SAVVY approach, all the members of the project team focus on the project objectives and every decision to iterate further is based on those objectives.

Invalid design assumptions cause misdirected production efforts.

While ISD does incorporate analysis and often feedback regarding the program design, the project stakeholders (e.g., subject-matter experts, clients, end users, managers, development team members) can imagine the program's functionality only on the basis of their interpretations of paper-based storyboards. Equipped with such feedback, the ISD development team then moves into production, only to discover later that the stakeholders did not understand the design. Costly modifications must be made to satisfy their needs. Instead, make sure the design is validated repeatedly by using functional and visual prototypes before production begins, reducing the risk of misunderstanding.

End user nonacceptance is a risk.

The ISD process commonly requires end user analysis, interviewing, and guidance before design begins. From the point of design until the storyboards are created, however, the end user is unable to experience and validate the design. One could question whether the personal interpretation of a storyboard is tangible enough to provide the dialogue necessary to validate the design. Without such a dialogue and the resulting validation, the members of the design team cannot be sure they have truly met the end user's needs. Make sure the project stakeholders are involved in the evolving program design. This can occur when functional prototypes are created early, shown to the stakeholders, and immediately modified in collaboration with the stakeholders on the basis of their feedback.

Media assets produced early in the development process are unusable.

In creating an interactive multimedia project with an iterative design, many multimedia assets (audio, video, three-dimensional graphics, and animation) are created later in the project. This makes design revolve around interactivity as opposed to the presentation elements. As a result, more media are usable because these assets are created in context of the final design rather than in anticipation of it.

Team Stress

Developing interactive multimedia is not an easy task. Dealing with the frustrations of technology, the pressure to maintain a budget and schedule, the wavering desires of a client, and the egos of team participants results in a tense and volatile environment, as shown below.

Reviews are characterized by fault finding and blaming.

Instead, use a process that calls for frequent reviews of small steps in which corrective feedback is actively sought and appreciated. With only modest amounts of effort invested at each step, designers and developers are less likely to have the strong sense of ownership that causes one to become defensive about criticism.

A linear-phased process generates misinterpretation and results in wasted development.

Miscommunication and missed expectations are the greatest causes of team stress. When direction is left to interpretation, such misunderstandings commonly occur. Instead, rely on functional prototypes to communicate throughout the design and development process. In this way, misunderstandings can be avoided or at least caught quickly.

Changes imply failure and express criticism.	Instead, use an iterative approach and a team environment in which changes in the program's design and direction are fundamental, expected, and appreciated. Each member of the team understands that a design direction cannot be understood fully until it is experienced in the final delivery medium by project stakeholders and therefore is subject to change.
Team members have fragmented project involvement.	When the phases of an interactive multimedia project are handled solely by a set of individuals who specialize in that phase and after the completion of a phase the project moves to a new group of individuals, team members feel fragmented and out of touch with the goals of the project. Instead, keep all the team members fully involved in the project from beginning to end. Such participation results in a tremendous sense of ownership and an increase in overall product quality.
Development becomes tedious, laborious, and monotonous.	Developers of interactive multimedia typically need to feel that they are contributing creatively to the product. If they are left in a production capacity, team members become bored. Allow each team member to participate in design, development, and evaluation. This results in a true sense of contribution.

Low User Acceptance and Unmet Objectives

The ultimate goal of an interactive multimedia project is to have the program accepted by the target population and have the defined objectives met. Because of the pervasiveness of mediocre multimedia, however, end users are quick to judge an application. If the application does not immediately prove to be easy to use or to meet their needs, the end users are very much willing to discard the program. For this reason it is important to ensure that the program will be a success with the end users, as shown below.

The final application is confusing, nonmotivating, and/or irrelevant.	We tend to assume that other people are pretty much like ourselves. This leads us to design interactive multimedia much as we'd like to see it for ourselves. However, learners are often very different from us. Their motivations, current knowledge and skills, views of management (and purposes in creating this learning "opportunity"), and comfort with computer technology probably differ greatly from ours. Requiring involvement of typical end users is vital to correcting potentially fatal design errors derived from faulty assumptions. Focus group tests are a common means of collecting feedback on the usability of an interactive multimedia application. Unfortunately, the findings from these sessions often are not implemented to the fullest extent because of the

	project time frame and budget constraints. Make sure end user validation occurs early in a project through the use of functional prototypes. In this way, feedback on usability, motivation, or content relevance may be implemented with little or no impact on the time frame and budget.
The final application performs poorly.	It's easy to design high-potency interactions that are soundly based on learning research, fit the content and learner profiles, have fascinating media, and look perfect in storyboards but perform so poorly on the chosen platform that they are worthless. Instead, use functional prototypes along the way to force the team to test the practicality of designs from the beginning and provide an important safeguard against overdesign errors.
There is an inadequate means to create early end user buy-in.	The best-designed content has little value in a program that end users are not willing to use. Learning that end users are not motivated by a program after development is of little value. With the use of functional prototypes all along the way, end users evaluate the program, contribute to its development, and with each iteration grow more enthusiastic about its implementation.

PUTTING AN ITERATIVE DESIGN PROCESS INTO PRACTICE

Before beginning an interactive multimedia project, you must remember that it requires an iterative and extremely collaborative methodology. Therefore, while the methodology is described in a linear fashion in this chapter, you must be willing to revisit events previously determined to be complete. For example, it is not uncommon to discover during design that further instructional analysis must be conducted or that during modelization additional SAVVY design must occur.

ENGAGEMENT PLANNING

Every multimedia development team, whether developing projects for internal use or as a production company, has preproject formalities that must be addressed. These activities are completed in the engagement planning phase. The following tasks are those we have found helpful. Those completed by your team may be very different.

Establish Project Administration Systems

Spending a little time before a project begins to determine what information you may want at the end of the project is a worthy exercise. For example, many development teams want to track how much time is contributed by each person on the team or how much cumulative time is dedicated to each phase of the project. Knowing this information before you begin a project makes it much easier to assemble such information at the end.

Assign a Project Team

Unless the entire development team is dedicated to every project, determine which specific individuals with their respective talents are appropriate for this initiative. Knowing all the players who ultimately will contribute is critical to the success of a project.

Develop a Management Plan

The entire project team should work together to create a plan that contains the initial problem statement, the stated goal, and a description of the phases to be undertaken throughout the project. Additionally, the plan should include a clear definition of the players and the role each one will play, a statement of project risks, and a plan for communicating throughout the project. Finally, the management plan should include a description of the desired deliverables and a means for managing change in those deliverables over the life of the project.

All project stakeholders should approve the management plan before instructional analysis begins.

Communicate the SAVVY Process

The overall success of development depends on the degree to which each individual involved understands the entire SAVVY process. Therefore, you should spend time at the beginning of each project to educate all the participants who will be involved in the project. If you are developing for an internal client, all development team personnel and subject-matter experts should be educated. If you are developing for a third-party client, that client should be included in the education process.

INSTRUCTIONAL ANALYSIS

The tangible creation of a project begins with instructional analysis. It is during this phase that you first explore the problem to be solved, the end user, the environment in which learning occurs, and the content. While incorporating professional practices for conducting analysis helps expose critical issues in each of these areas, you must accept the fact that additional items requiring analysis will arise once SAVVY design begins.

Instructional analysis consists of the following events.

Problem Analysis

Problem analysis incorporates methods for identifying what is preventing the desired behavior from happening and then selecting from among potential interventions or solutions. It determines whether instruction is an appropriate solution or only part of the solution. For example, technology-based noninstructional solutions such as information systems and electronic performance support systems may be more appropriate than training. Some problems may require process engineering, job redesign, compensation structures, feedback systems, or other interventions instead of or in addition to multimedia technology.

Learning Environment Analysis

In addition to identifying an instructional problem, activities in this area should lead to a description of the learning environment: the context in which the training is to be delivered. The hardware, software, and management structures for encouraging and monitoring completion of training delivery are extremely important variables in the learning environment.

Learning Task and/or Content Analysis

It is also necessary to analyze the job-related knowledge and skills related to desired performance. This involves identifying tasks that constitute competent performance, learners' current deficiencies regarding those tasks, and the problems learners are having performing each task. The purpose of task analysis is to develop performance objectives that describe the knowledge and skills that should result from instruction and develop measures for determining whether the desired learning has occurred.

Learner Analysis

Identifying and understanding the current situation and the desired outcome are necessary in creating an effective solution, but without a solid understanding of the learner, your interactive multimedia is unlikely to provide the desired outcome. Careful study of the learners must identify how they are motivated, what they find useful in performing the stated job-related skill, and what they believe would make the final product usable. The end user must be a primary influence in the design of the interactive multimedia application.

Analysis Sign-Off

At this point in the project it is important that all relevant stakeholders (client, end users, project team members, etc.) agree on the following:

- The defined problem and goal statement
- A description of the learner, including entry skills and a motivational profile
- A description of the instruction and other potential interventions
- A description of the learning environment and project constraints
- The performance objectives
- Sample test items and/or assessment measures

Therefore, you should seek acceptance of these definitions in the form of an analysis report by requiring key stakeholders to sign off.

SAVVY DESIGN

The SAVVY design phase consists of a series of analysis, synthesis, and evaluation cycles related to design decisions. The goal of this phase is to narrow the design choices and achieve agreement among all stakeholders about the design of navigation, interface, interactivity, assessment of learning, and so on.

Collaborative and iterative design requires several important elements:

- Instructional design skills to identify types of learning and select appropriate instructional methods
- Tools (and skills) that permit rapid functional and visual prototyping with minimal investment and delay
- Commitment to the goals of rapid collaborative prototyping (stakeholder participation and buy-in, more valid designs with internal and external consistency, more rapid design cycles, etc.)
- Commitment to rapid review and focused evaluation as well as rapid prototyping
- Skills in leading a group process of design inquiry and problem solving to create a solution design that meets the requirements and constraints identified in the learning analysis
- Commitment by the development team to adhere to the established budget and other constraints

SAVVY design consists of the following steps.

Sequence Primary Content and Classify Learning Types

Learners will be motivated if each learning step results in meaningful (i.e., useful) outcomes. Instead of attempting to sequence tasks according to hierarchical prerequisites, you should break the content into "chunks" that learners can easily see have functionally useful outcomes. Successfully completing modules of instruction in which learners acquire meaningful skills provides intrinsic feedback for the accomplishment. Such feedback is highly motivating for continued study.

As the content is organized into meaningful blocks that need to be validated by typical end users, it is also helpful to note the types of content that constitute each module. Although various theories of content codification can be used, we find it helpful to use Merrill's classifications of fact, concept, procedure, and principle together with the required performance classifications of remembrance, use, and find (Merrill 1983).

Prepare Functional Prototypes

A functional prototype (or model of the solution) provides the user with a tangible and dynamic look at an evolving solution to, and definition of, the problem. If a functional prototype is used to design an application, end users can point to features they don't like in an existing design (or indicate what feature is missing) rather than describing what they would like in an imaginary system described in paper-based storyboards. SAVVY facilitates a "design by doing" process in which the problems and the solution are discovered simultaneously.

Iteration is at the heart of SAVVY. Analytic, developmental, and evaluative activities tightly intertwine in recurring cycles, while minimal investment enables the design process to become a discovery process. Additionally, it is important to stress collaboration. End users are rightfully active participants, contributing to product design through both feedback and observed behavior. Through iteration and collaboration, stakeholders discover a level of interactivity that not only engages the end user but communicates the intended content.

Prepare Visual Prototypes

In much the same way that a functional prototype is created to communicate interactivity, navigation, sequence, and the like, a visual prototype is created to explore various options for metaphor, color, style, layout, and so forth. These prototypes should be presented not only independently of the functional prototypes but also married to the functional prototypes so that the stakeholders can experience the true context of the visuals.

Select Instructional Methods

In selecting instructional methods, develop several prototypes of varying instructional methods for each type of content to be learned, using the specific content as the base. Be careful not to perfect the details of these prototypes at this point; instead, look for creative interfaces that will relate well to both the end users and the content.

Then, still before refining the prototypes, go on to all the types of content to be included and develop experimental prototypes for them as well. After reviewing the prototypes with typical end users and subject-matter experts, select one or more of the better prototypes for each type of content and make a second effort to refine or replace them.

Next come steps to test the generality of the chosen instructional prototypes and test to see how well the structures can be integrated with each other. Of course, not all of them will integrate directly with each other, so look at the sequencing of content and its classifications to see which interactions do fit together. All interactions will need to use consistent user interface conventions. It's likely that you'll find variances in user interface that need to be worked out. This is a good time to do it.

The generality of selected prototypes is tested by substituting various segments of content that have the same type classification but deal with different topics. Try to find some topics that seem very dissimilar and some that seem quite similar to see if one prototype is sufficient or if multiple structures will be needed.

Select and Sequence Supporting Content

Traditional ISD developers are used to doing extensive content analysis in an attempt to determine every component of a task that must be learned before the task as a whole can be performed. These analyses are just as valuable to the SAVVY team, but the process more easily accommodates the inevitable errors and omissions. It's important to list all the items to be learned in the process of acquiring a new meaningful skill. Subject-matter experts and seasoned instructors give instructional designers their appraisals, but this only initiates the process of determining the best scope and sequence. The real experts on what's needed are the end users, but until they have something to react to, they are unable to contribute much.

This is where the iterative process and the experimental approach prove valuable. Observing learners working through hastily constructed instructional sequences helps designers verify the intuitive suggestions of the experts and designers. Being open and sensitive to the comments and behaviors of end users, designers usually can determine quickly where content components need to be added and where too many exist. Some areas may prove perplexing and several experiments may be needed to determine the best collections of content components, but getting this worked out to a "nearly correct" design is usually enough.

It will be possible to move things around later cost-effectively as long as this is done before the development of final media resources and one is using an authoring tool with the necessary flexibility. At this point all that's required is a reasonably thorough listing of all learning tasks organized into modules of manageable size, each of which clearly focuses on one or more outcomes that will be meaningful to the end users.

SAVVY Design Sign-Off

At this point it is important that all relevant stakeholders (the client, the end users, the project team members, etc.) agree to the functional and visual prototypes defining the

- Navigation options
- Menu structures
- Presentation methods
- Style of interactions and feedback
- Methods for student assessment

Additionally, all stakeholders should agree to a design plan that defines the

- Training program structure (scope and sequence)
- Selected instructional methods
- Student assessment techniques
- Implementation plan

At this point you can produce and confirm the

- Project budget and time frame
- Role definitions

MODELIZATION

The modelization phase prepares the project team for mass production and future maintenance of the interactive multimedia application. Functional prototypes are used to guide reengineering of the source code, resulting in clean, efficient structures that can be reproduced easily. Be sure you have truly validated the functional prototypes with the end users before beginning modelization, because later changes can be costly and disruptive.

For larger-scale projects or projects with significantly homogeneous interactive structures, modelization assumes that the original prototype will be thrown away. Lessons learned through the many prototypes created during SAVVY design will be used to create a more efficient and robust structure.

Functional prototypes also are used to indicate opportunities to separate the content from the code structure. Text files, external media files, and databases are common content repositories, and authoring tools are growing in the ability to link to and control content in those sources. Separating content from code allows much easier maintenance, modification, and additions of content.

Modelization consists of the following steps.

Build and Test the Navigation Shell and Interaction Models

Preparation of the navigation shell and interaction models involves engineering efficient code structures that can be used by the development team. Quality criteria assessing the functionality, modularity, ease of use, ease of interfile transport, and ease of maintenance must be established and managed. Throughout modelization you should identify opportunities to

- Review functional prototypes to confirm design intent and technical requirements
- Identify potential areas for replication, such as interaction types, variable settings, and function routines
- Identify areas for consolidation, such as repeated sequences, record keeping, and simulation
- Conduct quality assurance testing and make revisions as necessary (quality assurance is conducted to ensure that the models are error-free before mass replication)

The result of modelization is often source code with the following characteristics:

- Smaller file size
- Fewer icons or lines of code and/or script
- Greater use of content libraries and externally linked content resources
- More adaptability to modification or expansion

Finalize Graphic User Interface

Using the visual prototypes as a guide for color, design, layout, theme, and so on, and the functional prototypes as a guide for usage-related issues, at this point in the project you should build the final graphic user interface. This final iteration should include all the navigational elements, including button states, as well as the multimedia assets tied to those elements, such as sound effects.

Establish Structures and Procedures for Content Integration

Before content is collected, structures and procedures for preparing and integrating content (audio scripts, content narratives, video storyboards, etc.) should be established. These structures may be as simple as a word-processing template or as sophisticated as a database entry tool. Additionally, standards for text, graphics, audio, video, and animation elements should be defined and file-naming and asset management procedures should be established.

Acquire Modelization Sign-Off

At this point it is important that all relevant stakeholders agree to a content preparation plan that defines the

- Structures and procedures for preparing (audio scripts, content narratives, video storyboards, etc.) and integrating content
- Standards for text, graphics, audio, video, and animation elements
- File-naming and asset management procedures

Additionally, all stakeholders should agree to a project development plan that defines the

- Task and/or resource plan
- Quality assurance and quality control procedures
- Formative evaluation plan
- Implementation plan
- Project schedule
- Budget allocation

Finally, at this point you can confirm the

- Final graphic user interface
- Interaction model code

PRODUCTION

The goal of production is to implement the design faithfully, create and integrate the content, and assure the quality of the completed modules and program. It is not unusual for the production phase to overlap somewhat with the modelization and formative evaluation phases. In fact, it is often beneficial to gain experience in the use of the navigation shell and interaction models, content preparation methods, and the like, to guide refinements and plan resource needs more precisely. Similarly, lessons learned through end user trials of early modules can influence planning for later modules.

Production consists of the following steps.

Prepare the Content

Traditionally, the most tedious production task in an interactive learning application is the development of content. Subject-matter experts and writers spend hours being tossed between covering the content and maintaining an end user's interest.

Collecting content for an iterative-based project is very different from collecting content for a project with a traditional development approach. By following SAVVY design and modelization in which procedures and structures for collecting content are established, subject-matter experts and writers are able to develop content more easily. In many cases, as content is collected according to the established procedures, both content collectors and project team members can immediately see the content as it will appear in the final program.

Prepare Multimedia Assets

By using the functional prototypes to guide development, graphic artists begin replacing placeholder elements with final artwork, animators replace crude path animations with rich animation, and professionally produced assets replace scratch video and audio. Visual prototypes again are used to define the palette, style, and theme of the assets. Because design decisions have been confirmed through end user validation, multimedia assets can be created with confidence that few or no changes will be made.

Integrate Content and Multimedia Assets into Navigation Shell and Interaction Models

As content is harvested and multimedia assets are created, they may be integrated into the navigation shell and interaction models. This step can be simplified if a functional link is established to placeholder elements during modelization. When this is done, the final content assets appear in the final application as soon as they are created.

Conduct Quality Assurance, Client Review, and Testing

As content is integrated and modules of content become complete, they are eligible for formal quality assurance testing, client review, and formative evaluation. Delivering applications with a small number of completed modules allows testers to focus on those modules while providing feedback that may affect all the modules.

FORMATIVE EVALUATION

As described in the SAVVY design phase, end user collaboration in iterative design (or, at a minimum, end user review to validate design prototypes) is anticipated. This iterative and collaborative process improves the design.

When representative modules are completed in the production phase, the completed module or modules can be reviewed by the stakeholders and subjected to formative evaluation trials by end users. The purpose of formative evaluation is to verify functionality and improve the effectiveness of the instructional content while the program is being developed.

Formative evaluation consists of the following steps.

Conduct End User One-on-One Trials

One of the most valuable steps in a project is the collection of end user validation. As you near the end of the project, this collection should become more formal. Rather than casual sessions used to extract input regarding the design, steps should be taken to ensure usability, acceptance, and anticipation.

Conduct Small Group Pilot Reviews

As was mentioned above, collecting feedback from end users is a critical component. In many cases, collecting this feedback from several groups of end users at one time will result in information you may not otherwise have obtained. For example, it is not uncommon for a group of end users to begin discussing among themselves what they like and dislike about the program. Additionally, they may compare the program to other programs they have seen. This free-flowing feedback is more difficult to obtain in a one-on-one session.

Conduct Client Reviews

As soon as modules are completed, they should be subjected to review by the client, whether internal or external. Unlike traditional alpha or beta test cycles that deliver a significant amount of information about the usability of the application, the focus of this review is to secure buy-in, confirm that the application addresses the business need, and prepare for reproduction and distribution.

Correct Errors and Make Content Revisions

Throughout the formative evaluation process you will discover small errors in the content or errors caused by the integration of the modules as they were completed.

Because valid approaches regarding usability, motivation, functionality, relevance, and the like, were addressed during the SAVVY design phase, errors found at this point are rarely significant enough to warrant major budget or time frame modifications. Correcting errors and making necessary content revisions therefore become stress-free activities.

Acquire Sign-Off

At this point it is important that all relevant stakeholders agree to the results of formative evaluation. Specifically, the "final application" must be accepted before reproduction or distribution occurs.

PROJECT CLOSE

Many multimedia development teams rush to the next engagement as soon as production or formative evaluation is complete. Before abandoning a project, however, you should undertake a few simple activities.

Project close consists of the following steps.

Complete Administrative Activities

In the engagement planning phase several administrative activities were undertaken as the project began. You also should undertake a few administrative activities at the end of the project. For example, project-related files should be archived, source files backed up for easy retrieval in the future, and team members' notes stored for future reference.

Hold a Postmortem

In preparation for future projects, all project team members should gather to discuss what went well and in what areas improvements could be made. This exercise of collecting "continuous improvement" or "best practices" helps ensure that future projects go smoothly.

PROJECT MANAGEMENT TOOLS

While each multimedia team seems to develop or modify tools to meet its specific needs, the following checklists will serve as a starting point in developing technology-based training.

PROJECT REPORTS AND DELIVERABLES

	Completed	Date	Sign-Off
Project management plan report			
Analysis report			
Functional and visual prototypes			
Design plan report			
Navigation shell and initial interaction models			
Content preparation plan report			
Project development plan report			
Reproducible master			
Project archive			
Lessons learned report			

ENGAGEMENT PLANNING AND PROJECT INITIATION CHECKLIST

	Completed/Date	Reviewed/Date
Project initiation sheet		
Engagement code and project files		
Project planning and analysis team assigned		
Project initiation meeting		
Project management plan report		
Initial problem statement		
Goal statement		
Phase and/or process plan		
Roles and responsibilities		
Risk analysis and management		
Research and development requirements		
Communication plan		
Electronic file exchange plan		
Scope and change management		
Deliverable management		
Project management plan report sign-off		

INSTRUCTIONAL ANALYSIS CHECKLIST

	Completed/Date	Reviewed/Date
Analysis of problem(s)		
Analysis of learning environment		
Analysis of learning task(s) and content to be learned		
Analysis of learners		
Analysis report		
Refined problem and goal statement		
Learner description (entry skills and motivational profiles)		
Description of instruction (and other potential interventions)		
Description of learning environment and project constraints		
Performance objectives		
Sample test items and/or assessment measures		
Analysis report client sign-off		

SAVVY DESIGN CHECKLIST

	Completed/Date	Reviewed/Date
Select and sequence primary content and classify type of learning		
Select instructional methods appropriate for type of learning		
Select and sequence supporting content		
Prepare functional and visual prototypes per iterative and collaborative design procedures (i.e., rapid collaborative prototyping) and include learners and other stakeholders to collaborate in and/or validate emerging design of instruction aligned with objectives		
Navigation options		
Menu structure		
Presentation methods		
Style of interactions and feedback		
Methods of learner assessment		
Functional and visual prototypes client sign-off		

SAVVY DESIGN CHECKLIST (CONTINUED)

	Completed/Date	Reviewed/Date

Design Plan report

   Structure of training program (scope and sequence)

   Description of type of learning and selected instructional methods

   Learner assessment plan

   Implementation plan

   Confirmation of and establishment of budget, time frame, assumptions about roles, etc.

Design plan report client sign-off

MODELIZATION CHECKLIST

	Completed/Date	Reviewed/Date

Build and test navigation shell and initial interaction models

   Interface

   Logic

Finalize artwork for interface

Content preparation plan report

   Structures and procedures for preparing and integrating content

   Structures for content preparation (task grids, audio and video scripts, content narratives, storyboards, etc.)

   Standards for text, graphics, audio, video, and animation elements

   Content preparation procedures and file-naming and asset management procedures

Content preparation plan report client sign-off

Project development plan report

   Task and resource plan

   Quality assurance and quality control procedures

   Formative evaluation plan

   Implementation plan

   Development and evaluation schedule

   Confirmation of and establishment of budget, time frame, assumptions about roles, etc.

Project development plan report sign-off

PRODUCTION CHECKLIST

	Completed/Date	Reviewed/Date
Prepare content and multimedia assets		
Integrate content into shell and models		
Build and test additional interaction models, as deemed necessary		
Build and quality assure (QA) interim deliverables		
Client review and testing of interim deliverables		
Build and QA certified deliverables		
Application documentation		

FORMATIVE EVALUATION CHECKLIST

	Completed/Date	Reviewed/Date
Client reviews		
Learner one-on-one trials per formative evaluation plan and expectations established in management plan		
Small group pilot per formative evaluation plan and expectations established in management plan		
Error corrections and content revisions		
Implementation in learning environment		
Reproducible master		
Reproducible master client sign-off		

PROJECT CLOSE CHECKLIST

	Completed/Date	Reviewed/Date
Complete administrative activities		
Project archive		
Project archive client sign-off		
Project postmortem meeting		
Lessons learned report		
Contributions to library of best practices		
Feedback to account manager and client		

CASE STUDY: UNITED HEALTHCARE

Defining the Need

United HealthCare of Ohio needed to provide its employees with a better understanding of the complex health care services industry and how United HealthCare was positioned within it. Additionally, employees needed to understand how United differed from its competition regarding customers' needs. Recognizing this need, Bob Sheehy, then chief executive officer of United HealthCare, made the development of such education a top priority.

Sheehy and his management team concluded that an instructionally sound employee training and continued orientation program had to be in place within 5 months. To facilitate the development of the program, a $25,000 budget was established and Joan Busch was appointed project manager.

In the search for a cost-effective and time-sensitive solution, the senior management team suggested monthly classroom-based product training sessions that would each highlight a different product. It was determined, however, that a multimedia-based training program would be more effective, since the need was to orient employees continually with accurate and timely information.

Understanding the Challenge

United HealthCare, particularly Busch, faced two distinct challenges in the creation of employee training. First, the content matter had never been created or assembled. Therefore, a thorough instructional analysis was needed to confirm objectives, understand the learners and their need for the information, and determine a means to measure the effectiveness of the instruction. Second and perhaps more daunting, United had never been exposed to the creation of a multimedia-based training program. Busch therefore boldly relied on journal and magazine articles to create a strategy for completing the interactive multimedia program.

Busch began the initiative by developing a set of learning objectives as one would for any instructional program. After approval of the project's learning objectives, Busch began to prepare for development of the multimedia program by creating storyboards that graphically depicted every interaction envisioned for the program. As anxiety grew and the time frame decreased, Busch decided to enlist the assistance of an outside design and development firm, Allen Interactions Inc.

Engagement Planning

Allen's involvement began by clearly defining the problem identified by United HealthCare, the anticipated outcome of the training program, and a clarification of the roles to be played by Allen and United. A clear plan for communication, electronic file exchange, and change management was communicated.

After working through these project initiation details, United HealthCare and Allen Interactions had formed a collaborative team dedicated to the success of the final program. However, only 3 months remained to design and develop the final program.

Instructional Analysis

Busch was eager to share her initial analysis and design ideas. In the spirit of an iterative design process, however, she cautiously put aside her paper-based storyboards and agreed to return to the beginning of the project to readdress the learning objectives. Additionally, a thorough understanding of the learners was gained, including insight into how, when, and where they would experience the training program.

SAVVY Design

Once the learning objectives had been constructed as performance objectives and an initial understanding of the motivational factors of the end users had been determined, it was time to begin the SAVVY design phase.

For 2 days Busch, two members of the outside firm, a representative from United HealthCare's computer department, and a United subject-matter expert brainstormed instructionally sound, intrinsically motivating interactions based on the performance objectives. Rough ideas were communicated quickly through the use of whiteboard sketches. To explore a concept fully, however, by the middle of the first day functional prototypes were created. Those prototypes were reviewed by all project stakeholders: Busch, management, subject-matter experts, trainers, and, most important, end users.

By experiencing design ideas in fully functioning interactions, the project team was able to collect invaluable feedback regarding the mechanics of the interaction, the validity of the content, and issues involving motivation. Each comment was considered and then weighed against the performance objectives; if appropriate, it was incorporated immediately into the prototypes for further inspection and validation.

Completion of the SAVVY design phase brought several comforts. First, the United team felt for the first time that it was on target for creating a design that its employees would actually use. They knew that any investment of time or money made from that point on would be appropriate because the audience had confirmed that.

Additionally, the content for the application had been established. After 2 days of rapid prototyping, United actually had the skeleton of the total project. Twenty-six learning objectives were organized into four modules made up of four different interaction types.

After the functional prototypes were completed, a similar process was undertaken for the development of the visual prototypes. Ideas were hashed out using crude sketches, mock-ups were quickly created, stakeholders were given an opportunity to contribute, and modifications were made. Once again, the result included confidence in a direction validated by the end users.

The project—now named "We Are United: The Big Picture"—had a structure and a concept for the overall look. Busch was able to share this prototype with the chief executive officer and other senior management to get their buy-in and approval before further investments were made. The senior management team was able to experience how the program would work, not just see illustrations of what it would look like. Busch was able to make an impressive presentation to the executives because throughout the SAVVY design phase employees had validated the program.

Modelization

Using the functional prototypes as a design guide, the project development team began modelization for both the code and the content. Each interaction was rebuilt totally to be efficient and maintainable. As an interaction model was completed, it was subjected to quality assurance tests. Additionally, structures were created to allow the content to be harvested efficiently by the subject-matter experts under the direction of Busch.

Production

As soon as the content models were created, the subject-matter experts began harvesting the content. The next 2 months was spent working with subject-matter experts to acquire the right information for each objective and interaction. As content was collected, graphics produced, and animations created, they were incorporated into the functional models. Once again, stakeholders were able to see immediately how the content "worked," this time in the context of a refined application.

Formative Evaluation

Busch continued sharing the growing program with stakeholders as it developed. By roughly 4 months into the project, about 30 employees had tested at least a portion of the interactive multimedia-based learning program. Their feedback, now primarily content-related as opposed to being usability-oriented, was used to influence the modules that were still in development. When it was time to present a nearly completed version to the senior management team, Busch was confident that the program was what United HealthCare needed.

Project Close

As production and formative evaluation activities concluded, the project team began archiving project notes, source code, and other assets used during the project. Additionally, the entire team discussed the lessons learned during the project in an attempt to be better prepared for future efforts.

Conclusion

In the end "We are United: The Big Picture" was an exciting success that was delivered on time and within budget. It has become a part of United HealthCare's national orientation program, which will educate over 30,000 employees. Local follow-up surveys indicated that 83 percent of the respondents thought the program was very valuable, and 75 percent of the respondents achieved an "Expert" score on a self-assessment.

GLOSSARY

End User   A member of the population that will ultimately receive an interactive multimedia application.

Interactivity   The cognitive engagement of the end user expressed in involvement that goes beyond navigation, control, and assessment.

Prototype   The minimum investment to communicate an idea tangibly. A prototype is most useful when it is delivered in the final medium.

Stakeholder   Any individual directly affected by an interactive multimedia project, including team members, managers, end users, clients, and shareholders.

CHAPTER 18

Using Audio and Video
Over the Web

David S. Metcalf II, PhD

Objectives

This chapter focuses on the use of audio and video for the delivery of just-in-time training materials over the Web. Two basic techniques—downloadable files and streaming—are used to deliver audio and video content. Downloadable audio and video files must be sent to the user's computer in their entirety before they can be presented; streaming formats allow the audio or video content to be played as it is downloaded to the client with only a short delay at the beginning. Both techniques are examined in relation to Web-based training (WBT) delivery.

Typically, audio and video are two components that can make up a Web-based training solution. It is important to understand when their use is appropriate and recognize the potential problems and solutions associated with Web delivery. This chapter describes how to plan and implement effective audiovisual training over the Web. After reviewing best practices and several sites that use audio and video as part of a training solution, it reviews some of the latest technologies and future trends.

Many studies tout the effectiveness of multimedia for retention and understanding of information. Web-based training courses can improve retention and attention. There is a general belief in the training profession that you retain 10 percent of what you read, 20 percent of what you hear, 30 percent of what you see, and 50 percent of what you see and hear. Additionally, in a study by Lee and Bowers (1997), hearing spoken text and looking at graphics produced 91 percent more learning compared with a control group that did not study the same topic between standard pretests and posttests. The benefits of audio and video for learning can be extrapolated from such studies. These statistics indicate why so many organizations are exploring the addition of audio and video content to Web-delivered courses.

The key benefits of audio and video (AV) go back to the fundamentals of cognitive learning theory. Multisensory learning engages the learner as well as increasing retention. Audio and video often can convey feelings and the subtle contexts of learning more effectively than other tools can. Video is particularly effective when one is trying to demonstrate a kinetic task such as a tennis serve or the proper turning procedure for a bolt assembly. Another use of AV on the Web is personification. Audio and video can be used to restore the human element to technology-based training. For effective use, consider how AV media can help you meet learning objectives and accommodate particular learning styles.

Another benefit will be obvious to anyone with a large library of existing training content: The use of audio and video over the Web may allow you to reuse existing AV resources. While throwing existing video or audio training onto the Web most likely will prove ineffective, these resources can be valuable components in a well-designed Web curriculum. Each morsel of video and audio content forms a learning object that can be combined with objects such as interactive exercises, a written course curriculum, graphics, and tests to form an effective solution for the delivery of WBT.

With all these benefits, why are so few AV media used in WBT? A number of considerations must be addressed. First, there are equipment and logistic considerations. Even with the compression techniques that make audio and video as small as possible while maintaining sound and image quality, network resources often are strained by the use of audio and video. To use audio and video, additional network, computing, and software capacities are required. Networks must provide enough bandwidth to accommodate the increased volume of packets carrying large audio and video files. Computers must be able to process video and audio content while running the operating system, network services, and a Web browser. This computer resource requirement sometimes is increased by the requirement for a plug-in or helper application to run specialized audio and video functions. The network, computer, and software resource cost must be considered in planning the use of AV materials in a Web-delivered curriculum.

Another factor to consider in building training materials is the additional cost and time required to develop WBT with video or audio content. While new tools are making the integration of AV resources easier, it is still more expensive and time-consuming to develop than it is to design WBT without multimedia content. AV development can require video and audio production techniques that are unfamiliar to many trainers, specialized production tools and facilities, and expert knowledge about which delivery methods to use on the Web. As development and delivery tools become more advanced, these problems will be less of a concern and Web-delivered AV content will proliferate.

The following sections of this chapter discuss ways to capitalize on the benefits of AV content and minimize common problems in the development and delivery of

audio and video for the Web. You also will learn some of the best practices and potential uses of AV resources to promote effective learning.

TECHNIQUES

When to Use Audio and Video

Driscoll (1996) discusses the tendency to overuse multimedia in WBT. She believes
that the focus is too heavily on media and production and not on instructional design. It is important to use multimedia appropriately to meet learning objectives.
What are appropriate uses, and when should audio and video be used? Here are a
few examples.

Introduction of a Topic

Audio and video often serve as an engaging opening to a new concept or section
of instruction. The appeal to multisensory learning can promote greater initial understanding and the motivation to explore a topic in greater detail. This technique
works well in information design models that employ the newspaper-style in-
verted pyramid or the opening action of a dramaturgical model that uses theatri-
cal methods to convey instruction.

Kinetic Demonstrations

Video is an excellent choice for instructing people in activities that involve motion.
One of the few ways to show kinetic motion on the Web is through video. You typically will have a very small image size compared to full-frame video, especially if
you are attempting to send video over a standard dial-up connection. This smaller
image can make detailed actions difficult to see without using techniques specific
to Web requirements in shooting the footage. You may need to zoom in tighter on
the subject or crop the digital video before placing it on the Web. Realistic-looking
scenes with action are best suited to Web-delivered video as long as the focal point
of the scene does not require viewing small details that may not be visible at low
resolution. Distracting backgrounds should be avoided.

Multisensory Experiences

Seeing and hearing in synchronicity can promote better retention and understanding. Video and audio used in conjunction can present a powerful message, especially if the subject matter involves both visual and aural material. As a basic example, a narrator describing an assembly process as it is being put together is more
effective than the narrative voice description of the process and the visuals of the
process would be if they were presented independently. Capturing the sights and
sounds of an environment is a worthy objective in the delivery of WBT.

The Power of Audio

Few people realize the power of audio in everyday life. Noises alert us to our surroundings and can evoke emotion in subtle yet effective ways. Music, while a distracting agent if overused, can add to the power of a message. If music is not appropriate to the learning objectives, sound effects that convey meaning can provide both aural interface context cues and activity signals.

While music and sound effects can add impact to training that is delivered online, most of the power associated with audio for training purposes comes from the human voice. There is no substitute for the passion and power of a trainer's voice to add meaning, emotion, and character to a message. The members of your learning audience will respond to the warmth and richness of a human voice, especially if they learn best through aural means.

There are a number of reasons to use audio and video in a production and appropriate times to use them for WBT applications. Understanding why and when to use them are the first two steps in deploying these tools for training. Next, you'll see how to plan and implement audio and video for WBT.

HOW TO PLAN

The first step in the successful use of AV resources is knowing that preproduction is half the job. Proper planning will prevent excessive retakes using expensive studio time, equipment, and talent. Should you record your own audio and video for the production? Either way, you must perform the initial planning tasks. For example, legal issues must be addressed early. Before recording, make sure you have release forms for all participants agreeing that you can use their likeness and that they are old enough to enter into the agreement. You also may have to secure permits for certain activities or locations. Licensing and copyright are other legal issues that must be addressed if you are gathering content from outside sources or using existing footage or recordings. A one-time fee or royalty payment often is required for the use of file or stock footage.

The importance of planning and coordinating the recording sessions cannot be ignored. The logistics of equipment, studio or location setup, talent preparation, and proper recording conditions (weather, lighting, ambience) must be considered before you undertake your own production.

One of the best ways to ensure that you get what you want out of an audio or video recording session is to produce a script and/or storyboard. These items serve as the plan of action, road map, and backbone of the production. The script contains all the spoken information, and the storyboard carries the script a step further by adding graphic representations or descriptions of the visual aspects and actions of key frames.

Another important decision point in the planning stages is the choice of medium. While tape used to be the only way to go for recording, newer techniques are available. Digital tape often provides higher-quality audio and video reproduction. It is also possible to record directly into a digital format stored on a disk drive. It is usually a good idea to plan for and record on more than one media type or to have a redundant recording device if your budget allows it. It is cheaper to record the session on two devices than to pay for studio, equipment, and talent time twice if there is a technical problem. It is advisable to hire experienced professionals if the budget allows this. The additional cost is often recouped in terms of both time saved from fewer retakes or errors and avoidance of frustration caused by inexperience.

You should try to decide on the final delivery format over the Web during this planning stage. Making the decisions on which technology, frame size, image and/or sound quality, and compression techniques before beginning allows you to plan for some of the anomalies associated with implementing and delivering audio and video over the Web before the recording begins.

HOW TO IMPLEMENT

Once you have planned the work, it is time to begin the process. Whether you are producing your own audio or video or using AV resources from an outside organization, you will go through a series of steps. Figure 18–1 shows the typical steps.

This is a simplistic view of the process. There are a number of specific subtasks that depend on the particular tools. Some systems require a different ordering of these operations. For instance, editing may take place before digitization if you are

FIGURE 18–1

A Typical Web-Based Audio and Video Production Process

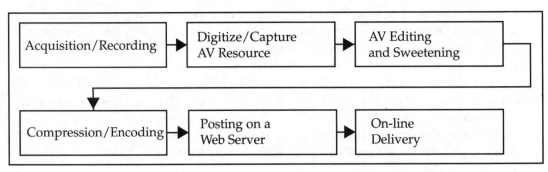

using an older analog editing system. Keep this process in mind as we look at techniques for delivering effective training using AV resources.

Develop Once, Deliver Many

One of the most important adages in the successful deployment of any project involving multimedia is to develop once, deliver many (Metcalf 1994). In essence, any content you take the time to develop should give you maximum return for the time and money spent by being flexible enough to be repurposed into several media, formats, or uses. This is especially true of video and audio, since they are two of the most expensive media types to produce. If you work from a high-quality source material, it is easier to repurpose and convert to formats that require less resolution or quality. You can always scale or convert an image or sound down, but it is extremely difficult to increase resolution, clarity, and size while maintaining the integrity of the original.

Once you have a high-quality original AV resource, you can convert it to a format for delivery through a videocassette recorder (VCR) or CD-ROM or over the Web, particularly in the case of video. As an example, some video segments produced for Web delivery also have been used as part of the curriculum in instructor-led training classes. It is not always easy to deliver in multiple formats, as the size variance requires different shooting techniques and shot choices. For example, in delivering video over the Web, it is important to use many more close-ups and extreme close-ups than it is in normal videography for television delivery, since the final delivery format usually will be quite small by comparison. These shot choices and editing decisions for Web delivery may appear odd when viewed on a television screen, as most people are used to greater shot variance (wide angles, medium shots, close-ups, extreme close-ups). It is usually even more problematic to take video developed for television display and maintain enough clarity in wide-angle shots that show a great deal of detail when delivered over the Web.

While develop once, deliver many should be the goal, this technique often is poorly executed when the requirements of different delivery formats are not taken into account. Careful planning can make reuse possible, but this often requires returning to the original unedited source material to provide the most effective training experience in different formats.

Downloadable Files versus Streaming

Typically, audio and video can be delivered over the Internet by means of two techniques. The first is a traditional download of the entire AV file. After a successful download, the Web browser launches a helper application or starts a plug-in capable of AV playback. The download process can take a long time on slower connections, and users generally grow bored waiting for the video unless they have a high-speed link. When this interruption occurs during instruction, the learner's attention is broken. Unless a large high-resolution file must be transmitted or the user can guarantee a fairly consistent data rate, this is not the best choice for delivering AV material.

Streaming is a much more effective technique. With streaming, an AV file can start playing before it is completely downloaded. This is accomplished by buffering (temporarily storing) a small portion of the video during the first few seconds after the AV file is launched and before play begins. While the file is playing, AV content continues to be loaded into the buffer. This process continues until the file is sent completely or the data transfer is slowed or stopped because of network congestion or other Internet difficulties. Streaming can be very effective for training even though the quality of the image and sound often suffers because of the high compression ratio necessary to deliver the AV files in near real time with minimal delays. Streaming can be effective on standard modem connections as it sends the AV content in manageable chunks while engaging the learner in the content as other parts of the file are being loaded.

Audio Formats

Streaming tools such as Real Networks RealAudio, Apple QuickTime audio, Macromedia Shockwave Audio, Xing Technologies StreamWorks, and Microsoft NetShow allow access to potentially large audio files in a matter of seconds. Streaming is a solution to the wait times associated with typical downloadable audio formats such as .au, .aiff, and .wav files.

Video Formats

Several streaming video technologies, such as Real Networks RealVideo, Xing Technologies StreamWorks, Apple QuickTime (streaming format), and Microsoft NetShow, provide video with just a few seconds' delay. These applications call for a particular video stream, buffer several seconds' worth of continuous video data, and then attempt to continue buffering and playing the video. Network traffic can cause breaks or delays in the video stream, but with enough bandwidth it is possible to keep a stream of video playing continuously without interruption or degradation in video quality. These streaming formats can take the place of downloadable formats such as Microsoft's previous de facto standard Video for Windows, .avi files, nonstreaming QuickTime files, and nonstreaming Motion Picture Experts Group (MPEG) files.

Compression

Compression can make low-bandwidth multimedia delivery possible over Internet connections. For example, the bandwidth required for streaming MPEG video could be around 96 kilobits per second (Kbps). The uncompressed segment at the same size and frame rate would need 1 megabit per second (Mbps), 10 times the bandwidth required with compression (Andleight and Thakrar 1996).

Intranet versus Internet Deployment

Tansy (1996) has noted the difference in the multimedia data that can be handled by Intranets and the Internet. Intranets can handle more data than can the Internet in much the same way that most local area networks (LANs) can handle more data than can the typical wide area network (WAN). Most Intranets are more than capable of handling audio and video. Heavy network traffic over the Internet and lower-bandwidth connections are frequently the reasons why multimedia cannot be accommodated effectively over the Internet.

Multiformat

One solution to the confusing variety of formats available for audio and video is to provide the learner with a choice. One approach is to provide resources consonant with the amount of bandwidth a learner has. For instance, a higher-quality format may be offered for delivery over an Intranet, with a lower-quality format available for Internet and dial-up connection support. The disadvantage of this technique is the extra time required to convert videos into multiple formats. Still, it is often worth the effort to accommodate a larger learning audience.

Transcripts

Transcripts are another format that can be provided in a multiple-format delivery system. Providing a transcript over the Web can be a lowest possible denominator solution for people who have a very slow connection, for those who do not have Web browsers or plug-ins that allow for video, and for the disabled. A transcript, with or without representative still images from an accompanying video, will help both hearing-impaired learners and the visually impaired who have text-to-speech readers.

Web-CD Hybrid

In the spirit of multiple formats and develop once, deliver many, it is possible to develop a hybrid Web and CD-ROM delivery method for training applications. For example, you could choose to put all the AV resources on a CD-ROM for fast delivery and playback. CD-ROM also can support the larger frame sizes and higher resolutions of video and audio files. In this example, the Web can be used for timely information that must be updated frequently and the associated CD-ROM can deliver general information and AV resources. The CD-ROM must be shipped to the learner, creating additional logistic considerations, but it is often worthwhile to have the increased reliability of CD-ROM, higher bandwidth, and larger file sizes.

AUDIO AND VIDEO PRODUCTION 101

Whether or not you are developing your own audio and video training content, it is important to understand a few of the fundamentals of audio and video production. A detailed exploration of audio and video production is beyond the scope of this book, but many resources are listed at the end of this chapter. Here you'll get a few basic tips about the specifics of audio and video production for WBT.

The following list provides information about the techniques involved in capturing audio and video training resources that are going to be digitized and delivered on-line.

Best Practices List

Because your product eventually will be delivered in a small, lower-resolution box, it is important to do all you can during video acquisition to make that transition work as well as possible. Most of the items that follow are standard best practices for shooting video and recording audio, with a few added considerations.

1. Start with the highest-quality video format available. If you can't shoot Beta SP or Digital Video, then choose Hi-8 or S-VHS over composite video.

2. Always shoot in the best light possible. Natural light is best, followed by tungsten. For most corporate presentation situations, be sure there is even lighting across the whole presentation area. If possible, do without standard overhead fluorescent lights, which put out an uneven spectrum and can add an annoying buzz to the audio track.

3. Don't forget to white balance the camera.

4. After lighting is set, set the exposure and lock it in. Do not use automatic exposure.

5. Always use a tripod and limit pans and zooms to those which are strictly necessary, keeping them slow and smooth. Compression artifacts are most evident when the whole frame changes.

6. When possible, keep the background simple and the subject or subjects far away from walls that could show shadows. (Some people have solved the background issue by using studio blue screens and adding the background later.)

7. Have the on-camera subjects avoid clothing with busy patterns. Plaids, checks, and thin stripes scintillate on video and further degrade after digital compression.

8. When the spoken word carries the message, be sure to shoot the speaker a little more tightly than usual. Use medium close-ups and close-ups for this.

9. In general, be aware that the usual big screen will be reduced to something slightly smaller than a baseball card. Therefore, think ahead and imagine the dynamics the shot will have as a 3-inch by 2-inch image. (Pull your head back from the viewfinder for a preview.)

10. With all the emphasis on image capture, don't forget audio. It is recommended that you plan for some audio redundancy. You may wish to capture audio in mono on more than one track and in more than one form for flexibility in translation. If you need to microphone a presenter and provide a room microphone to pick up audience questions, be prepared to mix the signals. Be sure to test audio levels before recording and monitor audio as it is being recorded. Often a small problem with a cable or low batteries can be caught before a significant amount of time has passed.

While everyone would like to get the best possible results when producing video, it is not always necessary to meet the production standards of broadcast specifications, especially in delivering smaller video sizes over the Web. A question to ask yourself is, Does it have to be professional-quality audio and video to be effective for learning? Certainly it has to be clear enough and of high enough quality to be comprehensible, but it does not have to be Academy Award–winning cinema to teach people how to do something. While many people with video and audio production backgrounds might disagree, not everyone has the time, budget, or know-how to produce high-quality AV resources. This does not mean you shouldn't try, especially if you are producing an internal video for an internal audience. "Industrial-quality" or corporate video has been used for years. Over the current Internet, video and audio that conform to the best practices listed above should be sufficient. The goal should be effective training, not an artistic masterpiece. If you need maximum quality in order to have a great reusable asset, it is best to seek out professionals and take the extra time and money to produce a top-notch AV resource.

CASE STUDIES

The following case studies give specific examples of some of the techniques described in this chapter. The first example is the NASA Web Interactive Training (WIT) project (Metcalf 1995). Video content was used at the beginning of each section of the training to introduce a topic and engage the learner. In this project a new methodology was used to deliver video content. Since not everyone had the proper bandwidth to receive higher-quality streaming video over the NASA Intranet, two other options were provided and explained. This gave the user a choice that depended on what helper applications or plug-ins he or she had loaded. The second option was a downloadable video file that was usually between 5 and 6 megabytes. The third option was a storyboard with all the transcribed text and representative images from the video for 28.8-Kbps modem users who could not accommodate either the larger-format streaming video or the downloadable movie file. This technique made it possible to lower the minimum requirements for the course and still give the learner the option to access the most engaging experience when the proper equipment was available (Figures 18–2 and 18–3).

Merrimac's CertificationNet provides on-line courses, tests, and certification programs to a global information technology audience. It is impossible to know exactly what user technologies are possible with a worldwide audience, but a technique was developed to identify and correct setup problems before the learners started a course. An automated Web browser and plug-in-detection setup pages checked for browser compatibility; RealMedia's RealPlayer plug-in Web-based lecture series for Cisco Systems and an introduction to SMC instruction are just two examples of CertificationNet courses that use streaming video or audio. The Merrimac development team created a Web lecture format for instruction that incorporates audio with synchronized still images of PowerPoint, live demonstrations, quizzes, and interactive exercises. This construction forms a more engaging learning experience than does watching an AV presentation. This is the basis of the Web lecture format (Figures 18–4 and 18–5).

Lawrence Livermore National Labs had a course developed that used streaming media to deliver integrated safety management (ISM) orientation training to a diverse group of new employees. To appeal to and engage a large portion of the learning population, personification was a desirable option for delivery. The initial prototype uses an on-screen agent or narrator guide transmitted as a streaming video file composited onto the Web page. The guide interacts with the content while engaging the learner, much like a buddy system in a new-hire orientation session. Audio recordings with media synchronization are used for the actual trainer presentations. This promotes the authority and passion necessary to convey the importance of safety at the facility (Fig. 18–6).

FUTURE USES

To fully appreciate the current state of the art and what is possible with Web-based delivery of AV resources, it is necessary to look to the cutting edge of technology and beyond.

F I G U R E 18–2

WIT Introduction with Video Choices

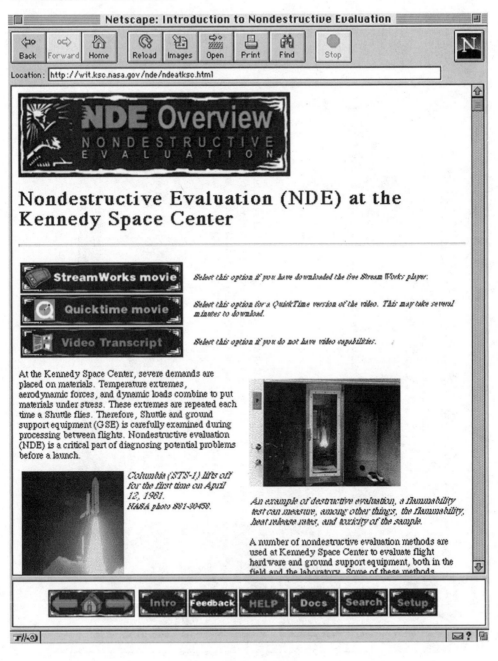

FIGURE 18-3

WIT On-Line Storyboard and Transcripts

Eddy Current Testing - Microsoft Internet Explorer

File   Edit   View   Go   Favorites   Help   Address

Introduction to Eddy Current Testing

The shuttle orbiter is both resilient and fragile, capable of withstanding the heat of reentry yet susceptible to a scratch.

Highly trained NDE inspectors at Kennedy Space Center respond quickly to perform an eddy current test on a suspect area on Columbia's wing. Eddy current testing can detect many types of discontinuities quickly and inexpensively.

Eddy current testing uses an induced electromagnetic field to inspect the surface or areas slightly below the surface of any electrically conductive metal, such as the aluminum alloy in Columbia's wing.

Intro   Feedback   HELP   Docs   Search   Setup

FIGURE 18-4

CertificationNet Setup Page

CertificationNet - Microsoft Internet Explorer

File Edit View Go Favorites Help

Address http://www.certificationnet.com/it/setup.asp?hasReal=false

Login Home Setup Course Programs Test Partners About CN Live! Demo! Help

CertificationNet Setup and Configuration Checklist

Depending on the speed of your Internet connection, this automated CertificationNet setup and configuration checklist may take up to three and a half minutes. Checked boxes will indicate that your system appears to contain a necessary component.

Browser Features - You appear to be using IE 4.0

Frames Support	Allows partitioning of the browser window into independent document display areas.	
Tables Support	Allows data to be organized in columns and rows as well as for the organized layout of any element of HTML pages.	
Cookie Support	A general mechanism which server side connections can use to both store and retrieve information on the client side of the connection. **Note**: If you are using a utility that disables cookie support, you will need to turn it off before proceeding through the CertificationNet instruction.	
JavaScript Support	JavaScript increases the aesthetics and friendliness of websites by adding author-specified user events to static pages. **Note**: If Java Script is disabled on your browser, you will need to enable it. Consult your System Administrator or the Help menu on your browser to determine how to enable Java Script.	
Java Support	Java is an object-oriented programming language. In this case it is used to deliver advanced content to your web browser. **Note**: If Java is disabled on your browser, you will need to enable it. Consult your System Administrator or the Help menu on your browser to determine how to enable Java. If you can see our CN logo fading in and out, your	

315

FIGURE 18-5

Cisco Web-Based Lecture Course

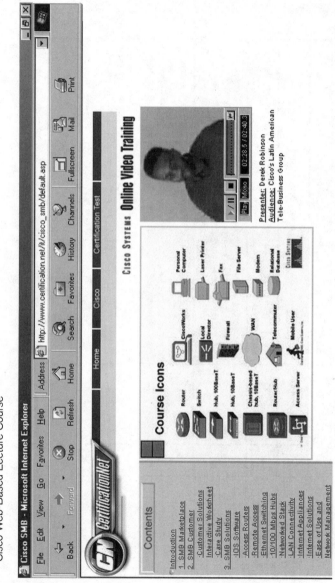

FIGURE 18–6

Lawrence Livermore National Labs ISM On-Screen Agent

New Standards

Standards play an important role in defining the compatibility of development tools and delivery systems. Several new standards have been proposed and/or approved in the area of streaming media. The first is Synchronized Multimedia Integration Language (SMIL), pronounced "smile." As the name implies, the goal of this new language is to make it easy to synchronize text, audio, video, and other elements to a fixed timeline. This standard was recommended by the W3 Consortium in June 1998. Real-Time Transport Protocol (RTP) and the proposed Real-Time Streaming Protocol have been put forth by the Internet Engineering Task Force (IETF). Both are responsible for the delivery of real-time data over the Internet. Another project to watch is Instructional Management System (IMS). This project group is building specifications for handling learning objects that could be created in any medium. The structure for the data about the audio or video files used in a training system will be part of this specification.

New Compression

New compression techniques are appearing that will allow even more video and audio data to be sent through low-bandwidth connections such as a dial-up modem. Fractal and wavelet compression techniques are already in use and are being improved to produce larger, crisper video images and higher-quality audio. It is only a matter of time before we see full-screen, full-motion video with CD-quality audio delivered through a dial-up connection.

A number of new techniques and technologies are becoming available as well. Because of the interactive nature of working with a computer versus the passive nature of televised video, new functions are possible. Some of these technologies may be a perfect fit for a learning objective. Consider an interactive video that allows the learner to select a hot spot in a moving video stream and change the course of action. This interactivity is offered by V-Active from Veon (formerly Ephyx). With this technology you can create dynamic, scenario-based case studies. Other important technologies include panorama tools such as QuickTimeVR, Microsoft's Surround Video, and LivePicture's PhotoVista. Panorama tools allow the learner to interactively pan and zoom around an object or through a view from a fixed point. While the technology uses a series of stills to form a 360-degree view, it gives the appearance of an interactive video window. True two-dimensional (2D) and three-dimensional (3D) animation is also possible through companion technologies to some of the new streaming media formats, such as RealNetworks RealFlash for streaming 2D animation and Virtual Reality Modeling Language (VRML) for 3D animation. These technologies may be on the fringes of video, but they offer a few more options to add to a Web-based training development tool kit. 3D sound is also a growing capability that expands the ability of an existing sound system to project complex sound scenarios. This may prove effective for certain types of aural training and for auditory effect.

This chapter has covered only the uses of one-way asynchronous audio and video. A host of other technologies allow for two-way AV communication and real-time AV broadcast delivery. Other chapters in this book provide more detailed information about these possibilities.

CONCLUSION

An understanding of the primary uses of audio and video to enhance learning is fundamental to effective deployment. The tips and techniques in this chapter will augment the core best practices and procedural flow for delivering audio and video over the Web. The case studies demonstrate some of these techniques in practice. Finally, you can look toward the bright future of new tools and techniques that will allow you to create advanced learning scenarios through the integration of multimedia and the Internet. This integration will form completely new constructs to convey meaningful training. It will advance the state of WBT training through the use of audio and video as integral components of a new experience rather than as stand-alone solutions.

GLOSSARY

Audio and Video Terms

Aspect Ratio   The relationship of height to width in an image size (e.g., 4:3 is a standard aspect ratio for NTSC television).

MPEG   The Motion Picture Experts Group has developed several formats for the delivery of compressed video in a variety of media.

NTSC   The National Television Standards Committee is responsible for the development of the broadcast specifications for television.

Pan   A pan operation involves a change in the view by rotating the camera angle.

Sweetening   The process of adjusting the sound for maximum quality. This includes filtering out unwanted sounds, adjusting the volume, and ensuring fidelity to the original sound.

White Balance   A camera adjustment that should be completed before a video shoot to ensure that the coloration of the video will be accurate, based on the type of lighting used and the shooting conditions. For example, if you do not white balance when shooting under fluorescent lights, everything will have a greenish cast.

Zoom   The process of tightening or widening the frame to focus in on details or pulling back to get more into a shot.

Web Terms

Buffer
A temporary storage area that is usually part of random access memory.

HTTP
HyperText Transport Protocol is the underlying protocol for standard World Wide Web data transmission.

IETF
The Internet Engineering Task Force is responsible for creating Internet standards and recommendations.

IMS
The Instructional Management System is an initiative sponsored by many organizations to develop specifications and standards for learning objects.

Internet
The Internet has become the global network of networks, connecting millions of computer users worldwide.

Intranet
A private network that is based on the Internet standards but serves a particular organization from behind a secure access point.

RTP
Real-Time Transport Protocol is an Internet standard from the IETF for real-time data.

RTSP
Real-Time Streaming Transport Protocol is an Internet recommendation from the IETF for real-time streaming data.

VRML
Virtual Reality Modeling Language is a standard for the delivery of 3D objects and animation over the Internet.

W3 Consortium
At the applications level, the MIT World Wide Web (WWW) Consortium plays the leading role in developing and promulgating Web standards.

Web AV Specific Terms

Codec
A compressor/decompressor is a technology or device used to compress and decompress data.

Compression
A series of techniques to reduce the size of data files, allowing more data to be transferred in the same amount of bandwidth.

Encoding
The process of converting data into a common format for transfer. The term is used in this context to describe the process of taking a video data file and encoding it to produce a streaming media file.

Fractal Compression
A compression technique that uses simple mathematical algorithms to define complex structures and thus achieve even greater compression than can more traditional methods.

SMIL
Synchronized Multimedia Integration Language is pronounced "smile." As the name implies, the goal of this new language is to make it easy to synchronize text, audio, video, and other elements in a fixed timeline.

Streaming
With this technique an AV file can start playing before it is completely downloaded. This is accomplished by buffering (temporarily storing) a small portion of the video during the first few seconds after the AV file is launched, after which play begins. While the file is playing the buffered segment, more AV content from the file is loaded into the buffer.

Wavelet Compression
Wavelets are mathematical functions that cut data into different frequency components to achieve higher-level compression.

CHAPTER 19

Virtual Reality: Is It for You?

Carol Gunther Mohr
Sam Field
Geoffrey Frank

Objectives

Virtual reality (VR) is a computer-based technology that gives learners a realistic, three-dimensional, interactive experience. It is a powerful tool that enhances learning by allowing the students to perform skills in a realistic, engaging simulation of a real-life environment. There is evidence that VR can improve learner motivation and retention of skills and reduce error rates. Like other forms of computer-based training, it can greatly reduce average learning time and therefore the cost associated with learning. For those interested in the results of the learning process, it provides new insights into performance-based evaluation techniques.

Virtual reality requires careful analysis and design to be implemented effectively. It requires a number of technologies and a range of skills to develop and deploy. There are investments, trade-offs, and risks to consider before embarking on a VR project.

Virtual reality is being used in many organizations to deliver performance-based learning solutions. Techniques have been developed to assist in the process of creating VR-based learning.

This chapter is organized around the questions the authors have heard most frequently from audiences interested in how VR can improve the effectiveness of learning. It is designed to help you answer questions about VR so that you can determine whether VR is for you.

WHAT IS VIRTUAL REALITY?

Virtual reality is a computer-based technology that gives learners a realistic, inter-active experience, or a sense of "being there." Virtual reality is

- Three-dimensional, representing real life with computer graphics that portray the functionality of complete objects or environments and allowing one to move around in those environments
- Interactive, responding immediately and realistically to users' actions
- Immersive, involving the learners in the physical process and putting them at the center of the experience

Unlike animations and video, in which images are played and replayed in preset sequences, VR can be viewed, interacted with, and examined from any num-ber of perspectives in any sequence. Learners select the viewpoint in accordance with the task at hand. This provides far greater flexibility than does conventional multimedia-based training, in which navigation around the program is more pro-scribed. VR provides multisensory input by enabling learners to

- See and hear
- Perform actions
- Perceive the consequences of actions through immediate, realistic feedback (visual and auditory), and in some cases experience tactile feedback in real time

VR technology can be used in a stand-alone virtual environment or integrated into a multimedia computer-based training application with media such as video, animations, and text. In this context, VR often is applied to simulation or scenario-based learning applications that enable the learner to perform skills and apply knowledge while working at his or her own pace.

BASIC TECHNIQUES

This section describes when, why, and how to develop VR-based learning programs.

How to Use Virtual Reality

Virtual reality is being applied to address a variety of training problems and situ-ations. It can be found in self-paced, instructor-led, and other learning methods, depending on factors such as cost, time to delivery, learning content, and learners.

Self-Paced Learning

VR is inherently a self-directed and self-paced experience. A single learner, im-mersed in a virtual environment, interacts with the objects surrounding him or her and experiences the results of those actions through visual, aural, and sometimes tactile feedback. This practice and feedback system depends on the learner in the loop to initiate actions or react to changing situations designed or scripted by the training designer. It is a commonly accepted tenet that adult learners appreciate and benefit from a degree of self-direction and a variety of learning media. The level of interactivity afforded by VR adds a layer of complexity and interest that takes the learner beyond the point-and-click operations afforded by other computer-based training (CBT) methods. VR can be a stand-alone environment or can be embedded in a multimedia computer-based training program as another medium. The latter method is the most common for VR-based learning systems.

VR-based, self-paced programs are most effective for teaching cognitive or procedural skills. These programs can be designed for

- Initial instruction for new staff
- Refresher or remedial instruction for experienced staff
- Practice and rehearsal of skills for all staff

A self-paced training application is not necessarily a single-learner application. By design or as a result of equipment limitations, two or three learners may use the same VR training station with some benefit. In a study of VR trainer utilization for the U.S. National Guard, the researchers found that pairs of learners at each training station received effective training. This may be due to the fact that the tasks being taught were inherently two-person operations, with one individual interacting with the work piece and the other ensuring that the correct procedure was followed. VR environments capable of simultaneously hosting several learners who may collaborate on a training problem is the logical next step, but there is insufficient research on the relative effectiveness of this type of application to provide guidance specific to the application of VR. To summarize, if resources are available to provide each learner with his or her own training station, this is the preferred approach. However, if pairing of learners is required or will make the training more similar to the actual job task, VR training devices are still applicable.

Instructor-Led Learning

Instructors teaching in classroom and lab settings are using VR-based programs to

- Illustrate complex equipment or procedures efficiently
- Demonstrate unusual conditions or circumstances that would be difficult or dangerous to reproduce on real equipment or under actual conditions
- Introduce the use of VR for training

Another benefit of using VR-based materials in classrooms involves the instructors' perception of the use of self-paced instruction in a classroom environment.

Some instructors fear that effective self-paced learning materials will replace them. Allowing instructors to interact with these materials to improve the quality of their instruction reduces those concerns.

While instructors can benefit from the use of VR-based materials, once the learners know how to use VR, it is best to let them interact directly and not interfere with their pacing in each lesson or module. Lockstep utilization of VR training devices reduces relatively expensive delivery platforms and courseware to an interactive slide show. The instructor also must take care not to allow this technique to elevate minor deviations between the virtual environment and the actual environment to the status of major discussion topics and opportunities for learners to vent their frustrations.

Integration with Other Training Methods

Virtual reality can be integrated effectively with other instructional techniques, specifically "live" or hands-on training, which use actual or partial mock-ups of equipment and environments. VR is a cost-effective tool for reducing reliance on expensive, hard-to-get, or hard-to-maintain equipment and for preparing learners to make the most of their time in the "real world." However, employing VR as a stand-alone solution is not an effective method for training motor skills. The most effective training strategy is to utilize a mix of virtual training for cognitive skills and "live" training for motor skills tailored to the availability of time, training materials, and learner attributes.

Assessment, Evaluation, and Certification

Ideally, the testing environment for a learner should be as close to the actual job situation as possible. However, these testing conditions rarely are achieved because of cost constraints and logistic factors. The use of VR to test mastery of skills and knowledge offers a cost-effective alternative whether the learning is delivered through traditional instruction, other types of computer-based training, or VR-based training. After a practice session in a virtual environment, learners can perform a self-assessment and instructors can review their performance.

VR is a particularly attractive option when hazards or extremely high costs are associated with the learning. For example, in a demolition course, the sizing, placement, and tamping of explosives might be practiced on actual small charges, but demolishing large structures may not be testable in any environment but a virtual one.

The design of the testing environment should be validated to ensure that the learner's success or failure in the test case cannot be attributed to shortcomings in the

VR simulation or other factors. Because of the liability issues associated with any certification process, this is particularly true if the test is used for certification. For example, driving simulators have long been used to teach foundation skills, but until recently the driving test has always been the domain of the road test. Just as simulators are now used to test student drivers before the issuance of a license, applications of VR, especially tactile feedback, will gain acceptance as certification mechanisms because of cost constraints, the availability of certification agents or locations, the destructive nature of testing, and so on. However, whether the level of fidelity and functionality provided by a VR application is sufficient to allow a certification to stand up in court has not been determined. Until this issue is decided, VR should be used for assessment and evaluation if the VR application is at least as realistic (in terms of functionality and fidelity) as any other component in the training.

What Are the Benefits of Using VR?

VR shares the benefits of all CBT technologies, including

- Reduced total cost of training
- Improved consistency of learning content
- Reduced average learning time
- Increased access to high-quality learning for large numbers of geographically dispersed trainees

In addition to these benefits, VR technology has unique characteristics that include its ability to

- Engage learners in the learning experience and increase their motivation to learn, particularly workers who typically learn on the job and prefer learning by doing
- Provide a wide variety of realistic conditions and feedback for effective practice and rehearsal of skills in a safe, risk-free environment
- Promote conceptual and procedural learning tasks
- Reduce errors in performing skills, particularly for complex tasks
- Increase retention

Evidence of these benefits is emerging as more practical applications are developed and evaluated. The following list highlights the results of several training initiatives that illustrate VR's benefits.

1. NASA used VR to prepare astronauts and flight controllers for the Hubble space telescope repair mission. The results of a formal posttraining survey showed that training time was reduced from hours to minutes for a complex set of tasks and that this contributed to the success of the mission.

2. Motorola found in a controlled study that students performed as well in the VR-based manufacturing line as they did in the real line and reported less fear of making mistakes that might damage the equipment. They also performed complex and critical tasks with far fewer errors (1 error in the VR group compared with 14 errors in the control group using the actual equipment).

3. Semiconductor manufacturers report dramatic savings as a result of reducing error rates from 25 percent to 2 percent, decreased damage to the equipment, and over 50 percent reductions in training time. In an industry where single errors can cost hundreds of thousands of dollars, the return on investment for VR-based training can be realized in 8 hours.

4. The U.S. National Guard conducted a controlled study of its VR-based equipment maintenance training system and found that it
   - Improves the acquisition of critical skills for initial and refresher training, reducing the overall cost of gaining and maintaining required skills
   - Increases the number of students who can be trained simultaneously in half the training time
   - Reduces reliance on expensive and hard-to-get or hard-to-maintain equipment
   - Is perceived by learners as improving their ability to retain knowledge

What Technologies Are Needed to Develop and Deliver VR?

As a sophisticated computer-based technology, VR requires a number of resources for the development and the delivery of learning applications. Different technologies are needed to develop and deliver different levels of VR training materials. The technology for developing and delivering VR training continues to evolve. This section provides a snapshot and makes predictions about how the technology will evolve.

VR Technology Introduction

VR requires a combination of computer software and hardware that offers many options for implementation, depending on

- The degree of realism required, both visual fidelity and the amount of real time, or immediately responsive, functional performance
- The amount of interaction between the user and the virtual environment
- The degree of immersion (whether the learner sees only the computer-generated images or views them through special glasses or watches a monitor)
- The degree of depth perception and tactile requirements

- The response time of the system (how fast and smooth the images, sounds, and/or movement appear to be)
- The current resources or budget

The hardware needed to display VR depends on these factors. Generally speaking, if the requirements are at the low end of the scale, a standard personal computer (PC) may be adequate, but as the requirements increase, higher-performance graphics work stations and specialized devices may be needed. The software that creates VR includes a number of programs for three-dimensional (3-D) graphics modeling and virtual environment building. Software requirements depend on the hardware selections and pertain to the development of virtual environments.

Technologies for VR Delivery

A basic implementation of VR can run on a standard multimedia PC with good graphics and audio capabilities. VR-based programs can be delivered on CD-ROMs, over networks, and to a limited degree over the Internet. For many learning applications, this readily available hardware is sufficient. However, depending on the requirements mentioned above, specialized equipment may be needed, including

- A head-mounted display (HMD) and tracker for greater immersion
- Stereoscopic (3-D) glasses to enhance depth perception
- Devices for enhanced tactile feedback, such as a joystick, a force-feedback steering wheel, a motion platform, and a data glove
- A graphics work station with more power than a standard PC for increased performance
- Other special high-resolution projection systems or environments for greater realism, response, and other factors

A major factor controlling the complexity of the VR that is developed is the delivery mechanism. Training analysis will determine which of these restrictions is most critical. It's important to consider the technical specifications (processor speed, random access memory, storage space, graphics acceleration, operating system, etc.) of the probable client computers that must host the training materials. In many instances one must design and test to the "lowest common denominator" system.

Some examples of the trade-offs are as follows.

- If the training materials must be delivered over the Internet, fidelity must be reduced to provide real-time interactions. The software developer may be able to design around bandwidth restrictions by requiring that the learner download the software and VR databases before running a lesson or by employing a hybrid approach. A hybrid design might incorporate large files and databases residing locally on a CD-ROM so that Internet traffic is limited to essential instructor-learner, learner-learner, and reference material interactions and other program control messages.

• Delivering the training materials over a local area network affords much more flexibility in the design of a VR application. Delivering training materials over a local area network provides better control over or insight into the types of client computers so that the VR application can include higher-fidelity simulations or visual models.

• An advanced learning environment (ALE) is a training lab environment that combines multiple forms of VR-based training with hands-on training. This environment supports a combination of learning methods, including VR-assisted instructor-led training for large groups, individual self-paced study on PCs with VR training courseware, and hands-on trainers for advanced students. By combining VR-based training on low-cost PCs with advanced training on actual equipment, an ALE can obtain many of the cost savings that can be achieved with VR but still have the actual equipment for the parts of the curriculum that require physical mock-ups or actual equipment.

Technologies for VR Development

Acquiring the technologies for VR development includes obtaining both hardware and software capabilities. This is an expensive and continuing investment, since the technology is changing rapidly and products developed with yesterday's technologies are not competitive in today's training marketplace.

The hardware platforms for VR development depend on the most sophisticated level of VR used in the complete project. Two aspects of VR development should be considered in selecting work stations for a VR development team: the storage space required to develop VR applications and the processing speed needed to render VR environments. The most critical issue is providing enough storage to support the development environment during the iterative design process. An effective VR training development effort must have a good configuration management plan. While VR models take up very little space, a multimedia VR training application uses a lot of storage space (several hundred megabytes), and typically, more than one version of a project will be on-line at the same time. During development, large portions of these databases change frequently, challenging the backup systems for the development team. These databases contain a lot of different media. Make sure the team's configuration management system can track and compress multiple revisions to the multimedia data files that will be delivered with the training application.

Rendering of VR is the process of computing what is shown on the screen from information about the model and the user's viewpoint as well as other considerations. High fidelity, real-time VR currently requires special-purpose graphics hardware. The task for the immediate future is to identify the graphics boards the VR application will employ early in the development effort so that client installations can be prepared for delivery and testing. As more applications now use complex graphics, powerful PC microprocessors and work stations equipped with the graphics hardware needed for VR are becoming more commonplace, and so this concern may dissipate over time. However, the customer's expectations for VR may exceed the available hardware, and unless they are dealt with in the development effort, those expectations grow at least as fast as does computer power.

The development environment should allow testing and user support of the final product hosted on the complete range of hardware and operating system platforms that are supported. To minimize user frustration, define what computer platforms are supported as early in the development effort as possible. For VR applications this may require specifying the graphics and boards that are supported as well as the processor, memory, and disk space requirements. If Internet delivery is used, communications bandwidths also should be specified. All this information must appear in the installation or downloading instructions and the user and instructor documentation.

An effective VR training development requires software tools that support the training development process from start to finish, including

- Training analysis
- Courseware development
- Multimedia material preparation
- VR model development
- Simulation development
- Web site development if required

In this section, only the technologies for VR model and simulation development are discussed. However, the creation of an effective VR-based learning environment also utilizes many of the multimedia tools that are used to create other multimedia applications.

VR Modeling Tools

VR models are three-dimensional visual representations of objects or environments. The specific tools required for a project are determined by the data standards selected for that project, the delivery environment, and the project team's resources and preferences. Generally, the available multimedia standards and the delivery options drive the selection of VR modeling tools. The VR modeling tools that are used include Multigen, 3DStudioMAX, ALIAS, and Softimage. Depending on the subject matter, VR modeling tools also may include conversion capabilities from design and/or architectural data (such as the DFX format) and terrain data (such as DTED and DFAD data).

VR Simulation Tools

A key part of the capability of high-end VR training systems is the ability of the objects in the VR world to simulate the actions of real objects and react to students' actions appropriately. Once the 3-D models have been constructed, the behaviors are associated and the scenarios are built to simulate the performance. Depending on the complexity of the simulation model required and the courseware, the simulation may be written in the courseware writing language or in a separate simulation programming language. These tools include Direct X, Active Service Page, Visual Basic Script, Java Script, Cold Fusion, Superscape, World-ToolKit, Vega, and VRML.

Multimedia Material Preparation Tools

The specific tools required for a project are determined by the data standards selected for the project, the delivery environment, and the project team's resources and preferences. These tools include

- Digital video and animations: QuickTime Movie, AVI
- Audio editing: Sound Forge, Audioworks
- Analogue video: ULead GIF Animator, Adobe Premiere, Microsoft Liquid Motion
- Digital graphics: JASC's Paint Shop Pro, Adobe Photoshop, Corel Draw, Microsoft Photo Editor

How Are VR Applications Developed?

Once a need is defined, the choice has been made to use VR as a medium, and the technologies for development and delivery have been sorted out, the development process can proceed. This section discusses each of these steps in VR development:

- Assemble a development team to create the virtual environment as a stand-alone application or as part of the courseware application
- Follow a process for creating what is required
- Define an approach for ensuring that the product provides effective training

Development Team

The size and makeup of the development team are largely dependent on the size and scope of the product. In some cases a project may be small enough and the expected product may be simple enough to allow a single developer or a developer working with an instructional designer to complete the effort. However, for a "professional-grade" product, VR requires people with specialized skills, including technical and artistic talent. Most VR development teams are made up of

- Instructional designer
- 3-D modeler and/or graphic artist
- Software engineer
- Subject-matter expert (SME)
- Project manager

The process of creating the discrete parts of the virtual environment defines the team's roles. The instructional designer bases the learning requirements on training analysis, oversees the instructional development process, and ensures that formative and summative evaluations occur. The 3-D modeler constructs a virtual environment populated with 3-D objects, and the graphic artist enhances it with textures. The software engineer codes the user interface, the behaviors of the objects, and the environments. The software engineer is also responsible for interfacing the VR application to special input and output devices (for example, a data glove or head-mounted display) and packaging the VR application as a stand-alone program or ensuring that the application integrates with another courseware application. The SME works with the development team to make sure the VR application is as accurate as possible. Additional roles may be defined to ensure that the look and feel of VR applications are adequate for the learners.

Development Process

Developing VR applications is an inherently cyclical process. Balancing the visual appeal of the virtual environment with the degree and types of interactivity and navigation required and the available processing power is an iterative process characterized by rapid prototyping, development, tuning, and revising. Superimposed on this process is the need for customer approval milestones to ensure progress toward product acceptance and ensure that budget and schedule goals are met.

Figure 19–1 shows how VR development interacts with courseware development to provide a VR-based training application. Many of the multimedia inputs are shared between the two processes. Both processes depend on an iterative approach to allow customer interaction and ensure that the customer gets what he or she wants.

The following process may be adapted to fit any size VR development effort.

1. *Requirements analysis.* This step includes definition of the application, followed by customer review and approval. Storyboarding is a good way to document the requirements for the VR components of the training course.

F I G U R E 19–1

An Approach to a Parallel Development Environment for Courseware and VR Models That Reduces Development Time and Allows Frequent Customer Interaction with Prototypes

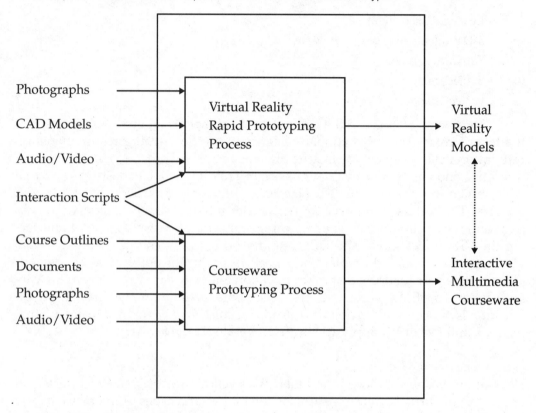

2. *Data collection.* This step can occur in parallel with analysis, and additional data collection efforts may be required throughout the job. Obtain geometric, textural, and functional information about everything that may be required in the virtual environment. Follow-up data collection can be costly. Be ready to take a lot of photographs, sift through a lot of computer-aided-design data, and examine a lot of off-the-shelf models.

3. *Prototype storyboarding.* This step can occur in parallel with the analysis phase. Figure out and document what is required to get the customer to approve the general design and serve as a starting point for discussions about trade-offs between the level of fidelity and interactivity in the virtual environment.

4. *Prototype development and review.* The sooner one can get the customer into a virtual environment that is a reasonable facsimile of the final product, the better.

Prototyping requires the development of an environment and a subset of the models required.

5. *Modeling guidelines.* The level of visual fidelity and interactivity, along with the delivery hardware, should be determined and documented at this point. Document the characteristics of the VR models and objects in terms of polygon budget per model and total, texture size, interactions, update rate, inputs to the simulation, and outputs from the simulation in light of the processing power and graphics capabilities of the target platform. Never trust component specifications to estimate system performance. Always try out the actual hardware with the prototype application. Obtain customer approval of the modeling guidelines.

6. *Full-scale model development.* Prototype models have to be updated. To obtain customer buy-in and participation, host a series of "working groups" where the SMEs work side by side with the modelers to obtain the required level of visual fidelity and build the models to support the desired level of interactivity. Make sure the modeling guidelines are adhered to strictly.

7. *Software development.* This step involves the creation of the software for simulation of the behaviors of the models. It gives the virtual environment its interactivity.

8. *Component integration and debugging.* This step involves verifying that the requirements are met and involves the whole team.

9. *Testing.* There are numerous ways to conduct usability testing to ensure that the application will perform adequately for the target learners. See the following section to learn how to map this process to formative and summative evaluations.

10. *Rework and testing.* Certain aspects of VR may require several iterations to get right. It's helpful to have the customer's SME work closely with the modelers and software engineers at their work stations to expedite this process.

Implications for Instructional Design

The VR development process follows the general model of the instructional system design process: analyze, design, develop, implement, and evaluate. VR projects benefit from iteration in the different stages of this process several times through formative evaluations, starting with the rapid prototype evaluation. In addition, small group trials and other summative evaluation techniques should be applied before the VR application is complete. By definition, there is a lot for the learner to see and do in the virtual environment, and you want to make sure that the purpose of the training is being reinforced, not eroded.

A strategy for ensuring that the application is moving toward a satisfactory end state is to conduct a series of one-on-one or small group evaluations with representative members of the learner audience, using successive iterations of the prototype during full-scale development. Each time the environment and software functionality are improved to include a measurable amount of additional fidelity and interactivity, run some learners through the system in a mock training course. Their feedback can be used to fine-tune aspects of the courseware before small group trials with the fully integrated system. Be sure to document the results of these evaluations rigorously, and keep the customer informed about the results and the changes you intend to make. Also, carefully monitor the desired improvements to avoid change to the contract without prior customer agreement.

What Does VR Cost?

Because VR is a multifaceted technology with numerous options for development and delivery, establishing cost guidelines is difficult. The factors that contribute most directly to the cost of VR are

- The complexity of the environment being represented (both visual and functional)
- The degree of realism required

These two factors drive the complexity and cost of the hardware needed to display VR and the software required to develop it. The goal is to create a virtual environment that performs with enough credibility to accomplish the required learning while using the most cost-effective resources.

A cost comparison can be made with PC-based multimedia instruction in which high-quality video production or VR is used. If VR replaces the video, the cost of multimedia CBT is similar. Often costs are represented in terms of the duration of the instruction. This is particularly difficult to measure in virtual environments, as the learning path is self-directed, with each learner's time on the system thus varying greatly.

Another cost variable is the ability to modify the materials during the development process and after delivery. Virtual environments are created in a modular fashion and, compared to video footage, can be modified easily. As SMEs review the learning content and inaccuracies are found, these factors can be corrected quickly. Also, as the work environment changes (equipment, processes, etc.), specific aspects of the virtual environment can be updated readily without re-creating the entire sequence, as is the case with video.

There is good news about the cost of VR: Trends indicate that the cost of including VR in a multimedia platform is coming down. The two key issues are as follows:

- The hardware to deliver VR is continuing to improve in terms of both performance and cost. By the end of 1998, 84 percent of computers were expected to be able to run 3-D images.
- The software tools to develop VR are improving and becoming standardized.

DOCUMENTS, JOB AIDS, AND HELPFUL HINTS

This section identifies additional resources to help you get started on a VR project.

The Virtual Reality Training Decision Tool

This tool is designed to help you decide whether VR is an appropriate technology to increase the effectiveness of your learning application. By working through 36 questions, you can assess the

- Learners
- Learning content
- Learning objectives
- Computing resources
- Organizational readiness

A scoring mechanism gives you guidelines for the suitability of VR for your application.

The Virtual Reality Training Decision Tool is available from the *1998 Training & Performance Sourcebook,* McGraw-Hill, 1998, and the Research Triangle Institute (RTI) Web site at http://www.rti.org/vr/w/decision.html.

Standards for VR Multimedia Applications

The use of standards is a key strategy for long-term success in developing VR training applications. A VR development team should learn the eccentricities of integrating VR applications from components using standard formats. Maintaining a focus on vendor-independent standards allows the development team to "mix and match" tools from different vendors and incrementally upgrade software tools to maintain a current development environment within a realistic investment budget.

Standards tools that are used in constructing VR environments include

- *3-D models:* 3DStudioMAX, Multigen, ALIAS, and Softimage
- *3-D environments:* DirectX, Direct3-D, ActiveX, Active Service Page, Visual Basic Script, Java Script, Cold Fusion, Superscape, WorldToolKit, and Vega
- *Multivendor standards:* OpenFlight, OpenGL, and Virtual Reality Modeling Language (VRML)

Multimedia standard tools that can be used include

- *Analog video:* VHS, BetacamSP
- *Digital graphics:* JPEG, GIF, TIF, TARGA
- *Digital video and animations:* MPEG 1, QuickTime Movie, AVI

The primary standard for simulation modeling is IEEE 1288.1, Distributed Interactive Simulation (DIS). The U.S. Department of Defense is spearheading an effort to establish a new and more sophisticated standard called the High Level Architecture (HLA). Interfacing a simulation model using either of these standards is an important step toward supporting collective training, in which several students interact with each other through the simulation. The network bandwidth required for these collective training applications limits the usefulness of this approach, but as bandwidth increases and tools and standards for interaction evolve, collective training over the Web will become practical.

PRACTICAL APPLICATIONS OF VR

In this section you will discover how VR is being employed by diverse organizations to improve learning effectiveness. While many of these implementations are regarded as pioneering efforts, the experience they accumulate will serve as a benchmark for others. *Training* magazine's 1998 Industry Report found that 2 percent of the 1828 respondents were using VR, while 88 percent relied on instructor-led classroom methods. As predictions for increased reliance on technology-based learning methods are realized, the use of VR is also expected to grow. Here is a survey of some of the practical applications of VR.

Maintenance Training

Vehicle maintenance training is a good VR application because the cost of the computer platform is many times less than the cost of an actual vehicle and the environment for training is safer. VR helps the users get familiar with the location of vehicle components and can support learning the diagnostic processes.

Research Triangle Institute is fielding its third generation of advanced VR-based training systems for the U.S. military. The evolution from first- to third-generation trainers demonstrates technology improvements in the computing platform, the use of standardized software, and the ability to reuse software and designs. It also represents an increasing integration of VR into the total learning system as VR materials move from prototypes to demonstration capabilities to installed training systems and from self-paced instruction to integration into the classroom and live training exercises (Table 19–1).

The Virtual Maintenance Trainer (VMAT) is a first-generation series of maintenance training devices for the M1A1 tank and two variations of the Bradley M2 personnel carrier. VMAT has been fielded to National Guard armories as a low-cost replacement for traditional training methods. VMAT used a personal computer and VR software ($10,000 per seat) for training instead of the traditional approach using actual vehicles (each of which costs several million dollars) or panel boards

TABLE 19-1

Evolution of Virtual Reality

First Generation	Second Generation	Third Generation
1994–1996	1995–1997	1997–present
Self-paced instruction	Classroom materials	Hands-on trainers
MS-DOS operating system on 486 PC platform	Windows 3.1 and 95 and upgrading of PC platform	Windows 95 and NT and upgrading of PC platform
Commercially available software for authoring only	Software for authoring and 3-D models	Software added for modeling, simulation, Web, etc.
No reusable components	RTI's VR-link software for integration with authoring	RTI extends integration to hardware devices

of components (each of which costs over $60,000). This cost reduction has made it possible to deliver the training to the armories and has allowed students to train on nights and weekends throughout the year instead of being limited to training at centralized institutions during the summer. Extensive reuse of materials across the three variations in the course has reduced the development expenses. Other features of the VMAT include

- Downloading of course modules and uploading of students' results.
- Integration of actual test equipment with the VR world for increased realism in the student experience.
- VR-based distant learning in which modems link VMAT to trainers over phone lines. This allows a remote instructor to manipulate a student's virtual model to explain a point.

Students working with VMAT have found the program especially beneficial for equipment familiarization. They can take the time to explore the VR model without risk and thus have greater confidence when first encountering the real vehicle. Experienced students can relearn procedures much more quickly than they could on the actual vehicle by using the VR models to skip many of the tedious and time-consuming parts of the actual procedure while concentrating on the cognitive issues.

The second-generation VR-based trainers took advantage of improvements in technology and extended the capabilities of the system. Technology enhancements included

- Moving high-fidelity VR models onto a computing platform that did not require special-purpose graphics accelerators. This freedom from special-purpose computers greatly expanded the potential distribution of the courseware.

- Developing image-based VR techniques as a low-cost alternative to traditional 3-D model-based VR. Image-based VR (IBVR) allows the user to explore a complex virtual environment but does not support the level of interaction and simulation that traditional VR provides. The cost of creating traditional VR models depends on the number and complexity of the objects in the environments, while IBVR is independent of the number of objects and their complexity, instead depending on the number of viewing locations supported. IBVR is ideally suited for familiarization and inspection tasks rather than operations or maintenance tasks. In addition, combining it with traditional VR may enhance the training benefits of IBVR. For example, the student can explore in the IBVR environment, and when he or she touches a "hot spot," a traditional 3-D interactive model appears with which the student can interact.

RTI's Maintenance Training System (MTS) for the M1A2 tank, a third-generation trainer, goes beyond VR-based training and integrates physical devices into a maintenance training system. Hands-on instrumented hardware devices provide a better learning environment for the retention of psychomotor skills, while the desktop VR simulator, implemented on a high-performance PC, is used to provide training in cognitive skills. The result has been a training system that provides over 200 hours of maintenance skills training.

The MTS training analysis identified 245 critical maintenance tasks. Development began with an analysis of vehicle data and traditional training materials provided by the U.S. Army. RTI worked with military instructors to base lessons on a task analysis and document the process by using tabular storyboards. The courseware for the MTS was developed using Authorware. The VR models and simulations were developed using WorldToolKit, Ada, and C++. The final step was on-site testing at Fort Knox by U.S. Army instructors and sample students.

Future generations of maintenance training systems will use natural language processing for spoken communication between the student and the computer. The program can play a passive role, as an assistant, by responding to students' inquiries or a more active role, as the instructor, by guiding students through the step-by-step process. The student can interrupt this process to ask questions, explore the virtual equipment, and take alternative paths to a solution. The computer will warn the student if he or she is taking a dangerous or potentially damaging action. Perhaps the greatest potential for this approach is the capacity for hands-free interactions with a computer as the ultimate talking repair manual.

Medical Training

VR is being used extensively in the training of medical personnel because it provides a safe, low-cost environment for practicing critical skills. One example is the Patient Assessment and Trauma Care Simulation, an interactive, multimedia VR-based simulator developed by RTI that offers realistic practice to trauma-care providers. Emergency medical technicians, medics, medical students, physician assistants, nurses, and physicians can sharpen their assessment and decision-making skills and develop an appreciation for patients' responses to appropriate and inappropriate treatments.

The learner is presented with a VR scenario in which a trauma incident has occurred. The user can navigate freely within the scene and view the scene and patient from any position. The trauma patient is a 3-D virtual model with realistic visible injuries and internal trauma who exhibits medical signs and symptoms with real-time, true-to-life physiological behavior. Records of all user interactions are maintained for postsession review, along with the pertinent physiological data. The application can be used for skill practice and student examination as well as introductory skill instruction with built-in guidance from standard protocols for trauma life support.

Safety Training

Virtual reality is proving to be beneficial in safety training because it allows learners to practice skills and receive feedback in a simulated work environment under a variety of conditions without harming themselves, the equipment, or the environment. True preparedness involves experiencing multiple worst-case scenarios, something that VR is uniquely suited to provide. This risk-free learning allows workers to learn and rehearse skills at their own pace.

The organizations that have employed VR for safety training include the following.

- Arizona Public Service Co. has a nuclear safety training program in which the learners perform job skills, demonstrate their understanding of radiation safety procedures, safely see the consequences of their actions on radiation exposure, and receive coaching.

- Fluor Daniel Hanford, Inc., has a nuclear safety training program for practicing waste transfer procedures under routine and emergency operating conditions.

- Portland Gas & Electric has an electric utility installation training program for learning and practicing line installation and grounding procedures under different conditions.

- The U.S. Bureau of Alcohol, Tobacco, and Firearms has an arson investigation training program for learning procedures and practicing investigations.

Manufacturing Training

Manufacturers with complex equipment and processes are finding that training in virtual environments reduces error rates, decreases training time, and improves production. VR allows trainees to experience processes under ideal as well as compromised conditions, something that is very costly to achieve with actual equipment. The benefits are particularly apparent in expanding industries, when skilled workers are scarce, and when prior training relied on learning on the job, resulting in reduced production capacity.

The organizations that have employed VR for manufacturing training include the following.

- Motorola pioneered the application of VR for new production worker training in its pager assembly line and now uses it in factories in 23 countries.
- IBM and other semiconductor manufacturers have used VR to train new workers in their complex and costly fabrication processes, reporting reductions in time and error rates.
- Ford Motor Company uses VR simulation to train new workers in forge operations and has found a 10 to 20 percent improvement in job performance.

Telecommunications Training

The telecommunications industry also provides several examples of the use of VR for training employees and customers.

- Southwestern Bell has created a large, complex virtual environment of an entire town to give technicians practical job training in the procedures for identifying and resolving telephone circuit problems.
- Nortel uses a VR-based training program to train customers to install and use its equipment.

GLOSSARY

Advanced Learning Environment (ALE)   A system of facilities (classrooms), infrastructure (computer hardware, software, and digital, audio, and video networks), and courseware that supports learning methods for realizing the potential of multimedia technologies for educational and training needs.

Hands-on Trainer (HOT)   A physical mock-up of a piece of equipment. It may be instrumented to allow downloading of diagnostic exercises and uploading of information about student performance. A HOT typically is designed to cost far less than an actual vehicle.

Head-Mounted Display (HMD)   A helmet or an oversized pair of glasses that monopolizes the user's field of view. An HMD is used to provide a high degree of immersion to a VR experience.

Image-Based Virtual Reality (IBVR)   A method for combining digitized photographs of the interior of a place (from a palace to a blood vessel) with computer navigation to allow the user to explore that place. IBVR provides realistic models of complex scenes at a fraction of the cost of fully interactive 3-D models.

Natural Language Processing (NLP)   A technology that supports a spoken human-computer dialogue. This goes a step beyond speech recognition, where the computer understands individual words, to provide complete dialogues. The dialogue processing allows the use of pronouns and context-specific references to objects and events.

Rendering   The process of computing what is shown on the screen from information about the model and the user's viewpoint as well as considerations such as lighting.

Virtual Reality (VR)   A computer-based technology that gives learners a realistic, interactive experience, or a sense of "being there." Virtual reality is

- *Three-dimensional:* represents real life with computer graphics that portray the functionality of complete objects or environments and provides the ability to move around in those environments
- Interactive: responds immediately and realistically to users' actions
- Immersive: involves learners in the physical process and puts them at the center of the experience

CHAPTER 20

Overview of Electronic Performance Support Systems

Deborah Stone
John Endicott

Objectives

After reading this chapter, you will be able to:

- Define electronic performance support systems (EPSSs).
- Describe how the components of an EPSS work.
- Describe basic strategies for maximizing the effectiveness of an EPSS.
- Describe how an EPSS was deployed using these strategies.
- Identify the resources for a more in-depth study of EPSSs.

OVERVIEW

Gloria Gery, who coined the term *electronic performance support system (EPSS)*, defines an EPSS as "an electronic system that provides integrated, on-demand access to information, advice, learning, and tools to enable a high level of job performance with a minimum amount of support from other people." Simply stated, an EPSS is a network of on-line and off-line job resources such as

- *Information,* including inventory databases and the contacts function in Microsoft Outlook. Information components typically contain reference or volatile information that end users need to access rather than master through training. Informational components store an organization's knowledge and deliver it on demand to end users on an as-needed basis.

For example, the information components of an EPSS at a securities firm could include information in the form of a graphic user interface to an existing database of customers, a repository of the securities in which the firm trades, and compiled research reports on the movements of those securities. All these information components may be linked to the stockbrokers' contact management software tree to identify potential sales.

• *Customized tools* such as embedded word-processing programs, templated presentation software, a preformulated spreadsheet, and filtered database applications. The most effective of these tools promote standardization, reduce errors, and reduce repetition through the use of customized templates, forms, or filters developed for a specific target audience.

For instance, once a stockbroker at a securities firm has made a sale, he or she can use an EPSS tool that displays a template for a confirmation, and then use a drag-and-drop function to automatically populate the template with the required customer and security information (drawn from the database).

• *Advisers* that provide context-sensitive, just-in-time advice for end users who encounter a situation they cannot handle on the job. Some EPSSs can apply advanced artificial intelligence (AI) technology to deliver nearly human coaching capabilities. A more low-tech example would be the wizards and cue cards used in Microsoft Word and other applications to walk users through complex procedures one step at a time.

A stockbroker who runs into a difficult customer situation could invoke a virtual adviser that provides tips on handling a talkative, angry, or harassing caller.

• *Training* in the context of an EPSS is considerably more modular than computer-based training (CBT). Rather than a lengthy course, an EPSS training component may deliver modules in the form of 5- to 10-minute "task bites" that end users can complete at their desks and then continue with their job tasks, immediately applying what they have just learned.

Given the ubiquity and increasing power of desktop computing, Intranets, and the Internet, many EPSS developers limit their description of EPSSs to electronic components that incorporate on-line advisers, wizards, expert systems, databases, custom application software, and instructional modules—all of which are navigable via a central interface.

At the broadest level, however, an EPSS can be seen as part of a larger performance support system (PSS) that can contain off-line components such as mentoring, problem-based learning workshops, references, training, audiotapes, videotapes, and paper job aids. Moreover, other off-line components, such as feedback systems, mentoring, incentives, and rewards, are often core components of a successful PSS.

Table 20–1 shows several other potential components to consider in implementing an EPSS. The key to all these examples is that the components work together to support individual and organizational performance.

TABLE 20-1

On-Line Electronic Performance Support System Options

Option	Description	Benefits and Applicability
Application Documentation: EPSS Components That Document Functions of the Application (How the System Works)		
On-line manual	A direct translation of a paper-based manual into an on-line tool. No hypertext or context-sensitive hot links.	Low cost of development; no linkage between application and document system.
		Always available when running application.
		Can be mainframe-based and distributed via dumb text-mode terminals.
Hypertext	Context-sensitive, hyperlinked descriptions of data entry fields and user-commanded system functions. Requires some integration between on-line document system and application.	Provides "just-in-time" information (i.e., when and where it's needed).
		Can be mainframe-based (e.g., CICS-TIMS/E) in some environments.
		Excellent PC-Windows system readily available (WinHelp).
Tool tips/bubble help	Pop-up description of application functions and tools whenever the user points at them; removes the pop-up when the user points elsewhere or performs another action.	Explains icons without requiring a lot of permanent screen space.
		Follows users based on what they want to do instead of directing them based on what the program wants them to do.
Task-based: EPSS Components That Help End Users Through a New System or New Tasks		
Cue cards	A single overlay that provides directions to users on how to perform a specific application function.	Gives users quick, easily referenced step-by-step instructions on how to use the program to perform their job tasks.
		Requires very little technical integration with the application.
		Should include corporate policies associated with job procedures.
Task guide (a type of wizard)	Step-by-step overlays in the application to interactively guide users while they are using the application. Activates only the application functions relevant to the task.	Interactivity assures that users perform tasks concisely, completely, and with fewer errors.
		Users can't get "off track" during the guided sequence since only the portions of the application that are relevant to the guided procedure are allowed.
		Since this option uses the application to perform tasks, it requires less underlying technical integration and ensures that users are using the application to perform tasks, thus "subliminally" learning it.

Term	Description
Task shell or mask (a type of wizard)	A focused, independent user interface overlay that cues users to perform very specific tasks. Presents highly customized user interface cues and data entry options as required to perform a very specific task; makes extremely efficient use of users' time.
Monitor adviser (a type of wizard)	A "monitor" that watches what users are doing and interrupts their activities to advise them on better ways to complete tasks. Provides training "on the spot" as users are using the application, generally improving their efficiency with the application even when they were already satisfied.
User macros	A shortcut that users develop (or practitioners provide) to automate frequently performed tasks on their own. Allows users who have diverse needs or different ways of accomplishing tasks to make the program more efficient for themselves individually. Requires highly trained expert users.

Computer-Based Training (CBT) and/or Multimedia: Teaches How to Use the Application and How to Perform the Job

Term	Description
Tutorial	Narrative instruction that describes and demonstrates how a job is performed and how the application is used to do that job. May incorporate multimedia to improve training effectiveness. Lowers development costs depending on level of interactivity implemented in the teaching. CBT combines job training and application training into a single, controlled training presentation. Passive (i.e., not interactive) demonstration of the application can be easily distributed to remote sites for increased flexibility in scheduling and reduced travel expenses.
Simulation CBT	Teaches both job and application via a simulation of the application developed through screen captures and interactive, logical simulation. Does not require the underlying application to be present for training to be delivered and may be easily distributed to remote sites for scheduling and travel efficiencies. Very little integration of training and application required.
Concurrent CBT	Similar to task guide but with significantly enhanced job task instruction. Requires highly sophisticated integration with the application to provide response judging and feedback instruction. Teaches novices how to perform the job while teaching them how to use the application. Can be developed so that novices can complete the training on the job, learning how to perform the job while doing it.
Multimedia	Introduces audio, video, and/or animation to CBT. Motivates end users, addresses readability or literacy issues, and/or models job tasks.
Computer-managed instruction	Record system to track students' training progress and performance. Required if training records are required to qualify students for promotion, job certification, scheduling and/or assignment availability, and so on.

345

Other qualities commonly attributed to EPSS include the following:

• *Flexibility.* A large part of this flexibility comes from a modular design that enables users to select components that support their requisite skill sets and responsibilities to perform on the job. When personnel and job descriptions evolve, the EPSS can be modified to meet the new sets of needs. In short, there is no "off-the-shelf" EPSS. It is not a product. It can take as many forms as the diversity of the target population and the robustness of the design allow.

• *Just-in-time delivery.* Some of the more sophisticated EPSSs use knowledge management strategies to simulate a flesh-and-blood coach or mentor to detect exactly which task a user is trying to perform, what form of support he or she needs, and at what level that support would be most valuable in accomplishing the task.

• *Day 1 performance.* Enabling end users to become productive the first day on the job is a central tenet of the EPSS model. Backed by studies that indicate that novices come up to speed more rapidly and with improved retention when they learn within the context of the job, EPSS practitioners have adopted day 1 performance as a central goal.

• *Extensibility.* Besides adopting EPSS components to match their own up-to-the-minute requirements, developers and/or end users can modify the system to reflect end users' experiences, updating information that is no longer current or adding embedded tools or tools of the users' creation. In this way an EPSS has an extensible shell that can go beyond supporting performance and become a vital tool for an organization's knowledge management.

• *Synergy.* EPSSs are integrated interventions whose components work together to support end users. These systems consist of not only the technologies workers use to perform their jobs but also the thought processes and mental models that make up those jobs.

The best-known examples of EPSSs include consumer software such as Quicken and TurboTax and software that includes context-sensitive help, cue cards, tutorials, and macros.

The remainder of this chapter provides a closer look at some design principles for ensuring that the components of an EPSS work together seamlessly to support performance and a real-life example of how those principles were applied to the creation of an award-winning EPSS. The bibliography lists resources for delving more deeply into EPSS theory and practice.

A DESCRIPTION OF THE BASIC APPROACH

In addition to functionality, an important attribute of EPSS components is their *approach,* or how they manifest themselves in the context of the job. Depending on several variables—such as performance requirements, whether the developer entered the project life cycle before or after the software was developed, and whether the source code can be accessed—an EPSS can be described as intrinsic, extrinsic, or external.

• *Intrinsic,* or integrated, EPSSs are part of the software's primary interface. In using intrinsic EPSSs, individuals are performing their job tasks. As a result, end users usually are unable to identify where the application stops and the EPSS starts, if they are conscious of using an EPSS at all. Often they know only that they are using well-designed software. Common examples of intrinsic EPSSs include automated teller machines and financial software packages such as Quicken and TurboTax. The easy-to-use intuitive interfaces of such programs enable users to master the task at hand instantly. While intrinsic EPSSs may be unobtrusive, the user cannot turn them off.

• *Extrinsic* EPSSs exist primarily to enable individuals to use existing software. They are generally separate from the software applications, although they often are accessible from within the software. Extrinsic components act as "sidecars" connected to the software's interface, and users can choose to use or disable them. Extrinsic EPSSs are often the result of efforts to make up for poor software design; thus, they sometimes are referred to as "bolted on." Common examples include the software application plus garden-variety CBT, on-line documentation, and/or electronic job aids.

• *External* EPSSs, unlike the other two types, occur off-line, are not integrated with the work context, and interrupt the user's job tasks. Examples include printed reference systems, traditional classroom or self-paced instruction, videotapes, printed policies manuals, and help desks.

DEVELOPING AN EPSS

The three approaches discussed above can be combined into a unified, effective EPSS if you follow several time-tested strategies throughout the development cycle.

Analysis

Double the Estimates and Add 10 Percent

In the experience of most practitioners, first EPSS efforts typically are underestimated in terms of both dollars and resources. The learning curve is steep. Therefore, in calculating budgets and schedules, it's wise to double the costs and add 10 percent; chances are, the project will take twice as long to complete as you think.

Think Systematically

By definition, an EPSS is systemic. Consequently, the first strategy for designing performance support systems is to identify and resolve systemic performance gaps. Too often people use subsystem solutions to address systemic problems, with poor or no results. The problem with this potential solution is that performance gaps travel in packs. That is, performance gaps rarely can be closed by one intervention. Rather, since performance gaps typically are caused by multiple, interacting sources, they frequently can be resolved by deploying interventions that increase transfer to the job, provide timely access to current context-sensitive information, and automate cumbersome manual tasks.

Assess Organizational Readiness

To facilitate expert-level performance, PSS developers often begin with a needs assessment that includes collecting data from novices, competent performers, and experts. While needs analyses are effective at identifying performance gaps, they seldom place enough emphasis on organizational issues. EPSSs without organizational sponsorship and readiness rarely get past the prototyping phase. To ensure that an EPSS clears this hurdle, organizational buy-in is crucial.

As Stan Malcolm puts it, "You must have real sponsorship, meaning dollars and resources, not just rhetoric. And you must figure out how to deliver something (a whole tool or a useful portion/release of a system) within the sponsor's 'window of enthusiasm.' "

An effective way to obtain sponsorship for an EPSS effort is to piggyback it onto technology efforts that are already under way. Organizations continue to invest in their computing infrastructures: providing E-mail and Internet access to employees, constructing World Wide Web sites, equipping workers with high-end desktop and laptop computers, establishing enterprise- and organizationwide data standards, and creating warehouses of regulatory data. Logically, organizations that make these major investments expect a return on them, and improved human performance can be an important part of that return.

To align an EPSS effort with an organization's technological investments, you must address the bottom-line considerations that probably sparked the investments in the first place. One way an EPSS can achieve this is by promoting *communities of practice.*

Investments in computing infrastructure also allow performance technologists to instill communities of practice in their organizations. E-mail, listservs, newsgroups, and Web pages provide opportunities for end users to "talk shop" across the boundaries of geographic location and time. These electronic venues are far more than a complement to the traditional help desk. By using them, end users can ask questions, receive answers, and learn from the successes and failures of everyone in the organization.

Making such job-related dialogues public enables novices and experts alike to upgrade their skills and knowledge on a continuing basis. Moreover, these venues allow novices to view alternative models of expert performance, expediting job mastery. Because this information is digital, a savvy EPSS practitioner can use these forums to capture "war stories" and best practices for use in future training or EPSS development efforts.

Design

Design the Components to Lead, Follow, or Get Out of the Way

To get the most mileage from an EPSS, make sure the design of the intervention leads, follows, or gets out of the way.

- The interface should gently lead new users through the appropriate activities, providing the scaffolding necessary for performance.
- For competent performers who are still honing their skills, the interface should quietly follow, interrupting only when requested or when the user makes an error.
- For experts and other seasoned veterans, the user interface should be transparent and unobtrusive, matching the mental models and procedures used on the job.

The user interface should help each group of users reflect on their performance and restructure it when appropriate. Common violations of this principle include confusing unnecessary menus, counterintuitive key combinations, confusing field identifiers, and "all-knowing yet never-revealing" on-line help.

Consider Making Information Filters Part of the Design

Whether an EPSS effectively supports end users depends on how it manages the flow and amount of information they use, which can be either too little or too much. Performance gaps arise when end users do not know where to find the information they need, must spend an inordinate amount of time locating it, or cannot trust the timeliness of the information they locate. The most common performance gap end users face is an overabundance of information. There is simply too much information out there, and end users must spend too much time managing it. Static and dynamic filters can cure this "information bulimia."

• Static filters act on information that already has been captured and internalized. They can take the form of shared databases that eliminate the need for end users to collect and organize personal libraries.

• Dynamic filters act on information as it is collected. Some dynamic filters act as "intelligent agents" that scour an organization's Intranet or the Web for information of interest, such as new legislation that affects an organization. Others ensure that the end user never sees "spam" and annoying marketing messages.

Ultimately, the filters should be customizable, easily accessible, and fitted to the tasks end users perform.

Prototype Early, Prototype Often

A prototype is a model or mock-up that produces successive approximations of the end product. For example, industrial designers often use prototyping processes that consist of sketches, foam-board mock-ups, and product prototypes to create a final version of a product and the manufacturing specifications for creating it.

Human performance technology (HPT) practitioners are increasingly using this powerful tool in developing EPSS because prototyping

• *Makes deliverables concrete.* End users seldom know what they want until they see it. Even if developers can picture a finished product on the basis of a topic outline or storyboard, most users cannot. In contrast, a series of prototypes lets end users and stakeholders view, comment on, and request changes in a prototype and then see their concerns addressed in the next prototype until they feel the intervention meets their needs. As a result, the entire project team shares a common vision of the look and feel of the CBT as well as the needs it must meet before development begins.

• *Minimizes costs in later phases of the project.* Errors or any other reasons for revisions are least expensive to fix during analysis and design, more expensive during development, and most expensive after implementation. This progressive increase in the cost of revisions exists because of the "ripple" effect: Changes in one part of an EPSS require corresponding changes to other parts. The more parts there are, the more changes can ripple. Through prototyping, a project team can identify and incorporate revisions while the ripples are still manageable.

• *Facilitates the selection of instructional approaches.* Because of the low costs of errors and revision, prototyping allows an EPSS team to experiment with competing prototypes and refine the most promising ones. After reviewing competing prototypes—perhaps demonstrating alternative instructional approaches, sequences, or media—developers and end users can negotiate revisions, select the best alternative, and refine it until it meets performance requirements and satisfies the users.

Make Cognitive Skills Visible

Much of the work end users perform is invisible; it occurs inside their heads. The final strategy for developing effective EPSSs is to develop components that make invisible cognitive skills visible. The capture and dissemination of these skills form the basis of the learning organization, help novices master their jobs, and leverage that expertise in the form of best practices. Because experts often cannot articulate what they do that makes them experts, performance technologists must extract, test, and disseminate those skills in the form of training, information, and tools. As was mentioned above, the communities of practice offered by tools such as chat forums are an ideal place to begin looking for these covert skills.

Development

Staff the Development Team with Experienced Specialists

An effective EPSS team consists of individuals from a wide spectrum of disciplines—on-line help, multimedia, software development, interface design, graphics and animation, instructional design, and the like—depending on the components of the EPSS. Your development team will look more like the credits from a Hollywood movie than a typical training development team.

The experience of the team is also critical. There's nothing like experience to help ensure the success of your first EPSS. Assemble a team that has worked together before, preferably on an EPSS project. If you don't have that experience in your organization, hire or "rent" it by using consultants.

Production

Build an Extensible Shell

Changes in products, performance requirements, and software are inevitable. Consequently, the shell of the EPSS should allow components to be added. Furthermore, it may be wise to build the entire EPSS to accommodate delivery over the World Wide Web even if you don't intend to use the Web right away. As technological issues such as bandwidth become less of a factor, Web delivery may become more feasible.

Implementation

Address Implementation Issues from the Outset

In a traditional HPT model, implementation begins after production. In creating a successful EPSS, implementation must begin the first day of the project, if not before. Implementation—including marketing and organizational change efforts and a provision for change management—must be an ongoing concern, from initial project planning through maintenance. Again, organizational sponsorship is a must to create a friendly environment for the implementation of the system.

In summary, a well-thought-out EPSS uses the five I's:

1. *Intuitiveness.* The EPSS uses a consistent, predictable graphic user interface that provides the metaphors and guidance that allow end users to reach mastery after spending minimal time (if any) learning about it.

2. *Integration.* EPSS components are designed to be used with each other and are seamlessly integrated.

3. *Immediacy.* EPSS offers on-demand access to custom tools, information, advice, training, and other components.

4. *Individualization.* EPSS supports a range of expertise and individual differences in learning, meeting the needs of novices, competent performers, and experts alike.

5. *Interactivity.* Interactions resemble a dynamic dialogue between end users and the EPSS.

A PRACTICAL APPLICATION

Over the last 4 years, DLS has collaborated with the National Association of Securities Dealers-Regulation (NASDR) to create an EPSS for its 450 examiners. These end users conduct examinations of over 5500 member securities firms throughout the United States and Puerto Rico to ensure that they possess sufficient financial reserves to safely trade securities and follow established sales practices.

NASDR contracted DLS to decrease the time required to train its novice examiners to mastery. At first glance this performance gap could have been attributed to a single source, such as a need for technology-based, self-paced training that would reduce overall training delivery time and costs and be available on day 1 of an examiner's career. However, a needs assessment and cause analysis revealed that the 2.5 years novice examiners required to master their jobs was also the result of more systematic issues.

To reduce time to mastery, NASDR and DLS created CORNERSTONE, a PSS that consisted of 21 different components using 10 different types of media. CORNERSTONE represents one of the largest EPSSs created to date.

The components of CORNERSTONE include the following:

• A hypertext information system (Figure 20–1). This static information filter describes existing securities products NASDR examiners are likely to encounter during an audit. As this information is easily updated, examiners know they can trust its contents and access them on demand. Since information describing each product is organized using the categorization system and questions expert examiners typically ask when they encounter new products, this information is accessible in a form examiners can use.

• Automated examination modules (AEMs). Examiners use AEMs, a custom software application that resides on their laptop computers, to automate the tedious paperwork associated with conducting an exam. The AEM replaces the paper forms examiners used to complete during these exams. On the surface, an AEM is a custom software tool that frees examiners from unnecessary paper shuffling and allows them to concentrate on the more substantive issues of an exam. In addition, AEM provides on-demand access to timely information on regulatory procedures and uses an extrinsic interface ("Exam Coach") that walks novice examiners through ex-

F I G U R E 20–1

CORNERSTONE Product Information Hypertext System

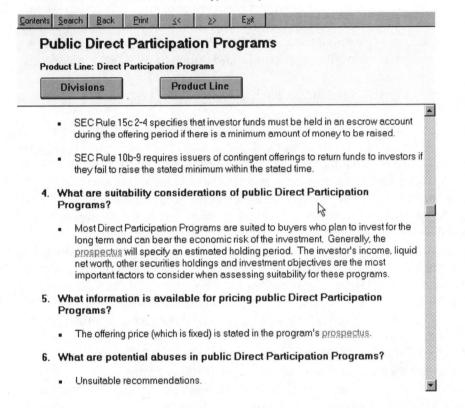

ams. AEM's user interface is based on the mental model and heuristics expert examiners use during an exam.

• A CBT component that applies the cognitive apprenticeship model described by Collins, Brown, and Holum (1991). In the CORNERSTONE CBT, expert examiners articulate their thought processes while novices reflect and articulate theirs. Because experts usually cannot articulate what they do, performance technologists must extract, test, and disseminate these skills in the form of training, information, and tools.

• A database of on-line test questions that assess end users' absorption of key teaching points. Like the CBT, these questions required hands-on participation from the learner. A randomizer and sets of alternative questions resulted in thousands of possible combinations, ensuring that no two learners would take the exact same test.

• A training management and administration tool that gives supervisors and mentors full computer-managed instruction (CMI) functionality. This tool enables supervisors to add and remove students and plan a new examiner's training path, on the basis of a set of tracks or a custom training path provided by the supervisors. Once an examiner's personal training plan is in place, the supervisor can track the examiner's progress through courses and hands-on activities and then provide remediation as necessary.

• Links to other NASDR resources, such as databases of regulations, notices to members, and interpretive memos.

DLS used prototyping to create an instructional approach and format for each medium. For instance, prototypes of the self-paced workbooks ensured that users ultimately would like their "look and feel." Prototypes of the CBT were used to illustrate how it would simulate the tools and processes examiners use on the job: file cabinets, computer- and paper-based source documents, logbooks, and so on. The requirements arising from this prototyping effort led to better designs that made these interventions easier to use.

A key to the success of this project was organizational sponsorship. Like other organizations, NASDR was deeply invested in its computing infrastructure. By obtaining the sponsorship of the executive vice president of regulation, DLS was able to align CORNERSTONE with the NASDR's ongoing efforts to upgrade its computing infrastructure. Like other organizations, the NASDR expected a return on this investment. They got it in the following areas:

• CORNERSTONE reduced initial time to mastery from 2.5 years to 1 year.

• Training delivery costs were reduced by $413,500 per year.

• CORNERSTONE eliminated the time all examiners spent building and maintaining their own libraries of product information and provided a new career path for senior examiners, who can become formal mentors.

• The 351 hours of training contact time provided in CORNERSTONE address high-level skills such as analyzing or synthesizing data and reviewing complex patterns of trades through real-world case studies and vignettes.

• CORNERSTONE is now distributed on the NASDR's Intranet, a much more efficient medium than paper for both delivery and maintenance.

• DLS and the NASDR explored the need for chat rooms or discussion groups for examiners to exchange "war stories" and solutions to challenging situations encountered in the field. This enhancement can promote a community of practice among NASDR examiners, as can an E-mail link to a "virtual mentor" who can answer regional or specialized questions (also under consideration).

• As DLS's and NASDR's computing infrastructures expanded, CORNERSTONE's review time and shipping costs were reduced considerably, allowing the project team to deliver CORNERSTONE within budget and on schedule. The leveraging power of this infrastructure is apparent in the ongoing maintenance effort surrounding CORNERSTONE's custom application, AEMs. As examination procedures change, NASDR sends vast volumes of information to DLS via E-mail. DLS uses these data to revise the procedures, schedules, and other information in AEM and then sends the resulting executable to the NASD for installation and distribution.

In summary, as the number of end users increases, performance technologists face growing challenges and opportunities in getting these workers on the job as quickly as possible and maintaining their performance once they have achieved mastery. Effective EPSSs are interventions that practitioners can use to support the performance of today's and tomorrow's end users.

CHAPTER 21

On-Line Training with a Distributed Learning Framework

Harvi Singh

Objectives

After reading this chapter, you will be able to:

- Identify the driving factors in the shift from traditional forms of training models, including the transition from stand-alone multimedia-based authoring tools to a distributed learning framework (DLF).
- Define a DLF.
- Describe the attributes and components of a DLF.
- Identify the benefits of a DLF approach.

WHAT IS A DISTRIBUTED LEARNING FRAMEWORK?

A distributed learning framework (DLF) is a software architecture that allows the integration of various processes and tools involved in training. These tools include front-end analysis, design of instruction, development of learning content, on-line delivery of content, and management of learning and results (Fig. 21-1).

A DLF operates in a network-based client-server environment that can be deployed in an enterprisewide capacity through the mechanisms afforded by the Internet and Intranets. Furthermore, a large repository based on relational databases can provide an underpinning for sharing the data between different processes, tools, applications, and learning content. The data repository ensures that the data across different processes are shared and that different projects can share data to avoid redundancy, resulting in consistency and time savings.

FIGURE 21-1

The Architecture of a Distributed Learning Framework

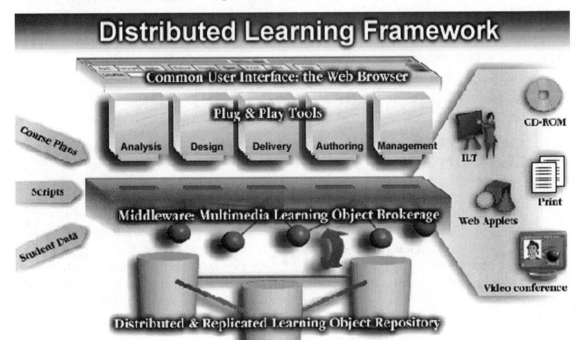

WHAT IS DRIVING THE SHIFT TOWARD INTEGRATED DISTRIBUTED LEARNING FRAMEWORKS?

The demand for a DLF can be understood by examining various distinct yet interconnected perspectives.

Learner's Perspective

The shifts from a learner's perspective include the following:

- From large courses to modular instructional content (learning objects)
- From learning once to continuous learning
- From classroom to on-the-job just-in-time and just-enough learning
- From mass to individualized and mixed-mode curriculum
- From individual learning to collaborative learning
- From passive learning to participatory learning and knowledge sharing
- From pay once to pay per use

Management's Perspective

The requirements from management's perspective include the following:

- Centrally administered and tracked progress and/or performance and evaluation
- Ease of registration, notification, reports, and other services
- Different levels of measurement and/or evaluation (Kirkpatrick's four levels of evaluation: reaction, learning, behavior, and results)

COMPONENTS OF A DISTRIBUTED LEARNING FRAMEWORK

Common User Interface: The Web Browser

The popularity of the Internet and the World Wide Web has resulted in the evolution of the Web browser as the most consistent cross-platform method for accessing multimedia data. A Web-enabled DLF can be accessed by users in a consistent and convenient manner from any location on the Internet or an Intranet. Web browsers will continue to evolve and support new multimedia, interactivity, and collaborative technologies. DLFs will benefit from these advancements.

Plug-and-Play Tools

A DLF provides a framework for many types of tools to be plugged into the infrastructure, depending on an organization's specific needs. Tools can vary from simple forms to very sophisticated interactive multimedia development environments.

Ideally, a DLF must support an open data architecture based on industry-standard components (data formats and protocols) that allow tools and content developed by multiple vendors to be integrated as the needs dictate and the technology advances.

A DLF integrates the processes for analysis, design, authoring, delivery and/or distribution, and management and/or evaluation.

Needs Assessment and Job Task Analysis Tools

Analysis tools provide templates and discrepancy matrices to quantify and accelerate the benchmarking and analysis process. Current performance needs are identified and analyzed, and performance improvement plans are easily generated. Furthermore, job-task analysis tools allow new or deficient tasks to be analyzed. This ensures that the resulting learning objects can be fine-tuned to the individual task and associated learning objectives.

Curriculum Design Tools

Curriculum design tools aid the curriculum designer in analyzing and specifying the audience profile and training goals. The process of determining learning objectives is accelerated by using templates and wizards.

Courseware Design Tools

A visual design tool allows the instructional designer to map training objectives to lessons and courses. Storyboarding tools automate the screen layout design and allow for easy transfer of instructional content into the authoring mode.

Authoring Tools and Templates

Authoring tools and templates assist instructional designers and content producers in creating learning objects. The learning objects may be based on a variety of instructional strategies embodied in the authoring template.

Content Metadata Tools

In building a large content repository and providing mechanisms to share content components, it is essential that each content component be tagged by certain searchable properties, such as author name, date of creation, and keywords. Industry efforts at creating standards are under way to provide metadata schemas that can be shared by different vendors to provide consistency in the use of content over different systems on the network.

Question and Answer Tools

Question and answer tools are a set of forms and wizards that allow the author to create a variety of learning activities, including

- True-false questions
- Multiple-choice questions
- Drag-and-drop exercises
- Clicking to identify objects
- Connecting the points with lines
- Matching the columns
- Simple interactive "challenge" games

Feedback, scoring, and a link back to course content can be specified.

Media Reuse Tools

Media reuse tools allow the author to reuse media elements (text, graphics, animation, audio, and video) by scanning the media repository through the use of thumbnail views. These tools support selection by object type and allow objects to be dragged and dropped directly into learning object screens. The learning tools provide presentation, navigation, feedback, and search capabilities.

Distribution Tools

Online Learning Infrastructure (OLI) distribution tools allow the learning objects or courseware to be exported out of the repository for distribution in a variety of formats, including print, instructor-led classroom presentation, CD-ROM, and Internet or Intranet delivery.

Administrative Tools

Administrative tools allow learners to view curriculum maps and register for courses. They help training administrators generate attendance and progress reports. These tools automate the time-intensive task of tracking the progress of all students through a training program.

Assessment Tools

Assessment tools provide management with different views of a learner's progress and performance. Using powerful database queries, a DLF provides different assessment metrics, for example, statistics about usage, progress, evaluation, and course success.

Collaborative Courseware Design and Development

Designing and developing courseware collaboratively on an Intranet or the Internet allow designers and developers to input up-to-the-minute content anytime, anywhere in the world. Geographically dispersed subject-matter experts are empowered to review courseware content simultaneously as an instructional designer makes the necessary revisions.

Collaborative Learning

A DLF may support several mechanisms to support collaborative learning: the chat mode, threaded discussions, and E-mail. The *chat mode* allows students to discuss course lessons and concepts synchronously. Students benefit in numerous ways from continuous input from other students as well as from immediate feedback from instructors during on-line office hours. *Threaded discussions* provide another convenient mechanism for collaborative learning. For each course, threaded discussions are maintained on a lesson-by-lesson basis. In addition, students can communicate with instructors and other students through E-mail.

Periodically, curriculum designers, courseware developers, and evaluators can benefit from the input generated from chat room discussions, discussion threads, and E-mail to improve courses and realign curricula. Over time a knowledge base can be built for each course, based on information garnered from conference discussions, to provide another source of help for students.

Distributed and Replicated Learning Object Repository

DLF can store all learning objects, student progress and/or performance data, and administrative and/or management data in an open architecture supported by a relational or similar database. Figure 21-2 shows the training content being pulled out of a relational database schema.

The database repository stores

- Clips and reusable multimedia elements
- Encrypted passwords and security information
- Student profiles
- A catalogue of lessons
- Results, scores, levels, and progress
- Links between nodes of training (as in a hypertext environment)

BENEFITS OF USING A WEB DATABASE SERVER TO SUPPORT DLF

Enterprisewide Support

A DLF system needs to operate in a client-server capacity where multiple work stations can access a shared repository of data and functionality on the server computer. A Web repository—a large database such as a relational database that can be accessed in a network environment—provides a multiuser environment that can support collaborative authoring, learning delivery, and management activities throughout the enterprise.

Cross-Platform and Open Repository

Ideally, the database repository in a DLF should be cross-platform. The popularity and widespread acceptance of data server solutions such as relational database management systems ensure their availability on almost every server platform.

FIGURE 21-2

Schema for a Relational Database

362

The learning object repository and application data, implemented as a relational database, therefore can reside on any Intranet server.

Efforts must be made to keep the data repository open and available for extensions by which different tools can be integrated into a DLF from different tool vendors to provide maximum value to the end users.

Sharable Data

Learning objects such as questions, simulations, and lessons, and media objects such as graphics and animations are stored in the repository; they are not tightly coupled to or embedded inside the training applications. The learning objects can be shared between multiple training applications or learning situations. The same holds true for other application data, such as learner profiles and progress data.

Scalability

Replication and distribution features, which are provided by most enterprise database management systems, allow a DLF's architecture to be scalable. The architecture can be used to deploy a large library of learning objects and support a large number of simultaneous users on the enterprisewide network.

Ongoing and Incremental Updates

As the enterprise learning needs expand, the learning object repository allows content to be added or updated in an incremental manner without affecting existing objects.

THE UNDERLYING HUMAN PERFORMANCE TECHNOLOGY MODEL IN A DLF

Human performance technology (HPT) provides a backdrop for DLFs from the standpoint of application functionality. A comprehensive HPT model suggests the involvement of not just learners and content authors but also management, analysts, designers, and administrators in a performance-oriented system. In fact, a dynamic HPT system that interconnects these perspectives is feasible in a network environment where data, knowledge, and processes are shared by all the stakeholders in the learning organization.

The latest thinking about on-line learning suggests that HPT processes need to be flexible and iterative. Flexibility in process steps means that one follows only the steps that make sense in a given scenario and context. Furthermore, the iterative principle suggests that a step not be fully completed but revisited on the basis of feedback from the next few steps.

Analysis

In front-end analysis tools, the performance consultant or business analyst can work with management to identify business issues that need attention and performance gaps between current and future business requirements. These gaps result in the identification of causal factors, resulting in solutions that may fix the problems. The fix may range from training to nontraining initiatives. Training solutions are linked with associated job, competencies and/or skills, and work-related tasks and practices that require training interventions.

Design

The design of training interventions needs to be linked to business issues that are identified in the analysis phase. The identification of job-task related learning goals and objectives lies at the heart of this process. The classification of learning outcomes defines the learning interventions and associated learning plans or blueprints and development storyboards where appropriate.

Development

The development of learning objects must be based on the viewpoint that there are multiple development strategies based on the situation: performance support or traditional training, directed or adoptive learning models, and self-paced or collaborative learning.

The open DLF environment should allow multiple authoring models that support multimedia authoring in addition to templates based on the development of content through which subject-matter experts can interface with the system and contribute knowledge content.

Delivery

A DLF delivers learning by providing network-based delivery of content. Separating the knowledge content from its presentation and delivery ensures that the content becomes more durable to the changing face of technology. Furthermore, the separation of intellectual capital and presentation affords an opportunity to create multimode delivery of content in several formats, including print, Web-based, and classroom.

In addition to content durability, the content must be managed and organized so that it can interoperate; that is, the content or parts of the content can be exchanged and reused between one system, application, or tool and another.

Administration and Management

What must be developed and delivered also must be managed and evaluated against results. These results must be evaluated at different levels, from a learner's satisfaction to business results.

In addition, a DLF automates the cumbersome process of learner and/or user enrollment, registration, records, transcripts, schedules, and reports.

UNDERSTANDING THE DATA AND CONTENT IN A DLF

Fundamentally, a DLF is a shared data repository in a network environment. The data can be categorized in the following way: learning content and metadata and application data.

Learning Content Components

There is a growing consensus in the industry that a building block approach is needed to construct the content for on-line delivery.

The content components can come from various sources and can include various data types (text, graphics, audio, video, animation, simulations, etc.). Content components also could include interactive activities, test questions, and games. These components can be sequenced into frames and pages and can be aggregated into topics and subtopics with navigational controls by using simple scripting or more complex adoptive algorithms.

The componentization of the content provides several benefits from a content development and delivery perspective.

From the content development perspective, components can be reused, decreasing the time and cost of content development at inter- and intraorganizational levels.

From the content delivery perspective, a higher level of individualization is feasible in late binding of curriculum with individual needs and interests.

Ideally, content should be deliverable in multiple modes—printed, CD-ROM, Web browser, or instructor-led—from the common repository.

Learning Content Metadata

The learning framework needs to support and manage not only the learning content but also metadata (searchable properties), administrative data, and management data.

Metadata allow the data to be "tagged" with searchable properties or attributes. The metadata need to be stored in a repository separate from (but linked to) the learning content. There is a need for the metadata to be published with or without the learning content.

Other Application Data

In addition to learning content, a DLF manages other application data, such as

- Registration
- Users
- Learner profiles (preferences, personal data)
- Schedules
- Progress and performance data
- Discussion forums
- E-mail
- Surveys

BENEFITS OF THE DLF APPROACH

A DLF provides substantial benefit over traditional silos-oriented approach to training development and delivery.

   • *Accessibility.* A DLF provides access to knowledge and related data on an enterprisewide, anywhere, anyplace basis.

   • *Flexibility.* A DLF environment provides a flexible work flow and process model that can be fine-tuned and configured to meet an organization's needs. At another level, a DLF supports different learning design paradigms, such as performance support and training and structured and unstructured forms of learning engagement.

   • *Extensibility.* As technology and requirement change and evolve, a DLF allows additional components to be integrated easily. This is attributed to the fact that a DLF is an open and component-based software architecture.

   • *Reusability.* Content reusability is critical in saving the time and cost of training development. In a DLF environment the content is created in components that are indexed on the basis of standardized metadata, allowing learning objects or constituent parts to be reused by the original creator or the consumers of the content. Value can be added rapidly.

   • *Interoperability.* A DLF must allow the content to swapped into and out of the system so that the data can be shared by disparate tools. Network and Web protocols and technologies allow the content structures to be exposed in a manner that allows the content package or part of it to be reused in another context.

• *Durability.* A DLF system manages the content in a way that separates it from its presentation and provides a porous interface that makes the content and data durable to technology advances.

CONCLUSION

In the future, learning frameworks will evolve to embrace new technologies such as electronic commerce and knowledge management best practices to solve business issues such as skills gaps, corporate virtual campuses, career development, and help desks. Distributed learning frameworks also will link to enterprise resource planning, human resources, and financial systems.

PART THREE

Design and Delivery of Self-Directed Training

George Piskurich

I would not want to say that this section is a catch-all area for the topics that didn't fit in the other two, so I won't. However, you will find a variety of concepts here.

For the most part they are all related to some aspect of individualized learning or self-instruction. Some people term the process *self-directed learning*, and this is what we've used as the title for this section.

There is probably a need to go into a long-winded academic discussion of self-directed versus self-instructional versus individualized versus self-paced learning, as purists will jump on this section title and say, "No it isn't self-directed; it's more this or that." However, this hairsplitting is not the purpose of this book, and so I'm not going to bore you with my definitions and thoughts on these concepts.

Suffice it to say that the chapters that follow look at various aspects of these and other concepts in no particular order of importance. From contract learning to performance support to transfer to the job, the emphasis is on the individual learner, not the group.

That is not to say that the applications of the concepts presented in this section relate only to individual learners. For example, Chapter 22 presents the design basis for much of technology-based training, which is only slightly different from good instructor-led design, while contracts (Chapter 23) are often used in classrooms as well as in individualized settings.

Chapters 26 and 27 deal with the relationship of training design and delivery to the practice of human performance technology (HPT). HPT is rapidly becoming a central issue in training, and no book on design and delivery should ignore its implications for the training process.

CHAPTER 22

Make It Easier for Them to Learn on Their Own: Instructional Design for Technology-Based, Self-Instructional Applications

George M. Piskurich

Objectives

After reading this chapter, you will be able to:

- Define the concept of individual technology-based training (I-TBT).
- State the four cornerstones of I-TBT.
- Describe the various types of analysis needed for I-TBT.
- Discuss the importance of objectives to the learner in I-TBT.
- Explain the use of chunking in developing I-TBT programs.
- List various factors related to media development for I-TBT programs.
- Discuss the evaluation aspects of I-TBT.
- State the two basic implementation scenarios of I-TBT.
- List the advantages of I-TBT.
- List the possible disadvantages of I-TBT.

This chapter discusses instructional design for self-instructional technology-based programs, or individual technology-based training (I-TBT). I-TBT scenarios can include videotapes, computers, digital video disks (DVD), CD-ROM, Net-based delivery, and learning center processes, but all these techniques have one thing in common: The trainee is expected to learn content without an instructor to provide guidance in the learning process. An understanding of this basic commonality by the instructional designer will make or break an I-TBT program.

I-TBT is one of the most useful training methodologies in the field of instructional technology. As a training intervention it can be effective in circumstances where no other training design is adequate. These situations often are characterized by factors such as a large employee population with diverse training requirements, a need for individualized development, multiple training sites where the same instruction must occur concurrently, the need for a high degree of consistency in the training, and high turnover rates that require continuous training.

DEFINITION

As with any TBT concept, there are a number of possible definitions for I-TBT and a number of terms that refer to the same process, at times erroneously. To simplify the issue, we will limit ourselves to a single definition of I-TBT: *a technology-based training design in which trainees work at their own pace, without the aid of an instructor, to master predetermined material.*

Let's look at what this definition means. The term *technology-based training design* indicates that I-TBT is only one of a number of technological approaches that can be employed to deal with a training problem. Other alternatives include satellite conferencing, Net-based synchronous classroom programming, and electronic performance support systems. Thus, the choice to use I-TBT is a design decision that usually is made after you've completed an analysis of the performance problem and/or training need. A key issue here is that I-TBT is not a training system. It is not the approach for designing all the training you need. It is simply one more design that works well in some circumstances but not in others. Looking at it as anything else, particularly as a way to create all the training for your company, invites big problems later.

To help you make the decision, Fig. 22–1 provides a list of questions that will help analyze your need for an I-TBT design.

In our definition, "trainees work at their own pace" is self-explanatory, though in the business environment this is often achieved within limitations that are set by the day-to-day needs of the company. Working at one's own pace is one of the major advantages of I-TBT and a reason for its high level of effectiveness and efficiency. However, it can also be a problem for trainees who are not used to the idea of learning on their own and for supervisors who are uncomfortable with the concept.

The phrase "without the aid of an instructor" means exactly that. An instructor is neither needed nor desirable for a good I-TBT process. All the content is delivered by the program, including further explanation, resource material, and remediation. If an I-TBT program does not deliver the proper content in the right amount, it will need assistance from an instructor or content expert, eliminating many of the advantages of the I-TBT concept.

"Master" specifies the evaluation criteria for I-TBT. It indicates that a certain level of expertise must be exhibited by the trainees through the process of criterion-referenced evaluation. This evaluation can have a number of different aspects, par-

F I G U R E 22–1

Is I-TBT the Right Approach for Your Organization?

A significant number of these items should be checked if you plan to initiate I-TBT in your organization
- [ ] Do you have a large training population?
- [ ] Do you have a number of dispersed training sites?
- [ ] Is there high turnover in your training population?
- [ ] Do you have more training needs than trainers to meet them?
- [ ] Do you need to train significant numbers of trainees in short periods of time?
- [ ] Do you have a large number of new hires or internal promotions who need training?
- [ ] Do you have classes that you need to repeat continually?
- [ ] Are a significant number of training classes poorly attended because of scheduling conflicts or last-minute cancellations?
- [ ] Do you need to decrease trainees' and/or trainers' travel expenditures?
- [ ] Do you need to do "downtime" or shift training regularly?
- [ ] Is standardization (consistency) of training important for your organization?
- [ ] Does your organization need just-in-time training?
- [ ] Do your development programs require a more individualized training system?
- [ ] Does your training population exhibit a sufficient degree of self-directedness?
- [ ] Do you have SMEs with knowledge that needs to be imparted but no time or ability to teach?
- [ ] Will your SMEs be given the time to support I-TBT content development and/or evaluation?
- [ ] Can you get commitment from management to support I-TBT's extra development time?
- [ ] Is there support in terms of funding and time for the implementation of I-TBT?
- [ ] Can you develop effective controls that will ensure proper I-TBT implementation?

ticularly as your technology reaches higher levels, but in a simple multiple-choice test or a complex computer-based simulation, the evaluation must be there and must be criterion-referenced if your I-TBT is going to be effective.

Finally, "predetermined material" is crucial to the I-TBT process. The content must undergo strong analysis and a number of reviews before it is presented to the trainees. Remember, there will be no instructor to deal with weak areas or trainee confusion when the I-TBT is delivered.

CREATING AN I-TBT PACKAGE

While defining I-TBT may lead to confusion at times, the way you create it should not. In fact, the process is basically the instructional systems design approach with a few simple modifications.

Analysis

You begin the creation of an I-TBT package with analysis. Since we've already defined I-TBT as a training design, you may feel that this is going backward, as you should have based your design decision to use I-TBT on a completed analysis. However, the data you used to make your design decision is of critical importance to how you proceed with the rest of the process. Now that you've chosen I-TBT as your design, you need to go back and reanalyze a number of factors for their I-TBT implications.

Job Analysis

The first and most important of these factors is the job analysis. If you ask, What job analysis? you've already got a problem, as you can't do a suitable job of developing I-TBT without a good job analysis. If you are unable or unwilling to do a proper job analysis, go back and choose another training design, because your I-TBT program will not work. A solid job analysis is the first cornerstone of the I-TBT process. Three more will be pointed out as this discussion continues. Ignoring even one of them will practically guarantee that your I-TBT package will not be effective.

Space limits the amount that can be said here about job analysis, but other chapters in this book discuss the process in detail. For I-TBT, the product and not the process is important, and that product is a complete listing of all the tasks that must be mastered for the topic at hand. In most cases these tasks also include the skills and knowledge that are important in mastering a task. There is a fine line here as to where you can stop the analysis. Some complex tasks require a deeper analysis. There is no rule of thumb here; it is something you learn through experience. If you are a novice designer, you may drill too deeply. You can always revise the analysis as you develop the content or even after finishing the pilot. If you don't analyze deeply enough, you will not provide the trainees with what they need or will have to go back and reanalyze later, when you realize your mistake.

Delivery Analysis

After the job analysis is complete, you need to analyze the best method for delivering the I-TBT program. The delivery method will have a large bearing on how you develop the program, and so you need to give this process some up-front consideration. There are two basic delivery processes in I-TBT: the learning center and distributed delivery. Basically, if you have or will have a learning center, you'll design the programs to be used there. If you aren't using a center, your packages most likely will be used at the work site, and so you will need to design and develop with that in mind. This is termed a *distributed implementation.*

There is a third delivery system: multiple learning centers at various locations. However, this type of delivery is a combination of the other two with the accent on the learning center aspect.

Technology Analysis

Next you need to do a technology analysis. The term *technology* can mean anything from print-based programs to the newest Net-based streaming audio and video processes. The choice depends on the resources that are available in your organization or the funds you have to buy the equipment and talent necessary to create and deliver technology-based programs. For example, you may be an excellent designer of multimedia-based training, but if you need to send your programs to 300 work sites, only half of which have computers, you probably should consider a different technology unless there is a lot of capital funding available. This may seem elementary, but many good I-TBT packages have failed because when they got to the site of the training, the technology was not available or was the wrong technology, negating one of the prime advantages of I-TBT: availability when the trainee needs it.

The technology analysis also should cover what your content and audience require. A major problem with TBT in general is that individuals become enamored of the technology and try to force content that does not belong into it. A rule of thumb is to use the least complex technology that will do the job. This may mean a videotape instead of Net-based training or a simple computer-based program instead of multimedia DVD, but always remember that your purpose is to present the content, not do "neat things." In the end, your trainees will thank you, and so will the company's bottom line.

As far as the audience is concerned, you will need to do an analysis of it as well. You need to find out what their technological competencies are and aren't, what they will be comfortable with, and how familiar they are with the technologies you are considering. Aspects such as reading level, language requirement, work environment, and cultural difference need to be understood. For example, your I-TBT program probably will be less successful in an environment where the trainees are so busy that they have no time to view it or when they are not comfortable using a mouse when this will be the main input device for the program. All good instructional designers do audience analysis, but in I-TBT it is even more critical, and there are entire new groupings of trainee characteristics you will need to find out about.

Facilitator Analysis

The last analysis you need to perform is a facilitator analysis. In this process you look at who will be facilitating the I-TBT packages in the learning center or, if you are using a distributed implementation, at the training sites. The facilitators' skills, abilities, and particularly time and motivation will be limiting factors in how you design the program, and so you need to consider them carefully before beginning. An example of what might go wrong without this type of analysis is the designer who added a performance evaluation that was to be monitored and graded by the facilitator to his Net-based program. Unfortunately, the designated facilitators in this distributed system were managers who were much too busy to spend the time necessary for the evaluation. The managers delegated the task to subordinates who weren't current on the correct methods of doing the tasks. Thus, the evaluations were poorly done, the trainees were undertrained and therefore unable to perform the tasks correctly on the job, and the I-TBT program was labeled a failure, all because the designer didn't consider whether the facilitators had the time to facilitate.

Notice, we did not say "teach" or "instruct." The facilitators in I-TBT systems perform administrative and often evaluative functions, but they do not present content. If you design a program in which you depend on the facilitators to deliver content or answer content-based questions, it is not truly a self-instructional process. That's not to say it's a bad design, only that you need to be careful about how you do the design and market it.

Content Development

Once you have done the various analyses and have a clear idea of what you can and can't do, you are ready to begin developing the I-TBT program.

Objectives

The first step is to write trainee-centered objectives and subobjectives, each one directly related to a task in the job analysis. These objectives take the place of the classroom instructor. They guide the trainees through the program, indicating what information is most important and what they must master.

This is the second cornerstone of I-TBT, and the same word of caution applies. If you are unable or unwilling to write proper trainee-centered objectives, do not attempt this type of training. Nothing has caused more I-TBT programs to fail than the slighting of this step. As an I-TBT developer you must remind yourself constantly that your package has to stand on its own. There will be no instructor to explain things, stress key points, and augment what the developer missed. The trainees go through the program alone, using only the guidance you give them, and the most important aspect of that guidance is the objectives. You must take the time to make sure the objectives cover all the tasks in the analysis, using the right verbs so that the trainees understand exactly what is expected of them. Your objectives should follow a logical sequence and be repeated often enough for the trainees to key in on them. When the objectives are done, review them. Have a subject-matter expert and another designer review them. Make sure they are as clear, concise, and useful as possible, because once they are in the trainee's hands, they will make or break the I-TBT program.

Content

The next task is to develop the actual content of the package. If you've chosen a text-based technology, this will be what the trainees read to help them master the objectives. In video or multimedia it's the script; in computer-based training (CBT), the screens. No matter what technology you have decided on, the important point is to use your objectives to write the material.

This is the third cornerstone of I-TBT. The content must relate directly to the objectives and cover them in enough detail for the trainees to achieve mastery. You may be able to create the content yourself, or you may need a subject-matter expert (SME) to help you or actually perform this function. Either way, if you've developed good objectives and based them on the job analysis, creating the content directly from the objectives should be the easiest part of the process.

As time is money, particularly in an I-TBT environment where training often occurs during small packets of downtime, try to keep away from nice-to-know information when you develop content. The content should be as concise as possible yet still give the trainees what they need to learn the material or skills the objectives demand. A good review process, particularly a proper pilot, will help ensure that you have reached this goal.

Chunking

The next important step in I-TBT development is to take the objectives and content and chunk them. This means dividing the mass of material you have developed into small digestible pieces so that the trainees can absorb them, and separating them with review and practice activities. Chunks have various titles, depending on the particular I-TBT system they are part of. Often the largest are termed *modules*. In print technologies a module is usually an entire book. Other terms for smaller chunks are *chapters, units, parts,* and *sections.* There are no absolute definitions for these terms. It's basically up to the I-TBT designer and the needs of the system. For example, a program is usually the largest discrete chunk, with smaller chunks contained within it.

Since the smallest chunks relate directly to a trainee's learning, they should be developed with the most consideration and planning. The larger chunks often are or become self-evident. A rule of thumb is that the smallest chunk should contain between three and five objectives. Of course, this depends on how much content is covered by an objective, but if you did a good job developing enough subobjectives to guide the trainees adequately, this rule should serve you well.

Chunks usually begin with a restatement of the objectives that will be covered in them and directions on how to go about the learning. These directions are normally boilerplate and simply remind the trainee of the most efficient way to do the learning, based on how the material has been developed. Chunks typically end with some form of separator that provides a summary, review, or activity. Often this includes a self-test in which the trainees answer questions and then check their answers or participate in a simulation that has a discernable outcome. There also may be some type of skills practice if the objectives are more performance-based.

This formalized beginning and ending, with some modification, is essential for all chunks, from the largest to the smallest. Whether it's a module, book, section, videotape, or new series of computer screens, the chunk should always state the objectives that will be covered in the coming material at the start and give the trainees a way to evaluate their learning at the end. The preorganizer and the postevaluation help the trainees become responsible for their own learning, one of the important elements of I-TBT.

Adding the Technology

With the chunking done, you need to add the technology. Depending on the technology you have chosen, you'll probably have media such as screens, video, sound, graphics, and animation to develop and a layout to plan.

Print

If you're using a simple paper-and-pencil format, you need to plan how the book will look. Plenty of white space is a must for easy reading. The right graphics are also important. Special techniques such as blocking, shading, borders, and different size fonts all add to the readability and effectiveness of the package. To accomplish these effects you need a good desktop publishing program combined with a high-quality laser printer and digital scanner. This equipment is not cheap, but it is more than worth the price. It not only makes the material more usable for the trainees, it also gives you an edge when you show the completed package to the executive committee and ask for its support in making self-directed learning a reality in your organization. Many good I-TBT programs have been given extra credibility when the chief executive noted that he was impressed by how the package "looked."

Many people do not consider print packages to be a technology because "they don't plug in." However, remember when we said that a good self-instructional designer uses the least complex technology that will do the job? In some cases that's print. Don't forget its capabilities as you analyze possible technologies for your I-TBT program.

Video

If you're using video as the technology, whether in tape format or digitized on the computer, you may feel that you can ignore these "print hints." However, many of the most successful I-TBT video-based programs come with a companion print segment that contains objectives, instructions, activities, and evaluation measures. That piece needs to look as good as the rest of the program and be just as usable as any stand-alone print process.

Along with the print segment, you'll need to develop the visuals and storyboards for the video format. This book contains other chapters on these processes, and so we won't go into detail here except to say that in I-TBT, as much as if not more than in any other training design, you must guard against cognitive dissonance. *Cognitive dissonance* is the displaying of a visual while the trainee reads, hears, or is otherwise told about something different from what the visual shows. Once again, in I-TBT there is no one to provide clarification if the trainee becomes confused because the visual uses different terminology, is too complex, or is not visible long enough to be digested. Be sure that all the visuals match the words and that the trainee is given enough time to benefit from them. This is also a major consideration in computer-based formats such as CD-ROM and Net-based training.

Computer Formats

Everything we've discussed so far concerning media formats goes double for CBT, CD-ROM, Net-based I-TBT, and all the more exotic technologies that may be just around the corner. While these processes provide their own print component in the form of a computer screen and often supply sound as well, the rules and techniques of good print formatting apply to these screens in the same way they apply to the written page. Don't forget the cardinal rule for any computer-mediated technology: Never develop an electronic page-turner. Blend in the activities, graphics, animations, simulations, and other learning activities that computer technologies do so well. Don't forget that when you add video or digital effects to your program, the rules of basic graphics and video development apply.

Computers can be marvelous instruments for learning and their uses are almost limitless, but high technology does not make up for poor development. Words and graphics must fit together and be of the highest possible quality whether the technology is as simple as a print booklet or as complicated as Net-based I-TBT. Other chapters in this book will help you develop these exotic designs properly.

Packaging

When a print package is nearing completion, one of the last steps is to plan for its binding. Your decision on the type of binding requires a consideration of what it will cost and how it will look and, most importantly, the program's need for revision. If you have to make a lot of copies and they have to be revised often, cheap binding such as staples or hot glue may be best. However, these copies look cheap and are not durable. For programs that will require a lot of single-page revisions, a ring binder, while initially expensive, may be cheaper and more practical in the long run.

Such "revision necessities" usually affect other technologies as well. For example, before you decide that a CD-ROM program is the only logical approach for the training, consider how often you may have to revise it, and how much it's going to cost each time you do. This may change your mind about the most logical approach.

EVALUATING I-TBT

Choosing and developing the evaluation methodology is the final aspect of I-TBT development. There are two types of evaluations to consider: evaluation of the trainee and evaluation of the program or system. Evaluation of the trainee is done through mechanisms such as the self-quizzes and activities that were discussed earlier as chunk separators, written exams, and performance evaluations.

Trainee Evaluation

In I-TBT these trainee evaluations are developed under a strict set of guidelines. Each question or activity outcome must relate directly to an objective, guaranteeing that the answer is covered in the material you developed. Cognitive objectives demand cognitive questions that expressly ask for the behaviors identified by the objectives' cognitive words. Performance objectives require performance evaluations. These techniques must measure the trainees' ability to accomplish the tasks that were delineated by the objective and exemplified in the material.

Criterion Referencing

Criterion referencing of trainee evaluation questions is the final cornerstone in the development of an I-TBT program. I-TBT test questions and evaluations are not formulated to trick the trainee. They are not developed to look for the "certain intangibles" that a "really good" test question can discern. They are written directly from the objectives, and can be answered directly from the material. This goes to the heart of proper I-TBT: no hidden meanings, no trick questions, no fishing for the right answer. The information is all there, right in front of the trainees and keyed so that they can find it and learn it. The concept of criterion referencing is relatively simple yet difficult for developers to achieve unless they remind themselves constantly of the fundamentals of I-TBT and I-TBT evaluation.

Criterion referencing is also the reason I-TBT can be considered a mastery process. If the trainees know what's expected, can find it in an efficient manner, and are evaluated on that and that alone, it is possible for them to master the materials on their own at relatively high levels. Eighty-five percent mastery for a well-designed I-TBT program is common, and 95 percent is not unusual.

Question Reviews

Once you have developed the questions, they must be reviewed to ensure that they are criterion-referenced. For the best results, each question should be reviewed at least twice. The first review should consider how well each question relates to its objective and to the rules of good question writing. This needs to be done by another instructional designer (not the original question developer) who understands these processes and knows what to look for.

The second review should be done by a subject-matter expert (SME) whose task is to make sure that the answers can be found in the material and that both the questions and the answers are accurate. Once again, the original developer, even if he or she is an SME, should not do this review. A fresh viewpoint from someone less involved in the writing will provide better results.

This review can be part of the overall SME review you should always perform on all the programs as part of the development process. The SME has a number of responsibilities in the review process, depending on the needs of the I-TBT system. An example of SME review directions and a checklist for their use are shown in Fig. 22–2.

A final review of the questions to determine whether the trainees can answer them accurately should occur as part of the piloting process you do before an I-TBT package is distributed. Use subjects for the pilot who are as closely matched in knowledge and learning characteristics to the target trainees as possible. If the program requires that the material be done on the job, you will have to get the program to the trainees at the job site for the pilot; otherwise, you can run it in your

F I G U R E 22-2

Subject-Matter Review Checklist

Used for the development of Regional Trainers.

SUBJECT MATTER REVIEW

The Checklist on the reverse side is intended to help subject-matter experts in the content review of written training materials. Your subject matter expertise is critical to the success of Revco's training programs. We hope the checklist and the following suggested process will facilitate your review by helping to focus your attention on specific subject matter issues.

Suggested Review Process

Read the checklist

First, read through the checklist and become familiar with the areas you are to focus your attention on, such as content accuracy and comprehensiveness.

Read the Table of Contents

Once you are comfortable with the topics on the checklist, begin reviewing the materials by reading the Table of Contents. The Table of Contents will give you an overview of the scope of the content.

Read the Objectives

The objectives will identify the audience and the specific behavior changes that are expected of those individuals as a result of training.

Read the materials quickly

Next, quickly read the training materials from beginning to end. This initial reading will give you a good sense of how the training materials cover the subject matter. As you read, make a check mark on the areas that you feel need further review and attention.

Reread the materials for details

Finally, reread the training materials, paying particular attention to those areas you checked the first time through. Use the topics listed on the Subject Review Checklist as a guide to make any appropriate notes about the content on the training materials themselves.

The Training and Development Department thanks you for your time and your expert advice.

SUBJECT MATTER REVIEW CHECKLIST

Value
Is the material relevant to daily operations? ☐
Is the material appropriate for the intended audience? ☐
Is the material necessary for the intended audience? ☐

Accuracy
Is the content accurate? ☐
Is any content misleading? ☐

Comprehensiveness
Is there too much information on any one topic? ☐
Is there too little information on any one topic? ☐
Are there additional topics that need to be covered? ☐
Does the content support Revco's philosophy? ☐

Coherence
Is the information presented in proper order and sequence? ☐
Is the vocabulary appropriate for the audience? ☐

Timely
Is the content up to date (concerning equipment etc.)? ☐
Does the content represent current policies and procedures? ☐

Graphics
Are the graphics (illustrations, charts, tables) accurate? ☐
Do the graphics enhance the content? ☐
Do the graphics detract from the content? ☐

Please review the attached training materials _____.
(title of materials)
The intended audience for these materials is _____.
Return to the Training and Development Department by _____.
(date)

own environment. Observe how the trainees work through the program and note where they have problems. After they have finished, ask them questions based on your observations. Analyze their answers to the test questions to determine what they missed and why. Fix the package as indicated, and then you are ready to distribute it.

Package or System Evaluation

The second aspect of I-TBT evaluation is evaluation of the program, or system if you have a series of programs. This occurs after the program is in use and can be broken down into five parameters.

- *Sufficiency.* Sufficiency indicates whether all the information the trainee needs to complete the objectives is available in the program. The pilot and other reviews should have caught most of the problems, but by asking those who have completed the program and, more important, have used the information on the job, you may find unsuspected areas that need augmentation. This parameter takes on more importance in an I-TBT system, where you want to know if you have all the programs or content that the trainees need.
- *Usability.* Usability determines whether the programs are as easy to use as possible. Once again you will need to ask the users and the facilitators to get this information.
- *Currency.* Currency determines whether the information in the program is up to date. For this you need to talk to SMEs and have them review the package for changes that have occurred since it was distributed.
- *Compliance.* Compliance indicates whether the programs actually are being used in the manner you designed them to be used to accomplish the training. Once again facilitators and users are the people to ask, but to really do a good job in this area the best method is personal observation.
- *Effectiveness.* Effectiveness means that the trainees mastered the objectives. You have already developed evaluation measures to assess this as part of the user evaluation, and so you need only collect the data from those evaluations and analyze them by using a good statistical technique.

The creation of an I-TBT program is a process of following a step-by-step approach. First do a proper job analysis so that you know what the trainees need to master. Next write good trainee-centered behavioral objectives that are based on the analysis so that the trainees know what they need to master. Then develop the content so that it reflects the objectives as closely as possible. Next use proper techniques to develop the technology component of the program, using the technology that your resources allow and that the trainees can use to master the content easily and thoroughly. Write proper criterion-referenced evaluations that are based on the objectives and the material. Have everything reviewed twice by other experts to check that it all relates properly and, then piloted to make sure it does what you planned. Now get the program to the trainees and let them do it.

If you follow these steps, you will develop an effective training design in which the trainees can work at their own pace, without the aid of an instructor, to master predetermined material—in other words, self-instructional technology-based training.

ADVANTAGES AND IMPLEMENTATION OF I-TBT: CASE STUDIES

So far we have not said much about the advantages and benefits of I-TBT. Also, there is the significant instructional systems design (ISD) step of implementation, which we skipped in going from development to evaluation in the previous discussion. To complete this chapter we'll combine a discussion of these two concepts with examples of how I-TBT has been used successfully in various corporate environments.

Individual Flexibility through Learning Center Implementation

Maximum benefit is obtained from I-TBT when a training need corresponds to one of its two major strengths: high individual flexibility and efficient multiple-site instruction. These advantages coincide with the two previously mentioned delivery scenarios for I-TBT: the learning centers and distributed delivery. An excellent example of a learning center implementation that provided individual flexibility can be found in the management development program of a large southern energy company. An assessment of the management and supervisory positions at this company showed that there was a large degree of variation in the skill levels of incumbents and in types of skills that were needed at the various management levels. Instead of following the usual corporate route of running a series of classes that covered the most obvious needs or the skills most common to all levels, the company developed a learning center. In this center it placed I-TBT programs that encompassed all the skills that were determined to be needs by the competency study. Most of these programs were purchased, which proved to be a time-effective approach as the information was fairly generic, while a few were developed in-house to meet the specialized needs of the company. Supervisors and managers use the center programs to remediate their individual weaknesses and develop new skills for higher-level positions. Figure 22–3 lists some questions to ask when considering the implementation of a learning resource center for I-TBT delivery.

FIGURE 22-3

Questions to Ask When Considering a Learning Center

General (reasons why you might need a learning center)
- Do you have more training needs than trainers to meet them?
- Are there a wide variety of developmental needs in the organization?
- Does the training need to be done on a just-in-time basis?
- Is it important that the training be consistent?
- Does the training require extensive use of multimedia formats?
- Can you provide a significant amount of training with prepackaged material?
- Doe the training require strong facilitation or control measures?

Developmental (considerations crucial to developing a learning center)
- Have you isolated a critical need that the learning center concept can support?
- Have you defined the center's main purpose and main users?
- Do you have accurate cost estimates for start-up and continuation?
- Have you designed an effective presentation to garner organizational support?
- Will your center be a designated facility?
- Will it have a full-time facilitator?
- Is the location you have chosen central to the training population?
- Will the trainees be given the time and opportunity to use the center?
- How self-directed is the trainee population?

Operation (things to consider while setting up and operating the center)
- Do I have the right kind of furniture (particularly comfortable chairs)?
- Is there sufficient storage space?
- Are lighting, HVAC, electricity, and interior decoration adequate?
- Do I have the hardware required for the programs I'll start out with?
- Have I obtained prepackaged materials where possible?
- Are my facilitators trained and ready?
- Have hours of operations been set and contingencies for shifts been developed?
- Have scheduling policies and procedures been set and announced?

- Do I have a program-cataloging system in place?
- Are directions for center use posted and clear to all users?
- Are directions for how to use the machines posted at each one?
- Do the programs include special directions for use where necessary?
- Has a new user orientation been developed?
- Have I done all the initial publicity I can think of?
- Are necessary center evaluation mechanisms developed and in place?

Efficient Multiple-Site Instruction Using a Distributed I-TBT Implementation

Multiple-site instruction was the problem for a major retailer with over 2000 stores in 28 states, each of which had to serve as a site for policy and procedure training for clerks. By using a distributed I-TBT implementation based on a simple print technology in which modules that dealt with every task a clerk had to perform were sent to each store, the company not only was able to train all 20,000 current employees simultaneously but also was able to deal effectively and efficiently with a 70 percent turnover rate. The number of trainers needed to do this with a classroom design would have been cost-prohibitive, and some type of mentoring or "buddy" system was too inconsistent for policy and procedure training. This organization found that a distributed I-TBT implementation was not only the best way but the only way to train in this situation.

Reducing Costs through an I-TBT Distributed Implementation

These two interventions also exemplify some of the other advantages of I-TBT. As was alluded to in the second example, one benefit is that I-TBT can reduce the administrative costs of doing training, particularly travel and possibly salary costs for field trainers. A direct example of this is provided by a large northeastern-based insurance company that was bringing its sales representatives to the main office for product knowledge training an average of three times a year. The cost of this process when travel and hotel costs and lost productive time were added together was approximately $4700 a year per sales rep. The company changed to a CD-ROM–based I-TBT approach in which all the reps received a new CD-ROM three to five times a year that dealt with new products and/or better ways to do their jobs. As a well designed I-TBT should, each disk included a series of simulations for the reps to complete after finishing the training. These simulations were reviewed by the district manager, and if weaknesses were noted, remedial training would be scheduled on an individual basis. The training director's guesstimate was that this program was saving the company close to $500,000 a year. This figure took into account the cost of developing, reproducing, and mailing the CD-ROM. Part of this cost saving was used to bring the reps together once a year for training on material that didn't fit the I-TBT mode, such as interactive sales training techniques, at a fancy resort instead of at the corporate offices. The rest of the savings went right into the corporate bottom line.

Time Effectiveness through an I-TBT Distributed Implementation

A large computer software firm that had to send trainers to their distributors each time it put a new or upgraded product on the market used an I-TBT Extranet-based approach to reduce travel costs. The I-TBT programs they now have available for their distributors in lieu of trainers are very interactive. Not only is the company saving on travel costs, it has reduced the need for a large cadre of trainers. Valuable developers who once spent time on the road training have been reassigned to software development activities. The decrease in road time with its associated wear and tear has made the permanent trainers more productive and a lot happier.

Downtime, Crisis Time, and Learning Center Implementation

Another I-TBT benefit is its relationship to downtime and crisis time. A major medical center has developed a learning center where both technical knowledge and self-improvement programs are available for the nursing staff. The technical programs are developed by a hospital I-TBT designer in concert with nursing SMEs, while much of the self-improvement and continuing education programming is bought off the shelf. When the patient load is light or staffing is high, creating downtime, a few of the nurses can leave their assigned floors and go to the center to take advantage of the programs. Using the center in lieu of classes for technical and continuing education programs also means that when the hospital is full or staffing is down because of illness or vacations, what might be termed "crisis time," the head nurse doesn't have to choose between making her floor short-handed to send people to a scheduled class and ignoring the class in the hope that it will be rescheduled. This is also efficient for the training department, which doesn't have to spend time giving half-full classes in which those in attendance may be called out for emergencies at any time.

To augment this downtime training system, the center prepares mobile carts with a number of programs and their associated hardware that are left on the patient floors for the night shift. As night shifts are often short-staffed, nurses usually can't leave the floor, but since the patients are normally asleep and require less care, there is often time for training using the I-TBT programs that are available at the nursing stations on the mobile carts. The plan for the future is to transfer many of the programs to the nursing station desktop, using the medical center's Intranet.

This I-TBT advantage of putting off the training until next week because this week has more than its share of crises is tremendously useful in environments with erratic work flow such as the health care setting or a just-in-time manufacturing environment.

I-TBT as Just-in-Time Training

Another I-TBT benefit, this one related to its application as a just-in-time training process that takes full advantage of trainee readiness, can be found at a specialty machining company. The work force here is small, but there are a number of different complex machines in use on the shop floor. Thus, there is minimal overlap of expertise among operators. Each machine has its own self-instructional video package that explains the basics of how to use it. When an employee calls in sick or resigns suddenly or if for any other reason someone new has to run a particular machine, the would-be operator completes its I-TBT package. The package includes a number of practice exercises and a final performance test that is evaluated by the shop supervisor. The trainee is motivated to learn because he or she will be using the machine immediately, and this immediate use also reinforces the learning so that the trainee rapidly gains confidence and proficiency. This method allows the company to quickly have someone ready to take the place of the missing or soon to be missing operator.

The company also uses its programs for cross-training and review. During slow periods it trains employees on machines they may not be using immediately and then has the I-TBT available as a quick review and reference tool when a cross-trained employee needs to operate the machine. This reduces the learning time even further when a crisis develops and gives the employees a sense of advancement as they learn new skills. Plans are in effect to take the I-TBT to the next level by developing self-instructional virtual reality programs for each machine. This will allow the company to train and cross-train without affecting the efficiency of the shop floor by tying up machines for training.

Individualizing Trainee Pacing through I-TBT

The final benefit of I-TBT we'll discuss here again concerns individualization: not the individualizing of self-development this time but allowing trainees to proceed at their own pace toward mastery. A hospital's training department was given the charge of training the institution's 750 nurses and aides, many of whom had never used a computer before, on newly computerized admission and discharge techniques. The I-TBT program employed the actual machines the staff members were going to use to teach them the tasks they needed to master. Ten of the machines were placed in a room with a trained facilitator, and informal classes were run every 2 hours for a few weeks. The classes were considered informal because the facilitator only introduced the topic and taught the trainees how to reach the main menu on the machine. From there on the accompanying workbook guided each trainee individually through the learning. Those with some computer experience and those who took to the process easily finished quickly and were back at their duty stations long before a typical instructor-mediated class would have ended. Trainees who had problems with the material or the concept of computerization were identified and aided by the facilitator. Since in most classes there were only one or two trainees who had major difficulties, the facilitator could work one-on-one with those individuals while the other trainees completed the training and went back to work.

Using this method, 98 percent of the trainees mastered the material and were able to do the tasks competently on the job. Further analysis found that the other 2 percent had reading disabilities that precluded their use of the computer completely. It's unlikely that this fact would have been discovered if the training had been done using a classroom approach.

Figure 22–4 lists many of the advantages of I-TBT.

FIGURE 22-4

Advantages of I-TBT

Trainee	
Available when trainee is ready	Trainee works at own pace
Individual choice of material	No surprises
Immediate feedback	Provides review and reference

Trainer/Developer	
No constantly repeated classes	Less time on road
More time to develop	

Corporation	
Multiple-site training	Reduced trainer travel cost
Requires fewer trainers	Reduced meeting room cost
Eliminates trainee travel costs	Just-in-time training
Downtime training	Captures SME knowledge
No training classes when busy	Easier shift training
Cross-training possible	Training consistency (quality)
Development programming	Less aggregate time spent

POSSIBLE DISADVANTAGES OF I-TBT

Distribution and Reproduction Costs

These examples of how I-TBT can be used to its best advantage are obviously not the whole story. I-TBT has disadvantages as well. One was mentioned in the example of the insurance company. For large distributed systems there are significant reproduction and distribution costs, particularly if complex technologies such as CD-ROM are used. Net-based technologies can reduce or eliminate these costs but have their own disadvantages, particularly in regard to speed and the ability to use video and high-level graphics. Unlike the company in the example, you are seldom lucky enough to be able to prove that these costs are outweighed by the costs associated with the previous training methods. Often there are no previous training methods to compare them with.

Time and Cost Disadvantages in Development

A second disadvantage is that the actual development costs of I-TBT are very high because development time is much greater. As we discussed earlier, if you are going to create a program that stands on its own, the analysis, development, and review processes must be much more extensive than they would be if you were putting together a classroom lesson plan in which the instructor could sew up the loose ends. You can add to this the cost of the technology development team to do tasks such as programming, video production, graphics, sound, and animation.

Increased development time and increased cost create another disadvantage: If your situation demands quick solutions, you may not have the time to do it right with strong analysis, good objectives, proper media, and the like. For I-TBT more than for any other training intervention, your motto must be, "If you can't do it right, don't do it at all."

Revision Problems in a Distributed System

Another disadvantage that was already mentioned is difficulty in revision, particularly in a distributed system where you have a large number of programs in the field or if you use higher-technology processes that are not easily revised.

The Problem of I-TBT as an Unknown Design

A final series of disadvantages relate to the fact that I-TBT is not a well-recognized form of instruction compared with, for example, the classroom approach. This is changing only slowly, and many people, particularly managers, do not see self-instruction as real training. This lack of recognition means that you will need to define, and in all probability sell, I-TBT to your company, starting at the top and working your way down. This preparation of the company must continue all the way to the first-line supervisors. These individuals will make the final decision on the program's effectiveness simply by giving their employees time to use your I-TBT packages or go to your learning center or not.

Other I-TBT Considerations

Selling the Concept

Selling is a simple process if you have a high-quality training program, which you will if you follow the steps of good I-TBT development. Some of the audience, particularly the first-line supervisors, will be sold by your thoroughness and the efficiency of your program, and others by how good it looks, but both reasons are acceptable. The point isn't how you impress them but that they are impressed so that at all levels you get the support you need to control the process of implementing I-TBT in the company.

Control

Control is critical to I-TBT implementation. A previously discussed advantage of I-TBT is that if this week is too busy, the training will be available next week. This is also a disadvantage, as in some companies next week never seems to come. Control measures such as completion records, management monitoring, and honest evaluation are necessary to ensure success, and they work only if there is plenty of commitment to the process from the top down. Many marvelous I-TBT packages were never used because the trainees' supervisors didn't believe in them and the process didn't have enough control measures built in to recognize and remedy that situation. This type of disaster can be averted by preparing everyone at every level for I-TBT; this gathers the support that leads to control.

Preparing the Trainees

Preparing everyone also means preparing the trainees. You need to prepare the trainees to be responsible for learning on their own, with no instructor to fall back on. Most important, you have to prepare them to believe that the objectives you have given them are truly all they need to know and that there aren't any hidden meanings, war stories full of useless information, or trick test questions in the I-TBT programs. This requires a lot of discussion and then completion of a program or two in which they find that what you promised is true. However, if you do the trainee preparation well and prepare the rest of the company so that the trainees are given the chance to use the programs, I-TBT programs will soon be the only way the trainees want to be trained. That can be another problem but an interesting one to have.

Figure 22—5 summarizes the possible disadvantages of an I-TBT design.

FIGURE 22-5

Disadvantages of I-TBT

Trainee
Not used to being a self-directed learner
Lack of an instructor
Not comfortable relying on objectives
Needs synergism of group

Trainer and/or Developer
Difficult to develop properly   Choice of media limited
Must revise more often   Selling concept harder
More trainee preparation needed   Control needs greater
Development time greater

Corporation
Production costs higher   Distribution costs
Reproduction costs   Revision costs

I-TBT disadvantages exist and have to be considered, but don't lose sight of the advantages we have discussed. There are other advantages of I-TBT that weren't explored here as well, such as its usefulness in structuring on-the-job training; ability to take advantage of SME expertise, even expertise that has left the company physically but is still available in an I-TBT program; and the ability to make large-scale training highly consistent, which is a prerequisite to any high-quality process.

However, in the final analysis you need to remember the first line of the definition. I-TBT is a design, and as a design, it can't be forced to work in situations that don't take advantage of its strengths or where its weaknesses prohibit its use. Add it to your training tool kit, do a strong analysis, decide if its advantages match your needs. If it's a good fit, do it right.

GLOSSARY

Chunking
The process of dividing a portion of training material into pieces that are smaller and easier to deal with.

Cognitive Dissonance
The incompatibility of a written or spoken message with the visuals that were developed to enhance the message.

Computer-Based Training (CBT)

A technology format in which a computer is the principal delivery method for disseminating the training content.

Criterion-Referenced Evaluation

An evaluation methodology in which each question or performance is written from and can be related to an objective in the learning process.

Distributed Implementation

An I-TBT delivery process in which there is no designated learning center. The packages are sent to the trainees' job locations and usually are facilitated by a supervisor or another line individual.

Individualized Instruction

A learning design in which each trainee works on materials without regard to what other trainees in the same class or facility are doing. Sometimes the learning is prescriptive, and often it is self-paced.

Instructional Systems Design (ISD)

A formalized process for producing training materials that requires the steps of analysis, design, development, implementation, and evaluation.

Learning Center

A designated facility, usually staffed by one or more facilitators, where trainees go to view I-TBT programs.

Mastery Learning

A design characteristic in which the trainee is expected to achieve a preset level of mastery of the material to be learned. This level usually is measured through a criterion-referenced evaluation.

Prescriptive Learning

A learning design in which each learner is measured against a set group of skills or competencies and then assigned work based on that measurement. The learning may be individualized and/or self-paced.

Self-Instructional Technology-Based Training (I-TBT)

A training design in which trainees work at their own pace without the aid of an instructor to master a set of predetermined material.

Self-Paced

A design characteristic in which the learner works at his or her own pace to complete the learning assignment.

Student-Centered Learning

A design characteristic in which objectives are written from the learner's point of view and activities are developed to relate more to the learner than to the instructor.

Subject-Matter Expert (SME)

An individual with specialized technical knowledge of a part0icular subject who is used to help analyze, write, or evaluate the training material for that topic.

White Space

The amount of blank space between areas of print in a piece of printed material.

CHAPTER 23

Learning Contracts:
A Learning Technique
and a Developmental Process

Lucy M. Guglielmino
Paul J. Guglielmino
Richard E. Durr

Objectives

After reading this chapter, you will be able to:

- Cite six reasons for using learning contracts.
- Describe the basic elements of learning contracts.
- Explain how to assess readiness, orient learners, and provide support systems.
- Explain how to institutionalize the learning contract process.
- Discuss how large and small organizations are benefiting from the use of learning contracts.

WHAT IS A LEARNING CONTRACT?

A learning contract provides a systematic way for an individual to take responsibility for his or her learning process and contribute to the growth of the organization. In essence, it is a plan for learning that is committed to writing. It is a tool to help individuals

- Determine what they need to learn
- Develop a plan for learning it
- Develop a time line for that learning
- Devise a means of evaluating how much learning has taken place
- Assess new learning needs

The word *contract* suggests a document that is formal, legal, complicated, and permanent, but that is not the case with a learning contract. A learning contract formalizes the commitment to learn but allows for flexibility. If a better approach becomes evident or new learning needs surface that have priority, the contract can and should be modified.

The term *learning contract* is used in this chapter because it is the most common term. If you are developing forms or supportive materials to introduce or expand the use of individualized learning in your organization, you may want to use a term such as *learning plan.*

WHY ARE LEARNING CONTRACTS BEING USED MORE FREQUENTLY IN TRAINING AND DEVELOPMENT?

Learning contracts are being used more frequently in training and development for six important reasons.

1. *To provide more appropriate learning for individuals with diverse backgrounds, experiences, and learning styles.* An individual's prior experience and background in an area have a major influence on how much time he or she will need to spend on new learning in that area. However, individuals have definite differences in their preferred ways of taking in information and learning new skills. Learners with a strong visual preference need pictures, videos, graphs, flowcharts, diagrams, and words on paper. Audio learners (a much smaller number) thrive on the traditional lecture approach and the use of audiocassettes. Haptic and kinesthetic learners learn best when they can touch or manipulate materials or practice skills. The use of learning contracts allows the learner to design a learning plan that builds on prior knowledge and experiences and makes use of preferred learning styles as much as possible.

2. *To meet the needs of learners in specialized areas.* In highly specialized areas there are often no appropriate commercially produced materials available and there are too few individuals at one site to justify bringing in a training consultant, yet currency and continued learning are essential. The learning contract format is especially appropriate for these individuals, who may benefit most from a combination of learning experiences based on attendance at conferences or symposia, scanning appropriate journals or Internet sites, consulting with experts or other specialists, and individual research and development activities.

3. *To meet needs of learners in rapidly changing fields when no appropriate curriculum or training is available.* The information and technology explosion is affecting almost every worker, but knowledge workers and those in rapidly changing fields where innovation is the norm often have needs for learning that outpace the development of appropriate curricula to address them. An organization that expects to maintain a competitive edge in this environment will find that individualized learning contracts are an especially valuable tool for maintaining worker currency.

4. *To meet the needs of learners at a distance.* Organizations with multiple sites or dispersed workers can use learning contracts as an extremely effective means for maintaining currency once familiarity with the process and some experience in using learning contracts have developed.

5. *To save training dollars.* Learning through individualized learning contracts, when appropriately implemented, can be economical as well as effective. The major savings lie in one of the most costly areas of training and development: participant time. When learning plans are developed on the basis of individual and organizational needs assessment, individuals do not waste time away from other responsibilities by going over information and skills already known in a lockstep, preplanned training session. The obvious savings in direct costs are in the areas of delivery, materials, equipment, and space for learning objectives that are pursued individually rather than in a group setting, although the learning plan may incorporate some group learning settings as well (see below).

6. *To develop self-directed, reflective, continuing learners who can contribute to the success and growth of the organization.* Everyone in the organization needs to learn and grow to contribute to the success of the organization and its ability to continue to function effectively or maintain a competitive edge. Zemke (1998, p. 60) asserts that

> the modus operandi that has worked for training departments in the past . . . isn't going to fly anymore. Too many people need too much training, and too much of it is individually idiosyncratic. . . . If the ideal of the learning organization is ever to become reality, the notion of self-directed learning has to move beyond the buzzword stage and become a major force in employee training.

The learning contract mode literally provides on-the-job training in becoming a self-aware, self-directed, reflective continuing learner. At the same time, it is a framework that allows the self-directed learning process to be documented so that accurate records of employee training and expertise can be kept.

HOW DOES THE LEARNING CONTRACT PROCESS WORK?

In essence, the learning contract process at the individual level is a microview of a systems approach to training design that has four major elements: *needs assessment, development, implementation,* and *evaluation.* In the learning contract process the learner takes the major responsibility for each of these steps, ensuring that the learning is relevant, important, and needed. The following box shows the learning contract process from the perspective of the individual learner.

THE LEARNING CONTRACT PROCESS FOR THE INDIVIDUAL LEARNER

Any of these steps may be done in consultation or collaboration with a colearner, work team, or supervisor.

Prework
- Analysis of self as learner
    - Learning styles
    - Learning preference
- Awareness of available learner support
    - Facilitation of the process
    - Learning resources
- Awareness of organizational procedures

Need and interest assessment
- Organizational assessment
- Job or task assessment
- Learner self-assessment
- Prioritization of learning needs

Learning plan development
- Development of learning objectives
- Selection of resources and activities for learning
- Setting time parameters
- Developing evaluation criteria
- Commitment
    - Learner sign-off
    - Supervisor or team leader sign-off

Implementation
- Schedule time for learning activities
- Obtain needed learning resources
- Arrange for participation in group learning activities (if used)
- Seek assistance, input, and feedback

continued

---

concluded

> Document new learning needs or opportunities discovered
>
> Renegotiate contract if necessary or desirable
>
> Evaluation
>
>> Review process and products
>>
>> Compare outcomes to evaluation criteria
>>
>> Seek feedback
>>
>> Summarize new and continuing learning needs (part of needs assessment for new learning plan)

If a transition is being made to the use of learning contracts as a major organizationwide initiative to contribute to the development of a learning organization, several steps have to be taken to prepare for the implementation of this approach and support its success, as shown in the following box. First we will examine the learning contract process from the individual perspective; then we will look at an example that shows the adoption and implementation of the process on a broad scale in Motorola's Paging Products Group.

OVERVIEW AND PROCESS CHART:

ORGANIZATIONAL ADOPTION OF A LEARNING CONTRACTS APPROACH

> Organizational assessment
>
>> Utility of the approach for the organization
>>
>> Learner readiness assessment
>
> Organizational commitment
>
>> Announcements
>>
>> Statements of support from top management
>>
>> Development of customized contract forms and explanatory materials
>>
>> Documentation and/or development of learner support systems
>
> Orientation of learners at all levels
>
>> Learner readiness assessment
>>
>> Benefits of learning contracts

continued

concluded

> Learners responsibilities
> Available learner support
>> Human
>> Material
> Learning needs assessment
>> Organization or unit
>> Individual
> Contract development
>> Basic elements (overview)
>> Collaboration
>>> Learner–manager
>>> Learner–learner
>> Practice with feedback
> Implementation
>> Evaluation
>> Learner reaction
>> Extent of adoption
>> Cost-benefit analysis

THE LEARNING CONTRACT PROCESS FOR THE INDIVIDUAL LEARNER

Prework

Before jumping into the learning contract process the first time, it is a good idea to do some preparation: assessing yourself as a learner, identifying available learning resources, and becoming familiar with the organization's procedures for contract learning.

Learner Self-Assessment

You can gain valuable information about yourself as a learner by using assessment instruments to explore your preferred learning styles and readiness for self-directed learning. While consideration of preferred learning styles is valuable in all learning, it is even more important in the design and implementation of self-planned learning. If you are tackling an especially difficult topic through a learning contract, you may want to begin by using the materials or methods most closely aligned with your pre-ferred learning style. Several learning style assessments are available on the Internet. Although they vary in complexity, one that provides some indication of preference for taking in information through audio, video, or kinesthetic approaches is proba-bly sufficient.

In addition, most learners preparing to undertake the increased responsibili-ties of self-planned, self-managed learning benefit from examining the process of self-directed learning and their attitudes, skills, and beliefs about that process. This can be accomplished in a workshop format or individually. Many organizations have used the Learning Preference Assessment (a self-scoring form of the Self-Directed Learning Readiness Scale) and an accompanying workbook, Enhancing Your Readiness for Self-Directed Learning (Guglielmino and Guglielmino 1991a, 1991b) for orientation to the use of a learning contract approach.

Available Learner Support: Learning Resources

Before planning your learning, you'll need to know what resources are available. Is there a reading room, a video or audiocassette library, a list of useful Internet sites? Are technology-based learning packages available? Is there a directory of in-house experts? Are all the resources on site, or is there an ordering process or a reservation process? Make sure to find out about all the available learning re-sources. Some organizations have cataloged on-site resources for self-directed learning and developed systems for accessing other resources through short-term rentals.

Available Learner Support: Facilitation

Through a Learning Resource Center   If your organization has a learning resource center, you may find individuals who can suggest good learning resources, help you access them, walk you through learning contract formats and reporting requirements, and suggest ways to overcome stumbling blocks. Be sure you clearly understand sign-up procedures, record-keeping procedures, and the review process. If there is a well-understood facilitation and support network, on-task learning can be maximized.

Through a Team or Supervisor   There may be a built-in learning sup-port system with team responsibility for the development of some of the learning objectives, or you may want to develop your own learning partnerships. Some company procedures call for collaborative development or review of learning con-tracts with your immediate supervisor. Both situations make it easy to tap the ex-perience and knowledge of others to identify good resources and resolve questions about the process.

LEARNING NEEDS AND INTEREST ASSESSMENT

As you prepare to develop a learning contract in an organizational setting, you will need to analyze learning needs and interests on two levels: yours and the organization's. What are the organization's needs and interests, present and future? What are your needs and interests in the organizational context? Once those questions have been answered, what are the priorities?

Organization or Unit

Both formal and informal assessments of organizational needs will be useful as you prepare to design a learning contract. Take a few minutes to review the latest revision of the organization's mission and goals, along with any unit or departmental goal statements or priorities. Alertness at meetings and in conversations with organizational leaders and careful observation of problem areas or potential areas of growth within the organization constitute valuable inputs for the organizational need and interest assessment.

Organizational projections also come into play. If, for example, some new computer equipment or programs will be put in use within 6 months, a means of preparing for this change must be incorporated in the learning contract. As a contributor to the organization, the learner also may anticipate needs or solutions. If you read in a trade journal about an innovation or alternative procedure that is working well for businesses or organizations similar to yours, a learning contract is an ideal vehicle for gathering more information and determining its feasibility for use in your organization.

Individual

Your individual need and interest assessment begins with an analysis of the knowledge, attitudes, skills, and habits (KASH) related to your work. Consider both your strengths and your areas of needed development. Reflection on practice (what you do and how well you do it) is a good way to begin. If performance standards, checklists, or competency lists are available, use them as benchmarks to assess your performance in your current work. Other guidelines can be sought out or suggested; for example, if average sales figures are available for a unit and you find yourself below the average, additional development in sales techniques would be a logical choice for your learning contract.

As you assess your needs for learning, take some time to look beyond the needs and interests that relate to your current work and think about the future. If you know that a new position will be opening up that you would be better qualified for if you had certain computer skills, include them in your learning plan.

When you complete your individual and organizational needs and interests assessments, you may find it helpful to develop a brief statement of prioritized needs and interests. Now that you know what learning is needed, you are ready to develop your leaning contract.

LEARNING CONTRACT DEVELOPMENT: BASIC ELEMENTS

The learning contract has been described as a tool to help individuals determine what they need to learn, develop a plan for learning it, set a timeline for that learning, and devise a means of evaluating how much learning has taken place. The logical parts of a learning contract, then, are learning objectives, learning activities or processes, time lines, and evaluation criteria. Most contracts also include a sign-off. Each of these components is described below.

Learning Objectives: What Do I Want to Know or Be Able to Do?

Learning objectives turn the most highly prioritized needs and interests into stated goals for learning that address the identified needs. Most learning objectives in a human resource development setting are stated as specific, measurable *actions,* using words such as *learn, improve,* and *develop.* Often they include a performance component such as the following.

For a New Employee

1. Learn the organizational structure and goals of the company.

For an Experienced Employee

2. Be able to design a computer tracking system for the new production lines' just-in-time component delivery.

3. Improve my sales by mastering at least three new sales techniques.

Use SMART objectives: *s*pecific, *m*easurable, *a*ttainable, *r*elevant, *t*ime-bound.

Learning Activities: What Will I Do to Achieve the Objectives?

In this section you list specific approaches to accomplishing the learning objectives, usually several approaches for each one. Remember to consider your learning style as you select the methods and resources to be used.

Examples for Objective 3 Above

1. Observe and reflect on the sales techniques of the three top salespersons in my unit. Write down my observations of their actions and customers' reactions.
2. Listen to "Top Sales Techniques" audiotape series during drive time.
3. Attend the company seminar on salesmanship.
4. Select three promising techniques to practice for 2 weeks.
5. Reflect on and record techniques used, customer constraints, and customers' responses to those techniques.
6. Analyze sales to determine impact.

Time Line: When Will I Start Each Learning Activity? When Will I Finish?

Target dates are set for the beginning and completion of each learning activity. For the activities described above, 1 and 2 probably would take place simultaneously, 3 would be based on the availability of the seminar (or a video could be substituted), and 4 might be planned for after 1, 2, and 3 have been completed but probably will begin, at least informally, as soon as the learning activities begin.

Evaluation Criteria: How Will I Decide If My Objectives Were Met?

In this section of the learning plan list the criteria to be used in judging whether your learning objectives have been achieved. When the objectives have a stated performance link, this task is simple. Was the tracking system designed? Did the sales improve?

Demonstrating the achievement of learning objectives that are not directly linked to performance require a bit more thought and usually can be done in more than one way. For example, a new employee who is learning the organizational structure and major goals of the company might use the following evaluative criteria:

1. I will be able to state the major goals of the organization and describe how my job contributes to those goals.
2. I will be able to visualize the position in the organizational chart of each department mentioned in the company newsletter.

Note that the obvious and unproductive "I will be able to reproduce from memory the organizational chart" is not included here as an example because the goal is directed toward initial orientation, not total recall. Learners should be encouraged to develop evaluative criteria that reflect learning for practical application or for innovation in the workplace rather than learning for memorization unless the goal dictates that (exact procedures for operating equipment or following safety regulations, for example).

Sign-Off

Most learning contract forms include a sign-off by the learner. Many also provide for supervisor sign-off.

- *Learner.* Your sign-off indicates your commitment to complete the learning outlined.
- *Learner and supervisor.* In many cases a supervisor also signs, indicating both agreement with the objectives of the contract and willingness to support the proposed learning.
- *Learner and collaborating learner.* If a peer mentoring system is being used in which two or more learners consult each other on the development of their learning contracts (an excellent introductory practice), both learners sign off, indicating agreement and support.

REVIEW OF PROGRESS

Some organizations incorporate learning contract review with performance review and examine both at the same intervals, usually annually or every 6 months. In the case of learning contracts, some intermediate review of progress is desirable. Contracts with shorter time frames or review dates are more likely to be addressed systematically rather than being set aside for later attention. Obviously, the ideal time frame depends on the objective, but a 3-month review interval usually is appropriate.

RECOGNITION OF COMPLETION OR NEW CONTRACT DEVELOPMENT

At the completion of the contract, there are several important questions to consider:

1. *a.* Were all learning objectives met?
   b. Were linked or implied performance objectives, if any, met?
   c. Have appropriate records been completed?

2. *a.* If learning goals were only partially met, what were the barriers?
   b. Are the goals still appropriate?
   c. If so, are there other ways of meeting those goals that might be tried?

The learning contracts approach is based on the concept that learning is a continuous developmental process that benefits both the learner and the organization, helping both maintain currency of knowledge, skills, and position. If adequate efforts were made, an unmet learning goal is not a cause for condemnation but a challenge to find a new way to meet it. This goal is included in the next learning contract, and the activities are amended.

3. *a.* Have the activities conducted during this learning contract uncovered new learning needs or opportunities?

 b. Is it appropriate to continue working on one or more of the prior learning goals to attain a higher level of KASH?

 c. Have new learning needs or interests surfaced since the last contract was developed?

If the answer to any of these questions is yes, the development of the new learning contract has already begun. Often the review of progress on the old contract and the initial draft of the new one are accomplished at the same session.

In the best organizations, continuous learning, reflection on that learning, and identification of new learning needs and interests are a vital part of the work of everyone in the organization. The use of learning contracts is an effective way to implement continuous, relevant, work-focused learning.

LEARNER RESPONSIBILITIES IN USING LEARNING CONTRACTS

The following steps are essential in using a learning contract.

• *Accept responsibility for your own learning.* Make a commitment to continuously be alert to learning needs and opportunities that could improve your performance and the performance of the organization. Rather than waiting for someone to tell you which training sessions to attend or what you need to learn, seek input from others and reflect on your needs, interests, and goals.

• *Assess yourself as a learner.* Do you learn best through listening, reading, discussing, observing, or another means? While you cannot always design your learning to match your preferred learning style, find out what it is. Ask if the organization has a learning styles inventory you can complete or find one on the Internet. How self-directed are you as a learner? Should you stick to prepackaged learning modules such as audiotapes, videotapes, planned workshops, and computer-assisted instruction, or are you ready to plan additional learning experiences for yourself, such as interviews with experts, seeking out information in books or articles or on the Internet, and experimenting? Do you find planning your own learning intimidating? If so, you might request a learning preference assessment and/or a workbook designed to enhance your readiness for self-directed learning.

• *Become an active planner of your learning.* You will need to develop a learning plan that includes your learning goals, the activities and resources you will use to achieve those goals, time lines for beginning and completing the activities, and criteria for evaluating learning.

• *Seek input from others as appropriate.* There normally will be at least one designated learning support person, and there may be several. Some organizations have developed learning laboratories staffed by full-time learning facilitators who can assist you with the wording of learning goals, identify available human and material resources for your learning, and suggest appropriate time lines and evaluative criteria. If you are new to learning contracts and a learning resource person is not available, ask for guidelines and samples and seek input from colleagues and supervisors. Your supervisor may assist you with an initial draft but certainly will expect you to come in with clear ideas about what you need to learn. As you gain more experience in planning your own learning, he or she probably will assume a less active role, suggesting learning alternatives or methods of evaluation, calling your attention to other needs, and approving the proposed plan. Keep an open mind as you discuss your learning plan, seeking to benefit from the experience, knowledge, and perspectives of others.

• *Don't apply the word* contract *too literally.* You have agreed to accomplish certain learning goals, but the learning contract can and should be renegotiated if more urgent learning needs surface. Come to an understanding with your supervisor about when formal renegotiation is necessary. Changing a major learning goal dictates renegotiation in most settings; substituting different means of reaching that goal usually does not.

• *Schedule time for learning.* Once you have made a commitment to your learning goals and time line, get out the calendar and schedule your learning time just as you would schedule a meeting or series of meetings. One employee who failed to do this, thinking he would "get around to it," and ended up looking foolish during the review session, immediately marked out weekly learning time enclosed in circles on his calendar for the next contract period. When asked what the circles stood for, he explained that they were "round tuits" (i.e., he would get "a-round-to-it"), and if you didn't plan for them, they didn't happen.

• *Jot down ideas for additional learning as they occur to you.* When the time comes to review your progress on the current learning contract and negotiate a new one, you will have an excellent list of options to begin with. In successful organizations, the lines between work and learning have blurred; learning and development are an important part of the work of each individual in the organization.

LEARNING CONTRACTS IN ACTION

Motorola: Using Learning Contracts to Develop Self-Directed Learners and Save Training Dollars

Deciding to Use Self-Directed Learning

Motorola, particularly the Paging Products Group of Motorola, Inc., in Boynton Beach, Florida, has consistently been on the leading edge of identifying training needs that meet specific business goals and are aimed at improving the performance of employees. A process of identifying critical business issues and matching training interventions to business issues had been a practice of the training department for many years.

In 1994 the management of the training department decided to find out how it could use the concept of self-directed learning (SDL) to make the learning and development process even more robust. The management team accepted the definition of SDL as being a matter of the learners taking major responsibility for planning, implementing, and evaluating their required learning. Although this was simple in concept, a very entrenched bureaucratic process was in place to support employees in the traditional instructor-led classroom delivery method. In the process used at that time the learner referenced the training course catalogue and decided what courses to take for a given year and when to take them. In many cases little consideration was given to the value of the course or ability in improving the employee's performance.

The training management team assigned to one of the training managers the task of developing a means to integrate SDL into the learning process at Boynton Beach. It was important that this be managed as a project so that appropriate focus and attention could be placed on determining and executing specific tasks that would allow the effective integration of SDL into the learning process.

Several factors inherent in the business environment at Motorola led the management team to believe that there was a high probability for success with this project. One was the corporatewide policy requiring every employee to receive a minimum of 40 hours of training each year. That 12-year-old policy was instrumental in evolving a culture that considered training a key part of any job. Over the years various public statements and monographs issued by the corporate training arm expressed to employees the need for continuous, lifelong learning and its contribution to the success of the corporation. Another important factor was the institutionalized approach employees used to gain access to training. Knowing the requirement to complete 40 hours of training each year (which was measured and reported all the way to the chief executive officer's office), employees made it a practice to consult the training catalogue and fill out a training plan form, which was used by the training department to schedule courses for the year.

Another important factor that brought additional support by business managers for this process related to the definition of SDL. By establishing the expectation that employees would "take major responsibility" for the process, the managers empowered employees to do more themselves than they ever had in the past. Conveying the concept of SDL to the employees gave permission to, or empowered, employees to take responsibility where previously responsibility at best had been shared with management and the training department.

Evaluating Readiness for Self-Directed Learning

Before the company established a methodology to integrate SDL into the learning process, a simple question was asked: What was the level of readiness for SDL of the Boynton Beach employee population? Although the environmental factors listed above indicated that one could decide intuitively that the readiness level was high, training management wanted greater confidence in the success of the deployment of SDL.

The calculation of the level of readiness for SDL was based on the results of administering the Self-Directed Learning Readiness Scale (SDLRS) (Guglielmino and Guglielmino 1991b). The instrument previously had been administered in a Motorola facility in Schaumburg, Illinois. The differences in regard to the locations of the facilities and the populations were significant enough that administration of the SDLRS was considered essential to confirm the assumption that employees were high in readiness, just as they had been in Schaumburg.

The results confirmed an above-average readiness level of the Boynton Beach employees, just as the Schaumburg SDLRS results had shown. Table 23–1 shows the results of the SDLRS administration for both Motorola facilities compared to the norm established by Guglielmino for the adult version of the SDLRS.

Orienting Managers and Employees to SDL

Attention must be paid to educating the management team from the top down regarding the plan to integrate SDL into the learning process. A series of orientation sessions for both managers and employees was presented. The presentation to

TABLE 23–1

SDLRS Score Comparison to Other Studies Using SDLRS with Adults, 1977–1997

Study	Number in Group	Mean Score	Manager Mean Score	Nonmanager Mean Score
Guglielmino norm (1977)		214		
Motorola, Schaumburg (1992)	607	234	238	232
Motorola, Boynton Beach (1996)	332	239	244	238

managers helped them understand the benefits to the employees as well as the potential cost advantage SDL would afford. It was at this presentation that the managers received a description of the empowering potential of SDL for employees. By requiring the employees to take major responsibility for planning, implementing, and evaluating their required learning, managers gave them an opportunity to be more involved in deciding on the training in which they would participate.

The idea of permitting employees to choose training was related to an important question managers raised: "How do we make sure employees choose the right training? During the management orientation the documentation that had been distributed to employees at the employee orientation was reviewed. This documentation consisted of a brief description of the value of SDL, a copy of the Learning Plan form (Figure 23–1) with instructions on what to consider in filling out the form, and a list of resources available from the training department to choose the training needed. This document also contained a section that guided learners in making decisions on training that were appropriate for them. When the learner considered what to enter in the column entitled "Learning Objectives: What Do I Need to Know or Be Able to Do?" the instructions stated that employees should consider learning objectives that would address one of three things: (1) improve performance on the job, (2) prepare them for the next job assignment, (3) fulfill organizational learning objectives (mandatory training to fulfill legal requirements). When employees focus on these areas, the manager is assured that the training selected will be aimed at improving the performance of the employees and consequently improve the performance of the organization.

An important implication of SDL is that learners have a broad selection of resources to choose from in completing their learning plans. The employee orientation documentation listed resources used by self-directed learners, including not only classroom-delivered training but also video workshops, computer-based training, interactive video, self-paced workbooks, conferences, seminars, and experts in the field. The list was not exhaustive but served as a starting point for employees to expand their thinking about training resources. To support this broadening of resource availability, the training department obtained acceptance of a proposal that allowed the construction of a technology-based learning lab that would support the use of vendor-available courseware. Managers were informed of studies that revealed at least a one-third savings by using technology-based delivery of training instead of classroom delivery. Both managers and employees were informed of studies showing that technology-based courseware resulted in shorter cycle time for learning, greater retention, and increased interest. Some additional benefits are the ability of learners to learn at their own rate and engage in the parts of courseware they need. The procedures to use the lab were also part of the orientations.

It was deemed important that employees understand the SDL process. The self-directed learning process indicates the need to (1) identify learning needs, (2) develop learning goals, (3) prepare a learning plan, (4) locate the necessary resources,

FIGURE 23–1

The Learning Plan at the Motorola Paging Products Group

Name	Social Security Number		
Learning Objectives: What Do I Need to Know or Be Able to Do?	Learning Process and Resources: What Resources Will I Use to Learn This?	Target Date	Evaluation Standard: I Will Have Succeeded in Learning What I Need to Learn If

(5) implement the learning plan, and (6) evaluate the results (Guglielmino and Guglielmino 1991a). As a result, the orientation sessions focused on the learning plan as the key catalyst to help employees understand the concept of SDL. Employees had already been engaged in completing a training plan each year, and the evolution to a learning plan that incorporated the concept of SDL was relatively easy. According to the documented SDL process, a learning plan consists of describing what the learner needs to learn, the activities and resources to be used, target dates to complete the plan, and evaluation standards (Guglielmino and Guglielmino 1991a). The Motorola training plan form already required the learners to list the courses they needed to take (activities and resources to be used) and target dates for getting the training. As a result, the form was renamed the Motorola Learning Plan and was modified to include a column to list learning objectives (what the learner needs to learn) and a column for listing evaluation standards (see Figure 23–1).

It became evident during the orientation sessions that Motorola employees were eager to engage in SDL. The orientations were held, and everything was ready for employees to engage in self-directed learning.

Getting Things Off the Ground

After the orientation sessions were held, it was decided that more than those sessions was required. Since the use of additional resources beyond classroom delivery was accepted as a legitimate learning means, different marketing techniques were needed to gain acceptance of other learning delivery methods so that the employees could gain a comfort level with them. Open houses were scheduled for the learning lab with tours of what was available and hands-on opportunities to try some of the courseware. Posters and electronic billboards advertised the need to complete individual learning plans and advertised the various means available with a hot line phone number for questions. The learning specialists from the training department took on additional roles as consultants and guides for SDL as it became necessary for them to serve employees beyond providing classroom training.

Measuring Results

Two months after the SDL orientation sessions were held, over 90 percent of the employees had submitted a learning plan. Over 60 percent had at least one technology-based learning course listed in their plans.

After 3 years of engaging in SDL, the metrics have been reported that signify that the engagement in SDL has been a success. The two key metrics—hours of learning and cost—have shown significant impact, which has been attributed to the integration of SDL into the learning process. There has been a cost saving of 50 percent for each hour an employee spends using technology-based courseware instead of classroom delivery. Figure 23–2 shows the number of hours employees spent in each type of learning. The significance of this chart is that while the percentage of hours of training for technology-based delivery has remained constant or dropped, employees are considering learning experiences such as seminars, conferences, experts in the field, and other identified activities as part of their self-directed learning. This is most evident in the large increase in training hours that were claimed in the "other self-study" category in 1997. Before the introduction of SDL, these other learning activities went largely unnoticed and unrecognized.

It generally has been accepted that the integration of self-directed learning into the learning process at Motorola's Boynton Beach facility has been a great success.

FIGURE 23–2

Number of Learning Hours

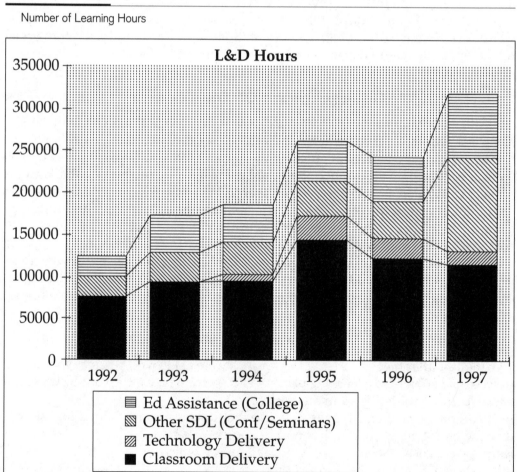

CHAPTER 24

Performance Support Systems and Job Aids

Saundra Wall Williams, Ed.D.

Objectives

After reading this chapter, you will be able to:

- Define the terms *performance support system* (PSS) and *job aid.*
- Differentiate between a job aid and a PSS.
- List and describe the benefits of a job aid.
- List and describe different types of job aids.
- List and describe the benefits of a PSS.
- Indicate when a PSS is appropriate.
- Indicate when a job aid is appropriate and describe the basic procedures for planning, developing, implementing, and maintaining a job aid.
- Utilize checklists to develop a job aid.

Huge amounts of information face us on the job every day. This information constantly changes and requires updates and enhancements. This constant change makes it almost impossible for a learner to comprehend all the information needed for a particular job. Therefore, the compelling task for an instructional designer is to respond to the question: How can learners be provided with the knowledge and skills they need to perform a task at the time they need to perform it? Answering this question can lead to the development of a job aid or a performance support system (PSS).

Job aids and PSSs provide just-in-time support and are only used when needed to complete a particular task. In addition, these tools are specifically designed to provide learners with the knowledge and skills needed to perform a task on the job. Using job aids and PSSs in the workplace can result in consistent performance improvement. User-friendly job aids and PSSs can provide essential information necessary for individuals, groups, and entire organizations to improve their performance. Using these tools in the workplace for performance support and improvement also can result in errorless performance. This level of performance is particularly important when wrong performance can lead to critical or dangerous outcomes.

As the complexity of current and future job tasks continues to grow, the need for support on the job will increase, and thus there is a need for effective job aids and PSSs. This chapter reviews PSSs and job aids as on-the-job tools that support performance. Helping the learner meet the daily challenges of work has become a responsibility of training practitioners. Utilizing job aids and PSSs can be a critical element in the successful design and delivery of training programs.

WHAT IS A PERFORMANCE SUPPORT SYSTEM?

Training programs alone cannot address the amount and complexity of information used in the workplace. There is so much material that must be integrated into job performance that retention of information can become a problem. For example, suppose a group of pharmaceutical sales representatives are responsible for 200 different drug products. Their company may be willing to spend the time and money to send them to training to learn about those 200 products, but how long will they be able to retain the information? In addition, with the continuous advancements in the pharmaceutical industry, how long will the information learned in training be accurate and current? These performance challenges can lead a company to develop a PSS.

Performance support systems can be any means of helping people do their jobs. They are systems that provide information or advising support that help a worker perform a task at the job site. The goal of a PSS is to provide the right corrective action the first time and eliminate rework. The PSS gives the worker immediate access to help that can be applied to challenging problems on the job. A PSS can be constructed before, during, or after the instructional design process as long as it is integrated into job performance (Rothwell and Kazanas 1998).

The term *performance support system* is difficult to define because it can refer to systems that range from simple to complex. For instance, a PSS can be manual, incorporating paper texts and tools such as job aids, or it can be electronic, using computers to guide a worker's performance [If a PSS is electronic, it is called an electronic performance support system (EPSS)]. Table 24–1 lists the most commonly used types of PSSs. A PSS also can be considered a mode of on-the-job training since it acts like a tutor who instructs a worker in the tasks needed to perform a job.

A PSS provides multiple types of information to support performance before or during a task. A PSS can provide the following benefits for an individual and an organization:

- Help workers improve their on-the-job performance in addition to their knowledge about the task

T A B L E   2 4 – 1

Types of Performance Support Systems

Type	Definition
Performance support system	Any information system that directly supports a worker in the performance of a task at the time of task performance
Electronic performance support system (also called integrated performance support or performance support tool)	A computer-based integration of one or more of the following: information databases, support procedures, on-line references, tools for decision making, learning experiences and simulations, productivity software, tools for task decision making
Help system	A desktop software-embedded system that provides just-in-time support to a worker
	Consists of help lines, documentation, error detection and correction methods and procedures, and tutoring
Expert system	An on-line aid that serves as an adviser or coach instead of only providing information or procedures
	Offers help from subject-matter experts, coaching, and explanations relating to recommendations

- Provide help just in time, when and where the worker needs it
- Provide instant access to information, methods, tools, job aids, and decision aids
- Assist with on-the-job training and retention of learning
- Help reduce training costs and time
- Allow for flexibility with worker assignments

COMPONENTS OF A PERFORMANCE SUPPORT SYSTEM

Performance support systems, whether manual or electronic, differ from job to job. However, all PSSs should have the following two components.

1. *References and documentation.* A PSS should contain an organization's complete references and documentation. This includes equipment manuals, detailed procedures, and process guides explaining why a decision should be made and the steps involved in making that decision. The references also may include the names, addresses, and phone numbers of subject-matter experts. The references and documentation should be organized in accordance with specific work requirements.

2. *Job aids.* Job aids are tools that support a worker's performance on the job. Although there are electronic job aids, a large range of manual job aids are used daily on the job.

A great deal of attention is necessary in designing job aids. To ensure that you have the tools needed to develop effective job aids, the remainder of this chapter reviews the definition of a job aid, its benefits, when it is appropriate to use one, the different types of job aids, and checklists that an instructional designer can use in developing job aids.

WHAT IS A JOB AID?

Job aids (also called performance aids) are tools that support or enhance the performance of a specific task. The user of a job aid utilizes it to complete a task that may be infrequent or new. Instead of storing the information in one's head for periodic use, a job aid can be used to guide and support the user during the task. Job aids provide examples, illustrations, or steps that help keep performance on track.

Some types of job aids are:

- Step-by-step lists
- Checklists
- Algorithms
- Flowcharts
- Worksheets
- Decision tables

Successful job aids may use any or all of these formats.

For an instructional designer, the key word in defining a job aid is *job*. For a support tool to qualify as a job aid, it must actually be used on the job. Therefore, when you use a job aid in conjunction with training, make sure it can be transferred from the classroom to the job.

JOB AIDS COMPARED TO PERFORMANCE SUPPORT SYSTEMS

It is important to understand the differences between job aids and PSSs. Many practitioners confuse the two terms. Although the terms are similar in their definitions and in supporting performance, they are distinct in content. PSSs are complex systems that can provide multiple types of structured information, tutoring, or advice, whereas a job aid is a product or tool that provides assistance in performing a task. Table 24–2 lists further differences that distinguish a job aid from a PSS (Reynolds and Araya 1995).

TABLE 24-2

Job Aid Compared to Performance Support System

Manual Job Aid	Performance Support System
Inexpensive (often a piece of paper)	Comparatively expensive (becoming more inexpensive)
No interaction with the user	High level of interaction (especially if electronic or on-line)
Stand-alone; cannot communicate actions or recommendations to others	Can be integrated with a computer network or another type of help system
Static; cannot adjust or modify automatically according to new conditions or recent enhancements	Adaptive; can learn by itself by analyzing recent performance
Cannot induce actions by itself	Can do calculations, offer advice and coaching, run programs, generate graphics and generate reports and house documentation and references
Practical only if it is no more than a page or two long	Very practical independent of length
Very portable if small	Very portable independent of length

BENEFITS OF JOB AIDS

There are several benefits to job aids for performance support. *A Handbook of Job Aids* (Rossett and Gautier-Downes 1991) lists the following benefits of using job aids to guide or support performance:

- Job aids save money and time.
- Job aids help people do their jobs better.
- Job aids help people feel better about new and challenging jobs.
- Job aids ensure more consistent performance across divisions.
- Job aids address the challenges of less skilled employees and rapid turnover.
- Job aids force instructional designers to be clear about the nature of the job and the skills and knowledge associated with it.
- Job aids decrease reliance on memory.
- Job aids support decision making and critical thinking and provide access to varied sources of knowledge and opinions.
- Job aids force their designers to be clear about how an organization wants jobs to be done.
- Job aids increase the relevance of training.

- Job aids support cross-training, the ability of people to transfer positions and responsibility readily.
- Job aids expand the perception and role of human resource development professionals.

Based on these benefits, job aids are an advantage to the organizational bottom line, the individual, the nature of work, and the training process.

WHEN TO USE AND NOT USE JOB AIDS

Although there are many benefits to using job aids for performance support, they are not appropriate for all job situations. Job aids are a good choice when the performance is infrequent or a task has multiple steps; they are not suitable when speed is critical to performance.

Rossett and Gautier-Downes (1991) and Rossett (1996) suggest designing job aids when

- Performance depends on a large body of information.
- Performance is dependent on knowledge, procedures, or approaches that change frequently.
- Employee performance can be improved through self-assessment and correction with new or emphasized standards in mind.
- The performance is infrequent
- The task is a complex, multistep, or multiattribute situation.
- The consequences of error are high.
- There is high turnover and the task is simple.
- Employees are expected to act in an empowered way with new standards in mind.
- There is little time or few resources for training.

According to *Selecting and Developing Media for Instruction* (Reynolds and Anderson 1992), job aids are the best choice for supporting an employee's performance in the following situations:

- Behavior sequences are long and complex.
- Tasks involve readings and tolerances.
- Tasks are aided by the presence of illustrations.
- Tasks use reference information such as tables, graphs, flowcharts, and schematic diagrams.
- Tasks have a branching step structure.
- Tasks are performed rarely or the consequences of error are high.

Recall there are some instances when a job aid is not appropriate (Rossett and Gautier-Downes 1991):

- *Job aids can damage credibility.* If an employee is expected to be knowledgeable about a topic, a job aid is a poor choice to support performance. For example, professionals such as doctors, financial advisers, engineers, and pilots are expected to respond to on-the-job challenges without the support of other sources. In cases like these, the instructional designer needs to determine whether, when people see this employee referring to other sources, they will question the employee's knowledge and skill. If this is the case, methods other than job aids must be used to support performance.

- *Speedy performance is a priority.* Speedy performance is most commonly required in two situations: when the processing of large number or people or products is critical and when life is in danger.

- *Surprising, different, or unpredicted situations are involved.* During a different or unpredictable circumstance, a job aid is not the best choice to support performance. For instance, pilots may experience unpredicted turbulence during a routine flight. Taking the time to consult a job aid could lead to dangerous circumstances.

- *The employee lacks sufficient reading, listening, or reference skills.* A job aid supports performance on the job only when it is used. If for any reason it is not used, a job aid is not appropriate for the job situation.

FORMATS FOR JOB AIDS

Job aids are designed to support or improve performance on the job. In these situations the job aid is a support tool before, during, or after a task. As was stated previously, job aids can be developed in several formats: step-by-step lists, checklists, decision tables and algorithms, flowcharts, and worksheets.

Step-by-Step Lists

The step-by-step list format represents actions in a particular order. If you choose this job aid format, ensure that the task is completed in a particular order. The steps can include numbers, verbs, and objects, as in a procedure manual. Table 24–3 describes a step-by-step job aid.

Checklists

A checklist is used to verify information before, during, or after a task. Checklists are different from step-by-step lists in that checklists do not require a particular order for completion. With checklists it is important that the items be considered or completed, but not necessarily in a particular order. Checklist job aids do not result in a particular answer; they list critical information to consider or complete while performing a task. Figure 24–1 gives a sample checklist from a workshop guide.

TABLE 24-3

Step-By-Step List Job Aid for Registering for a Training Course

Step	Activity
1	Review the course listing and determine which courses best fit the objectives.
2	Write down the course number, the date, and the location of the course.
3	Mail, call, E-mail, or fax the following to the registrar's office:
	•Name
	•Organization
	•Job title
	•Address, city, state, zip
	•Telephone number
	•Fax number
	•E-mail address
	•Course title
	•Course number
	•Course location
	•Payment method
4	Wait 3 days for confirmation. The confirmation will be sent by E-mail. If E-mail is not indicated, the confirmation will be faxed.

Decision Tables and Algorithms

Decision tables list "if-then" situations and allow the user to identify a solution to a problem on the basis of the conditions that present themselves in several ways. Developing a decision table (Table 24–4) requires accuracy and thought.

Algorithms are similar to decision tables; however, with an algorithm the decision-making process is too complex to represent in a table. Although algorithms may look like decision tables, they are different in that they are distinct steps to handle a narrow problem. Most algorithm job aids consist of steps, order, decision, alternatives, and results. An example of an algorithm job aid is the income tax table used by accountants in tax preparation.

FlowCharts

Flowcharts contain an orderly sequence of questions that can be answered yes or no. After making the selection, you move on to the next step or to the proper course of action. This process continues until enough information is received to reach a conclusion. Symbols such as rectangles and diamonds and connected lines are used to show step-by-step progress through a procedure. Figure 24–2 is an example of a flowchart job aid for selecting contractors (Rossett and Gautier-Downes 1991).

FIGURE 24–1

Checklist Job Aid for Workshop Room Set-Up

When previewing your room, be sure to check these items:

- Size of room: Room should not be too large or too small.
- Number of chairs in the room: Add extra chairs in case there is an overflow.
- Chairs arranged for best view, interaction, and closeness to workshop leader.
- Workshop leader's area proper distance from audience.
- Workshop leader's podium, table, and chairs present or absent according to your preference.
- Microphone present if needed.
- Audiovisual equipment set up in the proper place.
- Flip charts in the proper place if needed.
- Lighting sufficient. Be sure to test lighting.
- Temperature controls located and room at a comfortable temperature.
- Water available for participants.
- Stand at the rear and the extreme sides of the room to test the view for those who will be sitting in those areas.
- Registrations, handouts, or any other tables properly set up.
- All handouts ready for distribution.

TABLE 24–4

Decision Table for Choosing a Training Course

Job	Internal Certification Completed	Required Courses
Course designer	Yes	Advanced Instructional Design Designing Web-Based Training
	No	Writing Skills for Trainers Training Needs Analysis
Course instructor	Yes	Project Management for Trainers Advanced Instructional Techniques
	No	Presentation Skills for Trainers Training Basics for Trainers
Training manager	Yes	The Effective Training Manager Return on Investment Strategies
	No	Project Management Marketing Training Programs

F I G U R E 24–2

Flowchart Job Aid for Selecting Contractors

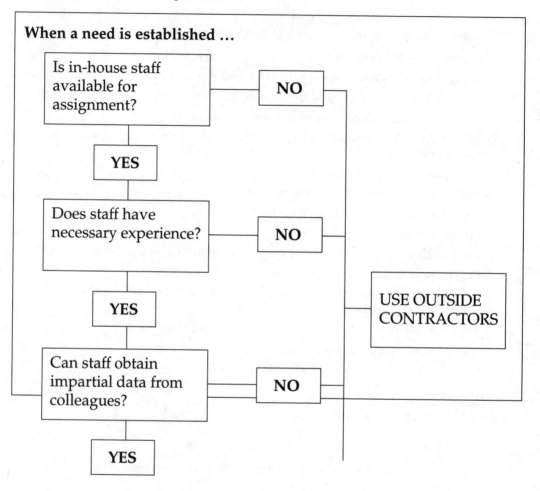

Worksheets

Worksheets are used when employees need a result, often a numerical answer. This format usually is characterized by steps that must be performed in sequence. In addition, worksheets require written responses from the user. Usually these responses are in the form of calculations. Figure 24–3 shows a worksheet job aid used to help determine workshop costs.

Worksheet for Calculating Workshop Costs

ACTIVITY	COSTS
Materials $_____/participant _____ participants	
Facilities $_____/participant _____ participants	
Lunch and breaks $_____/participant _____ participants (include instructor)	
Instructor Fees Mileage: $0.32/miles _____ miles Meals: $35/day _____ days Fees: $100/hour _____ hours	
Audiovisual charges (indicate the type of audiovisual equipment needed. _____ $_____/day _____ days _____ $_____/day _____ days _____ $_____/day _____ days	

CHECKLISTS FOR DEVELOPING JOB AIDS: PERFORMANCE SUPPORT TOOLS FOR THE INSTRUCTIONAL DESIGNER

Job aids can be successful only if they are carefully developed and used by the employee. A job aid that is not used is of no use to the employee, the organization, or the instructional designer. Therefore, before developing a job aid, study these 10 considerations from *A Handbook of Job Aids* (Rossett and Gautier-Downes 1991):

1. Good job aids are built on good needs assessments.
2. Job aids must be introduced into the environment carefully and systematically.
3. Job aids must be maintained and revised.
4. It is important to be aware of all types of job aids.
5. Formats should match the kind of job aid and the work site.
6. Instructional designers should seek out and use job aids that develop naturally within the organization.

7. Job aids should be tested before they are released to the organization.
8. Job aids should be evaluated for their impact on the individual, the unit, and organizational goals.
9. Job aids should be promoted in the organization as a valued performance tool.
10. Technology presents new opportunities for both the development and the delivery of job aids.

With these considerations in mind, how do you develop a successful job aid? The following steps and checklists (Tilaro and Rossett 1993) will help you plan, de-

FIGURE 24–4

Checklist for Planning Job Aids

WORKER

- What do the users need? What do the users want?
- How confident do workers feel about this part of the work?
- How are employees using and not using job aids already?
- How will cultural diversity, language differences, and literacy level be addressed?
- How will differences between experts and novices be managed?
- What factors will influence the attitudes of the user?
- What other concerns of the user might there be?

WORKPLACE

- Where, when, and how will the job aid be used?
- Will special auditory or tactile signals or special protective materials be needed for the job aid?
- What are the potential problems with getting the worker's attention?
- What factors will affect accessibility?
- What are management's attitudes toward using the job aid?
- How does management indicate that it values employees who use job aids?

WORK

- What information is needed to perform the task?
- What are the goals of the job aid?
- What do effective employees know and do?
- What work perspectives will be captured in the job aid?
- Can already existing job aids be adapted and made universally available?

velop, implement, and maintain a successful job aid. The questions in each checklist must be asked relative to the worker, the workplace, and the task to be completed.

Step 1. Clarify the problem to be solved by the job aid (Fig. 24–4).

Step 2. Choose the format and medium, prepare a draft, and pilot test the job aid (Fig. 24-5).

Step 3. Implement the job aid in the work site (Fig. 24-6).

Step 4. Maintain and manage the job aid (Fig. 24-7).

FIGURE 24–5

Checklist for Developing Job Aids

WORKER

- Is the job aid designed from the worker's point of view?
- Have potential problems with workers been examined and specific strategies devised to counteract those problems?

WORKPLACE

- Are there ways to link the job aid with performance and/or bottom-line results?
- Are there ways to link improved performance with organizational incentives and/or rewards?
- Has management been involved for buy-in and support?
- Has the job aid been pilot tested at the work site?
- Have subject-matter experts and management signed off on the draft of the job aid?

WORK

- Have key elements been grouped and chunked logically and naturally?
- Has need-to-know information been included and nice-to-know material been eliminated?
- Is critical information first?
- Is it possible to replace words with pictures?
- Can readability be improved by using color coding, highlighting, white space, bullets, or outlines?
- Is the job aid user-friendly, attractive, and aesthetically pleasing?
- Have all errors been eliminated?
- Can the job aid be simplified?
- Do design and function complement each other?

F I G U R E 24–6

Checklist for Implementing Job Aids

WORKER

- Have sessions been scheduled to train users in the use of the job aid?
- Have workers been shown the advantages and disadvantages of using the job aid?
- Will workers receive feedback on how well they are performing?

WORKPLACE

- Have environmental stumbling blocks been eliminated?
- Has the final version of the job aid been pilot tested for compatibility with the work site?
- Has use of the job aid been linked with performance and/or bottom-line results to gain management buy-in?
- Are incentives and/or reward systems in place for improved performance?
- Have subject-matter experts and management signed off on the final product?

WORK

- Is there an established method for evaluating use of the job aid after installation?

F I G U R E 24–7

Checklist for Maintaining Job Aids

WORKER

- Is there an established system for introducing new employees to available job aids?
- Is there a designated "owner" responsible for future updating?
- Are there incentives for an employee to take on the responsibility of ownership?

WORKPLACE

- Is there an established system for submitting changes for future updates?
- Has a revision schedule for future updates been prepared?

WORK

- Is there a list of job aids that have been created?
- Is there a list of who has received job aids?

SUMMARY

Job aids and performance support systems provide information and describe procedures and can offer advice when and where a user needs it. These on-the-job support systems and tools can enable an instructional designer to expand training beyond the classroom to the job. This chapter reviewed job aids and performance support systems and discussed how they can be used before, during, and after training. With the emergence of new technology in all areas of work, instructional designers are beginning to rely heavily on these tools to improve and support performance. As jobs become more complex, so will the tools needed to support performance on these jobs. Hence, there is a need to integrate effective job aids and performance support systems in training programs.

GLOSSARY

Algorithm Complex form of decision table. Often used as a job aid to show the steps, order, decision, and results of completing a task.

Checklist A list of critical information used as a job aid to verify or complete the performance of a particular task.

Decision Table Job aid that follows an "if-then" sequence for the completion of a task.

Flowchart A diagram consisting of a set of symbols (such as rectangles and diamonds) and connecting lines that shows step-by-step progression through a complicated procedure or path.

Job Aid (Performance Aid) A printed or on-line device, product, or tool designed for use on the job to provide guidance in the performance of a specific task.

Performance Support Systems Systems that provide information or advising support that helps a worker perform a task at the job site.

Subject-Matter Expert A content expert used in the instructional design process to assure accuracy of the factual material used in the development of training and performance support tools.

CHAPTER 25

Ensuring Transfer of Learning to the Job

Mary Broad

Objectives

After reading this chapter, you will be able to:

- Describe the shift in focus in organizations from training to performance.
- Discuss evidence that most organizations have problems in achieving high levels of performance.
- Identify six major organizational factors that affect performance.
- Define transfer of learning and identify its major stakeholders and barriers.
- Discuss recent research on transfer and what those studies indicate.
- Give examples of frequently used transfer strategies in many organizational settings.
- Describe exemplary transfer applications in public and private sector organizations.
- Discuss transfer strategies to support distance learning programs.

OVERVIEW

In a climate of increasing competition and fast-paced change, most organizations recognize that effective performance by the work force is essential to the survival and success of an enterprise. People in the performance improvement business—trainers, performance consultants, organization development specialists, managers, and others—frequently select training initiatives as the primary means to achieve effective performance, either to improve current deficient performance or to meet new performance requirements.

There is a growing consensus among experienced performance improvement professionals that excellence in training design and delivery is not enough. Estimates by these experts on the extent to which learning typically is transferred into performance range from 5 to 20 percent (see the next section), an embarrassingly low payoff for training investments. Several often unrecognized barriers have been identified in the typical workplace environment that prevent full performance by learners in applying new knowledge and skills.

This chapter focuses not only on the bad news of low payoff but also on the good news: the effective use of transfer strategies by key organizational stakeholders to eliminate barriers and support the full transfer of new behaviors by learners to their jobs.

The review of research and organizational best practices in the following pages clearly shows the need for and the successful use of planned and comprehensive support by key stakeholders for full transfer of learning. These stakeholders must work together to identify mutually supportive strategies to eliminate barriers and support transfer by learners.

This chapter also focuses on the necessity for planned evaluation throughout the training intervention. You must be able to measure with some confidence the level of learning achieved by trainees as a result of the training (Kirkpatrick's level 2), the extent of behavior or performance of new skills on the job (level 3), and often the organizational results of a training intervention (level 4). Without this evaluation evidence, you won't be able to demonstrate the impact of the training and the transfer of support strategies to organizational decision makers.

Finally, this chapter gives examples of effective transfer strategies used in various types of organizations for high-priority training requirements. Without such planned and comprehensive transfer support strategies by stakeholders before, during, and after a training intervention, the chances are slight that learners will find the necessary resources, opportunities, and rewards for transferring learning to full performance on the job.

FOCUS ON PERFORMANCE

For many years training professionals have had the luxury of having their functions seen as necessary for the organization without having to demonstrate the value of their contributions. That luxury has vanished in today's highly competitive environment as organizations seek greater efficiency and effectiveness in providing products and services.

In 1994 the Conference Board (a business research and information exchange organization) published the results of 166 responses to a survey of human resource executives in the United States and Europe. When asked how serious their organizations' problems were in regard to obtaining high performance from their work forces, 55 percent reported problems, 43 percent reported serious problems, and only 2 percent reported no problems (Fig. 25–1) (Csoka 1994).

The Conference Board report states a common assumption among many organizations: Increasing the skills and knowledge of the work force results in improved performance. Unfortunately, this assumption ignores the reality that organizations are complex systems with many factors affecting performance and productivity: "Continuing performance will only be achieved if it is supported by a performance improvement system that establishes a need for change and reinforces the change process" (Csoka 1994, p. 11).

Several experienced training professionals provide further evidence of the difficulty of achieving full performance. Their estimates of the limited extent to

FIGURE 25–1

Percentage of Companies (United States and Europe) Identifying Problems in Obtaining High Work Force Performance

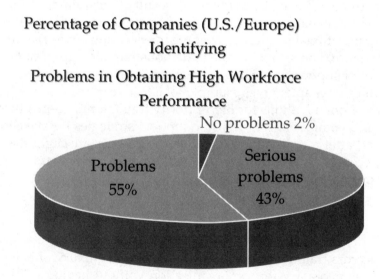

Percentage of Companies (U.S./Europe)
Identifying
Problems in Obtaining High Workforce
Performance

which knowledge and skills learned in training are typically applied in job performance are not good endorsements of the "value added" of training.

- In early research by John Newstrom (Broad and Newstrom 1992), training professionals estimated that only 15 percent of training content was still being transferred to the job by trainees 1 year after training.
- In a review of research on transfer, Baldwin and Ford (1988) found that no more than 10 percent of U.S. annual expenditures on training (up to $100 billion per year) result in the transfer of new skills and knowledge to the job.
- In a literature review, Tannenbaum and Yulk (1992) found that transfer of training was typically low, with as few as 5 percent of trainees claiming to have applied their learning on the job.
- In 1990 research (Broad, 1997b), Feldstein and Boothman surveyed trainees who had received Lotus 1-2-3 training. Only 15 percent of the respondents considered themselves "high-performance users" of what they had learned.
- The training experts Brinkerhoff and Gill (1994) found that the impact of typical training efforts is "shockingly small," with almost 80 percent of training investments wasted.
- In a research report Brinkerhoff and Montesino (1995) point to studies showing that no more than 20 percent of investments in training pay off in terms of transfer to performance on the job.

Taken together, these research reports and estimates by experienced professionals add up to bad news for performance improvement practitioners: We do not have a good track record, even among our own colleagues, for delivering training that results in significant performance improvement for the organizations we serve. The next sections of this chapter explore the ways in which some organizations have improved that track record.

FACTORS AFFECTING PERFORMANCE

A widely used model of the factors affecting performance is presented by Rummler and Brache (1995). The six factors listed below are adapted from their work. These factors in the workplace environment support effective performance by individuals, groups, and organizations and provide the foundation for effective transfer strategies.

- *Clear performance specifications.* Do performers and their managers know exactly what performance is required? What are the expected performance outputs and standards?

- *Necessary support in the workplace.* Are the required resources, clear responsibility, necessary time, and other support provided when needed?
- *Clear consequences for performance.* Are incentives, rewards, and reinforcement for the desired performance obvious and provided consistently? Are there disincentives for undesired performance?
- *Prompt feedback to performers.* Do the performers get necessary and timely information on how their performance compares to expectations?
- *Individual capability of performers.* Do the performers have the necessary mental, physical, and emotional capacities to perform the work? Are the right people in the right jobs?
- *Necessary skills and knowledge.* Do the performers know how to perform as expected? Have they had the necessary training or other learning opportunities to develop the desired behaviors?

Note that the first five factors are the responsibility of managers, who oversee the workplace environment and the resources, information, and work processes that involve performers. Only the last factor relates to training, and it implies responsibility by trainers to design and deliver effective training. Of course, managers also have an important responsibility for that factor: to authorize and provide training when it is necessary.

All these workplace environment factors are necessary to support effective performance. When there is a performance deficit or a requirement for new performance, all six factors should be addressed. Frequently, training will be a major part of the solution to a performance problem. However, providing training alone runs the risk of addressing only part of the problem.

We can design and deliver highly effective training that develops excellent potential performers. However, if the trainees are unable to perform in the workplace because of the lack of one or more of the other factors, the training solution will not correct the problem. As Rummler and Brache (1992) have said, "If you pit a good performer against a bad system, the system will win every time." Therefore, you must constantly consider all six factors when you are called on to improve performance. If we continue to think that training is the only solution to performance problems, we will deliver a solution that often will not be successful because one or more of the other five factors is almost inevitably part of the problem.

You as a trainer or other performance improvement professional can contribute to the sixth factor by providing effective training design and delivery, as authorized by managers. However, you also have the responsibility to educate managers about the importance of all these factors in supporting effective work force performance. All managers need to know about these factors and be able to recognize them or their absence in the workplace in order to support effective performance. Further, all performers need to know and be able to recognize these factors so that they can point out performance-supporting needs and gaps in the workplace to their managers.

The process now termed *performance consulting* (Robinson and Robinson 1995) incorporates educating managers and performers in these factors as part of the consulting process by performance improvement professionals. All the research-based barriers to performance discussed in the following page can be resolved by means of the application of one or more of the six factors listed above. The *transfer* process (identification of key stakeholders and barriers to performance and implementation of comprehensive transfer strategies to eliminate barriers) is an integral part of the performance consulting process.

TRANSFER OF TRAINING: WHAT DOES RESEARCH TELL US?

This section provides information on important research on transfer. These research results are included because many performance improvement practitioners have found them very useful in communicating with stakeholders about transfer issues. The research summaries are brief and are listed according to their key findings. References are provided at the end of the chapter.

Major Barriers to Transfer

In 1985 John Newstrom surveyed training professionals to identify the major barriers to the transfer of training. The barriers he found are shown in the first column of Table 25–1, listed in order of frequency. In 1996 (reported by Wall and White in Broad 1997b), Sharon Wall and Eleanor White of Saturn Corporation used this model to identify barriers for that organization that are very similar to Newstrom's; the Saturn barriers are shown in the second column of the table.

These barriers to transfer of training are, in effect, problem statements. The six factors Rummler and Brache (1995) identified can be considered categories of solutions that will eliminate or diminish the barriers. [Later in this chapter we present samples of many specific transfer strategies used by managers, trainers, and trainees identified by Broad and Newstrom (1992) that eliminate or bypass barriers and support transfer.]

The training professionals surveyed by Newstrom also identified managers as powerful stakeholders (particularly before and after training) who typically do not actively support transfer. Therefore, you should consider managers as prime "targets of opportunity," and persuade them to use their power and influence to increase transfer by implementing a range of transfer strategies.

TABLE 25-1

Barriers to the Transfer of Training

Barriers to Transfer of Training Identified by Training Professionals (in order of frequency)	Barriers to Transfer of Training at Saturn Corporation
1. Lack of reinforcement for new behaviors on the job	1. Lack of reinforcement on the job
2. Problems and/or obstacles in the work environment	2. Interference from the work environment
3. Nonsupportive organizational climate	3. Nonsupportive culture
4. Trainees' perception of new skills as impractical or irrelevant	4. Impractical, irrelevant training
5. Trainees' discomfort with change	5. Poor planning for training
6. Separation from trainer at the work site	6. Poor training design and development
7. Poor training design and/or delivery	7. Poor training delivery
8. Negative peer pressure	8. Lack of continual training improvement

Source: Newstrom (1985) and Wall and White (1997).

Factors Inhibiting Management Development Efforts

Kotter (1988) surveyed top executives in various organizations about barriers to the improvement of managers' performance through training and development efforts. Their responses can be summarized as finding a general lack of collaborative efforts among stakeholders (top executives, managers at several levels, and staff) to support behavioral change. Four specific factors stood out:

- Lack of top management involvement in training design, development, delivery, and follow-up
- Advocacy for change only from top executives without buy-in by middle-level and lower-level managers
- Staff-centered development efforts with little involvement by executives or managers
- Unrealistic and unattainable goals for change through training and development efforts

Learner and Work Environment Characteristics That Support Effective Transfer

Baldwin and Ford (1988) reviewed the research literature on transfer and identified characteristics of trainees and the work environment that supported transfer (Table 25–2). Practitioners have found the trainee characteristics interesting but not easy

TABLE 25-2

Trainee and Work Environment Characteristics That Support the Transfer of Training

Trainee Characteristics	*Work Environment Characteristics*
Ability	Supportive organizational climate
Aptitude	Precourse discussion with supervisor
Personality	Opportunities to apply learning on the job
Need for achievement	Postcourse goal setting and feedback
Strong internal locus of control	
Motivation	
Self-confidence	
High self-expectations	
Desire for success	
Voluntary attendance at training	
Interest in job	
Belief in value of training	

Source: Baldwin and Ford (1988).

to apply to the selection of trainees in typical organizational training situations. The work environment characteristics are much more applicable. They are included among many additional strategies in Broad and Newstrom (1992), and in the examples presented later in this chapter.

Major Stakeholders in Transfer: Roles and Time Frames

Broad and Newstrom (1992) identified three major stakeholders in the transfer process: managers (including executives, supervisors, and team leaders), trainers and other performance improvement practitioners, and trainees. They also identified three primary time frames in which transfer strategies occur: before, during, and after the training activity. Figure 25–2 shows the "transfer matrix" with stakeholders and time frames. This matrix has proved to be a very useful tool for planning, coordinating, and implementing comprehensive transfer strategies to support high-priority training efforts.

As we learn more about learning and performance, we find reasons to modify this basic model. Often there are several additional stakeholders beyond the original three: internal or external customers and suppliers, ad hoc trainers, mentors, quality specialists, and union officials and representatives, among others. Also, as learning becomes an ongoing process, transfer is becoming less event-focused and

FIGURE 25–2

The Transfer Matrix: Major Stakeholders and Time Frames

	BEFORE TRAINING	DURING TRAINING	AFTER TRAINING
MANAGER			
TRAINER			
TRAINEE			
OTHER STAKEHOLDERS			

Manager includes executives, all managers, supervisors, and team leaders. Trainer includes all performance improvement practitioners. Trainee includes all learners in the specific learning activity. To complete the matrix, show transfer strategies for each stakeholder in each time frame. Source: Broad and Newstrom (1992).

more of a continuing process. Thus, the time frame for transfer strategies during training may extend indefinitely in some continuous learning situations, with no separate after-training time frame.

Management Signals of Importance of Transfer

Baldwin and Magjuka (1991) identified four signals from managers that indicate to trainees that their transfer of new learning is important to the organization and heightens trainees' intentions to transfer learning. These signals, which trainees interpret as management encouragement for transfer, include the following:

- Trainees are held accountable for applying their learning to job performance.
- Trainees receive information about the training in advance.
- The training program is mandatory.

- Managers' presence in some aspect of the training demonstrates their support (introducing the program, participating in or leading sessions, etc.).

Managers' Pretraining and Posttraining Conferences with Learners

Brinkerhoff and Montesino (1995) conducted a control group study of the impact of management interventions in supporting transfer in a large Fortune 200 pharmaceutical company. For a randomly assigned group of trainees, their supervisors were asked to conduct pre- and postcourse discussions with the trainees on the importance of the training, expectations for performance after training, the resources and encouragement to be provided, feedback on training, and so forth. The supervisors of trainees in the control group were not asked to do anything. The trainees were not aware that they were part of a research study.

All the trainees in both groups were surveyed later. Those who had had pre- and postcourse discussions with supervisors reported significantly higher levels of transfer, fewer barriers to full performance, more practice opportunities, and greater support than did those who had not had discussions with supervisors.

Successful Transfer Strategies for Computer Applications Training

From 1989 through 1993 Harvey Feldstein and Terry Boothman of Logical Operations conducted research (Broad 1997b) to determine what events, attitudes, and behaviors before and after technology-related training had the most positive impact on a learner's long-term retention, application of learning to the job, and satisfaction.

In a survey of former trainees in a beginning Lotus 1-2-3 course, 212 respondents rated themselves on their success and satisfaction in applying learning to the job. Only 32 (15 percent of the respondents) rated themselves highly successful and satisfied (high-performance learners). Their responses to a range of questions were compared with those of the 32 respondents who rated themselves the lowest (low-performance learners). The researchers found eight factors that clearly distinguished the high- and low-performance learners, four factors related to learner attitudes and behaviors, and four factors related to learners' perceptions of managers' or supervisors' attitudes and behaviors. The eight factors and the responses of high- and low-performance learners are shown in Table 25–3.

Note the relatively high percentages for each factor for high-performance users. Also note the relatively low percentages (two at 0 percent) for the factors for low-performance users. Clearly, low-performance users heard little from supervisors or managers before or after training about the training's importance, how the training would be applied, or anything else supporting transfer.

TABLE 25-3

Factors Correlating to High Performance by Trainees on the Job

	High-Performance Learners	*Low-Performance Learners*
Learner Attitudes and Behaviors		
Explored or used software before training	72 percent had experience with software before training.	5 percent had experience with software before training.
Before training had a clear idea how to apply new skills	100 percent had at least some idea.	53 percent had no idea.
After training had three or more practice opportunities per week	62 percent practiced three or more times per week after training.	10 percent practiced three or more times per week after training.
After training were aware of many ways to apply new skills	93 percent saw many ways to apply new skills.	26 percent saw many ways to apply new skills.
Learner Perceptions of Managers' and Supervisors' Attitudes and Behaviors		
Managers/supervisors had reasonable expectations for performance change after training	75 percent reported reasonable manager/supervisor expectations.	75 percent reported no manager/supervisor expectations.
Managers/supervisors had adequate knowledge of how learners would use software	83 percent reported that manager/supervisor had adequate knowledge.	0 percent reported that manager/supervisor had adequate knowledge.
Learners felt supported by management in using software	80 percent felt well supported.	40 percent felt well supported.
Manager/supervisor noticed and communicated about productivity and process changes after training	62 percent reported that manager/supervisor had noticed and communicated about changes.	0 percent reported that manager/supervisor had noticed or communicated about changes.

Source: Feldstein and Boothman (1997).

CASE STUDY: TRAINING OF CHILD PROTECTION COUNSELORS AT THE FLORIDA DEPARTMENT OF CHILDREN AND FAMILIES

As we often hear in the news, ineffective performance by child protection workers threatens the health, safety, and lives of children. Thus, the transfer of learning into full job performance by new and current child protection workers is an important social priority. The state of Florida has incorporated transfer strategies into an innovative training and development program for child protection counselors in the Family Safety and Preservation Program of the Department of Children and Families.

The Professional Development Centre System has undertaken an effort to sharpen the focus on learning transfer. The system provides basic skills training and certification for new child protection counselors as well as in-service training and certification for existing staff of the Family Safety and Preservation Program. Training is delivered in six sites across the state, with program design and evaluation functions located in the program's main office in the state capital, Tallahassee.

The *Introduction to Child Protection* curriculum is a 12-week program for new counselors: 8 weeks of classroom training interspersed with 4 weeks of structured field training. The field training experience is closely linked to the classroom work. It is administered by full-time job coaches whose mission is to assist trainees in making the transition from training to the workplace. The job coaches work closely with trainers and trainees' supervisors to monitor trainee performance on the job and develop individualized training solutions as needed. Job coaches are experienced child protection counselors who are selected for their ability to coach, mentor, and develop counselors.

After completing the initial 12 weeks of training, including the field component, the trainees must pass a written assessment (level 2). Successful completion of this assessment allows them to move from trainee status to probationary status and brings a 5 percent pay increase. During the following 9-month probationary period employees continue to practice and develop skills while assuming a caseload. Before the end of the probationary period they must complete a field-based performance assessment (level 3) that focuses on their ability to interact with clients and others in a professional manner, document their work, complete products, and meet deadlines. Satisfactory performance on this assessment is rewarded with certification as a child protection professional, an additional 5 percent pay increase, and permanent employment with the department.

Centre leadership has set a high priority on involving stakeholders in using transfer strategies during the entire training design, development, delivery, and evaluation process. Table 25–4 presents a matrix showing transfer strategies by four groups of stakeholders (supervisors; trainers, including classroom trainers, the instructional design team, and the evaluation team; trainees; and job coaches) before, during, and after the 12-week training program.

As in many other organizational settings, supervisors are the stakeholder group that has presented the greatest challenge to the implementation of transfer strategies. Supervisors of child protection counselors are dispersed throughout the state; many do not sufficiently understand the rationale and design of the learning transfer strategies or their own role in implementing those strategies. The Professional Development Centre is meeting this deficit by conducting sessions with supervisors to outline the program, identify transfer roles, and enlist their support. In addition, a parallel certification program for supervisors is being developed and

TABLE 25-4

Introduction to Child Protection Learning Transfer Strategies Matrix

Stakeholder	Before Training	During Training	After Training
Supervisor	Sets expectations for trainee performance after training Sets expectations for trainee attendance and participation in training Reviews training content with trainee Provides time for trainee to complete training preview Promotes certification as performance incentive	Minimizes interruptions for trainee Plans for trainee's return to the field Works with job coach to schedule structured field training activities Reviews feedback from trainers on trainee participation in training Supports trainee's participation in structured field training	Reduces work environment distractions Reinforces performance expectations Reviews trainee's structured field training products and gives feedback Participates in feedback sessions with job coach
Trainer (including classroom trainers, instructional design team, evaluation team)	Designs competency-based curriculum Involves stakeholders from all levels in training design Reviews structured field training activities related to current course Works with job coach to develop prerequisite activities	Reinforces linkages between classroom instruction and on-the-job practice Provides practical examples of learning applications Incorporates the desk reference into instruction Provides job aids Gives individualized formal and/or informal feedback to trainees Assists trainees in creating individual action plans Follows up on field activities in next classroom session after field work	Provides feedback to job coaches and supervisors Conducts evaluation linked to training objectives Provides refresher information before to certification exam Recognizes trainees who become certified

Trainee	Attends training preview by job coach Meets with supervisor to identify performance expectations after training Completes prerequisite activities	Actively participates in classroom training Completes structured field training activities Links up with trainees from same district and/or unit Creates personalized booklet of job aids and helpful materials Creates action plan for applying learning on the job	Reviews content of training and practices skills Attends posttraining sessions with job coaches and other trainees Attends in-service training sessions Carries out action plan to apply learning on the job
Job coach	Conducts training preview Sets context for field activities for trainees Plans for structured field training weeks	Reviews feedback from trainers on trainee participation Works with supervisors to identify mentors for shadowing experiences Assists trainees with structured field training activities Models best practices in field training activities	Reviews trainee products and provides feedback to trainee, supervisor, and trainers Models best practices in follow-up work with trainees Serves as resource for supervisor Conducts posttraining follow-up with trainees who have passed written exam

Source: J. Michael Stephens, project manager.

will include a component that enhances supervisors' skills in working with and supporting trainees. This program, which was scheduled to go on-line in April 1999, will include specific information about learning transfer strategies used in the training for new counselors.

Job coaches are vital to the ongoing success of the program. This was demonstrated in 1997, when funding was available for only two job coaches for the entire state. Trainees who did not have access to a job coach were required to complete an early version of field training as self-study, with limited support from supervisors. Because of the demands of the unit environment and the lack of direct support for completing the activities, many were unable to complete the field training successfully.

A recent program redesign, as well as increased funding from the legislature, means that the program is now fully operational across the state. The enhanced structured field training was implemented in August 1998. The initial response from trainees, job coaches, and supervisors has been positive. Formal level 1 (trainee reactions) and level 2 (trainee learning) data were to be available for this program in November 1998. Information from the field-based performance assessment (level 3, performance on the job) was to be available in July 1999, since the trainees are not required to complete their field assessment until 9 months after training.

The current project is seen as a developmental environment for future training initiatives of the department. Within 2 years the nature of the work done by counselors is expected to change significantly as a new Statewide Automated Child Welfare Information System (SACWIS) comes on-line. This tool will be a vital part of the day-to-day work of counselors and will require in-depth training of new and existing staff. The Professional Development Centre will use the lessons learned in the development of the *Introduction to Child Protection* curriculum to ensure that SACWIS skills are integrated seamlessly into training and on-the-job performance.

TRANSFER STRATEGIES FREQUENTLY USED IN MANY ORGANIZATIONAL SETTINGS

Based on transfer-related research and on many innovative applications in a wide range of organizations and work settings, it is possible to identify some frequently used transfer strategies that can be applied or adapted to almost every training situation. Table 25–5 presents these commonly used transfer strategies, which can be adapted for classroom training or distance learning situations. You should consider these strategies as you begin to address any performance requirement for which training is part of the solution.

T A B L E 2 5 - 5

Frequently Used Transfer Strategies by Key Stakeholders in Many Organizational Settings

Stakeholders	Before Training	During Training	After Training
Managers (executives, managers, supervisors, team leaders)	Involve supervisors and trainees in needs analysis Coach supervisors in coaching skills Discuss training's value and importance with trainees Support trainees in completing prework	Prevent interruptions Introduce or participate in training activities Plan for trainees' return to job after training	Discuss training outcomes with trainees Provide frequent practice opportunities Give training-related work assignments Coach trainees in applying new learning Encourage and reward transfer of new skills Collect level 3 data
Trainers (performance improvement specialists, organization development professionals, instructional designers, etc.)	Involve managers and trainees in program planning and design Show alignment of program with strategic direction of organization Prepare prework to orient trainees to content	Use realistic examples in exercises Give individualized feedback to trainees Provide job aids for practice and later use Collect level 1 and level 2 evaluation data Help trainees plan for reentry to the job	Provide follow-up support and coaching Provide refresher and problem-solving sessions Review level 3 data to identify barriers Publicize transfer successes
Learners (performers at all levels	Provide input to program planning Discuss training's value and importance with supervisor Complete prework and other advance activities	Link with other trainees for practice Participate actively in training Form support groups for later mutual help Plan reentry to the job	Discuss training outcomes with supervisor Practice new skills frequently Maintain contact with support group
Others (coworkers, internal and external suppliers and customers, union officials and members, etc.)	Discuss training's importance with trainee Help plan how to handle trainee's work while in training	Participate in training activities Eliminate interruptions for trainees during training	Discuss training outcomes with trainee Provide support and encouragement for applying new skills Help eliminate barriers to performance on the job

Not all of these strategies are appropriate for all training situations. You must select only those which fit your organization's culture and practice and make sense for your specific training situation.

These methods by no means represent all useful transfer strategies. Every organization is different, and every training situation is different. Many organizations have developed tailored transfer strategies that are unique to their situations. Employ the commonly used strategies in Table 25–5 as triggers for your own unique and creative strategies for your organizational setting.

OTHER EXEMPLARY APPLICATIONS

Many public sector and private sector organizations have incorporated a focus on key stakeholders and transfer strategies into the development of new programs and the redesign of previously existing programs. The first six examples below are among those described in detail in Broad (1997b).

• In the Montgomery County (Maryland) Health Department an innovative career development program used coordinated transfer strategies by stakeholders at several levels to provide learning opportunities and qualifying experience for lower-graded employees, supporting their eligibility for promotion to higher-graded positions. One key transfer strategy involved a development "contract" among the employee, the supervisor, the top manager, and the director of human resources, outlining employee and supervisor responsibilities, projected completion dates, and termination rights by all parties (Broad 1997b).

• A rigorous evaluation study for a large federal government contractor showed significantly increased application of enhanced supervisory skills after a training program featuring transfer strategies by key stakeholders at several organizational levels. Part of the program's success was due to the transfer strategy of using specially trained employees rather than professional trainers as facilitators. The facilitators included managers, general line supervisors, human resource professionals, and employee involvement supervisors and professionals (Broad 1997b).

• A training program on clinical ethics for nurses cosponsored by the University of Kansas School of Nursing and the Midwest Bioethics Center incorporated transfer strategies throughout the planning, implementation, and follow-up components of the program. The project's outcomes brought ethics issues to the attention of large numbers of practicing nurses, nursing students, and members of the public. Important transfer strategies included development of the curriculum through focus groups of experienced nursing leaders, distribution of course information materials to the managers of potential participants, and careful selection of participants who were experienced nursing leaders with an interest in ethics and communications skills (Broad, 1997b).

- Learning International completely revised its Professional Selling Skills (PSS) system to incorporate transfer strategies throughout all components. The role of the sales manager as model and coach was strengthened throughout the system. One transfer strategy in particular has been widely copied in other settings: All sales managers must go through the basic selling skills training and a coaching training program before any of their salespeople can take the basic training (Broad 1997b).

- Organizational restructuring at the Connecticut Department of Labor resulted in new business practices and significant cross-training of many employees. A tailored instructional systems design process with rigorous evaluation procedures relied on well-tracked transfer support strategies by key stakeholders throughout the organization. Key stakeholders, formally involved throughout the organizational change and training processes, included the labor-management committee and the director of operations (Broad 1997b).

- The California State Automobile Association (CSAA), faced with a significant cross-training challenge, relied on an innovative electronic performance support system (EPSS). The EPSS was developed by a team that included the CSAA's reskilling department and two contractor partners. Constant stakeholder involvement (designers, managers, supervisors, coordinators, and end users) throughout the design, development, and installation process contributed to high levels of return on investment (ROI) for the project. An important example of stakeholder involvement was the ongoing review and approval process as the design was implemented. Experts and managers from the entire organization—main office, field offices, telephone centers, the reskilling department, and the legal department—attended frequent review meetings at which performance support issues were decided on the spot, and a mutually acceptable version of the EPSS was produced (Broad, 1997b).

Two other recent applications illustrate the growing attention to stakeholder involvement and use of transfer strategies.

- The Federal Aviation Administration's Aircraft Certification Service (FAA/AIR) has developed a comprehensive stakeholder involvement process (Figure 25–3) to support training for airframe engineers who work with aircraft manufacturers worldwide. The service has responsibility for certifying aircraft manufacturing systems to ensure aircraft airworthiness. Figure 25–3 shows a very simplified performance development process with stakeholder involvement at every step:

- Determination of vision, mission, goals, and business needs
- Specifications of desired performance to meet goals and needs, compared to actual performance, along with analysis of the performance gap
- Identification of causes for actual performance and appropriate training and/or solutions

FIGURE 25-3

Performance Development System at the Federal Aviation Administration's Aircraft Certification Service

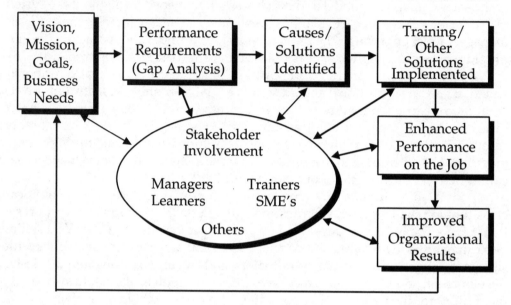

- Implementation of training and/or other solutions
- Assessment of enhanced performance on the job (level 3)
- Measurement of improved organizational results (level 4)

Key stakeholders include technical managers of specific work processes, top-level managers who provide leadership and oversight, the instructional systems design expert who manages the course development process, the FAA Academy course manager who oversees delivery of training, and experienced field professionals who serve as subject-matter experts. Teams and task forces involve these stakeholders in design, development, delivery, evaluation, and maintenance of the performance development system to prepare the engineers for high-visibility responsibilities (Broad 1997a).

- Bristol-Myers Squibb (BMS) is a Fortune 100 company with global sales of over $16 billion annually. In 1997 the organization began the international rollout of a marketing campaign for its number one product to sales forces in over 20 countries. Katy McWilliams, director of worldwide sales force effectiveness for BMS, managed a cross-functional program that involved multiple stakeholders in 40 transfer strategies, including the following:

Before the training of representatives, managers were given intensive preliminary training in demonstrating and coaching trainees to established standards of performance.

Before the training, trainees worked with their managers to complete prework directly related to their territories, which was then used during training.

During the training, trainees coached and role-played with peers in carefully designed realistic situations.

After training, trainees and their managers completed action plans and questionnaires to reinforce the value of new skills and aid in level 4 evaluation (measurement of market share increases).

Level 4 evaluations in pilot regions showed that market share increased 3 percent while market share remained flat in other regions. The project was immediately expanded to a global launch.

IMPORTANCE OF AN EVALUATION SYSTEM

This chapter focuses primarily on the need to ensure that new learning is transferred fully into performance on the job through identification of stakeholders and barriers to performance and through the use of comprehensive and integrated transfer strategies to support that performance. An important parallel process is the development and use of an evaluation system to measure outcomes of performance improvement efforts in terms of trainee reactions (level 1 in Kirkpatrick's model), learning accomplished by trainees during training (level 2), the extent of transfer of learning to the job (level 3), and the results in terms of organizational functioning (level 4).

The logic is compelling: If we don't know for sure how much trainees learned during training (level 2), we won't know if lack of performance on the job is due to ineffective training or to workplace barriers (level 3) and won't be able to demonstrate that improved organizational results are in any way the result of the training (level 4). Trainee reactions (level 1), which are the evaluation data most often captured by organizations, give useful information on course acceptability to learners but cannot help us know if the training is effective.

There is another reason for building evaluation into standard processes. Developing evaluation criteria and indicators of success at all levels provides an opportunity to involve managers and other stakeholders in the training and performance arena. Posing the question, What would success look like to you? to managers and other stakeholders gets them to contribute as partners in the training initiative. What evidence of learning at the end of training (level 2) do they hope to see? What performance on the job (level 3) would mean the training was successful? What organizational results (level 4) would they agree indicated that the training had an impact?

There are expert resources in this volume on designing and maintaining an evaluation system. Be sure to use evaluation data (when success is clear) as a marketing tool to build training's role as a partner in organizational performance improvement. When the data do not show success, use those results to determine what needs fixing in your performance improvement system. Often, poor results of training efforts are due to lack of stakeholder involvement in comprehensive transfer strategies.

TRANSFER SUPPORT FOR TECHNOLOGY-BASED LEARNING

One of the strongest trends in the performance improvement field is the movement toward technology-based training [e.g., computer-based training (CBT), Web-based training, and other forms and formats of distance learning]. This is understandable: The travel and per diem expenses to move trainees to learning events are escalating, while many organizations have already invested in hardware and software that may support nonclassroom learning activities.

As a performance improvement professional, however, you must recognize that support for transfer of learning is just as necessary for these new learning methodologies. The trendy technology does not change the barriers in many workplaces that inhibit or prevent full transfer of new learning into performance. As these new approaches become widely used, it is even more important to identify the key stakeholders, recognize barriers to full performance in the work setting, and implement comprehensive and collaborative transfer strategies to support full performance.

Sam Shmikler, principal of The Periscope Organization of Redwood City, California, is one of the rare "techies" who is an expert in advanced technologies for learning and is also very conscious of the barriers to performance and the need for transfer support (Broad 1997a). He sees several reasons why technology-based learning often does not result in improved workplace performance:

- Specific performance gaps (between desired and actual performance) are not clearly identified.
- Other factors affecting performance (besides lack of skills and knowledge) are not considered.

- Managers do not demonstrate strong and visible support for training.
- Supervisors are not coached in advance to demonstrate and support new performance requirements.
- Trainees are not informed about the purpose of training or rewarded for applying it on the job.

Shmikler has some strong suggestions to make sure that technology-based training is transferred to the job:

- Give managers and supervisors guidance and recognition for providing encouragement and support to trainees throughout the continuous learning process.
- Make sure the learning content is realistic and job-related and that the learning process provides opportunities for application practice and interaction with other trainees.
- Help trainees form user groups for mutual support and make sure their incentives for performance are clear and valued.

CONCLUSION

Your value to your organization will increase as you become proficient in focusing on *performance* as the goal of training interventions. The only way to ensure high levels of performance is to involve the many stakeholders who have an interest in achieving that performance. Each stakeholder can contribute by helping to identify and eliminate barriers in the workplace that prevent full performance by trainees. Because organizations are complex systems, there is no single "magic bullet" that will ensure high performance levels; we must use multiple transfer strategies by several key stakeholders to achieve the needed performance.

Your role is to teach organizational stakeholders to recognize barriers to performance and accept their important roles in supporting transfer. Together, you can become partners in gaining the performance needed for the organization's survival and success in a complex world.

GLOSSARY

Learners   Performers who are involved in some type of learning activity (e.g., independent study, action research, formal or informal training).

Performers   Members of the work force whose effective performance is necessary for an organization's success.

Stakeholders   Organizational members who have an interest in achieving effective performance (executives, managers, supervisors, performers, trainers and other performance improvement specialists, internal and external customers and suppliers, union officials and representatives, etc.).

Trainees   Learners who are involved specifically in formal or informal training activities.

Transfer of Learning   The effective and continuing application by learners of knowledge and skills gained in a learning activity to their jobs.

CHAPTER 26

Leveraging Technology for Human Performance Improvement

Roger E. Main

Objectives

After reading this chapter, you will be able to:

- Define performance as part of a performance system.
- Define human performance technology.
- Recognize the American Society for Training and Development and International Society for Performance Improvement human performance technology (HPT) models.
- Explain the relationship of instructional technology (IT) to HPT.
- Identify leveraging technology for IT and HPT.

The headline read, "Billions Wasted on Job-Skills Training." Front-page news? Not quite, but it was a front-page article in the "Money" section of *USA Today*. Training organizations are the target of this criticism for not improving business results and for costing businesses billions of dollars.

How can this be? Instructional technologists strive to produce high-quality training programs and materials. Job and task analysis, instructional objectives, adult learning principles, the use of accelerated learning techniques, and high-tech delivery platforms such as Web training programs are well designed and cost-effectively delivered. These actions are aimed at providing high-quality and cost-effective training for our clients. What is driving headlines like the one above?

At issue is the lack of the improved business outputs that clients expect. Clients continue to tell us that their workers' performances are not improving after they complete training programs. Over 80 percent of the time there is minimal or no improvement in a company's bottom-line profitability. Many senior executives have concluded that investment in training is a bad investment. As a result, training budgets and staffs are being cut, but we all know that well-designed training is a critical factor in enabling a worker to perform on the job.

Many books and articles call for training organizations to reengineer themselves into performance-consulting organizations. Why? Marc Rosenberg, 1990–1991 president of the National Society for Performance and Instruction [now the International Society for Performance Improvement (ISPI)], states the issue very well: "Remember, training is not what is ultimately important . . . performance is."

Human resource development (HRD) organizations and their staffs will be undergoing the greatest change in their history over the next 3 to 5 years. Several recent studies by the American Society for Training and Development (ASTD) have focused on this issue in great detail. The current business environment is driving the demand for the transformation of HRD organizations and practices. Training departments must change the most if they want to survive.

GOALS

In this chapter the primary goals are to

1. Highlight the current issues facing training organizations now and in the future
2. Introduce human performance technology (HPT) as a core technology for human performance improvement
3. Illustrate how instructional technology relates to HPT
4. Discuss how to leverage technology to support instructional and human performance technology and ultimately human performance improvement activities

PERFORMANCE SYSTEMS

When work systems are analyzed from a system perspective, it becomes clear that much more than workers' knowledge, skills, and abilities is used to produce outputs. Many additional factors are used to perform work: raw materials, equipment, machinery, information, processes, procedures, and company policies, among others.

Work is performed within work systems and subsystems. Work systems include all the elements that directly and indirectly influence a worker's performance. Performance consultants need effective diagnostic models to analyze performance systems. Like sound instructional design work, the quality of the analysis has a direct effect on the outcome and quality of the recommended performance interventions. The diagnostic models a performance consultant applies must ensure that all elements affecting, supporting, helping, or hindering a worker's performance are analyzed.

The current view is that not enough time is spent conducting diagnostic analysis work. Many feel that performance consultants should spend 40 to 50 percent of their time conducting diagnostic analyses. A significant focus of this analytic work should involve assessing the overall organizational and business goals and validating the quality of the alignment of three key elements: work, worker, and workplace.

Making the transition from a *training* to a *performance* focus requires an individual to develop the knowledge, skills, abilities, and attitude needed to *systematically* solve a client's *systemic* human performance problems. Many instructional technologists have taken this journey. If you ask them, they probably will agree that seldom does a singular intervention, such as training, solve a performance problem. Various researchers have reported on this specific topic. *Transfer of Training* by Mary Broad and John Newstrom (1992, p. ix) states: "Most of [the] investment in organizational training and development is wasted because most of the knowledge and skills gained in training (well over 80 percent by some estimates) are not fully applied by those employees on the job." Training alone seldom enables workers to reach their full potential. The usual culprit is the system a worker is trying to work in.

The transition from a training focus to a performance improvement focus requires that practitioner's learn an array of new skills and develop the ability to work in partnership with their clients. The title applied to this new role is written about extensively today: *performance consultant.*

A performance consultant knows it is his or her job to recommend interventions to enable a client's workers to reach their highest level of performance. Over the years, as a practicing performance consultant, I have found that I develop two primary categories of interventions: instructional interventions and noninstructional performance interventions.

Instructional technology (IT) is the technology I employ in delivering instructional interventions. A second technology must be employed to support noninstructional interventions: *human performance technology.* Figure 26–1 illustrates the relationship of two core technologies and two critical activities required to fulfill the role of *performance consulting.*

Figure 26–1 provides a mental model for two core technologies and two critical activities a performance consultant must employ. There are many other technologies and activities a performance consultant uses in her or his day-to-day life. Later in the chapter we will take a closer look at human performance technology, but first let us explore the concept of an integrated performance system.

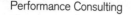

FIGURE 26–1

Performance Consulting

IT TAKES TIME FOR PEAK PERFORMANCE

Performance consultants must use various diagnostic models to identify the components and factors that influence human performance within the overall performance system. Achieving this requires the application of various diagnostic models to relate human performance to the larger performance system. Figure 26–2 shows a performance system diagnostic model developed by F & M Innovative Solutions, Inc. I have used this model for years and refine it when I see a need to. The performance clock model was developed to analyze a performance system by looking at four key interrelated components. The model uses an analogy of TIME and the supporting clock mechanisms that help the clock run smoothly and keep the right time.

THE PERFORMANCE CLOCK'S FOUR COMPONENTS

For the performance clock to run smoothly and on time, all four components must run in harmony, just as a human performance system does. Each of the four components is dependent on the others. Take any one away and the clock slows or stops. The loss of one of the components may not necessarily cause the clock to stop; the clock may just gradually start to lose time.

- *Training.* The goal of training is to provide workers with the knowledge, skills, and abilities to perform their work.
- *Incentives and motivation.* These are the intrinsic and extrinsic factors that affect a person's will to perform. All factors internal and external to the worker should be reviewed.

FIGURE 26–2

The Performance Clock

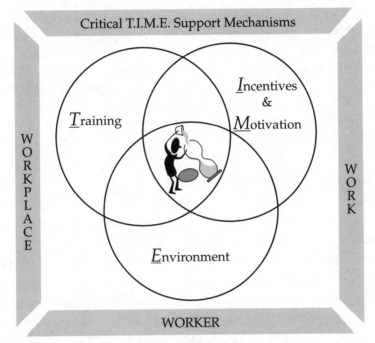

- *Environment.* These are the extrinsic environmental factors that affect a person's work and working environment.
- *TIME support mechanisms: The performance clock's frame.* These represent the cultural environment and the relationship of work, worker, and workplace. All of them must be aligned properly to support the performance system.

All four of these components must constantly work together in harmony to enable a worker to perform at a peak level. A mental reminder I like to use is, It takes TIME for peak performance. Whenever I am working with a client, I keep this question in mind. I know that if just one of these components falls out of harmony with the others, the performance system will become unstable and, in the worst cases, fail completely. Our job as performance consultants is to keep the performance clock ticking.

The center of the performance clock is where all the elements merge to form the point of optimal performance. At the center of the Performance Clock there is everything a performer needs to perform the job at the highest level of proficiency.

Every element is in perfect harmony, and the clock's framework is providing all the support necessary to keep the clock running all the time and on time. Unfortunately, in today's business world this point of optimal performance is seldom achieved. The center of the performance clock is the desired destination.

Having used this model with clients and having taught it in our "Fundamentals of HPT" workshop, I have found the analogy of a performance clock to be an easy-to-understand performance system model. To remember the key components of a performance system, keep asking the following question: Do the performers have the right TIME to achieve peak performance? Reminders are all around us: on our arms, the walls, the desk, and even our computers. Any time we see a clock, it should make us think about TIME.

These questions are a high-level starting point for a system diagnostic:

1. Do the workers have the right *training?*
2. Are sufficient *incentives* to perform present?
3. Do the workers have the *motivation* to perform?
4. Is the work *environment* supporting them?
5. Is there a shared commitment and/or vision that aligns the work, the worker, and the workplace?

Getting the answers to these five questions will help develop a foundational picture of the current performance system and its performance level. In addition to the five questions, I have found that conducting a SWOT (strength, weakness, opportunities, and threats) analysis of the performance system can provide a different view of analysis data. However, these models are only the beginning of an in-depth performance system analysis. I designed the performance clock model as a tool to develop a global picture of a performance system, but now we need to use the data and apply them to a second key technology for human performance: *human performance technology.*

HUMAN PERFORMANCE TECHNOLOGY

Human performance technology evolved primarily from general systems theory and behavioral psychology in the early 1950s. Many practitioners and theorists came out of the training profession. Many others came from related fields:

- Information and feedback systems
- Ergonomics
- Human factors
- Organizational development
- Change and chaos theory

- Human resource management
- Information systems

It is not my intent to delve deeply into the history of HPT. If you are interested in conducting further research on HPT, refer to any of the current publications from ASTD or ISPI or any of the many books currently available. Each month new publications are being released on HPT, human performance improvement, and performance consulting; there is plenty to research. A major criterion for being a successful performance consultant is to be committed to continuous learning. No one can be successful without a well-stocked resource library. An HPT library of books covering the major concepts and theories would include books written by B. F. Skinner, Tom Gilbert, Robert Mager, Joe Harless, Geary Rummler, Odin Westgaard, Judith Hale, Dana and James Robinson, and Danny Langdon. Practicing HPTers know these names and are familiar with their writings and philosophies. Start your HPT library today. Table 26–1 provides a few of the key concepts of some of these authors.

I am not sure of the origin of this phrase, but it applies to all of us: "Leaders are readers, and readers are leaders."

Successful performance consultants make a commitment to continuing self-development and lifelong learning. They understand the need to stay current with the constantly evolving field of performance consulting and commit to conducting ongoing research, learning, and self-assessment. A performance consultant must read more than the average professional does because of the nature of our work. Performance consultants must stay up to date on new and evolving philosophies and technologies that can affect workplace performance.

While HPT's roots have been growing since the early 1950s, HPT is still an evolving field and the roots are still growing. Every year new models and research add to, improve, challenge, and expand on the basic performance models and practitioners' understanding of HPT.

No single HPT model or conceptual approach can meet every practitioner's needs. These days everyone is trying to develop *the* model to follow. However, four criteria can serve as a basis for defining a basic HPT model:

1. HPT functions within a *systematic framework.*
2. HPT mandates a *comprehensive analytic process.*
3. Practitioners must utilize a *nonlinear perspective* to solve performance problems or take advantage of performance improvement opportunities.
4. HPT practitioners must develop a network of professionals to serve on *diverse teams* because no individual can possess all the required skills.

As with HPT models, there are also several published definitions for human performance technology. ASTD, ISPI, and numerous other professional groups have

TABLE 26-1

Key Contributors to the Field of HPT

Contributor	Key Concepts
B. F. Skinner	Behavior is influenced by the responses that are elicited by the behavior.
Tom Gilbert	The work environment, not the absence of knowledge or skill, is the greatest block to peak performance.
Robert Mager	Learning objectives must be written in performance terms. An objective must have three key elements: • The performance: what the worker must do • The conditions under which the performance or work is done • The standard or criterion that is considered acceptable performance
Joe Harless	There must be an analysis of the system in which the performer is working. Harless invented the term *front-end analysis* (FEA). He also is well known for job aid design and the belief that in every training course there is a job aid screaming to get out.
Geary Rummler	Three levels of performance must be aligned to sustain exemplary performance: • Process • Organization • Job/performer
Danny Langdon	His *The New Language of Work* (1995) is a systems analysis approach to the work system that looks at: • The business unit • Departments • Processes • The individual This method provides a fully integrated approach to the daily management and execution of work.

published definitions. This is another issue causing confusion in regard to human performance technology. As a result of the lack of a single definition and HPT model, new practitioners experience varying degrees of difficulty understanding HPT and its basic philosophies. Professional organizations as well as individual practitioners continue to add to and refine HPT models and philosophies on an ongoing basis. Possibly one day in the near future we can all agree on *one* definition and model. Here is my working definition of HPT:

> A systems view of human performance that is used to systematically analyze both performance gap and performance system. It is necessary to select and design cost-effective and efficient interventions that are strategically aligned to support organizational goals and values.

By breaking down this definition, one will find that it contains several significant implications for anyone who wants to be an HPT practitioner.

HPT Practitioners

- Maintain a systems view of human performance. They conduct systems analysis based on sound data, clearly defined competence, and objective evaluation. They must maintain a perspective that views human performance as part of the performance system.
- Systematically analyze both the performance gap and the performance system. They develop a cause-and-effect model for each component of the performance system that illustrates the effects of one component on the others.
- Remember that performance systems are fluid and constantly in a state of change.
- Design cost-effective and efficient performance interventions. They understand that the most cost-effective way may not always be the most efficient.
- Ensure that recommended interventions will support the client's business goals and organizational values. Practitioners must develop an understanding of the client's written and unwritten goals and values. Practitioners should ensure that clients' goals are clear, understood, and measured.
- Analyze performance feedback systems. They verify their existence or nonexistence. This is one of the first things a performance consultant should examine. Lack of a working feedback system is one of the most common causes of performance problems.

Much of this is logical and practical. You may have concluded that applying HPT would not be a hard transition for you or your training organization. Today almost everyone is encouraging training organizations to make the transition to performance consulting, but this journey is long and filled with hazards. The journey from training to performance consulting takes 2 to 5 years for most organizations. Numerous obstacles have to be overcome to be successful. One of the hardest is culture.

THE CULTURE CHALLENGE

Let us start with a diagnostic question. Today, when you are approached with a performance problem, in which component of the performance clock (Figure 26–2) do you find yourself spending the largest amount of time? Before you answer, think about what I have asked. I am not asking which component you *should* be spending the majority of your time in; rather, I am asking which component you *do* spend the majority of your time in.

Many people answer, "The training component." Actually, there are historical reasons driving this answer. Many current business cultures drive management's expectations to focus our efforts on training. Three waves of change have played a significant role in shaping current organizational structures and cultures as well as management's current views:

- *The first wave* came when we moved from a hunter-gatherer culture to an agricultural culture.
- *The second wave* came when we moved from an agricultural culture to an industrial age culture.
- *The third wave* came when we moved from the industrial age to the information age.

Training organization roles in the industrial age have been solidly defined over the years. Training is the obvious place trainers are expected to be working. However, time and the third wave have changed current work environments and organizational needs. Companies that want to remain competitive must demand that we change our focus to one of work, worker, and workplace performance.

Training professionals must understand that many senior leaders and managers quickly become uncomfortable when training professionals attempt to expand their roles to encompass all the components of the performance clock. Unfortunately, most HRD managers do not understand human performance systems. As a result, they challenge or stop training professionals from expanding into other traditional HRD-related fields.

Figure 26–3 shows a traditional HRD organization with its structured and reporting relationships of traditional functions. All are neatly organized and normally *siloed,* or expected to work in their respective areas of expertise. This structure seldom supports cross-functional relationships. If the functions attempt to

FIGURE 26-3

A Traditional HRD Organizational Structure

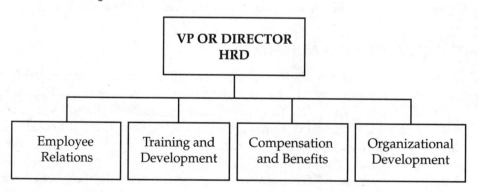

cross over into the others, turf wars erupt. This current paradigm of an HRD structure must be changed to meet the business needs of the future.

Business survival demands new roles for training organization and staff. Today's training organizations must be transformed into performance consulting organizations. This does not happen through a simple name change; it requires cultural and structural change. Organizations that realize this and change will survive; those that don't, won't. Much work has to be done. Hard work and dedicated commitment will overcome the current lack of understanding among managers and organizations. Training organizations must start the transition today. The business world is fast-paced and unforgiving. The transition period for this level of change from a training to a performance focus is normally 2 to 5 years. Unfortunately, today's business leaders have developed an extremely low tolerance for rocking the boat. Find a champion or sponsor and build a case for change.

Performance consultants know that it is an absolute business necessity to apply a system view to today's working environment. They also understand no single HRD function such as organizational development (OD), training and development, or compensation and benefits can deliver the required business results. Performance interventions require the collective expertise of several HRD disciplines. Many times the cross-functional teams are led by an experienced performance consultant. Cross-functional performance teams will become a key way to address the business challenges of the future.

The road from training to performance consulting is uphill, bumpy, and at times dangerous; the journey is one of survival. This is truly an issue of business survival. If businesses don't survive, neither will we. Therefore, challenge the status quo. Push the envelope every chance you get. Move toward understanding performance systems. Take little steps; start with small projects that can ensure success. Once business leaders understand the importance of partnering with performance consultants, they will be calling. You need to be ready, and a place to start is by understanding the basic HPT models.

HUMAN PERFORMANCE TECHNOLOGY: THE MODELS

There are two HPT models we will look at: the ASTD model and the ISPI model. Figure 26–4 shows the ASTD model.

It is not my intent to recommend one model over the other. You should decide which model would be more useful to you. I encourage you to research each model beyond what is covered here. ISPI publishes a handbook for human performance technology, and ASTD has several publications that support its model. You will not have to look far to find additional information about each model.

FIGURE 26–4

HPT ASTD View

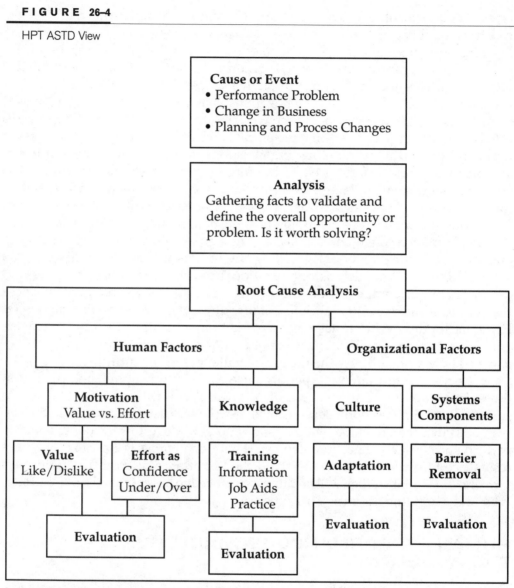

Source: ASAD-WSC Training Institute 1996. Reprinted with permission.

After reading this chapter, you will *not* be an expert on either of the models. The goal here is for you to develop a basic understanding of the two models and get interested enough to look further.

Before looking at HPT models, let's review a standard instructional systems design (ISD) model. Many know this as the ADDIE (*a*nalysis, *d*esign, *d*evelopment, *i*mplementation, *e*valuation) model. The traditional ADDIE model is designed to analyze and produce training interventions. It is a sound model and has been used for years.

The two models are distinctively different. Each is designed to produce specific outputs. The ISD model is a *training* model, and the HPT model is a *performance system* model.

Each HPT model starts by looking at a performance gap or opportunity. The ISPI model starts with performance analysis and moves into cause analysis. The ASTD model identifies the cause and determines whether the problem is worth solving. The ASTD model then moves into conducting a root cause analysis that is similar to the ISPI's cause analysis. Each model in this phase is looking for the root causes of the performance issues. Each model looks beyond the human factors. The result is a sound analysis of the performance system. Both models then move into intervention selection, design, and implementation. Each ends with ongoing evaluation phases. Either model can work. Which one fits your needs is for you to decide. The key is to use *a* model. Models such as the HPT models are road maps for solving a client's performance problems. Like highway maps, use them or you can end up getting lost. There are many roads, but only a few actually get you to your destination.

The International Society for Performance Improvement (ISPI)

Founded in 1962, the International Society for Performance Improvement is the leading international association dedicated to improving productivity and performance in the workplace. ISPI represents more than 10,000 international and chapter members throughout the United States, Canada, and 40 other countries. ISPI's mission is to improve the performance of organizations in systematic and reproducible ways through the application of HPT. Assembling an annual conference and exposition and other educational events, publishing several periodicals, and producing a full line of publications and resources are some of the ways ISPI works toward achieving this mission. For more information, write ISPI, 1300 L Street, N.W., Suite 1250, Washington, D.C. 20005, www.ispi.org; info@ispiorg.

COMPARING INSTRUCTIONAL TECHNOLOGY TO HUMAN PERFORMANCE TECHNOLOGY

Instructional technology can address knowledge, skills, and ability problems. When knowledge and skills are involved, it is an appropriate intervention to employ. No one disputes that there will always be a need for workers to acquire new knowledge and skills. In fact, with the current rate of change and advancement in technology, the need for training programs and instructional designers will continue to grow. High-technology delivery platforms such as web-based training

TABLE 26-2

Performance Clock Intervention Grouping

Performance Clock Component	Intervention Group
Training	Interventions that support the acquisition of knowledge, skills, and abilities
Incentives and motivation	Interventions designed to motivate desired human performance
Environment	Interventions designed to adjust or modify the work environment
Clock frame	Interventions designed to align the key components of work, worker, and workplace

(WBT) and multimedia-based training (MBT) require instructional designers more than the more traditional methods of training delivery do. *All* training must be designed using sound instructional design principles. We all have seen training programs fail because they were not well designed and resulted in flash and fizzle programs.

Performance technology is based on years of research in behavioral psychology and systems thinking. Practitioners understand that multiple interventions are required. I have seen lists of human performance improvement interventions running anywhere from 100 to 150 items; I have even seen one with as many as 200. The point is that training is only one intervention. HPT practitioners must develop a solid understanding of *a majority* of interventions. The 80-20 rule applies to HPT interventions; I have found that I use 30 to 40 different interventions most of the time. The main point is not to force fit an intervention just because you like it or know how to use it.

I have found the performance clock to be an effective tool for intervention selection and grouping. Refer back to Fig. 26–2. There are four major components of the performance clock. Table 26–2 lists intervention groups in relation to the performance clock's components.

Instructional design skills provide a solid foundation for anyone considering moving into the field of HPT and ultimately performance consulting. The two technologies differ substantially, and it is important to understand the key differences (Table 26–3).

What does this mean for an instructional technologist who has decided to make the transition to performance consulting? Several issues have to be considered. One significant change is that a commitment to lifelong learning is a necessity. Having a strong foundation in instructional design is a good starting point,

TABLE 26-3

Comparing Human Performance Technology to Instructional Technology

Human Performance Technology	Instructional Technology
Centers on worker and organizational accomplishments	Centers on knowledge and skill deficiencies
Systems and systemic issues are central themes	Centers on jobs, duties, and tasks
Performance issues are the result of multiple causes	Assumes primary cause is knowledge and skill deficiencies
Ensures support of organizational mission, vision, goals, and business objectives	Normally does not consider alignment a key factor
Requires networking with specialists in other disciplines and specialties	Works primarily within the instructional design community
Requires advanced project management skills	Requires basic project management skills
Requires continuous learning	Instructional design skills are the end goal
Partners with clients	Normally siloed in the training department
Philosophies are being expanded and developed constantly	Philosophies are firmly developed and not easily changed

but remember the over 100 different interventions mentioned above. Performance consulting requires practitioners to be very familiar with most of them and, more important, know when to use each of them to solve a client's performance problems. The fact that the field of performance consulting is fluid and changes on a daily basis adds to the challenge.

Comparisons of the key differences between instructional technology and performance technology have been written about extensively elsewhere. My intent in this section is to point out some of the more significant differences and highlight some of the challenges you can expect to encounter if you decide to expand your world from instructional technology to performance technology.

The next section looks at leveraging technology to support both instructional and human performance technologies. Both technologies support the larger umbrella of human performance improvement.

LEVERAGING TECHNOLOGY FOR IT AND HPT

Knowing how to leverage technology in everyday work is becoming critical for instructional and human performance technologists. IT and HPT are two core technologies performance consultants apply to address their clients' performance issues.

It is no secret that businesses have cut everything from people to capital with the goal of becoming lean and mean. However, many, if not most, businesses have cut too deeply and actually cut into organizational muscle. However, the expectation to do more with less, deliver more, and not lower quality is a real expectation in these flawed management philosophies at a time when change has become our constant companion and the business environment is so fluid that much of what worked today won't work tomorrow.

To survive we need help, and technology can provide much of what we need. Let's start by clarifying what we mean by technology. If you grab a current dictionary and look up *technology,* you most likely will find a definition that reads something similar to the following:

> *Technology n:* Theoretical knowledge of industry and the industrial arts. The application of science and technical advances in industry, the arts, etc.
> The technical language of an art, science, etc.
> The means by which material things are produced, as in a particular civilization.

This handbook was written to focus on IT and several supporting technologies. I encourage you to look through the various chapters and pick several to research further.

There are numerous technology-based techniques that practitioners could and should be using in their day-to-day work. Software packages are available that have been specifically designed to reduce analysis time, improve quality, and assist in the decision-making process. With the cost of computers dropping almost daily, a laptop loaded with supporting software programs has become extremely useful in leveraging time and effort. Today's word-processing software can do desktop publishing that used to require specific desktop software. Any tool that reduces time, improves the quality of output, and enables us to communicate more clearly with our clients is worthy of our time and effort. Hardware such as digital cameras will become indispensable for designers. Delivery of training using the Internet, Intranets, and distant learning technologies is here to stay and provides opportunities to provide high-quality and low-cost training for our clients. So how can we leverage technology to support our work?

Designing a Job Aid: A Traditional Approach

A traditional method of developing a job or training aid involves the use of computers, word-processing software, printers, and instructional design skills. The basic process involves determining which process or task the job aid should illustrate and, through the use of a computer and software, designing the job aid and printing a hard copy for use by the worker. If we needed pictures of the actual equipment, we would use a standard camera to take the pictures, have them developed, and use a scanner to scan them into a format we could use in the computer software. We would print the job aid, have the client review it, find out the client wanted something different, and go through the whole process again.

Designing a Job Aid: Leveraging Technology

Now let's look at what is possible today. We still use many of the traditional tools, but we have better tools to leverage our time and greatly improve the quality of the output. Today one could use a digital camera at the production site and take the pictures of the equipment to include in the job aid. With a digital camera we can see immediately what the picture will look like. If it isn't what we want, we simply take another picture. The next step would be to plug the camera into a laptop computer (the camera is specially designed to dock to the laptop) and download the graphic images. Then, using standard word-processing software, as powerful a desktop publishing tool as we need, we insert the images into the job aid and complete the job. Still at the production site, the client validates the job aid and we secure the client's buy-in immediately. On the quality side, the client is able to see exactly what he or she is getting. We still haven't printed a thing. Instead of printing a master copy for the client, we use the laptop to connect to the client's computer network and upload the job aid to the client's corporate Intranet. The job aid is now immediately available for any of the company's workers. An additional benefit to the client is that the job aid is easily controlled and updatable. This is an important issue in a business world where document control is becoming a critical issue.

Developing a Training Design Document: A Traditional Approach

To complete a training design document we would conduct a front-end analysis and use our word-processing and spreadsheet software to develop a document to provide to the client. We might use the spreadsheet software to work up a cost-benefit analysis to show a return on investment (ROI) for the client. The client usually would offer a few recommendations for changes. After this we would revise the design document and conduct a final alignment meeting to finalize the design document for the training program. During this time the client would have questioned us about different delivery methods and other options that we could address through our years of practical experience.

Developing a Training Design Document: Leveraging Technology

We send the client a diskette or instruct the client to go to our Internet site and work through an analysis wizard. The client sends the document back to us, and we plug the data into the decision support software on our laptop. This software package is intuitive and is in reality an electronic performance support tool for us. The software works us through diagnostic wizard interviews and develops a comprehensive assessment of the training program. The software calculates the break-even point for the course and simultaneously generates a cost-benefit report. This software constantly compares over 25 different delivery options and ranks them in order of applicability. A cost-benefit analysis has been computed, and we are ready to meet with the client.

We meet with the client and, using the laptop, display the data in graphs and charts the client finds easy to interpret and understand. The client asks several what-if questions, which we address by simply changing the answers in the software and the software recalculates the data. The client can then make a final decision. Once done, we export the file to the master training design document and give the client a detailed document for the proposed training program or course. Much less time is involved, and the client feels very comfortable about the decision.

LEVERAGING TECHNOLOGY: FINDING IT AND LEARNING TO USE IT

These are just a few examples of what can be accomplished if we look for and use leveraging technology to perform our jobs. But how do we know what is available? We must research new technologies by attending technical trade shows, reading technology-related magazines, exploring the Internet, and networking with peers locally and on the Internet.

There is more information available today than ever before. The challenge is to hone our research skills and consistently set aside time to conduct research. Want to find current publications on a subject? Hit the Internet and search the major bookstores on-line. Want office supplies? Hit one of the on-line supply stores and place an order. Want to book airline reservations? Hit the Net.

The ability to use the Internet to conduct research has become a critical skill for instructional and human performance technologists. If you have not developed your Internet research skills, start working on them today. Take a class, buy a book, find a local expert, or just get on the Net and start surfing.

We must become proficient at using new supporting technology hardware as well. You don't want to wait until you are working for a client before you learn how to use a digital camera.

How do you position yourself to use technology? The steps are fairly straightforward. All it takes is commitment.

- You have to know what is available. This requires a commitment to constant research. When was the last time you went to a technology trade show or read a trade journal?
- You have to learn how and when to use technology. Read books, attend workshops, engage in self-study activities, and find experts to work with.
- Watch for opportunities to use the technology. Resist the temptation to rely on traditional methodologies.
- Check to be sure that the current work environment supports the use of the technology. If the environment is not ready for it, do not use it.
- Share your newly discovered knowledge with peers or anyone else who could benefit from it. You will be rewarded greatly, for you truly learn only when you teach.

I have used this five-step approach for several years. Tables 26–4 and 26–5 provide additional examples of leveraging technologies for IT and HPT.

TABLE 26–4

Leveraging Technologies for IT

If You Are Doing	Consider Using
Analysis	Software programs designed specifically for instructional analysis
	Video cameras
	Digital cameras
	Internet searches
Design	Rapid prototyping techniques
	Templates and design models
	Module databases
Development	On-line copy shops
	Desktop publishing software
	Color printers
Implementation	Local area network delivery
	Intranet/Internet delivery
	Computer-based training
	WBT
	Distance learning techniques
Evaluation	Level 3 and 4 evaluations
	Intranets for attendees to post responses on
	Forms that can be E-mailed

TABLE 26-5

Leveraging Technologies for HPT

If You Are Doing	Consider Using
Gap/cause analysis	Software programs designed specifically for process/system mapping
	Video cameras
	Digital cameras
	Internet search techniques
Intervention selection	Network of interventionists
	Decision templates and matrices
	Culture analysis techniques
Implementation	Partnership building
	Performance support systems
	Intervention teams

SUMMARY

Today's problems demand tomorrow's solutions. This chapter has compared two core technologies: instructional and human performance. We have examined how we can use supporting technologies to leverage our output and improve client satisfaction. To survive in the future we must move beyond our traditional roles of instructional and human performance technologists and focus on becoming competent performance consultants.

Today's problems demand complex and integrated solutions. Training by itself is not the answer. We must be willing to research and adopt additional mental models and constantly add to our performance consulting tool kits. Networking with peers in supporting disciplines, leveraging the use of the Internet, and making a commitment to lifelong learning are some of the keys to future success. Leveraging new technology and exploring new mental models will enable us to continue to develop our professional skills.

It is not my intent to assert that human performance technology is better than instructional technology. Rather, my point is to emphasize the fact that many training organizations are fighting for survival. To win this war requires new tactics and weapons. Technological weapons are powerful tools in the performance battle, but we must know how and when to use them. Remember that *performance* is what is important. Improving *human performance* is our job. To do this we must produce and/or enhance two primary outputs: instructional systems and performance systems. Work requires both. One will not survive without the other.

Using technology for technology's sake must be avoided. It is tempting, and new advances are made every day. However, unless the technology results in improved business performance, we should not use it.

CHAPTER 27

The Relevance of Performance Improvement to Instructional Design

Dale M. Brethower, Ph.D.

Objectives

After reading this chapter, you will be able to:

- Describe at least three major implications of performance improvement considerations for instructional design.
- Identify at least three training mandates for which performance improvement considerations have secondary or minor implications for instructional design.
- Describe a strategy for responding to pressures and opportunities generated by the performance improvement bandwagon.
- Describe similarities and differences between the performance-based instruction design process and similar instructional system design approaches
- List at least five questions to ask to determine whether vendors are focusing instruction on performance improvement or merely using the term *performance improvement* to increase sales.

OVERVIEW: BEYOND THE PERFORMANCE IMPROVEMENT BANDWAGON

The Performance Improvement Bandwagon

The Present

The performance improvement bandwagon is rolling through human resource development territory festooned with banners proclaiming the virtues of training that improves performance. This bandwagon is powered by at least three forces. The first is the widely recognized importance of skilling the work force in developing countries and reskilling the work force in developed countries such as the United States, Germany, and Japan. The second force is the pressure for rapid change that is inspired by global competition, market differentiation, and the opportunities and pressures afforded by technological developments. The third force is the increasing awareness of the extremely high opportunity cost of training that is intended to improve performance but does not transfer to the workplace.

The Past

Bandwagons are attractive vehicles for those who want to buy the latest thing; they also are attractive for vendors who seek "new and improved" labels to use in packaging their wares. Competent instructional designers, by contrast, know that the "latest things" have great potential for use and misuse, with misuse being the easier to accomplish. They have seen the latest things come and go, by their very newness costly, too new to be proven, and too little understood to be used wisely.

Competent instructional designers prefer to use the latest thing only when it increases the value or reduces the cost of training. The real value of the latest things in training has always depended on competent instructional design. The real value of filmstrips and audiotapes and movies and videos and computer-assisted instruction has always depended on good instructional design.

The Future

The goal of improving performance will always be with us, but the excitement that sometimes surrounds performance improvement will wane. It will be replaced by a new bandwagon. At the same time, the implications of performance improvement for instructional design will become more widely and fully understood, substantially benefiting human resources development (HRD) and organizations that focus much of their training on performance improvement.

THREE INSTRUCTIONAL DESIGN CONSTRAINTS

Let us review three basic and well-known constraints on instructional design.

First, different purposes require different instructional tactics. If the purpose is to assure high levels of expertise, a design intended only to increase awareness will not do the job; if the purpose is to increase awareness, a design intended to assure expertise will be far too costly. A design intended to improve knowledge will not produce applications automatically. Instructional designers know that there is a vast difference between "knowing about" and "using on the job."

Second, there are at least three training mandates that specify purposes other than performance improvement:

1. Some training is externally mandated, for example, that people receive a minimum number of hours of safety training or be trained in a specific content. It may be clear to the designer that training for the mandated amount of time in the mandated content will not yield improved on-the-job safety performance or increased use of safety procedures or equipment, but the designer must fulfill the mandate.

2. Some training is internally mandated, for example, when a senior manager wants to launch a major (and perhaps career-enhancing) initiative or organizational policy dictates that people receive a certain amount of diversity training or training in gender-related issues or material on how to do a performance appraisal interview. The mandate typically includes training time and content specifications that if followed will not yield positive effects on workplace performance.

3. Some training is considered as a perk, for example, as a way to recognize high-potential employees or give executives or line workers a break from daily stresses.

Third, even when performance improvement truly is the goal, mandated constraints can make it impossible to achieve. Even a very competent instructional designer will be unable to design instruction that enables people to learn well enough to perform better on the job if

- Too little training time is allowed for participants to practice and master key skills
- Too little lead time is provided
- Too little access to key people is provided
- Equipment is not provided to enable participants to practice essential skills

These obstacles and constraints are familiar. Experienced instructional designers encounter them often.

PERFORMANCE IMPROVEMENT IMPLICATIONS

Understanding the implications of performance improvement for instructional design requires an understanding of the meaning of two words: *performance* and *improvement*. These words are used so commonly that they have taken on a variety of meanings. *Performance* can mean anything from "behavior" to "financial results" to "peak power potential." Similarly, *improvement* has multiple meanings in an organizational setting.

The problem of definition is compounded by people eager to use current buzzwords. When a client or a vendor talks about *performance, improvement,* or *performance improvement,* a streetwise instructional designer will ask questions to determine the definitions the speaker is using. The words themselves convey little meaning. Definition or exemplification is needed.

Defining Performance

There is agreement on the definition of *performance* among many opinion leaders in the International Society for Performance Improvement and the American Association for Training and Development. As articulated by Gilbert (1996), performance has two components: a behavior or activity and whatever that behavior or activity accomplishes. For example, the performance of "closing a sale" has an activity component (the things done to close the sale) and an outcome or accomplishment (a transaction of money for goods or services).

Similarly, the performance of "making a widget" has an activity component (making) and an outcome or accomplishment component (a widget). The first component—the activity—always adds cost. Whenever we set up a training program to increase people's knowledge and skill, we are increasing cost: We are a cost-adding profession. We like to think that the new knowledge or skill will add value, but whether it does is determined not by our thinking it will but by the uses to which it is put. The second component—accomplishment—is the component that adds value.

Consider the design of training in "interpersonal communications." Many different communications behaviors can be taught, such as active listening, reflective listening, making I statements, making feeling statements, clarifying, confirming, making factual versus interpretive statements, asking for agreement, and probing for hidden problems. Any of these behaviors can be important in improving actual communications: Used well and at the right time, a behavior may improve communication; used poorly or at the wrong time, it may make communication worse.

Thus, if an instructional designer focuses only on an activity or behavior, the design is *not* a design for performance improvement: Behavior is not the same thing as performance. Just as teaching tennis behaviors is not the same as improving tennis performance, teaching communication behaviors is not the same as improving communication performance. People must have or acquire communication skills, but using a communication skill at the wrong time, in the wrong place, or for the wrong purpose does not yield improved communication. Well-practiced behaviors used improperly interfere with performance; we call such behaviors "bad habits."

Table 27–1 shows several examples of performance and several examples that, though sometimes referred to as performance, are not performance. The bottom part of the table shows activities and results, but unless specific activities are con-

TABLE 27-1

Performance and Nonperformance

Performance	Activity	Accomplishment or Result
Widget making	Widget-making process	Widget
Instructional design	An ISD process	Designs
Instruction	Presentation/facilitation, etc., according to the design	Participant learning
Leadership	Providing direction, resources, etc.	People moving together in the same direction
A piano recital	Playing the piano	Audience satisfaction
It's Called "Performance" But It's Not		
Communicating	Sending an E-mail (or memo or letter) or giving a speech	?
Computer performance	Peak levels possible for a variety of computing tasks	?
Division performance	?	Financial data, e.g., profit margin, RONA
Leadership	Acting like great leaders of the past	?
Team performance	?	Win-lose record
Managing	?	Focusing on results
Managing	Focusing on activities	?

nected to specific results, it is not performance. Focusing on activities alone is a management activity that eventually results in poor performance. Focusing on results alone also leads to poor performance. It doesn't take a genius to figure out why both components are necessary: Results do not occur without action; actions that do not yield results are wasteful.

Defining Improvement

Improvement is another term that is so widely used that it has acquired multiple meanings. In the performance improvement context there are only three possible meanings. If performance is improved, it is (1) reduced in cost, (2) increased in value, or (3) both.

If we improve persuasion skills, what have we improved? Persuasion skills. Does improving persuasion skills make one more persuasive? Not unless the persuasion skills are used. Does using the skills improve persuasive performance? Not unless the skills are used to add value. If the person applies the skills to persuade others more easily, has persuasive performance improved? Not if the person persuades people to do the wrong things. Performance is improved only if persuasion occurs in ways that add value.

BASIC TECHNIQUES

People use thousands of little techniques to improve workplace performance. Fortunately, all the techniques can be captured in two categories: techniques that support good performance and techniques that support poor performance. Having two extremely long lists of techniques that sometimes work and techniques that usually interfere with good performance would be a step in the right direction, but more is required because any technique is only part of the solution, only one of several essential supports for good performance. Excellent performance support requires an integrated set of techniques. The essential supports can be captured by a set of only six categories (Gilbert 1996, pp. 73–93; Zigon 1994, pp. 258–262). The six categories are shown in Fig. 27–1. Improving performance requires assuring that the six categories of variables are managed so that the variables that support good performance are present and the variables that support poor performance are absent.

There are three points to note about Fig. 27–1. First, the variables shown in all 12 cells must be optimal if excellent performance is to be supported: No one cell is more essential than the others. Second, professional specialties have been established to deal with the variables in each of the six rows. There are specialists in

1. Reward and recognition systems (but fewer specialists in feedback systems)
2. Tools and materials (typically industrial engineers and human factors engineers)
3. Guidance (typically industrial engineers and organizational communications specialists)
4. Knowledge, skills, and attitudes (typically HRD professionals)
5. Abilities (typically selection specialists and human factors psychologists)
6. Motives (typically organizational psychologists, motivation researchers, and motivational speakers)

Third, training departments tend to be boxed into the fourth of the six rows, the "Knowledge, Skills, and Attitudes" row.

The implications of the figure for instructional designers who want to board the performance improvement bandwagon are strong. Unless you are willing and

Supporting and Destroying Excellence

	Supporting Good Performance	Supporting Poor Performance
Incentives and Feedback	1. Providing rewards or recognitions that (a) connect to people's motives and goals and (b) are attained only by performing well 2. Providing timely feedback on progress and performance quality	Providing rewards or recognition attainable without performing well, e.g., by doing something else Choosing rewards and recognitions that do not connect to people's motives and goals; providing weak or conflicting feedback or providing feedback to the wrong people or at the wrong time
Tools and Materials	Matching tools and materials to work requirements by providing adequate tools, materials, and work processes	Providing inadequate tools and materials for good performance, perhaps by providing better tools and materials for doing something else
Guidance	Matching guidance to workplace demands by providing clear and nonconflicting goals, priorities, and work procedures; walking the talk, e.g., by assuring that management deeds match management words	Providing goals, exhortations, etc., that confuse or conflict rather than guide one in appropriate directions; saying one thing but doing conflicting things; Acting as if having leaders "say it" is equivalent to assuring that people "do it."
Knowledge, Skills, & Attitudes	Matching KSA available to KSA required by selecting people with some of the required KSA and providing training that enables people to acquire the additional KSA and apply it in the workplace	Providing training that enables people to acquire relevant KSA but does not connect to the workplace in ways that support the transfer of training; allowing on-the-job training to be the sharing of bad habits, misinformation, and interfering attitudes; changing hiring practices without changing training
Abilities	Matching work requirements with human abilities, e.g., by placing people in work for which they have the required abilities or designing work so that it can be done by people with the abilities they have	Designing work in ways that require unnecessarily high levels of physical or intellectual exertion and then developing a culture that rewards the unnecessary exertions
Motives	Matching incentives, recognitions, and cultural practices in the organization to the goals and motivations of people in the work force	Exhorting people to perform and "be motivated" without providing WIIFMs (What's In It For Me) that match their motives; supporting a work culture in which there are rewards and recognition for poor performance

able to partner with many others in your organization to "cover the territory" of all 12 cells,

1. Don't even try to get on the performance improvement bandwagon.
2. Don't promise anything other than level 1 (Did they like it?) and level 2 (Did they learn it?) results.
3. Justify your existence on the basis of accomplishing level 2 learning outcomes rather than on the basis of workplace results.
4. If you want to become more proactive, advocate a systems approach. Use this figure as a tool for showing what must be in place, in addition to high-quality training, to assure workplace utilization (level 3—Did they use it?) and workplace impact (level 4—Did performance improve?).

A wise strategy for many instructional designers might be to stay in the HRD box but seek opportunities to partner with others to improve organizationally significant performances. Instead of the "performance improvement" bandwagon, jump on a "program of the month" bandwagon that you believe can make a significant contribution. At worst, doing so demonstrates that you are a loyal, forward-thinking team player. At best, one of the bandwagons will pay off handsomely and you'll be part of the victory celebration. There are bandwagons aplenty; if you do not jump on, it is at the very least prudent to avoid getting run over.

Regardless of the bandwagon you try to leap on—or the bandwagon wheels you try to avoid being run over by, there are ISD tools that focus on performance improvement that you can use to implement your strategy. Instructional designers who see the performance improvement bandwagon as an opportunity to position HRD for greater impact can put those tools to good use.

TOOLS: WORKSHEETS, CHECKLISTS, AND OTHER JOB AIDS

Many opinion leaders in the American Society for Training and Development (ASTD) and the International Society for Performance and Instruction (ISPI) have been grappling for years with issues involving organizational interventions that actually improve workplace performance. Their work has produced numerous tools that have been published in a variety of places. These worksheets, checklists, and other tools can be helpful in scanning organizations for opportunities to improve performance and in supporting performance.

Table 27–2 compares the performance-based instructional design process with a generic ISD process. The table is structured to clarify the ISD process for performance-based instruction and show that it is similar to ISD processes that are widely known and advocated in HRD.

TABLE 27-2

Performance-Based versus Generic ISD

Project Phase	Performance-Based ISD Questions	Generic ISD Questions
Needs assessment	What is the strategic or current business need for performance improvement?	What training needs do key stakeholders see? Who needs what KSA?
Specification of outcomes	What performance products are needed? What standards? What performance support?	What are the instructional objectives?
Design phase 1: Specification of content	How can people do it? What processes can people use to produce the products? How will we guide practice?	What KSA is needed?
Design phase 2: Specification of instructional processes	How does the overall design link learners and workplace? How does each unit?	How will we teach it?
Implementation and Evaluation	Are analysis and design done properly? Do the design and implementation reflect principles of adult learning and performance? Do they actually work?	How can we implement the instruction? How will we determine the extent to which people learn it? How will we determine how satisfied people are with the instruction?

The view of ISD shown in Table 27–2 is simplified; however, it contains enough detail to show major similarities and differences.

- *Similarities.* The approaches are similar in that both are orderly, beginning with a determination of need for the training. Both have a method for determining the content of instruction, the instructional techniques, and the success of the HRD project.
- *Differences.* The processes differ in focus. The generic ISD process focuses on getting expert opinion from clients and subject-matter experts, whereas the performance-based instruction ISD process focuses on identifying business issues and analyzing workplace performance.

The performance-based ISD process focuses on application, whereas the generic ISD process typically focuses on content. For example, the generic ISD process might be used to design the lecture portion of a typical college chemistry course, whereas the performance-based ISD process might fit the lab portion more readily.

The performance-based ISD process shown in Table 27–2 is a tool that can be used to design instruction that improves performance. Opinion leaders in the performance improvement arena use many worksheets, checklists, and other job aids. Kaufman, Thiagarajan, and MacGillis (1997) edited a volume that contains many such tools. Brethower and Dams (in press), Lineberry and Bullock (1980), and Harless (1978) describe additional tools. Other volumes that contain performance improvement tools include Dean (1994), Dean and Ripley (1997), Stolovitch and Keeps (1992), and Stolovitch and Keeps (in press).

Table 27–3 is intended to help instructional designers and others determine whether a vendor or an upper-level manager is really talking about performance improvement or is just using buzzwords from the performance improvement bandwagon.

APPLICATIONS

Phillips (1994) includes 18 cases that demonstrate that instruction can have a positive impact on workplace performance. The cases include work in both not-for-profit organizations and for-profit organizations in a variety of industries. LaFleur and Brethower (1998) report a series of performance improvement initiatives, some involving training, in a small business. Esque and Patterson (1998) provide 22 cases showing improvement in workplace performance, with many of them involving training. Brethower and Smalley (1998) describe 12 cases that illustrate how instruction can be designed and implemented so that training contributes to improved workplace performance.

Additional cases are described by Kopelman (1986), who reviewed interventions that focus on all six categories of variables necessary to support workplace performance. Interestingly, Kopelman's review of the research and validated practice literatures supports a point also made by Dean (1994, p. 25): Workplace feedback deficiencies are quite common. Indeed, Kopelman's review supports the view that feedback interventions tend to be both lower in cost and higher in impact than training interventions.

Successfully improving performance with training requires that the instruction be connected in very specific ways to workplace standards and performance support variables. Brethower and Smalley (1998), for example, describe systematic and reproducible techniques instructional designers can use to assure that instruction has a positive impact on workplace performance. Broad and Newstrom (1992) provide similar guidelines for the transfer of training.

The following scenario illustrates these techniques:

Client: Pat, we need a training program in finance for nonfinancial managers.

Designer: Sounds good to me. (Confirming.) There are good books on that topic. Maybe we could buy copies of one of the best ones and give it to some of our nonfinancial managers. (Offering a quick and inexpensive approach.)

TABLE 27-3

Buzzword Versus Substance

What You Hear	What You Suspect	Things You Might Ask
A vendor says, "Our proprietary performance improvement process offers distinct advantages."	The advantages aren't distinct except by their use to justify pricey services.	"What theoretical models and research evidence is your proprietary process based on?" (to find out if they know what makes it work) or "How do you know we'll experience those advantages?" "Would you be willing to write a guarantee into the purchase agreement?"
A vendor says, "All our training programs are designed with performance improvement in mind."	Their intentions may be good, but their execution and results are weak.	"What specific performance improvement can I expect to see in my organization?" "What better results will people produce after being trained?" "How do you tailor your training to the performance support conditions that actually exist in our organization?" "How do you measure performance during the training? How should we measure performance after training?" "How do people practice the specific work they'll be doing on the job?"
A manager says, "I want you to improve the performance of our supervisors."	The manager has already tried several things that haven't worked and is hoping that training will do the trick.	"I'd be happy to help. What operating results do you want to see improved?" "May I talk to the three supervisors who are performing the best right now?" "What have you already tried?"
A manager says, "I just came back from a conference on performance improvement. We have to focus our training on that."	The manager will be a good ally if you can act quickly, before he goes to another conference.	"Good idea. What did people at the conference mean by performance?" "Let's work together on this. When can we get together to get started on a pilot project?"
A manager says, "This is an extremely important project. If we don't get the cost of materials down, we are in big trouble."	The manager means it and is ready to work with you.	"Let's get started. Let's schedule an hour later today to zero in on all that we'd have to do to get cost of materials down. May I show you something then? It shows six things that have to be done to support good performance and six things that support poor performance."

483

Client: I don't think that would do it. I'm not sure they'd read it.

Designer: You are probably right. (Confirming.) And they might not be able to see right away how they could apply the information even if they read the book. (Pausing. Waiting for a response.)

Client: That's why we need a training program.

Designer: So they can apply what they learn? (Confirming.)

Client: Yes.

Designer: What are some of the things you see that tell you that some of our managers could make good use of financial information? (Probing.)

Client: They just make bad decisions. (Pause. The designer waits.) Like some of them don't really understand their budgets.

Designer: And that leads to bad decisions? (Probing.)

Client: Right.

Designer: Is there one specific bad decision that lots of managers make that we should focus on?

Client: I don't think so. Every manager's situation is different.

Designer: So different managers might make different bad decisions. (Confirming.) I guess about the only thing their bad decisions have in common is that they waste money in some way. Is that what you are saying? (Clarifying.)

Client: Yes.

Designer: I know that in our shop we really have to do a better and better job of using our financial resources. That's actually why I'm asking all these questions. I just don't want to spend people's time and money running training programs that don't help. If you and I worked together to run a course that spends a lot of time training people in financial concepts but doesn't focus on how they can make decisions that are "on the money," that would be wasteful, wouldn't it?

Client: Yes.

Designer: When do you want this training offered?

Client: Soon. It came up in a management meeting last week. Bart (the chief executive officer) was fuming about it and told us we had to do something about it right away.

Designer: Okay. Let's schedule it now so Bart will know it's in the works. (Knowing that timeliness is required if customers are to be satisfied.) We'll run a session with about five or six people. Do you think Bart wants us to spend a lot of time training them?

Client: Absolutely not. I think one of the reasons people make bad decisions is that they are overloaded. They just don't have the time to think things through. Spending a lot of time in a training course isn't what we want.

Designer: They probably want to see some quick results, too. (Probing for customer expectations.)

Client: Tell me about it.

Designer: Did Bart really tag you with getting something going? Or did he just toss the idea out there to see who would pick it up and run with it?

Client: He just tossed it out, but nobody said anything. So he told me to deal with it. That's why I came to you.

Designer: Okay. Then let's check calendars. We'll schedule three 1-hour sessions. (Probing.) I'll put an agenda together. It'll be a training agenda in the form of an action agenda for a meeting. You and I can decide later which one of us leads the meeting.

Client: What will that accomplish? How are they going to learn finance in three sessions?

Designer: Don't worry. I'll take care of that. They're not going to learn finance; they're going to practice financial decision making. What we'll do is bring in some examples of good and bad financial decisions. Did Bart mention specifics in that meeting?

Client: Yes, but they're not ones I can share with everyone.

Designer: No problem. Did he mention any good financial decisions? Ones that would have been bad if the manager hadn't known what she was doing?

Client: Probably. I'd have to check with Bart. I'm sure I could bring one of mine.

Designer: Good. Get one of Bart's if you can so he'll know we are taking action here. Are you strong enough in financial decision making that you could coach the managers we invite to the meeting? Or would you need some backup? (Probing.)

Client: I probably could coach on some things. Depends on what we get into.

Designer: Okay. If we get into anything you can't handle, we'll bring in some backup for the second session. Now let's decide who we should invite to the meeting. Maybe a couple of people who are relatively new and a couple of people who make some reasonably large financial decisions.

Client: I can give that some thought. You want people who are at roughly the same level, don't you?

Designer: Same level? Like in position?

Client: No. At the same level of knowledge about finance.

Designer: No. Let's not worry about that. If we were just teaching content, we might want that, but we're teaching financial decision making. We want people who make financial decisions; I'd guess that's about every manager in the place. For this first session we want people who represent areas that Bart thinks can have a big impact if they make bad decisions.

Client: I see. I'm not quite sure how that will work, but I can put together a list of people.

Designer: Good. We're a team. You came to me because you didn't see how to do this yourself. You can count on me to make that session work. (Reassuring. Promising.) I'll talk to each of the people on your list beforehand to prep them for the meeting. We'll have them each define at least one area where good financial decision making is important, and we'll work with those.

Client: I'm still not sure how it will work, but I have to run. I just wanted to raise the issue with you.

Designer: You've accomplished a lot more than that. I'll call you later to get about a half hour of your time before I contact the people who'll be attending the training. Do you think we can get them all together for the first session sometime this month?

Client: Probably. It seems to take about that long to get a meeting set up, as busy as we all are.

Designer: Good. You can tell Bart that we are trucking right along and that he'll have some results soon.

This scenario illustrates the practical nature of the design process for performance-based instruction. Table 27–4 shows a generic model for developing performance-based instruction (modified from Brethower and Smalley 1998, p. 9). The figure shows how the designer could have "roughed in" the training design during the 10-minute conversation. The designer's notes represent mental notes the designer might have made during the conversation.

The conversation with the client is just the beginning. The ISD process for performance improvement requires lead time, but note that the designer has already committed to delivery dates. Clients appreciate the prompt action symbolized by a commitment to dates. The date provides time for analysis, especially if it turns out to be difficult to get the meeting scheduled.

However, much remains to be done. First, the designer will talk with managers one on one to clarify and confirm the value of the project. A subjective assessment will be done by conveying Bart's concern and (1) asking the manager one on one how many dollars are involved in their financial decisions, (2) asking for their estimates of the number of dollars that are actually lost through bad financial

T A B L E 2 7 – 4

Developing Performance-Based Instruction

Project Phase	Key Questions	Designer's Notes
Specification of business need	What is the strategic or current business need for performance improvement?	Bart believes many managers are making bad financial decisions. If he's right, it could have a significant impact on current business results.
Specification of performance requirements	What performance products are needed? What standards? What performance support?	"Good financial decisions" are the products, but I'm not sure yet about where they show up and what the standards are. My guess is that performance support is weak, especially in the area of feedback; it probably exists, but the timing probably is off.
Design phase 1: Specification of work processes	How can people do it? What processes can people use to produce the products? How will we guide practice?	We'll figure this out with each manager in the first or second training session. They all know something about the content and, by pooling their knowledge, probably know enough. If not, we'll bring in someone with that knowledge to coach people during the second or third session.
Design phase 2: Specification of instructional processes	How does the overall design link learners and workplace? How does each unit?	We'll bring in some examples of good and bad financial decisions and get each manager to begin reviewing his or her actual decisions. We'll get more information as we go and help managers get ready for upcoming decisions.
Implementation and evaluation	Are analysis and design done properly? Do the design and implementation reflect principles of adult learning and performance? Do they actually work?	I'd like more lead time, but the way I like to do analyses of problems like this is to convene a focus group. That's essentially what we are doing. But instead of just "using" people's time in the analysis, we are involving them in the solution, applying it to their own work, and treating them like the intelligent adults they are. If I can really get them involved, it will work.

decisions each year in the organization, and (3) asking for their estimates of how much value they could add if they made better financial decisions. Done tactfully, such conversations would give concrete meaning to Bart's general concern.

The people interviewed will know about examples of costly financial decisions, supporting the subjective assessment with data that confirm and support Bart's hunch. If the opposite is true and managers don't corroborate Bart's hunch, the instructional designer can go to Bart or the client and say, "Maybe things aren't as bad as we feared," getting permission to investigate further or switch to a more promising project.

Second, the designer will collect from the prospective trainees examples of their best and worst (or at least suboptimal) decisions. The designer is looking for performance standards: What are the defining characteristics of good (versus bad) financial decisions? (If the people were making widgets instead of making decisions, the designer would search for characteristics of good versus bad widgets.)

At the same time the designer will try to collect examples of the processes managers use to make the best (in contrast to the worst) decisions. Note that the examples of good and bad decisions, the standards, and the good and bad processes constitute the content of the instruction. (The content is "how to make good financial decisions," not, for example, "basic concepts of finance.")

Third, the designer will position each participant as an expert in financial decision making in his or her own area, emphasizing that he or she was selected because of current expertise and a willingness to learn. In addition, the designer will be positioning the training program as an important pilot program that is career-enhancing for the participants.

In short, the designer is positioning the training program as important, the participant as a valued partner, and the training as a cooperative partnership in which the trainer works with the participants to achieve a goal. At the same time, the designer is assuring the participants that it will not be a session in which someone talks at them about finance, interfering with their work and not providing them with information tailored to their specific situations. It will be "just-enough, just-in-time, just-for-me" training.

If the designer had had more lead time, the analysis would have been similar. People would have been questioned as representatives of a population of participants rather than as colleagues in a specific project. Of course it would have taken longer and been more costly, and the examples and processes collected would have been prepared more elegantly for presentation during the training. In addition, the designer might have worked with one or more of the managers to analyze financial records in some detail to verify or disprove Bart's hunch.

Note that the design for each session is roughed but the details of the design of later sessions will emerge from information gained during the first sessions. This feature of rapid prototyping approaches assures that the performance improvement ISD process supports timely and tailored instruction. The process is inherently flexible, tailored to the specific situations and capabilities of each set of participants. (If the pilot is successful, the same ISD process will be used with subsequent groups; the design would not be "rolled out" as if one size fit all the second time around.)

A Caveat

Some designers may suspect that this approach relies too much on (1) what participants already know, (2) encouraging participants to share what they know, and (3) the demands of a specific application project. As a result, they fear, people will not gain a thorough grounding in basic principles of finance. These worries are understandable. However, these features are a strength, not a weakness, of the approach. Good instruction builds on what people already know; that is a fundamental characteristic of adult learning. Realistic approaches to organizational problem solving or innovation require people to share what they know; that is why people from multiple areas are chosen for work on cross-functional teams and new product development teams. Recent research in the cognitive sciences supports earlier findings: Learning is connected to the situation in which it is acquired, such as the classroom or the workplace. Learning does not occur by absorbing huge masses of material and then applying it all; expertise is constructed by encountering many different situations, each of which demands only a small amount of knowledge. (Researchers use the words *situated learning* to describe this fundamental finding.)

How would people like Bart's managers acquire a thorough grounding in finance if that were the goal? By calling on experts in finance when the expertise is needed to solve current management problems, working with financial experts on cross-functional teams, or going back to school and majoring in finance. (However, if they went back to school, they would probably assert that while they were exposed to many concepts of finance in school, they did not really learn finance until they returned to the job and had to use those concepts: Learning really is situated.) Fortunately, Bart is interested in good financial decisions, not in demanding that all his managers have an academic understanding and credentials in finance.

CONCLUDING IMPLICATIONS

HRD can play a significant role in improving performance in organizations. Instructional designers can use a performance-based ISD process to connect training to current and strategic business goals. In doing so, instructional designers must partner with others in the organization because performer knowledge, skills, and attitudes (KSA) constitute only one of six categories of variables that are essential in supporting good performance. KSA is necessary but not sufficient: Performers who have the physical and intellectual abilities must be recruited and retained and work must be designed so that it can be performed effectively by the people who are available, the incentives and rewards provided for staying on the job and performing well must be designed to match the motives of the performers, people must be given adequate tools and materials, and the work processes must be well designed. People must have adequate guidance both in how to do the work and in how to respond to changing and challenging priorities. People must have adequate feedback and incentives. HRD can't do it all, but it can't be done at all if people aren't trained properly.

GLOSSARY

Abilities   The physical and intellectual capacities of people. From the perspective of the instructional designer, abilities are constraints rather than controllable variables. Our task is to design instruction that enables people to use their physical and intellectual abilities to perform competently at work.

Feedback   Information about performance that is used to guide or improve performance. Feedback is essential to guide complex performances at work and during learning. Providing people with data that they do not use is not feedback. Telling people things they do not hear and use is not feedback. Data received too late to use for correcting performance are not feedback.

Guidance   Information intended to guide performance. Job aids, beginning-of-shift announcements, memos describing priorities, hints from supervisors or coworkers, mission and vision statements, and policy statements are all forms of guidance.

Incentives   Items intended to reward performance. Money, stamps, letters of commendation, and opportunities for promotion are common incentives. If incentives connect to people's performances and motives, they tend to work as rewards; otherwise, they do not.

Improvement   A measurable change for the better. In the case of improvements in performance, the change must occur in an activity or process that reduces cost or be a change in the quality, timeliness, or value of the product or result.

Instructional systems design (ISD)   An orderly procedure for the systematic design of instruction that typically follows an analysis, design, develop, implement, and evaluate sequence.

Job Aid   A tool that supports performance on the job or supports acquiring the performance during training. To-do lists, lists of steps, quality checklists, flowcharts, worksheets, recipes, and electronic performance support systems are common examples.

Knowledge, skills, and attitudes (KSA)   The traditional domain of instructional content, described by the cognitive, affective, and psychomotor taxonomies of instructional objectives. In performance-based instruction, KSA are viewed as enablers of performance, as means, not as ends.

Motives   Processes an individual uses to channel energy. Motives are typically but not always related to a person's goals, values, and attitudes. A person typically has multiple motives, some of which conflict with others. Wishes and wants become motives only if a person works to attain them.

Performance   A process or activity *and* the product or result of that activity. The activity or process component is necessary but costly; the product or result should add value.

Performance-Based Instruction   Instruction that focuses on performance. Characterized by exercises that simulate work. Contrasts with "traditional" instruction, which focuses on the transmission of content.

Tools and Materials   Tools are the machines, hand tools, and decision aids that are used to enable or support performance. Materials are the consumables used in doing work, such as raw materials, supplies, electricity, and forms.

CHAPTER 1

Armstrong, T. *7 Kinds of Smarts.* Penguin.

Brewer, C., and D. G. Campbell. *Rhythms of Learning.* Zephyr Press.

Buzan, T. *Brain Users Guide.* Dutton.

Buzan, T. *Make the Most of Your Mind.* Simon & Schuster.

Buzan, T. *Use Both Sides of the Brain.* Dutton.

Caine, R. *Making Connections.* Innovative Learning.

De Bono, E. *De Bono's Thinking Course.* Facts on File.

De Bono, E. *Lateral Thinking.* Harper & Row.

DePorter, B. *Quantum Learning.* The Learning Forum Success Products.

Dhority, L. *The Act Approach.* Gordon & Breach.

Edwards. *Drawing on the Right Side of the Brain.* J. P. Tarcher.

Fuller, B. *On Education.* Amherst: University of Massachusetts Press.

Gardner, H. *Frames of Mind.* Basic Books.

Gazzaniga, M. *The Social Brain: Discovering the Networks of the Mind.* New York: Basic Books.

Hampden-Turner, C. *Maps of the Mind.* Collier Books.

Hanks, K., and J. A. Parry. *Wake Up Your Creative Genius.* William Kaufman.

Hooper, J., and D. Teresi. *The 3-Pound Universe.* Macmillan.

Jensen, E. *Superteaching.* Turning Point for Teachers. P.O. Box 2551, Del Mar, CA 92014.

Joseph, R. *The Right Brain and the Unconscious: Discovering the Stranger Within.* New York: Plenum.

Knowles, M. *The Adult Learner: A Neglected Species.* Gulf.

Kolb, D. *Xperiential Learning: Experience as the Source of Learning and Development.* Englewoods Cliffs, N.J.: Prentice-Hall.

Lazaer, D. *Multiple Intelligence Approach to Assessment.* Zephyr Press.

Lazear, D. *Seven Ways of Teaching.* Skylight.

McKim, R. *Experiences in Visual Thinking.* Brooks/Cole.

Mellander, K. *The Power of Learning.* Business One Irwin.

Oech, V. *A Whack on the Side of the Head.*

Ornstein, R., and R. Thompson. *The Amazing Brain.* Houghton Mifflin.

Ostrander, and Schroeder. *Superlearning.* Delacorte.

Rico, G. *Writing the Natural Way.* Tarcher.

Rose, C. *Accelerated Learning.* Dell.

Russell. *Global Brain.* Tarcher.

Russell. *The Brain Book.* Dutton.

Sample, B. *The Metaphoric Mind.* Addison-Wesley.

Springer, S. P., and G. Deutsch. *Left Brain, Right Brain.* Freeman.

Williams, L. *Teaching for the Two Sided Room.* Prentice-Hall.

CHAPTER 2

Anderson, J. R. 1982. Acquisition of cognitive skill. *Psychological Review* 89:369–406.

Anderson, J. R. 1983. *The Architecture of Cognition.* Cambridge, Mass.: Harvard University Press.

Anderson, J. R. 1983. *Cognitive Psychology and Its Implications.* New York: Freeman.

Andrews, D. H., and L. A. Goodson. 1980. A comparative analysis of models of instructional design. *Journal of Instructional Development* 3(4):2–16.

Banathy, B. H. 1968. *Instructional Systems.* Palo Alto, Calif.: Fearon. Cognition and Technology Group at Vanderbilt. 1990. Anchored instruction and its relationship to situated cognition. *Educational Researcher* 19(5):2–10.

Cohen, S. Alan. 1987. Instructional alignment: Searching for a magic bullet. *Educational Researcher.* November, pp: 16–20.

Davidson, G. V. 1990. Matching learning styles with teaching styles: Is it a useful concept in instruction? *Performance & Instruction* 29:36–38.

Dick, Walter. 1996. The Dick and Carey model: Will it survive the decade? *Educational Technology Research and Development* 44(3):55–63.

Gagne, R. M. 1984. Learning outcomes and their effects: Useful categories of human performances. *American Psychologist* 39: 377–385.

Gagne, R. M. 1985. *The Conditions of Learning,* 4th ed. New York: Holt, Rinehart and Winston.

Gagne, R. M. 1992. *Principles of Instructional Design.* Fort Worth: Harcourt Brace Jovanovich.

Gagne, R. M., and L. Briggs. 1979. *Principles of Instruction Design,* 2d ed. New York: Holt, Rinehart & Winston.

Gott, S. P. 1988. Apprenticeship instruction for real-world tasks: The coordination of procedures, mental models, and strategies. In E. Z. Rothkopf (ed.), *Review of Educational Research.* 15: 97–169. Washington, D.C.: AERA.

Handbook for Designers of Instructional Systems, vol. 2. 1973. Washington, D.C.: U.S. Department of the Air Force. AFP 50–58.

Harless, J. H. 1987. An analysis of front-end analysis. *The Best of Performance & Instruction* 26(2):7–9.

Jonassen, D. H. 1988. *Instructional Designs for Microcomputer Courseware.* Hillsdale, N.J.: Erlbaum.

Jonassen, D. H. 1990. Thinking technology: Toward a constructivist view of instructional design. *Educational Technology* 30(9):32–34.

Jonassen, D. H., R. S. Grabinger, and N. D. C. Harris. 1990. Analyzing and selecting instructional strategies and tactics. *Performance Improvement Quarterly* 3(2):29–47.

Kaufman, R. 1990. Strategic planning and thinking: Alternative views. *Performance & Instruction* 29: 1–7.

Kyllonen, P. C., and V. J. Shute. 1988. *Taxonomy of Learning Skills.* Brooks Air Force Base, Texas: Air Force Human Resources Laboratory (AFHRL-TP-87-39).

Landa, L. 1984. Algo-heuristic theory of performance, learning and instruction: Subject, problems, principles. *Contemporary Educational Psychology* 9(3):26–30.

Landa, L. 1987. The creation of expert performers without years of conventional experience: The Landamatics method. *Journal of Management Development* 6(4):122.

Mager, R. F. 1997. *Making Instruction Work, or, Skillbloomers: A Step-by-Step Guide to Designing and Developing Instruction That Works.* Atlanta: Center for Effective Performance.

Mager, R. F. 1997. *Preparing Instructional Objectives,* (3d ed.) Atlanta: Center for Effective Performance.

Mager, R. P., and P. Pipe. 1997. *Analyzing Performance Problems, or, You Really Oughta Wanna: How to Figure Out Why People Aren't Doing What They Should Be, and What to Do About It,* (3d ed.). Atlanta: Center for Effective Performance.

McFarland, R. D., and R. Parker. 1990. *Expert Systems in Education and Training.* Englewood Cliffs, N.J.: Educational Technology Publications.

Merrill, M. D., Z. Li, and M. K. Jones. 1990. Limitations of first generation instructional design. *Educational Technology* 30(1):7–11.

Merrill, M. D., Z. Li, and M. K. Jones. 1990. Second generation instructional design (ID$_2$). *Educational Technology* 30(2):7–14.

Merrill, M. D., Z. Li, and M. K. Jones. 1990. Second generation instructional design research program. *Educational Technology* 30(3):26–31.

Merrill, M. D., Z. Li, and M. K. Jones. 1990. (ID$_2$) and constructivist theory. *Educational Technology* 30(2):52–55.

Muraida, D. J., and M. Spector. 1990. The advanced instructional design advisor (AIDA): An Air Force project to improve instructional design. *Educational Technology* 30(3):66.

Norman, D. A. 1980. Twelve issues for cognitive science. *Cognitive Science* 4:1–32.

Norman, D. A., and S. Draper. 1986. *User Centered System Design.* Hillsdale, N.J.: Erlbaum.

Reigeluth, C. M., ed. 1983. *Instructional Design Theories and Models: An Overview of Their Current Status.* Hillsdale, N.J.: Erlbaum.

Romiszowski, A. J. 1981. *Designing Instructional Systems: Decision Making in Course Planning and Curriculum Design.* New York: Nichols.

Rossett, A. 1987. What your professor never told you about the mundane practice of instructional design. *TechTrents* 32(1):10–13.

Snelbecker, G. E. 1977. The educational psychologist as architect. Paper presented during the Symposium "Implementing the Call for New Directions in Educational Psychology," American Educational Research Association Annual Meeting, New York. ERIC Document 141 227.

Snelbecker, G. E. 1987. Contrasting and complementary approaches to instructional design. In C. M. Reigeluth, ed., *Instructional Theories in Action: Lessons Illustrating Selected Theories and Models,* pp. 321–337. Hillsdale, N.J.: Erlbaum.

Snelbecker, D. E., and D. S. Stepansky. 1985. "GIGO" (Garbage In, Garbage Out)—How Does It Apply to Computer-Based Instruction? In *26th ADCIS Conference Proceedings,* pp. 29–33. Bellingham, Wash.: ADCIS.

Spector, J. M. 1990. *Designing and Developing and Advanced Instructional Design Advisor.* Brooks Air Force Base, Texas: Air Force Human Resources Laboratory. (AFHRL-TP-90-52).

Tennyson, R. D. 1990. *A Framework for an Automated Instructional Systems Development Advisor.* Unpublished manuscript. Minneapolis: University of Minnesota.

Tennyson, R. D. 1990. *Prototype AIDA: A Modified ISD Model for Mei Associates, Inc. Phase II. Cycle 1 Report.*

Tennyson, R. D. 1990. Cognitive learning theory linked to instructional theory. *Journal of Structural Learning* 10(3):249–258.

Tennyson, R. D. 1990. Integrated instructional design theory: Advances from cognitive science and instructional technology. *Educational Technology* 30(7):9–15.

Tessmer, M., and J. F. Wedman. 1989. A layers-of-necessity instructional development model. *Educational Technology Research and Development* 38(2):77–85.

Twitchell, D. 1990 and 1991. Robert M. Gagne and M. David Merrill: In conversation (series of seven articles). *Educational Technology* 30(7):34–39; (8):36–41; (9):36–42; (10):37–44; (11):35–39; (12):35–46; January and June 1991.

Vogt, J. L., E. R. N. Robinson, B. E. Taylor, and W. H. Wulfeck II. 1989. *Authoring Instructional Materials (AIM): Automated Curriculum Development.* San Diego: Navy Personnel Research and Development Center (NPRDC TR 89–12).

CHAPTER 3

Developing Human Resources. 1972–1978. San Francisco: Jossey-Bass/Pfeiffer.

Eitington, Julius E. 1984. *The Winning Trainer.* Houston: Gulf.

Lawson, Karen. 1998. *The Trainer's Handbook.* San Francisco: Jossey-Bass/Pfeiffer.

Lawson, Karen. 1998. *Train-the-Trainer Facilitator's Guide.* San Francisco: Jossey-Bass/Pfeiffer.

Mill, Cyril R. 1980. *Activities for Trainers: 50 Useful Designs.* San Diego: University Associates.

Newstrom, John W., and Edward E. Scannell. 1980. *Games Trainers Play.* New York: McGraw-Hill.

Scannell, Edward E., and John W. Newstrom. 1983. *More Games Trainers Play.* New York: McGraw-Hill.

Scannell, Edward E., and John W. Newstrom. 1991. *Still More Games Trainers Play.* New York: Mc-Graw-Hill.

Silberman, Mel. 1992. *Twenty Active Training Programs.* San Diego: Pfeiffer & Company.

Silberman, Mel. 1994. *Twenty Active Training Programs, Vol. II.* San Diego: Pfeiffer & Company.

Silberman, Mel. 1997. *Twenty Active Training Programs, Vol. III.* San Francisco: Jossey-Bass/Pfeiffer.

Silberman, Mel. 1998. *Active Training: A Handbook of Techniques, Designs, Case Examples, and Tips,* 2d ed. San Francisco: Jossey-Bass/Pfeiffer.

Silberman, Mel, and Karen Lawson. 1995. *101 Ways to Make Training Active.* San Diego: Pfeiffer & Company.

Sugar, Steve. 1998. *Games That Teach.* San Francisco: Jossey-Bass/Pfeiffer.

CHAPTER 4

Clark, Ruth Colvin. 1989. *Developing Technical Training.* Reading, Mass.: Addison-Wesley.

Jonassen, David H., Katherine Beissner, and Michael Yacci. 1993. *Structural Knowledge: Techniques for Representing, Conveying, Acquiring Structural Knowledge.* Hillsdale, N.J.: Erlbaum.

Leshin, Cynthia B., Joellyn Pollock, and Charles M. Reigeluth. 1992. *Instructional Design Strategies and Tactics.* Englewood Cliffs, N.J.: Educational Technology.

Rossett, Allison. 1999. *First Things Fast: A Handbook for Performance Analysis.* San Francisco: Jossey-Bass/Pfeiffer.

Rothwell, William J., and H. C. Kazanas. 1992. *Mastering the Instructional Design Process.* San Francisco: Jossey-Bass.

Thiagarajan, Sivasailam. 1998. *Frame Games.* Amherst, Mass.: HRD Press.

CHAPTER 5

Accelerated Learning Sometimes written as *accelerative learning* or used interchangeably with *experiential learning* or *active learning.* While purists may dispute whether the terms are interchangeable, they agree that accelerated learning includes the use of a highly interactive and reinforcing style designed to promote learning by engaging the emotional centers of the brain.

Active Listening A set of techniques that includes repeating what you have heard in your own words to see if you have understood the intent of the speaker.

Consultative Skills This term refers generally to the skills of listening, analysis, and facilitation that are used by consultants. We use these skills as trainers all the time, but that doesn't necessarily make us consultants. To learn more about consulting, including a specific process to follow, read *Flawless Consulting* by Peter Block (Pfeiffer).

Corporate Culture The idea here is that when groups of people get together, they negotiate the meanings of ideas and words, ways of doing things, and ways of teaching and learning through their daily interactions. The sum total of these negotiations at any given time is the culture of the group. An awareness of a group's culture can help the group change and help a consultant or facilitator identify ways to work with what seems like resistance to learning. One of the first books to discuss corporate culture was *Corporate Cultures: The Rites and Rituals of Corporate Life* by Deal and Kennedy (Addison-Wesley). To learn more about how organizational cultures interact and affect ethnic and/or national cultures, pick up *Beyond Race and Gender* by

R. Roosevelt Thomas, Jr. (Amacom), and *Beyond Race and Gender: Software of the Mind* by Geert Hofstede (McGraw-Hill).

Diaphragm The large muscle just below the lungs that aids in breathing. Breathing from the diaphragm helps one project the voice and speak for longer periods without getting tired.

Facilitate Literally, "to make easier." As facilitators we guide and enable learning, as opposed to dumping information or imposing our opinions. While some training requires "right" and "wrong" answers, a facilitator strives to create an environment where people discover what they need to know and learn it in the way that works best for them.

Learning Organization A term used to describe a company or another organization that not only changes as it learns but possesses an awareness of how to develop its capacity for learning continuously. A great deal of what it takes to get an organization to learn applies directly to the environment trainers want to design for classrooms. A seminal book on learning organizations is *The Fifth Discipline: The Art and Practice of the Learning Organization* by Peter M. Senge (Doubleday, New York, 1992).

Learning Style Based on past success in various learning situations, we develop a particular way that works for us. Researchers have divided learners into various style groups. It is valuable for you to know your learning style because it will probably influence the way you teach. (If you learn well from listening, you may tend to lecture a great deal, for example.) Knowing learners' individual styles can help you modify your approach. In general, it is a good idea to present so that people can learn by watching what you do, practicing, interacting with others, and taking time to discuss and think about the material.

Left-Hand Column The format for the examples of what the trainer is thinking versus what is being said was borrowed from the work of Chris Argyris. This format is best used as a tool for two or more people to reflect on what is happening when they talk with each other. For a fuller explanation and some great exercises, look in *The Fifth Discipline Fieldbook* by Peter Senge et al. (Doubleday).

Level 1 Evaluation This term is usually associated with the work of DeWald Kirkpatrick. Level 1 evaluation usually is characterized by the evaluations trainers distribute at the end of a class to measure training effectiveness. Some trainers dismiss level 1 evaluation as frivolous because it does not address the important issue of behavioral change on the part of the learner. For presentation purposes, level 1 evaluation can be a valuable tool. Use it to learn about learners' reactions to your approach. Track responses over time to determine your own or a particular program's improvement.

Needs Analysis When you want to find out what people need to learn, you conduct a needs analysis. This may take many forms, including surveys, interviews, and focus groups. A good needs analysis can help you find out about group learning paradigms and individual learning styles and cultural differences.

Process This term can mean the step-by-step method of working toward a desired outcome. It also is used to mean the analytic and reflective discussions that take place after an exercise, game, or role play. When you ask, "Now, why in the world did we just do that?" you are *processing* the exercise.

CHAPTER 6

Burzan, Tony. 1983. *Use Both Sides of Your Brain.* New York: Dutton.

Hooper, Judith, and Dick Teresi. 1996. *The Three Pound Universe.* New York: Macmillan.

Smith, Terry. 1991. *Making Successful Presentations.* New York: Wiley.

Wilder, Cauludyne. 1990. *The Presentations Kit.* New York: Wiley.

CHAPTER 7

Books

Costello, M. 1991. *The Greatest Games of All Time.* New York: Wiley.
Ellington, H., E. Addinall, and F. Percival. 1982. *A Handbook of Game Design.* New York: Nichols.
Horn, R. E., and A. Cleaves. 1980. *The Guide to Simulation Games for Education and Training,* 4th ed. Beverly Hills, Calif.: Sage.
Gredler, M. 1994. *Designing and Evaluating Games and Simulations.* Houston: Gulf.
Jones, K. 1988. *Interactive Learning Events.* New York: Nichols.
Newstrom, J. W., and E. E. Scannell. 1994. *Even More Games Trainers Play.* New York: McGraw-Hill.
Newstrom, J. W., and E. E. Scannell. 1980. *Games Trainers Play.* New York: McGraw-Hill.
Newstrom, J. W., and E. E. Scannell. 1983. *More Games Trainers Play.* New York: McGraw-Hill.
Newstrom, J. W., and E. E. Scannell. 1991. *Still More Games Trainers Play.* New York: McGraw-Hill.
Sikes, S. 1995. *Feeding the Zircon Gorilla.* Tulsa: Learning Unlimited.
Sugar, S. 1998. *Games That Teach.* San Francisco: Jossey-Bass.
Sugar, S., and G. J. Takacs. 1999. *Games That Teach Teams.* San Francisco: Jossey-Bass.
Thiagarajan, S. 1997. *FrameGames.* Bloomington: Workshops by Thiagi.
Thiagarajan, S. 1997. *Interactive Learning Designs.* Bloomington: Workshops by Thiagi.
Thiagarajan, S. 1997. *Simulation Games.* Bloomington: Workshops by Thiagi.
Wujec, T. 1988. *Pumping Ions.* New York: Doubleday.

Helpful Publications

Games by Thiagi. Amherst: HRD Press. Alexandria: ASTD
INFO-LINE. 1984. *10 Great Games and How to Use Them.*
INFO-LINE. 1984. *Get Results from Simulation and Role Play.* Amherst: HRD Press. Alexandria, ASTD.
INFO-LINE. 1991. *More Great Games.* Amherst: HRD Press. Alexandria, ASTD.
Performance & Instruction. International Society for Performance and Instruction. Washington, D.C.
Simulation & Gaming. London: Sage Periodicals Press.
Thiagi Game Letter. San Francisco: Jossey-Bass.

CHAPTER 9

Kirkpatrick, D. L. 1998. *Evaluating Training Programs: The Four Levels,* 2d ed. San Francisco: Berrett-Koehler.
Knowles, M. 1986. *Using Learning Contracts.* San Francisco: Jossey-Bass.

CHAPTER 11

Bennis, Warren, and Joan Goldsmith. 1994. *Learning to Lead: A Workbook on Becoming a Leader.* Reading, Mass.: Addison-Wesley.

Leaders are made and not born, and this practical workbook shows how to become a more effective
    leader.
Hammer, Michael, and James Champy. 1993. *Reengineering the Corporation: A Manifesto for Business
    Revolution.* New York: HarperCollins.
When applied to training and learning, Hammer and Champy's concepts stretch thinking about how
    to radically redesign a training organization and how technology can be used to transform
    work and learning.
Kotter, John P. 1996. *Leading Change.* Boston, Harvard Business School Press.
This excellent book on organizational change also addresses strategy implementation. The author's
    eight-step process of creating major change is brilliant.
Piskurich, George M., and Ethan S. Sanders. 1998. *ASTD Models for Learning Technologies: Roles, Com-
    petencies, and Outputs.* Alexandria, Va.: American Society for Training and Development.
This the definitive book on learning technologies, from the technologies themselves to the compe-
    tencies required to build them and methods for implementing them.
Shandler, Donald. 1996. *Reengineering the Training Function: How to Align Training with the New Corpo-
    rate Agenda.* Boca Raton, Fla.: St. Lucie Press.
Shandler delivers what he promises: a practical approach to aligning training with the corporate
    agenda.
Smith, Douglas K. 1996. *Taking Charge of Change: Ten Principles for Managing People and Performance.*
    Reading, Mass.: Addison-Wesley.
Smith's 10 principles for managing people and performance are effective and to the point, increasing
    the odds of success.
Svenson, Raynold A., and Monica J. Rinderer. 1991. *The Training and Development Strategic Plan Work-
    book.* Englewood Cliffs, N.J.: Prentice-Hall.
This book contains a wealth of tested tools and techniques to help with the design and implementa-
    tion of an effective training organization customized to a specific company. It also includes an
    excellent section on the strategic planning process itself.
Winslow, Charles D., and William L. Bramer. 1994. *FutureWork: Putting Knowledge to Work in the
    Knowledge Economy.* New York: Free Press.
Winslow and Bramer challenge conventional thinking on the relationship between knowledge, busi-
    ness results, and human performance with reference to what work looks like today and what
    it will look like in the future.

CHAPTER 12

Brood, Mary L., and John W. Newstrom. 1992. *Transfer of Training.* Reading Mass: Addison-Wesley.
Carr, Clay. 1992. *Smart Training.* New York: McGraw Hill.
Clark, Ruth C. 1989. *Developing Technical Training.* Phoenix: Buzzards Bay Press.
Clothier, Paul. 1996. *The Complete Computer Trainer.* New York: McGraw-Hill.
Hall, Brandon. 1997. *Web-Based Training Cookbook.* New York: Wiley.
Jackson, Terence. 1989. *Evaluation: Relating Training to Business Performance.* San Diego: University As-
    sociates.
Pepitone, James S. 1995. *Future Training.* Dallas: AddVantage.
Phillips, Jack. 1991. *Handbook of Training Evaluation and Measurement Methods,* 2d ed. Houston: Gulf.
Robinson, Dana Gaines, and James C. Robinson. 1996. *Training for Impact.* San Francisco: Berrett-
    Koehler.

Tobin, Daniel R. 1993. *Re-Educating the Corporation.* Essex Junction, Vt.: Oliver Wight.

Merrill, M. David. 1997. "Instructional Strategies That Teach." *CBT Solutions,* December, p. 1.

"Is There a Learning Curve in This Business?" *Training.* February, p. 28.

Woodall, Dorman. 1997. "The Power Shopper's Guide to Acquiring Valuable CBT." *CBT Solutions,* December, p. 32.

Zemke, Ron, and Judy Armstrong. 1996. "A Bluffer's Guide to Multimedia." *Training,* June, p. 36.

Zemke, Ron, and Judy Armstrong. 1996. "Evaluating Multimedia Developers." *Training,* November, p. 32.

Zemke, Ron, and Judy Armstrong. 1996. "Evaluating Multimedia." *Training,* August, p. 48.

CHAPTER 13

Anderson, L. W., and L. A. Sosniak. 1994. *Bloom's Taxonomy: A Forty-Year Retrospective.* Chicago. University of Chicago Press.

Baker, E. L., and H. F. O'Neil. 1994. *Technology Assessment in Education and Training.* Hillsdale, N.J.: Erlbaum.

Ginsburg, H., and S. Opper. 1969. *Piaget's Theory of Intellectual Development: An Introduction.* Englewood Cliffs, N.J.: Prentice-Hall.

Hall, B. 1997. *Web-Based Training Cookbook.* New York: Wiley.

Leshin, C. B., J. Pollock, and C. M. Reigeluth. 1992. *Instructional Design Strategies and Tactics.* Englewood Cliffs, N.J.: Educational Technology.

Mager, R. F. 1984. *Preparing Instructional Objectives.* Belmont, Calif.: Pitman Learning.

Reiser, R. R., and R. M. Gagne. 1983. *Selecting Media for Instruction.* Englewood Cliffs, N.J.: Educational Technology.

Reynolds A., and R. H. Anderson. 1992. *Selecting and Developing Media for Instruction.* New York: Van Nostrand Reinhold.

Romiszowski, A. J. 1988. *The Selection and Use of Instructional Media.* New York: Nichols.

Sive, M. R. 1983. *Media Selection Handbook.* Littleton, Colo.: Libraries Unlimited.

Towne, D. M. 1995. *Learning and Instruction in Simulation Environments.* Englewood Cliffs, N.J.: Educational Technology.

CHAPTER 14

Gery G. 1996. *Electronic Performance Support Systems.* Cambridge, Mass.: Ziff Institute.

Keen, Peter G. W., and Craigg Balance. 1997. *On-Line Profits: A Manager's Guide to Electronic Commerce.* Boston: Massachusetts: Harvard Business School Press.

Kirkpatrick, D. 1998. *Evaluating Training Programs—The Four Levels,* 2d ed. San Francisco: Berrett-Koehler.

Parry, Scott B. 1997. *Evaluating the Impact of Training.* Alexandria, Va.: American Society of Training and Development.

Pepitone, James S. 1995. *Future Training: A Roadmap for Restructuring the Training Function.* Dallas: Add Vantage Learning Press.

Phillips, Jack J. 1997. *Handbook of Training Evaluation and Measurement Methods,* 3d ed. Houston: Gulf.

Phillips, Jack J. 1997. *Return on Investment in Training and Performance Improvement Programs.* Houston: Gulf.

Phillips, Jack J., ed. 1994. *Measuring Return on Investment,* vol. 1. Alexandria, Va.: American Society for Training and Development.

Phillips, Jack J., ed. 1997. *Measuring Return on Investment*, vol. 2. Alexandria, Va.: American Society for Training and Development.

Ravet, Serge, and Maureen Layte. 1997. *Technology-Based Training*. Houston: Gulf.

Stevens, E., and G. Stevens. 1995. *Designing Electronic Performance Support Tools*. Englewood Cliffs, N.J.: Educational Technology.

Zielinski, Dave. 1997. *Selling Technology-Delivered Learning in Your Organization*. Minneapolis: Lakewood.

CHAPTER 15

One of the challenges of selecting a training management system is the lack of information available. Below are a few of the available resources. Also look for white papers provided by vendors.

Hall, Brandon. 1998. "Training Management Systems: How to Choose a System Your Company Can Live With." Industry report. brandon-hall.com.

Hall, Brandon. 1998. "The Next Big Thing in Training." Multimedia presentation. www.eloquent.com.

Hall, Brandon. 1998. "Training Management Systems." Videotape. brandon-hall.com.

CHAPTER 17

Allen, Michael W. 1993. Toward ideal authoring systems. In G. M. Piskurich, ed., *The ASTD Handbook of Instructional Technology*. New York: McGraw Hill.

Apple Computer, Inc. 1989. *HyperCard Stack Design Guidelines*. Reading, Mass.: Addison-Wesley.

Apple Computer, Inc. 1992. *Macintosh Human Interface Guidelines*. Reading, Mass.: Addison-Wesley.

Apple Computer, Inc. 1994. *Multimedia Demystified*. New York: Random House.

Berk, R. A. 1980. *Criterion-Referenced Measurement: The State of the Art*. Baltimore: John Hopkins University Press.

Bloom, B. S., ed. 1956. *Taxonomy of Educational Objectives: Book 1: The Cognitive Domain*. White Plains, N.Y.: Longman.

Briggs, L. J., K. L. Gufstafson, and M. H. Tillman. eds. 1991. *Instructional Design: Principles and Applications*, 2d ed. Englewood Cliffs, N.J.: Educational Technology.

Carlisle, K. E. 1986. *Analyzing Jobs and Tasks*. Englewood Cliffs, N.J.: Educational Technology.

Cooper, A. 1995. *About Face: The Essentials of User Interface Design*. Foster City, Calif.: IDG.

Dick, W., and L. Carey. 1990. *The Systematic Design of Instruction*, 3d ed. New York: HarperCollins.

Dick, W., and R. A. Reiser. 1989. *Planning Effective Instruction*. Englewood Cliffs, N.J.: Prentice-Hall.

Fernandes, T. 1995. *Global Interface Design: A Guide to Designing International User Interfaces*. Boston: Academic Press.

Filipczak, Bob. 1996. Engaged! The nature of computer interactivity. *Training*, November, pp. 53–58.

Filipczak, Bob. 1996. To ISD or not to ISD. *Training*, March, pp. 73–74.

Fleming, M., and W. H. Levie, eds. 1993. *Instructional Message Design: Principles from Behavioral and Cognitive Sciences*, 2d ed. Englewood Cliffs, N.J.: Educational Technology.

Gagné, R. M. 1975. *Essentials of Learning for Instruction*. New York: Holt, Rinehart, and Winston.

Gagné, R. M., L. J. Briggs, and W. W. Wager. 1992. *Principles of Instructional Design*, 4th ed. Orlando: Harcourt, Brace, Jovanovich.

Hannafin, M. J., and K. L. Peck. 1988. *The Design, Development & Evaluation of Instructional Software*. New York: Macmillan.

Heckel, P. 1984. *The Elements of Friendly Software Design*. San Francisco: Sybex.

Kemp, J. E., G. R. Morrison, and S. M. Ross. 1994. *Designing Effective Instruction.* New York: Merrill.

Kristof, R., and A. Satra. 1995. *Interactivity by Design: Creating and Communicating with New Media.* Mountain View, Calif.: Adobe.

Jonassen, D. H., ed. 1988. *Instructional Designs for Microcomputer Courseware.* Hillsdale, N.J.: Erlbaum.

Leshin, C. B., J. Pollock, and C. M. Reigeluth. 1992. *Instructional Design Strategies and Tactics.* Englewood Cliffs, N.J.: Educational Technology.

Lopuck, L. 1996. *Designing Multimedia: A Visual Guide to Multimedia and Online Graphic Design.* Berkeley, Calif.: Peachpit Press.

Merrill, M. D. 1983. Component display theory. In C. M. Reigeluth, ed., *Instructional Design Theories and Models: An Overview of Their Current Status.* Hillsdale, N.J.: Erlbaum.

Merrill, M. D. 1994. *Instructional Design Theory.* Englewood Cliffs, N.J.: Educational Technology.

Merrill, M. D., and R. D. Tennyson. 1977. *Teaching Concepts: An Instructional Design Guide.* Englewood Cliffs, N.J.: Educational Technology.

Norman, D. A. 1990. *The Design of Everyday Things.* New York: Doubleday (originally published as *The Psychology of Everyday Things.* 1988. New York: Basic Books.

Reigeluth, C. M. 1983. *Instructional-Design Theories and Models: An Overview of Their Current Status.* Hillsdale, N.J.: Erlbaum.

Reigeluth, C. M. 1987. *Instructional Theories in Action: Lessons Illustrating Selected Theories and Models.* Hillsdale, N.J.: Erlbaum.

Rothwell, W. J., and H. C. Kazanas. 1992. *Mastering the Instructional Design Process.* San Francisco: Jossey-Bass.

Schneiderman, B. 1992. *Designing the User Interface: Strategies for Effective Human-Computer Interaction.* Reading, Mass.: Addison-Wesley.

Seels, B., and Z. Glagow. 1990. *Excercises In Instructional Design.* Columbus, Ohio: Merrill.

Smith, P. L., and T. J. Ragan. 1992. *Instructional Design.* New York: Merrill.

Sullivan, H., and N. Higgins. 1983. *Teaching for Competence.* New York: Teachers College, Columbia University.

West, C. K., J. A. Farmer, and P. M. Wolff. 1991. *Instructional Design: Implications from Cognitive Science.* Engelwood Cliffs, N.J.: Prentice-Hall.

Zielinski, Robert S. 1996. *Special Edition Using Macromedia Authorware® 3.5.* Indianapolis: QUE Corporation.

CHAPTER 18

Andleight, P. K., and K. Thakrar. 1996. *Multimedia Systems Design.* Upper Saddle River, N.J.: Prentice Hall.

Angel, J. 1998. *Realmedia Complete: Streaming Audio and Video over the Web.* Hightstown, N.J.: McGraw-Hill.

Builder.com. 1998. *Emerging Web Standards: Synchronized Multimedia Integration Language (SMIL): Multimedia Made Easy* (on-line) http://builder.com/Authoring/Standards/ss01.html.

Deivert, B., and D. Harries. 1996. *Film & Video on the Internet: The Top 500 Sites.* New York: Edmond H. Weiss.

Deluca, S. 1990. *Instructional Video.* New York: Focal.

Driscoll, M. 1996. Three Web-based training trends worth watching. *Multimedia Training Newsletter.* 3(11):6–7.

Johnson, N. 1996. *Web Developer's Guide to Multimedia and Video: Your Complete Guide to Creating Live Video for the Internet.* New York: Coriolis Group.

Johnson, N. 1997. Embedded Web video. *DV*, August, pp. 64–66.

Johnson, N. 1997. Tools of the Trade. *DV*, December, pp. 76–77.

Kennedy Consulting 1998. *JustSMIL* (on-line). http://www.justsmil.com/news/.

Lee, A. Y., and A. N. Bowers. 1997. "Displaying Information: The Effect of Multimedia Components on Learning." Proceedings of the Human Factors and Ergonomics Society, 41st Annual Meeting, pp. 340–344.

Metcalf, D. S. 1994. "I-NET Multimedia Information Exchange." Multicomm '94 Conference Proceedings. Vancouver, Canada: University of British Columbia.

Metcalf, D. S. 1995. "Web Interactive Training: New Delivery Mechanisms for Remote Training at Kennedy Space Center. *"Congreso Internacional: Tecnologia y Educacion a Distancia Memoria* (conference proceedings). San Jose, Costa Rica: EUNED, Nova Southeastern University.

Nemzow, M. A. 1997. *Web Video Complete*. Hightstown, N.J.: McGraw-Hill.

Tansy, G. 1996. Designing Internet-based and intranet-based training. *Multimedia Training Newsletter* 3(11):7.

Waggoner, B. 1998. Everything's coming up QuickTime. *Interactivity*, August, pp. 64–65.

Waggoner, B. 1998. Streaming media. *Interactivity*, September, pp. 22–29.

VRML Consortium. 1998. *VRML Consortium home page* (on-line). http://www.vrml.org/.

General References

DV magazine

Interactivity magazine

New Media magazine

http://www.webopedia.com. A technical on-line encyclopedia.

CHAPTER 19

Bell, James. 1998. A new dimension in CBT. *Inside Technology Training*, 2(9):

Frank, Geoffrey, and Jorge Montoya. 1997. *"On the Design of Classrooms for the 21st Century."* Interservice/Industry Training Systems and Education Conference.

Greengard, Samuel. 1998. "Virtual" training becomes reality, *Industry Week* 247(2):

Guinn, Curry, and Jorge Montoya. 1997. "Natural Language Processing in Virtual Reality Training Environments." Interservice/Industry Training Systems and Education Conference.

Hubal, Robert. 1997. "Evidence of Effectiveness of Virtual Reality Training Applications." Research Triangle Institute.

Hubal, Robert, Robert Helms, and Suzanne Triplett. 1997. "Advanced Learning Environments." Interservice/Industry Training Systems and Education Conference.

Industry Report. 1998. *Training* 35(10).

Kenyon, Henry. 1998. Virtual reality in training—virtually here. *Corporate University Review* 6(3).

Lewis, Darcy. 1997. Will virtual reality become the standard in safety training?, *Safety + Health*.

Marquardt, Michael J., and Greg Kearsley. 1999. *Technology-Based Learning*. St. Lucie Press.

Research Triangle Institute. *Virtual Reality Multimedia Training*. http://www.rti.org/vr/w/vrtrain.html.

University of Washington, Human Interface Laboratory. *Information Resources in Virtual Reality*. Technical Report No. B-93-1. http://www.hitl.washington.edu/kb/irvr/irvr.html.

CHAPTER 20

A good starting point for learning EPSS on the World Wide Web can be found at http://itech1.coe.uga.edu/EPSS/EPSS.html. Sponsored by the Birmingham Education Center, this site contains articles, criteria for deciding whether an organization needs an EPSS, and links to other Web resources, including Gloria Gery's excellent epss.com! site at www.epss.com.
Other valuable sources for further review include the following:

Carr, C. 1992. PSS! Help when you need it. *Training & Development* 46(6):30–38.

Clark, R. C. 1995. 21st century human performance. *Training* 32(6):85–90.

Collins, Allan, John Seely Brown, and Ann Holum. 1991. Cognitive apprenticeship: Making thinking visible. *American Educator,* Fall 1991, pp. 6–11, 38–46.

Dickelman, G. J. 1995. Things that help us perform: Commentary on ideas from Donald A. Norman. *Performance Improvement Quarterly* 8(1):23–30.

Dublin, L. E. 1993. Learn while you work. *Computerworld* 27(35):81–82.

Gery, G. 1991. *Electronic performance support systems: How and Why to Remake the Workplace through the Strategic Application of Technology.* Tolland, Mass.: Gery Performance Press.

Raybould, B. 1995. Making a case for EPSS. *Innovations in Education and Training International* 32(1):65–69.

Rossett, A. 1991. Electronic job aids. *Data Training* 10(7):24–29.

Sherry, L., and B. Wilson. 1996. Supporting human performance across disciplines: A converging of roles and tools. *Performance Improvement Quarterly* 9(4):19–36.

Witt, C. L., and W. Wager. 1994. A comparison of instructional systems design and electronic performance support systems design. *Educational Technology* 34(6):20–24.

CHAPTER 21

Clark, Ruth. 1998. *Building Expertise.* International Society for Performance Improvement.

Dubois, David. 1993. *Completency-Based Performance Improvement.* HRD Press.

Gagne, Robert, Leslie J. Bridges, and Walter W. Wagner. 1992. *Principles of Instructional Design.* Harcourt Brace Jovanovich.

Khan, Badrul. 1997. *Web Based Instruction.* Educational Technology Publications.

Kirkpatrick, Donald. 1996. *Evaluating Training Programs: The Four Levels.* Berrett-Koehler.

Dills, R. Charles, and J. Alexander Romiszowki. 1997. *Instructional Development Paradigms.* Educational Technology Publications.

Phillips, Jack. 1997. *Handbook of Training Evaluation and Measurement Methods.* Gulf.

CHAPTER 22

Boud, D., and N. Falchikov. 1989. Quantitative studies of student self-assessment in higher education: A critical analysis of findings. *Higher Education* 18:529–549.

Bynum, M., and Nate Rosenblatt. 1984. Self-study: Boon or bust? *Training,* November, pp. 61–64.

Cox, John H. 1982. A new look at learner-controlled instruction. *Training and Development*, March, pp. 90–94.

Dewey, F. J. 1938. *Experience and Education.* New York: Collier.

Even, M. J. 1982. Adapting cognitive style theory in practice. *Lifelong Learning: The Adult Years,* 5(5):14–17.

Feeney, Edward J. 1981. Beat the high cost of training through LCI. *Training and Development*, September, pp. 41–43.

Hammond, M., and R. Collins. 1991. *Self-Directed Learning: Critical Practice*. New York: Nichols/GP Publishing.

Hiemstra, R., and B. Sisco. 1990. *Individualizing Instruction*. San Francisco: Jossey-Bass.

Howard, Melinda. 1985. *Modeling a Training and Development System and Employee Motivation to Learn*. Norman: University of Oklahoma Press.

Huff, J. O. 1984–1985. How to determine what course design will be most effective. *Journal of Educational Technology Systems* 13(3):227–232.

Kearsley, G. 1982. *Costs, Benefits, and Productivity in Training Systems*. Reading, Mass.: Addison-Wesley.

Kirkpatrick, D. 1977. Evaluation of training programs: Evidence vs. proof. *Training and Development*, November.

Knowles, M. K. 1980. *The Modern Practice of Adult Education*, rev. ed. New York: Cambridge University Press.

Knowles, M. K. 1980. How do you get people to be self-directed learners? *Training and Development*, May, pp. 96–99.

Loacker, G., and A. Doherty. 1984. Self-directed undergraduate study. In M. S. Knowles and associates, eds., *Andragogy in Action*. San Francisco: Jossey-Bass.

Long, H. 1989. Truth unguessed and yet to be discovered. In H. Long and associates, eds., *Self-Directed Learning: Emerging Theory and Practice*. Norman: University of Oklahoma Press.

Long, H. 1990. Changing concepts of self-direction in learning. In H. Long and associates, eds., *Advances in Research and Practice in Self-Directed Learning*. Norman: University of Oklahoma Press.

Mentzer, Dean. 1974. *The Effect of Response Mode upon the Achievement and Retention of Student-Nurses Taught Life-Science by Audio-Tutorial Instruction*. Ann Arbor, Mich.: University Microfilms International.

Penland, P. 1979. Self-initiated learning. *Adult Education* 29:170–179.

Piskurich, G. 1983. Individualized media instruction: A dream come true? *Training and Development*, December pp. 68–69.

Piskurich, G. 1989. *Self-Directed Learning*. San Francisco: Jossey-Bass.

Piskurich, G. 1991. Ensure quality and quality training through self-directed learning. *Training and Development*, September.

Piskurich, G. 1991. Preparing the learner for self-directed learning. In H. Long and associates, eds., *Journal of the 5th Annual Symposium on Self-directed Learning*. Norman: University of Oklahoma Press.

Reisman, D. 1950. *The Lonely Crowd: A Study of Changing American Culture*. New Haven, Conn.: Yale University Press.

Romiszowski, A. J. 1986. *Developing Auto-Instructional Materials*. London: Kogan Page.

Rowntree, Derek 1986. *Teaching through Self-Instruction*. London: Kogan Page.

Snow, R. E. 1980. Aptitude, learner control, and adaptive instruction. *Educational Psychologist* 15:151–158.

Steinberg, E. R. 1984. *Teaching Computers to Teach*. Hillsdale, N.J.: Erlbaum.

Thompson, M. 1980. *Benefit-Cost Analysis for Program Evaluation*. Beverly Hills, Calif.: Sage.

Young, Deborah. 1986. *An Exploratory Study of the Relationship between Organizational Climate and Self-Directed Learning among Organizational Managers*. Kansas City: University of Missouri Press.

CHAPTER 23

Anderson, G., D. Boud, and J. Sampson. 1996. Learning contracts.

Durr, R. E. 1995. Integration of self-directed learning into the learning process at Motorola. In H. B. Long and Associates, eds., *New Dimensions in Self-directed Learning*. Norman: Public Managers Center, University of Oklahoma, pp. 335–344.

Guglielmino, L. M., and P. J. Guglielmino. 1991a. *Enhancing Your Readiness for Self-Directed Learning.* King of Prussia, Penn.: HRD Press.

Guglielmino, L. M., and P. J. Guglielmino. 1991b. *Learning Preference Assessment Facilitators' Guide.* King of Prussia, Penn.: HRD Press.

Guglielmino, L. M., and P. J. Guglielmino. 1994. Practical experience with self-directed learning in business and industry human resource development. In R. Hiemstra and R. Brockett, eds., *Overcoming Resistance to Self-Direction in Adult Learning. New Directions for Adult and Continuing Education* 64:39–46.

Knowles, M. S. 1977. *Self-Directed Learning: Guide for Learners and Teachers.*

Knowles, M. S. 1986. *Using Learning Contracts.* San Francisco: Jossey-Bass.

O'Donnell, J., and R. Caffarella. 1998. Learning contracts. In M. Galbraith, ed., *Adult Learning Methods.* Malabar, Fla.: Krieger.

Zemke, R. 1998. In search of self-directed learning. *Training,* May, pp.

CHAPTER 24

Broad, M., and J. Newstrom. 1992. *Transfer of Training: Action Packed Strategies to Ensure High Payoff from Training Investments.* Reading, Mass.: Addison-Wesley.

Cline, R., and R. Pearlstein. 1993. Using job aids to supplement manuals. *Performance and Instruction,* July 1993, pp. 12–14.

Lineberry, C., and D. Bullock. 1980. *Job Aids.* Englewood Cliffs, N.J.: Educational Technology Publications.

Mitchell, D. 1993. On using job aids in lieu of or as an adjunct to training. *Performance and Instruction,* May–June 1993, pp. 32–33.

Piskurich, G., editor in chief. 1993. *The American Society for Training and Development Handbook of Instructional Technology.* New York: McGraw-Hill.

Reynolds, A., and R. Anderson. 1992. *Selecting and Developing Media for Instruction.* New York: Van Nostrand Reinhold.

Reynolds, A., and R. Araya. 1995. *Building Multimedia Performance Support Systems.* New York: McGraw-Hill.

Rossett, A. 1996. Job aids and electronic performance support systems. In R. Craig, editor in chief, *The ASTD Training and Development Handbook.* New York: McGraw-Hill.

Rossett, A., and J. Gautier-Downes. 1991. *A Handbook of Job Aids.* San Diego: Pfeiffer.

Rothwell, W., and H. C. Kazanas. 1998. *Mastering the Instructional Design Process: A Systematic Approach.* San Francisco: Jossey-Bass.

Saltzman, P. 1998. The comeback of cheat sheets. *Technical Training,* November–December 1998, pp. 30–32.

Tilaro, A., and A. Rossett. 1993. Creating motivating job aids. *Performance and Instruction,* October 1998, pp. 13–20.

CHAPTER 25

General References

Broad, Mary L. 1997a. Overview of transfer of training: From learning to performance. *Performance Improvement Quarterly* 10(2):7–21.

Broad, Mary L. ed. 1997b. *Transferring Learning to the Workplace.* Alexandria, Va.: American Society for Training and Development.

Broad, Mary L., and John W. Newstrom. 1992. *Transfer of Training: Action-Packed Strategies to Ensure High Payoff from Training Investments.* Reading, Mass.: Addison-Wesley.

Robinson, Dana Gaines, and James C. Robinson. 1995. *Performance Consulting: Moving Beyond Training.* San Francisco: Berrett-Koehler.

Rummler, Geary A., and Alan P. Brache. 1992. Transforming organizations through human performance technology. In Harold D. Stolovitch and Erica Keeps, eds., *Handbook of Human Performance Technology.* San Francisco: Jossey-Bass, pp. 32–49.

Rummler, Geary A., and Brache. 1995. *Improving Performance: How to Manage the White Space on the Organization Chart,* 2d ed. San Francisco: Jossey-Bass.

Research and Applications References

Baldwin, Timothy T., and Kevin Ford. 1988. Transfer of training: A review and directions for future research. *Personnel Psychology* 41:63–105.

Baldwin, Timothy T., and Richard J. Magjuka. 1991. Organizational training and signals of importance: Linking pretraining perceptions to intentions to transfer. *Human Resource Development Quarterly,* 2(1): 25–36.

Brinkerhoff, Robert O., and Stephen J. Gill. 1994. *The Learning Alliance: Systems Thinking in Human Resource Development.* San Francisco: Jossey-Bass.

Brinkerhoff, Robert O., and Max Montesino. 1995. Partnerships for training transfer: Lessons from a corporate study. *Human Resource Development Quarterly* 6(3): pp. 263–274.

Csoka, Louis. 1994. *Closing the Human Performance Gap.* New York: The Conference Board, Research Report 1065-94-RR.

Kotter, J. P. 1988. *The Leadership Factor.* New York: Free Press.

Tannenbaum, S. I. and G. Yulk. 1992. Training and development in work organizations. *Annual Review of Psychology* 43:399–441.

CHAPTER 26

Broad, M. L., and J. W. Newstrom. 1992. *Transfer of Training.* Reading, Mass.: Addison-Wesley.

Esque, T. J., and P. A. Patterson. eds. 1998. *Getting Results: Case Studies in Performance Improvement.* Amherst, Mass.: HRD Press International Society for Performance Improvement.

Findley, B. F., and R. E. Main. 1995. *Fundamentals of Human Performance Technology Workshop.* Belton, Mo.:

Gilbert, T. F. 1978. *Human Competence: Engineering Worthy Performance.* New York: McGraw-Hill.

Hale, J. 1998. *The Performance Consultant's Handbook.* San Francisco: Pfiffer.

James-Catalano, C. N. 1996. *Researching on the WORLD WIDE WEB : Spend More Time Learning, Not Searching.* Rocklin, Calif.: Prima.

Langdon, D. 1995. *The New Language of Work.* Amherst, Mass.: HRD Press.

Mager, R. F., and P. Pipe. 1997. *Analyzing Performance Problems.* Atlanta: Center for Effective Performance.

Norman, D. A. 1998. *The Invisible Computer.* Cambridge, Mass.: MIT Press.

Robinson, D. G., and J. C. Robinson. 1996. *Performance Consulting: Moving beyond Training.* San Francisco: Berrett-Koehler.

Robinson, D. G., and J. C. Robinson. eds. 1998. *Moving from Training to Performance.* San Francisco: Berrett-Koehler.

Stolovitch, H. D., and E. J. Keeps. eds. 1992. *Handbook of Human Performance Technology.* San Francisco: Jossey-Bass.

Swanson, R. A. 1996. *Analysis for Improving Performance.* San Francisco: Berrett-Koehler.

CHAPTER 27

Brethower, D. M., and P. C. Dams. In press. Systems thinking and systems doing. *Performance Improvement.*

Brethower, D. M., and K. Smalley. 1998. *Performance-Based Instruction: Linking Training to Business Results.* Washington, D.C.: ISPI/Jossey-Bass.

Broad, M., and J. Newstrom. 1992. *Transfer of Training: Action-Packed Strategies to Ensure High Payoff from Training Investments.* New York: Addison-Wesley.

Dean, P. J., ed. 1994. *Performance Engineering at Work.* Batavia, Ill.: International Board of Standards for Training, Performance, and Instruction.

Dean, P. J., and D. E. Ripley, eds. 1997. *Performance Improvement Pathfinders: Models for Organizational Learning Systems.* Washington, D.C.: International Society for Performance Improvement.

Esque, T. J., and P. A. Patterson, eds. 1998. *Getting Results—Case Studies in Performance Improvement.* Washington, D.C.: International Society for Performance Improvement.

Gilbert, T. 1996. *Human Competence: Engineering Worthy Performance.* Amherst, Mass., and Washington, D.C.: HRD Press and International Society for Performance Improvement.

Harless, J. H. 1978. *Job Aid for Selection and Construction of Job Aids.* Newman, Ga.: Harless Performance Guild.

Kaufman, R., S. Thiagarajan, and P. MacGillis. eds. 1997. *The Guidebook for Performance Improvement: Working with Individuals and Organizations.* San Francisco: Pfeiffer.

Kopelman, R. E. 1986. *Managing Productivity in Organizations: A Practical, People Oriented Approach.* New York: McGraw-Hill.

LaFleur, D., and D. M. Brethower. 1998. *The Transformation: Management Techniques for the 21st Century.*

Langdon, D. 1995. *The New Language of Work.* Amherst, Mass.: HRD Press.

Lineberry, C. S., and D. H. Bullock. 1980. *Job Aids.* Englewook Cliffs, N.J.: Educational Technology Publications.

Phillips, J. J., ed. 1994. *In Action: Measuring Return on Investment.* Alexandria, Va.: ASTD.

Rummler, G. A., and A. P. Brache. 1995. *Improving Performance: How to Manage the White Space on the Organization Chart,* 2d ed. San Francisco: Jossey-Bass.

Stolovitch, H. D., and E. J. Keeps, eds. 1992. *Handbook of Human Performance Technology: A Comprehensive Guide for Analyzing and Solving Performance Problems in Organizations.* San Francisco: Jossey-Bass.

Stolovitch, H. D., and E. J. Keeps, eds. In press. *Handbook of Human Performance Technology: A Comprehensive Guide for Analyzing and Solving Performance Problems in Organizations,* 2d ed. San Francisco: Jossey-Bass.

Zigon, J. 1994. Performance management training. In J. J. Phillips, ed., *Action: Measuring Return on Investment.* Alexandria, Va.: ASTD, pp. 258–262.

George Piskurich is presently consulting in instructional design and technology-based training implementation. He has been in the training profession in various positions and industry settings for over 20 years. His areas of special interest include self-directed learning, performance improvement, customer service, and management/supervisory development.

He has been a presenter at over 30 conferences and symposia, including the International Self-Directed Learning Symposium and the ISPI and ASTD international conferences, speaking on topics ranging from mentoring systems to interactive distance learning to telecommuting.

He has authored books on learning technology, self-directed learning, and telecommuting, written extensively in his areas of interest for a number of periodicals, and is currently working on a book on practical instructional design.

Currently residing in the Raleigh/Durham area of North Carolina, he can be reached at 919-968-0878.

GMP1@Compuserve.com

Peter F. Beckschi joined Merck-Medco as director of training and education in March 1997 and has close to 30 years' experience as a training and human performance specialist in industry and government. His initial assignment as a trainer was for the U.S. Navy, where he learned instructional systems development (ISD) and conducted team training for U.S. and NATO forces. After several years as a marketing specialist for GATX Corporation, Beckschi was selected to develop and provide technical training for turnkey operations around the world. He started the first training department for this organization and introduced competency-based methodologies for headquarters and field personnel.

In 1982 Beckschi joined the faculty at the American University in Cairo, Egypt, where he served as director of commercial and industrial training. His unit was responsible for providing technical and commercial skills for clients throughout the Middle East. Upon completion of this contract, he returned to developing and conducting training programs as a senior human resources and development consultant for Holderbank Management and Consulting out of Switzerland. He provided training and organizational development services (primarily team training) for a variety of the firm's clients, including the World Bank. Projects were based in Iraq, Saudi Arabia, India, Egypt, Korea, Japan, Brazil, Germany, Costa Rica, the Baltic states, and Pakistan.

Returning to the United States, Beckschi undertook research and development training projects for the Air Force Human Resources Laboratory in the application of cognitive psychology to modern training methods while employed by Pacer Systems, a training systems developer. During this period he coauthored the *Handbook for Instructional Technology* published by the American Society for Training and Development.

Beckschi performed training design as a solutions integrator for Astra Merck and produced workshops for executives at SmithKline Beecham, Baxter Healthcare, Bristol-Myers Squibb, Bellcore, Sprint, Avon, Ford 2000, GE Finance, and the World Bank. He provides pro bono workshops for a number of organizations, including the Philadelphia Museum of Art.

Beckschi was awarded the American Society for Training and Development Technical Trainer of the Year award in 1982 and the International Leadership Award in 1995.

Beckschi is a graduate of the University of California, Berkeley, with a master of science degree from Temple University in Philadelphia and is embarked on a doctoral program that will be completed when he decides to stop traveling so much. His wife, Trudy, would like that too.

www.peter_beckschi@merck.com

Brandon Hall is editor of brandon-hall.com, an independent research organization on technology for training. He is a frequent speaker at conferences on industry trends and advises organizations on strategic issues related to on-line learning. Hall is recognized as an independent analyst, and his publications include *Training Management Systems* and the *Web-Based Training Cookbook.* He chairs an annual awards program that recognizes the best on-line learning programs. Hall has been a columnist for *Inside Technology Training* and a contributing editor to ASTD's *Training & Development.* He has been interviewed by *Fortune, The New York Times, The Wall Street Journal, Business Week,* and other magazines.

brandon@brandon-hall.com